Classical Mechanics

Classical Mechanics

Vimal Kumar Jain
Professor of Physics
Maharshi Dayanand University,
Rohtak

Ane Books Pvt. Ltd.
New Delhi ♦ Chennai

Classical Mechanics

Vimal Kumar Jain

Pages : xii + 284 = 296 (PB)
Size : Royal (6¼" × 9½")
Paper Quality (GSM) : 80
Price : Rs. 495/-

Published by

Ane Books Pvt. Ltd.

4821, Parwana Bhawan, 1st Floor, 24 Ansari Road, Darya Ganj,
New Delhi - 110 002, Tel.: +91(011) 23276843-44, Fax: +91(011) 23276863
e-mail: kapoor@anebooks.com, Website: www.anebooks.com

Branch Office:

- Avantika Niwas, 1st Floor, 19 Doraiswamy Road, T. Nagar,
  Chennai - 600 017, Tel.: +91(044) 28141554, 28141209
  e-mail: anebookschennai@gmail.com, rathinam@anebooks.com

ISBN : 978-81-9084-061-3

Printed at : R.K. Offset Process, New Delhi.

Dedicated to
my wife Minakshi

Preface

Mechanics is not only the oldest branch of physics but is also the basis of theoretical physics. The '*Classical Mechanics*' is an introductory text for graduate and post graduate students in physics taking a standard classical mechanics course. This textbook has grown out of many years of 'course notes' that I developed for M.Sc. students covering many aspects of mechanics of particle, system of particles and rigid bodies.

A large number of solved, unsolved problems and objective questions based on the articles are given at the end of each chapter to supplement the text. The students will find a fair amount of detail in the examples and derivations given in the text. The phrase *'it can be shown that'* has been avoided wherever possible. The vectors are denoted with bold face in the book.

I am grateful to the authors whose work I have consulted in the process of developing this book. A list of some of these is given at the end. I must also acknowledge the unreserved cooperation and support of my dear parents and my children Ira, Manu and Manish. Finally, I must thank Mr. J. R. Kapoor of Ane Books Pvt. Ltd. for readily agreeing to undertake this project.

Vimal Kumar Jain

Contents

CHAPTER 1

Introduction to Particle Dynamics

1.1 NEWTON'S LAWS OF MOTION

One of the fundamental concepts of mechanics is that of a particle. A particle is defined as a body whose dimensions may be neglected in describing its motion. For example, the earth may be regarded as a particle in considering its motion about the sun but not in considering its rotation about its own axis. Initially, bodies will be taken to be mass point, point like particles of mass m. These are objects that have no spatial extension but do carry a finite mass. The study of the motion of particles in terms of forces associated with that motion is called particle dynamics. The principles that relate force and motion were formulated by Isaac Newton. These principles are referred to as Newton's laws of motion.

1. A body remains at rest or in uniform motion unless acted upon by a force.

To say that a body is in uniform motion means that the body experiences no acceleration. This law does not apply to all reference frames, the coordinate system in which the motion is specified. The first law is valid only in an unaccelerated frame of reference. The implication of the first law is that every physical body possesses an intrinsic characteristic called Inertia, the tendency of the body at rest to remain at rest. If the body is in uniform motion it tends to remain in uniform motion. The Newton's first law establishes the notation of inertia and inertial frame.

2. A body acted upon by a force **F** moves in such a manner that the time rate of change of momentum equal to the force.

The momentum **p** is defined as the product of mass m and the velocity **v**

$$\mathbf{p} = m\,\mathbf{v}$$

The second law can be expressed as

$$\mathbf{F} = \frac{d\mathbf{p}}{dt} = \frac{d}{dt}(m\mathbf{v}) = m\mathbf{a}$$

$$m = \frac{\mathbf{F}}{\mathbf{a}}$$

where **a** is acceleration. According to the second law, for same acceleration large value of **F** is required for larger value of m in comparison with the smaller value of m. The mass m is thus measure of the reluctance of the body to accelerate under the influence of net force. Whereas, the first law implies the existence of inertia, the second law establishes mass as the measure of the inertia. Thus, the mass which determines the acceleration of a body under the action of a given force is called inertial mass. One of the more common methods of determining mass of the object is by weighing. In the gravitational field, the weight of the body is just the gravitational force acting on the body. Thus, gravitational mass is defined as which determine, gravitational force between a body and other bodies. In this case, Newton's second law takes the form

$$W = m\,g$$

where **F** is replaced by W and g is acceleration due to gravity.

3. If two bodies exert forces on each other, these forces are equal in magnitude and opposite in direction.

According to third law, the forces come in pair. A pushes on B only if B pushes back on A. Let $\mathbf{F}_{12}$ represent the force body 1 exerts on body 2. Then, there exists a force $\mathbf{F}_{21}$, the force that body 2 exerts on body 1. These forces are related by

$$\mathbf{F}_{12} = -\,\mathbf{F}_{21}$$

The negative sign points out that the pair of forces are oppositely directed. The subscripts emphasize that the forces under consideration are on different bodies.

1.2 MECHANICS OF A PARTICLE

The motion of the particle is governed according to Newton's second law

$$\mathbf{F} = \frac{d\mathbf{p}}{dt} \qquad ...(1.1)$$

where **F** is the total force acting on the particle and **p** is the linear momentum. The linear momentum is defined as

$$\mathbf{p} = m\mathbf{v} = m\frac{d\mathbf{r}}{dt} \qquad ...(1.2)$$

where $\mathbf{r}$ is the position vector and m is the mass of the particle. The force is therefore,

$$\mathbf{F} = \frac{d\mathbf{p}}{dt} = \frac{d}{dt}(m\mathbf{v}) = m\frac{d^2\mathbf{r}}{dt^2} = m\mathbf{a} \qquad ...(1.3)$$

assuming m does not vary with time and $\mathbf{a}$ is acceleration and

$$\mathbf{a} = \frac{d^2\mathbf{r}}{dt^2} \qquad ...\ (1.4)$$

If the total force acting on the particle vanishes, then

$$\frac{d\mathbf{p}}{dt} = 0 \qquad ...(1.5)$$

or $\mathbf{p}$ is constant in time and the linear momentum is conserved. The result is obtained from the Eq.(1.5) and therefore applies for each component of the linear momentum. Let $\mathbf{s}$ be some constant vector such that

$$\dot{\mathbf{p}} \cdot \mathbf{s} = \mathbf{F} \cdot \mathbf{s} = 0$$

on integrating with respect to time

$$\mathbf{p.s.} = \text{constant} \qquad ...(1.6)$$

which states that the component of linear momentum in a direction in which the force vanishes is constant in time.

The angular momentum $\mathbf{L}$ of the particle with respect to an origin from which $\mathbf{r}$ is measured as

$$\mathbf{L} = \mathbf{r} \times \mathbf{p} \qquad ...(1.7)$$

The moment of force or torque $\mathbf{N}$ about the same origin is defined as

$$\mathbf{N} = \mathbf{r} \times \mathbf{F} = \mathbf{r} \times \frac{d\mathbf{p}}{dt} \qquad ...(1.8)$$

On differentiating Eq.(1.7)

$$\frac{d\mathbf{L}}{dt} = \frac{d\mathbf{r}}{dt} \times \mathbf{p} + \mathbf{r} \times \frac{d\mathbf{p}}{dt} = \dot{\mathbf{r}} \times m\dot{\mathbf{r}} + \mathbf{r} \times \mathbf{F} \qquad ...(1.9)$$

The first term on the right hand side of Eq.(1.9) vanishes. Thus, from Eqs. (1.8) and (1.9)

$$\frac{d\mathbf{L}}{dt} = \mathbf{r} \times \mathbf{F} = \mathbf{r} \times \dot{\mathbf{p}} = \mathbf{N} \qquad ...(1.10)$$

If the total torque acting on the particle vanishes, then

$$\frac{d\mathbf{L}}{dt} = 0 \qquad ...(1.11)$$

and L is constant in time. Thus, Total angular momentum of a particle is conserved if the total torque acting on it vanishes.

Consider the work done by a force **F** on a particle is going from point 1 to point 2. The work done by definition is

$$W_{12} = \int_1^2 \mathbf{F}\cdot d\mathbf{r} \qquad ...(1.12)$$

$$\mathbf{F}\cdot d\mathbf{r} = \dot{\mathbf{p}}\cdot d\mathbf{r} = m\frac{d\mathbf{v}}{dt}\cdot d\mathbf{r} = m\frac{d\mathbf{v}}{dt}\cdot\frac{d\mathbf{r}}{dt}dt = \frac{d}{dt}\left(\frac{1}{2}m\mathbf{v}^2\right)dt \quad (1.13)$$

Substituting Eq.(1.13) in Eq.(1.12)

$$W_{12} = \frac{m}{2}\int_1^2 d(\mathbf{v}^2)$$

$$W_{12} = \frac{m}{2}(\mathbf{v}_2^2 - \mathbf{v}_1^2) \qquad ...(1.14)$$

The scalar quantity T given by

$$\frac{1}{2}m\mathbf{v}^2 = T$$

is called kinetic energy. Hence Eq.(1.14) is

$$W_{12} = T_2 - T_1 \qquad ...(1.15)$$

If $T_1 > T_2$, then $W_{12} < 0$ and the particle has done work with a resulting decrease in kinetic energy. If the force field is such that the work W done around a closed orbit is zero, that is,

$$\oint \mathbf{F}\cdot d\mathbf{r} = 0 \qquad ...(1.16)$$

then the force is said to be conservative. By Stoke's theorem, the condition for conservative forces can be written as

$$\nabla\times\mathbf{F} = 0 \qquad ...(1.17)$$

We may define the potential energy V of a particle in terms of the work required to move the particle from a position 1 to a position 2 with no net change in kinetic energy

$$\int_1^2 \mathbf{F}\cdot d\mathbf{r} = V_1 - V_2 \qquad ...(1.18)$$

where V_1 and V_2 are the potential energies at points 1 and 2, respectively. Since curl of a gradient always vanishes, therefore from Eq.(1.17) we have

$$\mathbf{F} = -\nabla V \qquad ...(1.19)$$

The potential energy is defined to within an additive constant. That is force defined by Eq.(1.19) is not different from that defined as $-\nabla\,(V + \text{constant})$. Therefore, the potential energy has no absolute meaning, only difference of potential energy is physically meaningful. The zero level of V is therefore arbitrary.

$$\int_1^2 \mathbf{F}\cdot d\mathbf{r} = -\int_1^2 (\nabla V)\cdot d\mathbf{r} = -\int_1^2 \left(\frac{\partial V}{\partial x}dx + \frac{\partial V}{\partial y}dy + \frac{\partial V}{\partial z}dz\right)$$

$$W_{12} = \int_1^2 \mathbf{F}\cdot d\mathbf{r} = -\int_1^2 dV = V_1 - V_2 \qquad ...(1.20)$$

From Eqs.(1.15) and (1.20)

$$T_2 - T_1 = V_1 - V_2$$

$$T_2 + V_2 = V_1 + T_1 = E \qquad ...(1.21)$$

Thus, if the forces acting on a particle are conservative then the total energy E is conserved. The total time derivative of E is

$$\frac{dE}{dt} = \frac{dT}{dt} + \frac{dV}{dt} \qquad ...(1.22)$$

From Eq.(1.13)

$$\mathbf{F}\cdot d\mathbf{r} = d\left(\frac{1}{2}m\mathbf{v}^2\right) = dT$$

dividing by dt

$$\mathbf{F}\cdot\frac{d\mathbf{r}}{dt} = \mathbf{F}\cdot\dot{\mathbf{r}} = \frac{dT}{dt} \qquad ...(1.23)$$

$$\frac{dV}{dt} = \left(\frac{\partial V}{\partial x}\frac{dx}{dt} + \frac{\partial V}{\partial y}\frac{dy}{dt} + \frac{\partial V}{\partial z}\frac{dz}{dt}\right) + \frac{\partial V}{\partial t} = (\nabla V)\cdot\dot{\mathbf{r}} + \frac{\partial V}{\partial t} \qquad ...(1.24)$$

on substitution of Eqs.(1.23) and (1.24) in Eq.(1.22)

$$\frac{dE}{dt} = \mathbf{F}\cdot\dot{\mathbf{r}} + (\nabla V)\cdot\dot{\mathbf{r}} + \frac{\partial V}{\partial t} = (\mathbf{F} + \nabla V)\cdot\dot{\mathbf{r}} + \frac{\partial V}{\partial t}$$

But

$$\mathbf{F} = -\nabla V$$

Therefore,

$$\frac{dE}{dt} = \frac{\partial V}{\partial t}$$

If V is not an explicit function of time then, the force field represented by **F** is conservative. The total energy E of a particle in a conservative force field is a constant in time.

1.3 MECHANICS OF A SYSTEM OF PARTICLES

A system of particles with all its interaction constitutes a dynamical system of great generality. Let us consider, the behaviour of a mechanical system containing two or more particles acted upon by (i) internal forces exerted by the particles upon one another (ii) external forces exerted upon particles of the system by agents not belonging to the system. We assume the particles to be point masses each specified by radius vector **r** (having components x,y,z) in space.

Suppose a system contains N particles and they are numbered as 1, 2, 3,..., N. The masses of the particles are designated by m_1, m_2, ..., m_N. The position of the particles are r_1, r_2,...., r_N relative to an inertial frame. The total force acting on the ith particle will be the sum of the internal forces exerted on particle i by all the other $(N-1)$ particles in the system, plus any external force which may be applied to the particle i. Equation of motion according to Newton's second law is

$$\dot{\mathbf{p}}_i = m\,\dot{\mathbf{v}}_i = \mathbf{F}_i = \mathbf{f}_i + \sum_{j=1}^{N} \mathbf{f}_{ij} \qquad ...(1.25)$$

where $\mathbf{f}_i$ is an external force, and $\mathbf{f}_{ij}$ is the internal force on the ith particle due to jth particle and $\mathbf{f}_{ii} = 0$, that is particle cannot act on itself to influence the motion. $\mathbf{f}_{ij}$ (like $\mathbf{f}_i$) obeys Newton's third law of action and reaction. Summing the right and left hand sides of the Eq.(1.25) over all the particles

$$\sum_{i=1}^{N} \dot{\mathbf{p}}_i = \frac{d^2}{dt^2} \sum_{i=1}^{N} m_i\,\mathbf{r}_i = \sum_{i=1}^{N} \mathbf{f}_i + \sum_{i=1}^{N} \sum_{j=1}^{N} \mathbf{f}_{ij} \qquad ...(1.26)$$

The first term on the right hand side of the equation is total external force **F.** Because of Newton's law of action and reaction we have

$$\mathbf{f}_{ij} = -\mathbf{f}_{ji}$$

Consider the last term on the right hand side of the Eq.(1.26), that is,

$$\sum_{i=1}^{N} \sum_{j=1}^{N} \mathbf{f}_{ij}$$

In this term the summation is carried out over both i and j, these indices are dummies, that is, we may interchange i and j without affecting the sum.

Thus

$$\sum_{i,j\neq i}\mathbf{f}_{ij}=\sum_{j,i\neq j}\mathbf{f}_{ji}$$

But $\mathbf{f}_{ij}=-\mathbf{f}_{ji}$, so that

$$\sum_{i,j\neq i}\mathbf{f}_{ij}=-\sum_{i,j\neq i}\mathbf{f}_{ij}$$

If the quantity is equal to its negative, it must vanish identically, that is

$$\sum_{i=1}^{N}\sum_{j=1}^{N}\mathbf{f}_{ij}=0 \qquad \text{... (1.27)}$$

The centre of mass (Fig.1.1) of the system of particles is defined as

$$\mathbf{R}=\frac{m_1\mathbf{r}_1+m_2\mathbf{r}_2+.......+m_N\mathbf{r}_N}{m_1+m_2+....+m_N}=\frac{\sum_i m_i\mathbf{r}_i}{\sum_i m_i}=\frac{\sum_i m_i\mathbf{r}_i}{M} \qquad \text{...(1.28)}$$

where M is total mass, that is,

$$M=\sum_i m_i$$

Differentiating Eq.(1.28)

$$\dot{\mathbf{R}}=\frac{\sum_i m_i\dot{\mathbf{r}}_i}{\sum_i m_i}=\frac{\sum_i m_i\mathbf{v}_i}{M} \qquad \text{...(1.29)}$$

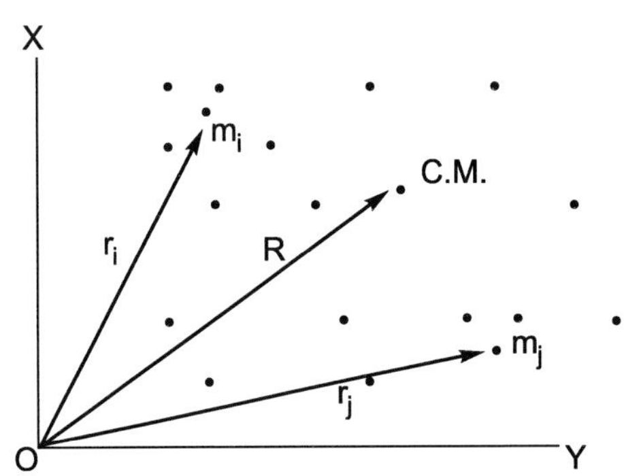

Fig 1.1 The centre of mass (C.M.) of a system of particles.

where $\sum_i m_i \mathbf{v}_i$ is the total momentum of the system. In the absence of external forces, the total momentum is constant, so that

$$\dot{\mathbf{R}} = \text{constant} \qquad \text{...(1.30)}$$

Thus velocity of centre of mass is constant in the absence of external force. From Eq.(1.29)

$$\sum_i m_i \dot{\mathbf{R}} = \sum_i m_i \mathbf{v}_i$$

Differentiating

$$\sum_i m_i \ddot{\mathbf{R}} = \sum_i m_i \dot{\mathbf{v}}_i = \sum_i \mathbf{F}_i \qquad \text{...(1.31)}$$

From Eqs.(1.26) and (1.27)

$$\sum_i m_i \ddot{\mathbf{R}} = \sum_i \mathbf{F}_i = \sum_i \mathbf{f}_i + \sum_{i,j} \mathbf{f}_{ij} = \sum_i \mathbf{f}_i \qquad \text{...(1.32)}$$

Thus

$$M\ddot{\mathbf{R}} = \sum_i \mathbf{f}_i = \mathbf{f} \qquad \text{...(1.33)}$$

This result shows that the centre of mass moves as if total external force is acting on the entire mass of the system concentrated at the centre of mass. Purely internal forces therefore have no effect on the motion of the centre of mass.

The total linear momentum **P** of a system of N particles is equal to the N vector sum of the momenta of the individual particles

$$\mathbf{P} = \sum_i m_i \dot{\mathbf{r}}_i = \sum_i \mathbf{p}_i = M\dot{\mathbf{R}} \qquad \text{...(1.34)}$$

The total linear momentum of the system is the total mass of the system times the velocity of centre of mass.

$$\dot{\mathbf{P}} = \sum_i \dot{\mathbf{p}}_i = \sum m_i \ddot{\mathbf{r}}_i = M\ddot{\mathbf{R}} = \mathbf{f} \qquad \text{...(1.35)}$$

If **f** remains equal to zero over some time interval, the linear momentum remains constant during the interval. If a component of **f** in a certain fixed direction remains at zero then the corresponding component of **P** is conserved.

The angular momentum of the ith particle of mass m_i about fixed reference point O is

$$\mathbf{L}_i = \mathbf{r}_i \times m_i \dot{\mathbf{r}}_i = \mathbf{r}_i \times \mathbf{p}_i \qquad \text{...(1.36)}$$

Upon summation over N particles, the angular momentum of the system about O is

$$\mathbf{L} = \sum_i \mathbf{L}_i = \sum_i \mathbf{r}_i \times \mathbf{p}_i$$

The torque **N** is

$$\mathbf{N} = \sum_i (\mathbf{r}_i \times \mathbf{F}_i) = \sum_i \mathbf{r}_i \times \dot{\mathbf{p}}_i = \sum \frac{d}{dt}(\mathbf{r}_i \times \mathbf{p}_i) - \sum \frac{d\mathbf{r}_i}{dt} \times \mathbf{p}_i$$

$$\mathbf{N} = \sum_i \frac{d}{dt}(\mathbf{r}_i \times \mathbf{p}_i) - \sum_i \mathbf{v}_i \times m_i \mathbf{v}_i \qquad \text{...(1.37)}$$

$$\mathbf{N} = \sum_i \mathbf{r}_i \times \dot{\mathbf{p}}_i = \sum_i \mathbf{r}_i \times (\mathbf{f}_i + \sum_j \mathbf{f}_{ij}) \qquad \text{...(1.38)}$$

the term $\mathbf{r}_i \times \mathbf{f}_{ij}$ can be considered as a sum of the pairs of the form

$$\mathbf{r}_i \times \mathbf{f}_{ij} + \mathbf{r}_j \times \mathbf{f}_{ji} = \mathbf{r}_i \times \mathbf{f}_{ij} - \mathbf{r}_j \times \mathbf{f}_{ij} = (\mathbf{r}_i - \mathbf{r}_j) \times \mathbf{f}_{ij} \qquad \text{...(1.39)}$$

But $\mathbf{r}_i - \mathbf{r}_j$ is identical with the vector $\mathbf{r}_{ij}$ from i to j (Fig.1.2) and the law of action and reaction states that

$$\mathbf{r}_{ij} \times \mathbf{f}_{ij} = 0 \qquad \text{...(1.40)}$$

since the vector $\mathbf{r}_{ij}$ has the direction of the line joining the particle i and j. If $\mathbf{f}_{ij}$ acts along this line the cross product $\mathbf{r}_{ij} \times \mathbf{f}_{ij}$ vanishes. Thus

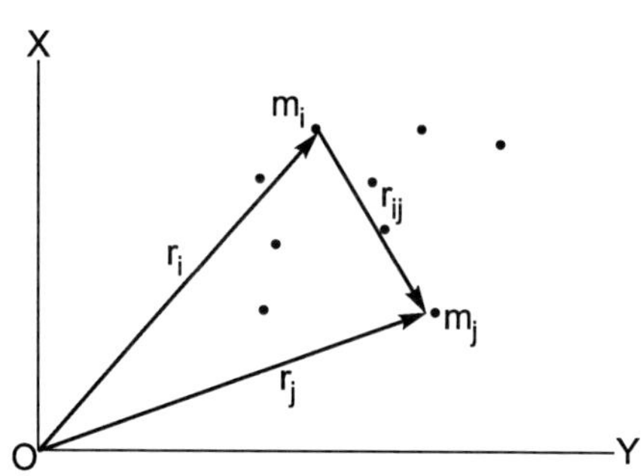

Fig 1.2 The vector $\mathbf{r}_{ij}$ between the i th and j th particles.

$$\mathbf{N} = \frac{d\mathbf{L}}{dt} \qquad \text{...(1.41)}$$

The time derivative of total angular momentum is thus equal to the moment of the external force about a given point and angular momentum of an isolated system cannot be altered with the application of an external force or torque.

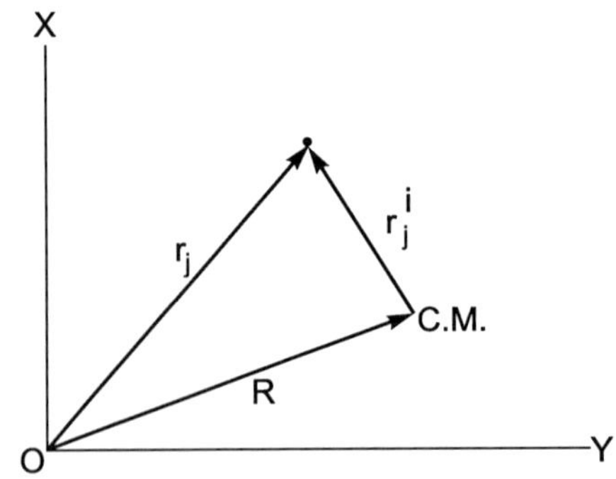

Fig 1.3 The vectors involved in the shift of reference point for the angular momentum.

Let **R** be the radius vector from O to the centre of mass and $\mathbf{r}_i'$ be the radius vector from centre of mass to the ith particle (Fig.1.3)

$$\mathbf{r}_i = \mathbf{R} + \mathbf{r}_i' \qquad ...(1.42)$$

$$\mathbf{v}_i = \dot{\mathbf{r}}_i = \dot{\mathbf{R}} + \dot{\mathbf{r}}_i' = \mathbf{V} + \mathbf{v}_i' \qquad ...(1.43)$$

where velocity of centre of mass relative to O is given by **V** and velocity of ith particle relative to centre of mass of the system is $\mathbf{v}_i$'

Total angular momentum

$$\mathbf{L} = \sum_i \mathbf{r}_i \times \mathbf{p}_i = \sum m_i(\mathbf{R} + \mathbf{r}_i') \times (\mathbf{V} + \mathbf{v}_i')$$

$$\mathbf{L} = \sum_i m_i(\mathbf{R} \times \mathbf{V} + \mathbf{R} \times \mathbf{v}_i' + \mathbf{r}_i' \times \mathbf{V} + \mathbf{r}_i' \times \mathbf{v}_i') \qquad ...(1.44)$$

$$\mathbf{L} = \sum_i \mathbf{R} \times m_i \mathbf{V} + \sum_i \mathbf{r}_i' \times m_i \mathbf{v}_i' + \left(\sum_i m_i \mathbf{r}_i'\right) \times \mathbf{V} + \mathbf{R} \times \frac{d}{dt}\sum_i m_i \mathbf{r}_i' \qquad ...(1.45)$$

Putting the value of $\mathbf{r}_i$ from Eq.(1.42) in Eq.(1.28)

$$\mathbf{R} = \frac{\sum_i m_i(\mathbf{R} + \mathbf{r}_i')}{M} = \frac{\mathbf{R}\sum_i m_i}{M} + \frac{\sum_i m_i \mathbf{r}_i'}{M} = \mathbf{R} + \frac{\sum_i m_i \mathbf{r}_i'}{M} \qquad ...(1.46)$$

The left hand side and right hand side of the Eq.(1.46) are equal if

$$\sum_i m_i \mathbf{r}_i' = 0 \qquad ...(1.47)$$

Differentiating Eq.(1.46)

$$\dot{\mathbf{R}} = \dot{\mathbf{R}} + \frac{1}{M}\frac{d}{dt}\sum_i m_i \mathbf{r}_i' \qquad ...(1.48)$$

The left hand side and right hand side of the Eq.(1.48) are equal if

$$\frac{d}{dt}\sum_i m_i \mathbf{r}_i' = 0 \qquad ...(1.49)$$

On substitution of Eqs.(1.48) and (1.49) in Eq.(1.45), the total angular momentum about O is

$$\mathbf{L} = \sum_i \mathbf{R}\times m_i \mathbf{V} + \sum_i \mathbf{r}_i' \times m_i \mathbf{v}_i' = M\,\mathbf{R}\times\mathbf{V} + \sum_i \mathbf{r}_i' \times \mathbf{p}_i' \qquad ...(1.50)$$

The total angular momentum about a point O is the angular momentum of the system concentrated at the centre of mass plus the angular momentum of the motion about the centre of mass. If centre of mass is at rest with respect to O, the angular momentum will be independent of the point of reference and **L** will always reduce to the angular momentum taken about the centre of mass.

Consider the work done by all forces in moving the system from an initial configuration 1 to final configuration 2

$$W_{12} = \sum_i \int_1^2 \mathbf{F}_i \cdot d\mathbf{r}_i = \sum_i \int_1^2 \mathbf{f}_i \cdot d\mathbf{r}_i + \sum_{i\neq j} \int_1^2 \mathbf{f}_{ij} \cdot d\mathbf{r}_i \qquad ...(1.51)$$

$$\sum_i \int_1^2 \mathbf{f}_i \cdot d\mathbf{r}_i = \sum_i \int_1^2 m_i\, \dot{\mathbf{v}}_i \cdot \frac{d\mathbf{r}_i}{dt} dt = \sum_i \int_1^2 m_i\, \dot{\mathbf{v}}_i \cdot \mathbf{v}_i\, dt = \sum_i \int_1^2 d\left(\frac{m_i\, \mathbf{v}_i^2}{2}\right) dt \qquad ...(1.52)$$

$$\sum_i \int_1^2 \mathbf{F}_i \cdot d\mathbf{r}_i = \sum_i \frac{1}{2} m_i\, \mathbf{v}_i^2 \Big|_1^2 = T_2 - T_1 \qquad ...(1.53)$$

where

$$T = \frac{1}{2}\sum_i m_i\, \mathbf{v}_i^2 \qquad ...(1.54)$$

In centre of mass coordinates

$$\mathbf{v}_i^2 = (\mathbf{V} + \mathbf{v}_i')\cdot(\mathbf{V} + \mathbf{v}_i') = (\mathbf{V}^2 + 2\mathbf{V}\cdot\mathbf{v}_i' + \mathbf{v}_i'^2) \qquad ...(1.55)$$

Substituting Eq.(1.55) in Eq.(1.54),the kinetic energy is

$$T = \frac{1}{2}\sum_i m_i (\mathbf{V}^2 + 2\mathbf{V}\cdot\mathbf{v}_i' + \mathbf{v}_i'^2) = \frac{1}{2}\sum_i m_i\, \mathbf{V}^2 + \mathbf{V}\cdot\frac{d}{dt}\sum_i m_i\, \mathbf{r}_i' + \frac{1}{2}\sum_i m_i\, \mathbf{v}_i'^2 \qquad ...(1.56)$$

Using Eq.(1.49) in Eq.(1.56)

$$T = \frac{1}{2} M \mathbf{V}^2 + \frac{1}{2} \sum_i m_i \mathbf{v}_i'^2 \qquad ...(1.57)$$

The total kinetic energy of the system is equal to the sum of the kinetic energy of the particle of mass M moving with velocity of the centre of mass and kinetic energy of motion of the individual particles relative to the centre of mass.

If the forces $\mathbf{f}_i$ and $\mathbf{f}_{ij}$ are conservative, then they are derivable from potential function

$$\mathbf{f}_i = -\nabla_i V_i \;,\; \mathbf{f}_{ij} = -\nabla_i V_{ij} \qquad ...(1.58)$$

V_i and V_{ij} are potential functions. The notation ∇_i means that the gradient operation is performed with respect to the coordinates of the ith particle.

Consider the right hand side of the Eq.(1.51) and equating it with W_{12}

$$W_{12} = \sum_i \int_1^2 \mathbf{f}_i \cdot d\mathbf{r}_i + \sum_{i,j\neq i} \int_1^2 \mathbf{f}_{ij} \cdot d\mathbf{r}_i \qquad ...(1.59)$$

The first term on the right hand side of Eq.(1.59) is

$$\sum_i \int_1^2 \mathbf{f}_i \cdot d\mathbf{r}_i = -\sum_i \int_1^2 (\nabla_i V_i) \cdot d\mathbf{r}_i = -\sum_i V_i \Big|_1^2 \qquad ...(1.60)$$

The second term on the right hand side of Eq.(1.59) is

$$\sum_{i,j\neq i} \int_1^2 \mathbf{f}_{ij} \cdot d\mathbf{r}_i = \sum_{i,j\neq i} \int_1^2 (\mathbf{f}_{ij} \cdot d\mathbf{r}_i + \mathbf{f}_{ji} \cdot d\mathbf{r}_j) = \sum_{i,j\neq i} \int_1^2 \mathbf{f}_{ij} \cdot (d\mathbf{r}_i - d\mathbf{r}_j) = \sum_{i,j\neq i} \int_1^2 \mathbf{f}_{ij} \cdot d\mathbf{r}_{ij}$$

...(1.61)

where

$$d\mathbf{r}_{ij} = d\mathbf{r}_i - d\mathbf{r}_j$$

V_{ij} is a function of distance between particles i and j therefore V_{ij} depends on six quantities, that is, three coordinates of particle i and three coordinates of particle j. The total derivative of V_{ij} is therefore

$$dV_{ij} = \frac{\partial V_{ij}}{\partial x_i} dx_i + \frac{\partial V_{ij}}{\partial y_i} dy_i + \frac{\partial V_{ij}}{\partial z_i} dz_i + \frac{\partial V_{ij}}{\partial x_j} dx_j + \frac{\partial V_{ij}}{\partial y_j} dy_j + \frac{\partial V_{ij}}{\partial z_j} dz_j$$

$$dV_{ij} = (\nabla_i V_{ij}) \cdot d\mathbf{r}_i + (\nabla_j V_{ij}) \cdot d\mathbf{r}_j$$

Now

$$\nabla_i V_{ij} = -\mathbf{f}_{ij}$$

Since

$$V_{ij} = V_{ji}$$

we have

$$\nabla_j V_{ij} = \nabla_j V_{ji} = -\mathbf{f}_{ji} = \mathbf{f}_{ij}$$

therefore

$$dV_{ij} = \mathbf{f}_{ij} \cdot (d\mathbf{r}_i - d\mathbf{r}_j) = \mathbf{f}_{ij} \cdot d\mathbf{r}_{ij}$$

On substitution of Eq.(1.58) in Eq.(1.61)

$$\sum_{i,j\neq i} \int_1^2 \mathbf{f}_{ij} \cdot d\mathbf{r}_i = \sum_{i<j} \int_1^2 dV_{ij} = -\sum_{i<j} V_{ij}\Big|_1^2 \qquad ...(1.62)$$

On substitution of Eqs.(1.60) and (1.62) in Eq.(1.59)

$$W_{12} = -\sum_i V_i\Big|_1^2 - \sum_{i<j} V_{ij}\Big|_1^2 \qquad ...(1.63)$$

If the external and internal forces are derivable from potential function, then the potential energy V is

$$V = \sum_i V_i + \sum_{i<j} V_{ij} \qquad ...(1.64)$$

$$W_{12} = -V\Big|_1^2 = V_1 - V_2 \qquad ...(1.65)$$

Equating Eqs.(1.53) and (1.65)

$$T_2 - T_1 = V_1 - V_2$$

$$T_1 + V_1 = T_2 + V_2 = E \qquad ...(1.66)$$

which expresses the conservation of energy.

1.4 MOTION WITH VARIABLE MASS- THE ROCKET EQUATION

The operation of a rocket depends upon the law of conservation of momentum as applied to a system of particles, where the system is the rocket plus its ejected fuel. Let the velocity of the rocket with respect to a certain fixed coordinate system be $V(t)$ and let the mass of the rocket plus fuel is $M + \Delta m$. As a rocket moves in a free space, some of its mass is released in the form of ejected gases its momentum changes. Since the ejected gases acquire some momentum, the rocket receives a compensating momentum in the opposite direction.

Let the rocket ejects some fuel of mass Δm and the rockets speed therefore increases to $\mathbf{V} + \Delta \mathbf{V}$. Let the velocity of the ejected fuel is $\mathbf{V}_e$ relative to the rocket., then velocity of the fuel relative to fixed coordinate system is $\mathbf{V} - \mathbf{V}_e$. From law of conservation of momentum

$$(M + \Delta m)\mathbf{V} = M(\mathbf{V} + \Delta\mathbf{V}) + \Delta m(\mathbf{V} - \mathbf{V}_e)$$

$$M\,\Delta\mathbf{V} = \mathbf{V}_e\,\Delta m \qquad ...(1.67)$$

Since the expelled fuel represents a decrease in rocket mass, that is, the change ΔM in the rocket mass is given by

$$\Delta M = -\,\Delta m$$

the negative sign indicates a decrease in mass. The Eq.(1.67) is therefore,

$$M\,\Delta\mathbf{V} = -\,\mathbf{V}_e\,\Delta M \qquad ...(1.68)$$

Dividing by the time Δt over which the fuel is expelled, the Eq.(1.68) becomes

$$M\frac{\Delta\mathbf{V}}{\Delta t} = -\mathbf{V}_e\frac{\Delta M}{\Delta t} \qquad ...(1.69)$$

For a vanishingly small fuel mass expelled over a vanishingly small time , the velocity change becomes negligible and Eq.(1.69) becomes exact. In this limit ratio Eq.(1.69) becomes derivative

$$M\frac{d\mathbf{V}}{dt} = -\mathbf{V}_e\frac{dM}{dt} \qquad ...(1.70)$$

The quantity on the right hand side of the Eq.(1.70) is called thrust. On integrating Eq.(1.70)

$$\int_{V_i}^{V_f} d\mathbf{V} = -\,\mathbf{V}_e\int_{M_i}^{M_f}\frac{dM}{M}$$

where M_i is the initial mass of the rocket plus fuel and M_f is the final mass of the rocket and remaining fuel

$$V_f = V_i + V_e \ln\frac{M_i}{M_f} \qquad ...(1.71)$$

The increase in the velocity of the rocket is proportional to velocity of exhaust gases. Further, increase in velocity is proportional to logarithm of the ratio of initial and final mass. Therefore, this ratio should be as large as possible, that is, fuel to payload ratio must be quite large.

1.5 CONSTRAINTS

Consider a particle. The position of the particle can be specified by a radius vector **r** or three Cartesian coordinates x,y,z with reference to some fixed set of axes. If a system contains N particles then position of the system is specified by giving the position of all the particles . For example, position of particle 1 is given by radius vector $\mathbf{r}_1$ (having components x_1,y_1,z_1), particle 2 by radius vector $\mathbf{r}_2$ and so forth. Thus N radius vectors or $3N$ Cartesian coordinates are required to describe the position of the system. The N particle system has $3N$ coordinates or degrees of freedom, that is, the number of independent coordinate variables. The state of the system can be represented by a point in $3N$ dimensional space called configuration space. Every dimension of this corresponds to one of the coordinates. The time history of a system may be represented by a curve in the configuration space. Each point specifies the configuration of the system at a particular instant.

The particles of the system cannot move completely independently because they are subjected to certain constraints. A constraint is a restriction on the freedom of the system of particles in the form of a condition which must be satisfied by their coordinates or by the allowed changes in their coordinates. The constraint reduces the number of degrees of freedom and therefore changes the equation of motion. For example if there are α constraint conditions, then the degrees of freedom for N particles equal $n = 3N - \alpha$. In this case configuration space is of n dimension without violating the constraints. Constraints are classified as

(1) Holonomic Constraints

The constraints are said to be holonomic if they can be described by a set of independent equations of the form

$$h_i(\mathbf{r}_1,\mathbf{r}_2,..........,\mathbf{r}_N,t) = 0 \quad (i=1,2,....,\alpha) \qquad ...(1.72)$$

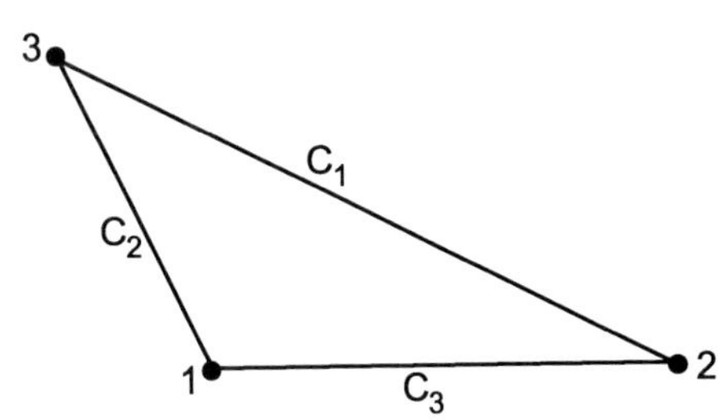

Fig 1.4 A system of three mass points at constant distance from one another.

In this case the corresponding constraint forces are always perpendicular to constraining surface. A dynamical system whose constraint equations, if any, are all of the holonomic form is called a holonomic system. As an example, consider a body consisting of three particles (Fig.1.4) such that inter particle distance is constant and equation is

$$h_1 = |\mathbf{r}_1 - \mathbf{r}_2| - c_3 = 0$$

$$h_2 = |\mathbf{r}_2 - \mathbf{r}_3| - c_1 = 0$$

$$h_3 = |\mathbf{r}_3 - \mathbf{r}_1| - c_2 = 0$$

without constraints the number of degrees of freedom = $3N = 3 \times 3 = 9$. There are three constraints conditions thereby reducing the number of degrees of freedom to $n = 3N - \alpha = 9 - 3 = 6$. Another example of a holonomic constraint is provided by a particle which is forced to move on a sphere of radius R centred at the origin of a cartesian coordinate system. The equation of the constraint is

$$h = (x^2 + y^2 + z^2) - R^2 = 0$$

where x, y, z are coordinates of the particle.

(2) Non-holonomic Constraints

The constraints are said to be nonholonomic if they take the form

$$h_i = \sum_{j=1}^{N} a_{ij}(\mathbf{r},t)\dot{\mathbf{r}}_j + a_{it}(\mathbf{r},t) = 0 \quad (i=1,2,.....,\alpha) \qquad ...(1.73)$$

or the differential form

$$\sum_{j=1}^{N} a_{ij}(\mathbf{r},t)d\mathbf{r}_j + a_{it}(\mathbf{r},t)dt = 0 \quad (i=1,2,.....,\alpha)$$

but cannot be integrated to the form (1.72). If either expression were integrable, then a function h would exist and Eq.(1.72) would apply, indicating that the constraint is actually holonomic. From Eq.(1.72)

$$\dot{h}_i = \sum_j \frac{\partial h_i}{\partial r_j}\dot{\mathbf{r}}_j + \frac{\partial h_i}{\partial t} = 0$$

Comparing it with Eq.(1.70)

$$a_{ij} = \frac{\partial h_i}{\partial r_j}, \; a_{it} = \frac{\partial h_i}{\partial t}$$

for the holonomic constraints. An example of non holonomic constraint is gas in a spherical container of radius b such that

$$r_i^2 \le b^2$$

where $\mathbf{r}_i$ is the position vector of the ith gas molecule.

(3) Scleronomic Constraints

A constraint is classified as scleronomic if the time t does not appear explicitly in the equation of the constraint. The scleronomic holonomic constraint has the form

$$h_i(\mathbf{r}) = 0 \qquad ...(1.74)$$

The form of scleronomic non-holonomic constraint is obtained by putting in Eq.(1.73)

$$h_i = \sum_{j=1}^{N} a_{ij}(\mathbf{r},t)\dot{\mathbf{r}}_j = 0 \ (i=1,2,......,\alpha) \qquad ...(1.75)$$

(4) Rheonomic Constraints

Constraint that depend on time is called rheonomic constraint. For rheonomic constraints we have

$$a_{ik}(\mathbf{r},t) \neq 0 \qquad ...(1.76)$$

in Eq.(1.73) and

$$h_i = h_i(\mathbf{r}_1, \mathbf{r}_2, ..., \mathbf{r}_N, t) \qquad ...(1.77)$$

example of rheonomic constraint is rod of varying length connecting two particles in the holonomic case

(5) Unilateral

The constraints which are expressed in the form of inequalities, such as

$$h(\mathbf{r},\dot{\mathbf{r}},t) \geq 0 \qquad ...(1.78)$$

Such constraints arise for instance, when an N-particle system (a gas, for example) is enclosed in a box; the particles move freely inside the box but cannot penetrate its boundaries.

(6) Bilateral

The constraints which are expressed in the form

$$h(\mathbf{r},\dot{\mathbf{r}},t) = 0 \qquad ...(1.79)$$

are called bilateral constraints.

(7) Conservative and Dissipative Constraints

A constraint is conservative if the total mechanical energy of the system is conserved while performing the constraint motion. Constraint forces do not do any work. The constraint is dissipative if constraint forces do work and mechanical energy is not conserved.

If a constraint equation involve coordinates as well as their derivatives, the corresponding constraint is termed as differential or kinematics. The constraints whose equations involve only coordinates are called geometric. Holonomic and non-holonomic constraints put restriction on the possible motion of the system. There is an important difference in their possible motion that distinguish holonomic and nonholonomic systems. Because of holonomic constraints, the configuration point moves in n dimensional space. Therefore, certain region of 3N dimensional space is no longer accessible, In contrast, for non-holonomic constraints, it is the differential motion which are constraints. Since these differential equations representing non holonomic constraints are not integrable, there are no finite constraint surface in the configuration space and there is no reduction of accessible region.

1.6 GENERALIZED COORDINATES

A system of N particles free from constraints has 3N independent coordinates or degrees of freedom. If there exists holonomic constraints expressed in α equations of the form (1.72), then we may use these equations to eliminate α of $3N$ coordinates and we are left with $3N - \alpha = n$ independent coordinates and the system is said to have n degrees of freedom. Table 1.1 gives some examples of various degrees of freedom.

This elimination of the dependent coordinates can be expressed in another way by introducing new n independent variables. These quantities are designated as generalized coordinates and it is customary to denote them by $q_1, q_2, \ldots, q_n$. The generalized coordinates form the n dimensional configuration space and axes of this space may have different dimensions. In terms of q_k (k = 1,2, ...,n) old coordinates are expressed as

$$\begin{aligned} \mathbf{r}_1 &= \mathbf{r}_1 (q_1, q_2, \ldots\ldots\ldots\ldots, q_n, t) \\ \mathbf{r}_2 &= \mathbf{r}_2 (q_1, q_2, \ldots\ldots\ldots\ldots, q_n, t) \\ &\ldots\ldots \; \ldots\ldots \; \ldots\ldots \; \ldots\ldots \; \ldots\ldots \\ \mathbf{r}_N &= \mathbf{r}_N (q_1, q_2, \ldots\ldots\ldots\ldots, q_n, t) \end{aligned} \qquad \ldots(1.80)$$

Table 1.1 Examples of systems having various degrees of freedom

Degrees of freedom	Examples of systems
1.	Bead sliding along a smooth parabolic wire, a piston moving up and down, a rigid body rotating about a fixed axis, simple pendulum, particle of mass m free to move in the interior of a given fixed smooth tube of small bore, motion of a homogeneous solid right circular cone on a perfectly rough inclined plane, motion of a discone of whose points is forced to move in a given manner, motion of a disc rolling on a constrained disc and linked to it, simple harmonic oscillator.
2.	A particle moving on a given surface, motion of the particle which is constrained to move on the surface of a cone, rod passing through ring on a horizontal plane, one cylinder rolling on the another under gravity, axle with pair of wheels rolling on a plane.
3.	A rigid body moving parallel to a plane, a particle moving in a space, rigid body rotating about a fixed point, sphere rolling on a horizontal plane, circular disc rolling on a horizontal plane.
4.	Two components of a double star revolving in the same plane.
5.	Two particles kept at a constant distance from each other, rigid body in contact with a fixed plane.
6.	Two planets revolving about a fixed sun, a rigid body moving freely in space.

The generalized coordinates need not have thc dimensions of length. Depending on the problem, it may prove more convenient to choose some of the generalized coordinates with dimension of energy, some with dimension of $(\text{length})^2$, some which are dimensionless etc. The choice of a set of generalized coordinates for the description of a system is not unique; there are in general many set of quantities which will completely specify the state of a given system.

Consider the motion of a particle in the xy plane. The position of the particle can be specified by Cartesian coordinates x and y. The position of the particle in the plane can also be specified by the plane polar coordinates $\mathbf{r}$ and θ. The ultimate test of the suitability of a particular set of generalized coordinates is whether the resulting equations of motion are sufficiently simple to allow a straight forward interpretation. In addition to the generalized coordinates, we may define a set of quantities which consists of the time derivative of the or simply the generalized velocities.

1.7 VIRTUAL DISPLACEMENT

A mechanical system is said to be in equilibrium if the sum of all the forces acting on it is zero. The system can have several positions of equilibrium (consistent with the constraints imposed on it) at any given time. To go from one such configuration of the system of particles at a particular instant to another configuration we need only give the ith particle a displacement $\delta \mathbf{r}_i$ from the old position to the new position. $\delta \mathbf{r}_i$ is called virtual displacement to distinguish it from true displacement, denoted by $d\mathbf{r}_i$, which occur in a time interval where forces and constraints could be changing.

1.8 VIRTUAL WORK

For a system to be in equilibrium, the resultant force acting on each particle of the system must be zero, that is,

$$\mathbf{F}_i = 0$$

The virtual work done by a force $\mathbf{F}_i$ during a virtual displacement is

$$\delta W = \mathbf{F}_i \cdot \delta \mathbf{r}_i = 0$$

By adding these we have

$$\sum_{i=1}^{N} \mathbf{F}_i \cdot \delta \mathbf{r}_i = 0 \qquad \text{...(1.81)}$$

where $\mathbf{F}_i$ is the total force applied to the particle i. Suppose the constraint is taken care by applying an additional force $\mathbf{R}_i$ (force of constraint) to every particle i, then

$$\mathbf{F}_i = \mathbf{f}_i + \mathbf{R}_i \qquad \text{...(1.82)}$$

where $\mathbf{f}_i$ is real dynamic force. Substituting Eq.(1.82) in Eq.(1.81).

$$\sum_{i=1}^{N} \mathbf{F}_i \cdot \delta \mathbf{r}_i = \sum_{i=1}^{N} (\mathbf{f}_i + \mathbf{R}_i) \cdot \delta \mathbf{r}_i = 0 \qquad ...(1.83)$$

Total work of the force of constraint vanishes, that is,

$$\sum_{i=1}^{N} \mathbf{R}_i \cdot \delta \mathbf{r}_i = 0 \qquad ...(1.84)$$

and Eq.(1.83) is then

$$\sum_{i=1}^{N} \mathbf{f}_i \cdot \delta \mathbf{r}_i = 0 \qquad ...(1.85)$$

This equation does not imply that the individual term vanishes as $\delta \mathbf{r}_i$ are not independent.

1.9 D'ALEMBERT'S PRINCIPLE

Consider a system of N particles. For the ith particle Newton's law of motion is

$$\mathbf{F}_i = m_i \ddot{\mathbf{r}}_i \qquad ...(1.86)$$

where m_i is the mass and $\mathbf{r}_i$ is position vector of ith particle. Total force acting on the ith particle is $\mathbf{F}_i$. The total force acting on the particle is sum of applied force $\mathbf{f}_i$ and constraint force $\mathbf{R}_i$. Then Eq.(1.86) is

$$(\mathbf{F}_i - m_i \ddot{\mathbf{r}}_i) = (\mathbf{f}_i + \mathbf{R}_i - m_i \ddot{\mathbf{r}}_i) = 0 \qquad ...(1.87)$$

Taking the scalar product with virtual displacement $\delta \mathbf{r}_i$

$$\sum_{i} (\mathbf{f}_i + \mathbf{R}_i - m_i \ddot{\mathbf{r}}_i) \cdot \delta \mathbf{r}_i = 0 \qquad ...(1.88)$$

Restricting to those systems for which work of the force of constraint vanishes, that is,

$$\sum_{i} \mathbf{R}_i \cdot \delta \mathbf{r}_i = 0 \qquad ...(1.89)$$

The Eq.(1.88) is thus

$$\sum_{i} (\mathbf{f}_i - m_i \ddot{\mathbf{r}}_i) \cdot \delta \mathbf{r}_i = 0 \qquad ...(1.90)$$

The vector $m_i \ddot{\mathbf{r}}_i = \dot{\mathbf{p}}_i$ is called effective force and this vector reverse $-m_i \ddot{\mathbf{r}}_i$ is called reverse effective force or forces of inertia.

$$\sum_{i} (\mathbf{f}_i - \dot{\mathbf{p}}_i) \cdot \delta \mathbf{r}_i = 0 \qquad ...(1.91)$$

This is called D'Alembert's principle. The importance of D'Alembert's principle lies in two facts (a) a set of vector equations is replaced by a single scalar equation (b) δW involves only those forces which do work in the displacement $\delta \mathbf{r}$. The D'Alembert's principle eliminates workless reaction of constraints.

Solved Examples

Example 1. *A ball rolls without friction on the inside of a circular annulus. The annulus is put upright in the earth's gravitational field. Obtain equation of motion using D'Alembert's principle.*

Solution: Choose the *xy* plane to coincide with the annulus and takes it centre to be the origin. Let **n** be the unit vector in the direction of increasing r while ***l*** is the unit vector in the direction of θ as shown in the Fig.1.5

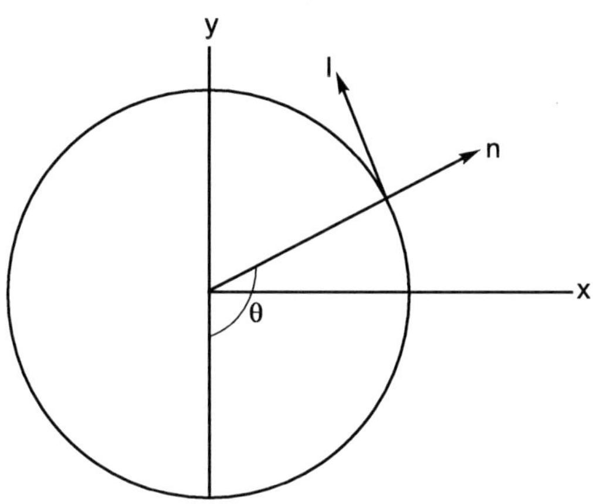

Fig.1.5

From the Fig.1.5

$$\mathbf{l} = \cos\theta\,\mathbf{i} + \sin\theta\,\mathbf{j} \qquad ...(1.92)$$

$$\mathbf{n} = \sin\theta\,\mathbf{i} - \cos\theta\,\mathbf{j} \qquad ...(1.93)$$

The position vector **r** is given by

$$\mathbf{r} = \mathrm{r}\,\mathbf{n}(\theta) \qquad ...(1.94)$$

$$\dot{\mathbf{r}} = \dot{\mathrm{r}}\,\mathbf{n} + \mathrm{r}\,\dot{\mathbf{n}} = \dot{\mathrm{r}}\,\mathbf{n} + \mathrm{r}(\cos\theta\,\dot{\theta}\,\mathbf{i} + \sin\theta\,\dot{\theta}\,\mathbf{j}) = \dot{\mathrm{r}}\,\mathbf{n} + \mathrm{r}\,\mathbf{l}\,\dot{\theta} = \mathrm{r}\,\mathbf{l}\,\dot{\theta}$$

since r = R (R is the radius)

$$\ddot{\mathbf{r}} = \mathrm{r}\,\dot{\mathbf{l}}\,\dot{\theta} + \mathrm{r}\,\mathbf{l}\,\ddot{\theta} = -\,\mathrm{r}\,\mathbf{n}\,\dot{\theta}^2 + \mathrm{r}\,\mathbf{l}\,\ddot{\theta} = -\,\mathrm{R}\,\mathbf{n}\,\dot{\theta}^2 + \mathrm{R}\,\mathbf{l}\,\ddot{\theta} \qquad ...(1.95)$$

we have from Eq.(1.94)

$$\delta\mathbf{r} = \mathrm{R}\,\delta(\mathbf{n}) = R(\cos\theta\,\mathbf{i} + \sin\theta\,\mathbf{j})\,\delta\theta = R\,\mathbf{l}\,\delta\theta \qquad ...(1.96)$$

The force acting on the system

$$\mathbf{f} = -mg\,\mathbf{j}$$

From D'Alembert's principle, using Eqs.(1.91), (1.95) and (1.96)

$$(-mg\,\mathbf{j} - m\ddot{\mathbf{r}})\delta\mathbf{r} = [-mg\,\mathbf{j} - m(-\mathrm{R}\,\mathbf{n}\dot{\theta}^2 + \mathrm{R}\,\mathbf{l}\ddot{\theta})]\cdot R\mathbf{l}\delta\theta = 0$$

$$[-mg\,\mathbf{j}\cdot\mathbf{l} - m(-\mathrm{R}\,\mathbf{n}\cdot\mathbf{l}\dot{\theta}^2 + \mathrm{R}\,\mathbf{l}\cdot\mathbf{l}\ddot{\theta})]\,R\,\delta\theta = [-mg\,\mathbf{j}\cdot\mathbf{l} - m\,\mathrm{R}\,\ddot{\theta}]\,R\,\delta\theta = 0$$

$$= [-mg\sin\theta - m\,\mathrm{R}\,\ddot{\theta}]\,R\,\delta\theta = 0 \qquad ...(1.97)$$

Since $\delta\theta$ is freely variable so the coefficient must be equal to zero. Therefore,

$$\ddot{\theta} + \frac{g\sin\theta}{R} = 0 \qquad ...(1.98)$$

Example 2. *A particle is constrained to move in a circle in the vertical plane xy. Using the D'Alembert's principle show that for equilibrium*

$$\ddot{x}y - \ddot{y}x - gx = 0$$

Solution: Consider a circle of radius a. The equation of the circle is

$$x^2 + y^2 = a^2$$

and

$$2x\delta x + 2y\delta y = 0$$

$$\delta x = -\frac{y}{x}\delta y \qquad ...(1.99)$$

From D'Alembert's principle (Eq.1.91)

$$\sum_i (\mathbf{f}_i - \dot{\mathbf{p}}_i)\cdot\delta\mathbf{r}_i = (f_x - m\ddot{x})\delta x + (f_y - m\ddot{y})\delta y = 0 \qquad ...(1.100)$$

Now,

$$f_x = 0,\ f_y = -mg \qquad (1.101)$$

From Eqs.(1.91) and (1.99-1.101)

$$(-m\ddot{x})\delta x + (-mg - m\ddot{y})\delta y = 0$$

$$[m\ddot{x}\frac{y}{x} + (-mg - m\ddot{y})]\delta y = 0$$

Since δy is freely variable so the coefficient must be equal to zero. Therefore

$$\ddot{x}y - \ddot{y}x - gx = 0$$

Example 3. *A particle of mass m can move without friction on the inside surface of a paraboloid of revolution*

$$\phi = x^2 + y^2 - z = 0 \qquad ...(1.102)$$

under the action of a uniform gravitational field in the negative z direction. Obtain the equation of motion using D'Alembert's principle.

Solution: The forces are

$$f_x = 0, f_y = 0, f_z = -mg \quad ...(1.103)$$

In order to obtain constraint equation for virtual displacement

$$\dot{\phi} = 2x\delta x + 2y\delta y - \delta z = 0 \quad ...(1.104)$$

$$2x\delta x + 2y\delta y - \delta z = 0 \quad ...(1.105)$$

We require to obtain 3N - m = 2 independent virtual displacements satisfying the Eq.(1.105)

$$\delta y = 0, \delta z = 2x\delta x \quad ...(1.106)$$

$$\delta x = 0, \delta z = 2y\delta y \quad ...(1.107)$$

From D'Alembert's principle (Eq.1.91)

$$(0 - m\ddot{x})\delta x + (-mg - m\ddot{z})2x\delta x = [-m\ddot{x} - 2mx\,(g + \ddot{z})\}\delta x = 0$$

Since δx is freely variable so the coefficient must be equal to zero. Therefore

$$\ddot{x} + 2x\,(g + \ddot{z}) = 0$$

Similarly taking $\delta x = 0, \delta z = 2y\delta y$, we have

$$\ddot{y} + 2y\,(g + \ddot{z}) = 0$$

Example 4. *Discuss the kind of constraint obeyed by a cylinder rolling without slipping down a rough inclined plane.*

Solution:

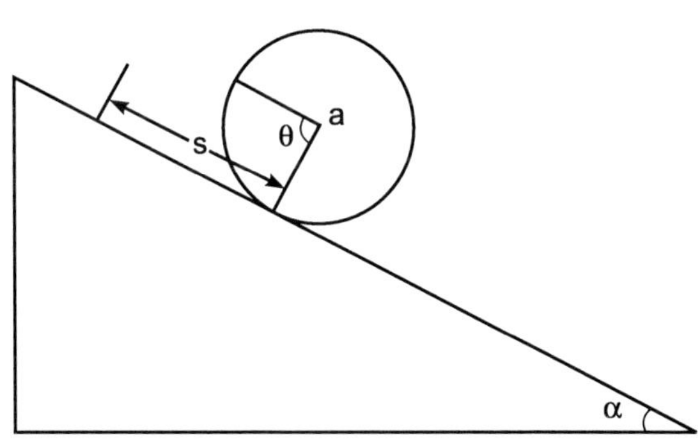

Fig.1.6

The cylinder can be located by two coordinatess and θ (Fig.1.6). The coordinate s measures the distance the cylinder moves down the plane and the coordinate θ is the angle that a fixed radius in the has rotated from the radius to the point of contact. The velocities $\dot{s}$ are θ related by the equation

$$\dot{s} = a\dot{\theta}$$

$$ds = a\,d\theta$$

$$s - a\theta = \text{constant}$$

Though the initial relation is among the velocities but on integration we obtain relations between coordinates. Thus constraint is holonomic, is, independent of time hence scleronomic, bilateral (because of equal sign) and conservative as cylinder rolls because of gravity.

OBJECTIVE TYPE QUESTIONS

1. Consider a point particle which moves on the surface of a hemisphere of radius R whose centre is at the origin. The number of generalized coordinates required to specify the position of the particle is

(*a*) Four (*b*) Two
(*c*) Three (*d*) One

2. Consider the motion of the particle of mass *m* which is constrained to move on the surface of a cone of half angle α and which is subjected to a gravitational force. The number of generalized coordinates required to specify the position of the particle is

(*a*) One (*b*) Three
(*c*) Two (*d*) Four

3. The number of degrees of freedom for a rigid body with fixed point is

(*a*) Three (*b*) Six
(*c*) Four (*d*) Five

4. The number of degrees of freedom for a circular disc rolling on a horizontal plane is

(*a*) One (*b*) Six
(*c*) Four (*d*) Three

5. The constraint on the motion of the particle in a plane reduces the number of degrees of freedom by

(*a*) Four (*b*) Three
(*c*) One (*d*) Two

6. The number of degree's of freedom is in general

(*a*) a property of the system (*b*) choice of the coordinates
(*c*) both (*a*) and (*b*) (*d*) none of these

7. Degrees of freedom for a bead of mass *m* slides along a smooth parabolic wire is

(*a*) 1
(*b*) 4
(*c*) 5
(*d*) none of these

8. The number of degrees of freedom for the case when a sphere is constrained to roll without slipping on a plane are

(*a*) 2
(*b*) 5
(*c*) 3
(*d*) 6

9. Name the type of constraint that may be expressed in the form of an equation relating the coordinates of the system and time

(*a*) Holonomic
(*b*) Non-Holonomic
(*c*) Scleronomous
(*d*) all of these

10. Name the type of constraint for a sphere rolling down from the top of a fixed sphere.

(*a*) Scleronomic and conservative
(*b*) Non-holonomic
(*c*) Unilateral
(*d*) Scleronomic, conservative, non-holonomic and Unilateral.

11. The generalized coordinates of a system

(*a*) need not necessarily have the same dimension
(*b*) must have the same dimension
(*c*) are unique
(*d*) have dimensions of length

12. A particle is forced to move on a sphere of radius R centred at the origin of a Cartesian frame of reference. The constraint is

(*a*) Holonomic
(*b* Rheonomic
(*c*) Non-Holonomic
(*d*) None of these

13. Certain regions of n-dimensional configuration space are not accessible in case of

(*a*) Holonomic
(*b*) Non-Holonomic
(*c*) both (*a*) and (*b*)
(*d*) None of these

14. Which is not an example of ideal constraint?

(*a*) frictionless constraint surface
(*b*) rolling contact without slipping

(*c*) internal forces on a rigid body (*d*) applied forces on a rigid body

15. Which one of the following expression gives the torque about the origin of a particle of mass *m* with position vector **r**.

(*a*) $\mathbf{r} \times m\mathbf{r}$ (*b*) $\mathbf{r} \times m\dot{\mathbf{r}}$

(*c*) $\mathbf{r} \times m\ddot{\mathbf{r}}$ (*d*) $\dot{\mathbf{r}} \times m\ddot{\mathbf{r}}$

16. Which is not true for the constraint in the case when a sphere rolls down another which is rolling with uniform speed along a horizontal plane

(*a*) rheonomic (*b*) non-holonomic
(*c*) conservative (*d*) holonomic

17. Which is not true for the constraint in the case when a cylinder is rolling without slipping down a rough inclined plane of angle β.

(*a*) scleronomic (*b*) non-holonomic

(*c*) conservation (*d*) holonomic

PROBLEMS

1. A small rigid rod of length l is allowed to move in any manner inside a sphere of radius $a > l$. Obtain the equation of constraint.

2. Show that constraint for a simple pendulum with rigid support is scleronomic, holonomic, bilateral and conservative.

3. Show that for the rigid body, the constraint is holonomic, scleronomic and bilateral.

4. Show that for a pendulum with variable length $l = l(\mathrm{t})$, the constraint is rheonomic, holonomic, bilateral and dissipative.

5. Show that the constraint represented by the relation

$$(yz - 2x + y)\dot{x} + (xz - 2y + x)\dot{y} + xy\dot{z} = 0$$

is holonomic.

6. A lever ABC has weights w_1 and w_2 at distances a_1 and a_2 from fixed support. Using the principle of virtual work, obtain the necessary and sufficient condition for equilibrium.

7. Show that in the case of rocket motion in free space, the greater the ratio of mass of fuel to mass of vehicle, the greater is the maximum speed attained by the rocket. Determine the distance travelled by the rocket in time *t*.

8. A spacc vehicle ejects fuel at a velocity $-\mathbf{V}_0$ relative to the vehicle. The rate of change of mass of the vehicle is $dM/dt = -\alpha$ a constant. Set up and solve the equation of motion of space vehicle, neglecting gravity.

9. Two particles of masses m_1 and m_2 are located on a frictionless double inclined and connected by an inextensible mass less string passing over a smooth peg. Using the principle of virtual work show that for equilibrium

$$\frac{\sin\alpha_1}{\sin\alpha_2} = \frac{m_2}{m_1}$$

where α_1 and α_2 are the angles of the incline. Use D'Alembert's principle to describe the motion of the masses.

❑❑❑

CHAPTER 2

Lagrangian Formulation

2.1 LAGRANGE'S EQUATIONS

Consider a system of N mass points with masses $\{m_i\}$ and coordinates $\{r_i\}$, i = 1,2, …, N subject to the holonomic constraints

$$h_j(\mathbf{r}_1,\mathbf{r}_2,......,\mathbf{r}_N,t) = 0, \qquad (j=1,2,..........., \alpha) \qquad ...(2.1)$$

The number of degrees of freedom is therefore $3N-\alpha = n$. As the conditions (2.1) are independent they can be solved locally for the coordinates r_i, that is,

$$\mathbf{r}_i = \mathbf{r}_i(q_1,q_2,..........,q_n,t), \qquad (i=1,2,......,N) \qquad ...(2.2)$$

where q_k's are generalized coordinates

From equation (2.2)

$$\dot{\mathbf{r}} = \mathbf{v}_i = \frac{d\mathbf{r}_i}{dt} = \frac{\partial \mathbf{r}_i}{\partial q_1}\dot{q}_1 + \frac{\partial \mathbf{r}_i}{\partial q_2}\dot{q}_2 + ..., + \frac{\partial \mathbf{r}_i}{\partial q_n}\dot{q}_n + \frac{\partial \mathbf{r}_i}{\partial t} = \sum_{k=1}^{n}\frac{\partial \mathbf{r}_i}{\partial q_k}\dot{q}_k + \frac{\partial \mathbf{r}_i}{\partial t} \qquad ...(2.3)$$

Differentiating $\mathbf{v}_i$ with respect to $\dot{q}_k$

$$\frac{\partial \mathbf{v}_i}{\partial \dot{q}_k} = \frac{\partial \dot{r}_i}{\partial \dot{q}_k} = \frac{\partial r_i}{\partial q_k} \qquad ...(2.4)$$

The arbitrary virtual displacement $\delta \boldsymbol{r}_i$ is connected with the virtual displacement δq_i by

$$\delta r_i = \frac{\partial r_i}{\partial q_1}\delta q_1 + \frac{\partial r_i}{\partial q_2}\delta q_2 + ... + \frac{\partial r_i}{\partial q_n}\delta q_n = \sum_{k=1}^{n}\frac{\partial r_i}{\partial q_k}\delta q_k \qquad ...(2.5)$$

Since the virtual displacements are made at a fixed time, hence there is no time derivative in equation (2.5).

The D'Alembert's principle is given by the Eq. (1.91)

$$\sum_{i=1}^{N}(\mathbf{f}_i - \dot{\mathbf{p}}_i)\cdot\delta\mathbf{r}_i = 0 \qquad ...(2.6)$$

The first term on the left hand side of equation (2.6) can be written as

$$\sum_{i=1}^{N}\mathbf{f}_i\cdot\delta\mathbf{r}_i = \sum_{i=1}^{N}\sum_{k=1}^{n}\mathbf{f}_i\cdot\frac{\partial\mathbf{r}_1}{\partial q_k}\delta q_k = \sum_{k=1}^{n}Q_k\,\delta q_k \qquad ...(2.7)$$

with

$$Q_k = \sum_{i=1}^{N}\mathbf{f}_i\cdot\frac{\partial\mathbf{r}_i}{\partial q_k} \qquad ...(2.8)$$

where Q_k are called the components of the generalized forces. They need not have the dimensions of the force but $Q_k\delta q_k$ must always have the dimensions of work. The generalized force has a dimension determined by the generalized coordinate in such a way that the product $Q_k q_k$ is an energy. For example, if Q_k is angular momentum, q_k is angle and if Q_k has dimensions of work then q_k is dimensionless.

The second term of Equation (2.6) is

$$\sum_{i=1}^{N}\dot{\mathbf{p}}_i\cdot\delta\mathbf{r}_i = \sum m_i\ddot{\mathbf{r}}_i\cdot\delta\mathbf{r}_i = \sum_{i=1}^{N}m_i\sum\ddot{\mathbf{r}}_i\cdot\frac{\partial\mathbf{r}_i}{\partial q_k}\delta q_k \qquad ...(2.9)$$

Now

$$\ddot{\mathbf{r}}_i\cdot\frac{\partial\mathbf{r}_i}{\partial q_k} = \frac{d}{dt}\left(\dot{\mathbf{r}}_1\cdot\frac{\partial\mathbf{r}_i}{\partial q_k}\right) - \dot{\mathbf{r}}_i\cdot\frac{d}{dt}\frac{\partial\mathbf{r}_i}{\partial q_k} \qquad ...(2.10)$$

and

$$\frac{d}{dt}\left(\frac{\partial\mathbf{r}_i}{\partial q_k}\right) = \sum_{j=1}^{n}\frac{\partial^2\mathbf{r}_i}{\partial q_k\partial q_j}\dot{q}_j + \frac{\partial^2\mathbf{r}_i}{\partial q_k\partial t} = \frac{\partial}{\partial q_k}\left(\sum_j\frac{\partial\mathbf{r}_i}{\partial q_j}\dot{q}_j + \frac{\partial\mathbf{r}_i}{\partial t}\right) \qquad ...(2.11)$$

Using Eq.(2.3) in Eq.(2.11)

$$\frac{d}{dt}\left(\frac{\partial\mathbf{r}_i}{\partial q_k}\right) = \frac{\partial\dot{\mathbf{r}}_i}{\partial q_k} \qquad ...(2.12)$$

Substituting Eqs.(2.4) and (2.12) in Eq.(2.10)

$$\ddot{\mathbf{r}}_i\cdot\frac{\partial\mathbf{r}_i}{\partial q_k} = \frac{d}{dt}\left(\dot{\mathbf{r}}_i\cdot\frac{\partial\dot{\mathbf{r}}}{\partial\dot{q}_k}\right) - \dot{\mathbf{r}}_i\cdot\frac{\partial\dot{\mathbf{r}}_i}{\partial q_k} = \frac{d}{dt}\left(\mathbf{v}_i\cdot\frac{\partial\mathbf{v}_1}{\partial\dot{q}_k}\right) - \mathbf{v}_i\cdot\frac{\partial\mathbf{v}_i}{\partial q_k} = \frac{1}{2}\frac{d}{dt}\left(\frac{\partial\mathbf{v}_i^2}{\partial\dot{q}_k}\right) - \frac{1}{2}\frac{\partial\mathbf{v}_i^2}{\partial q_k}$$

...(2.13)

$$\sum_i \dot{\mathbf{p}}_i \cdot \delta \mathbf{r}_1 = \sum_i m_i \left[\sum_k \frac{1}{2} \frac{d}{dt} \left(\frac{\partial \mathbf{v}_i^2}{\partial \dot{q}_k} \right) - \frac{1}{2} \frac{\partial \mathbf{v}_i^2}{\partial q_k} \right]$$

$$= \sum_k \left\{ \frac{d}{dt} \left[\frac{\partial}{\partial \dot{q}_k} \sum_i \frac{1}{2} m_i \mathbf{v}_i^2 \right] - \frac{\partial}{\partial q_k} \sum \frac{1}{2} m_i \mathbf{v}_i^2 \right\} \qquad ...(2.14)$$

The kinetic energy T is

$$T = \frac{1}{2} \sum_i m_i \mathbf{v}_i^2 \qquad ...(2.15)$$

The Eq. (2.14) is therefore,

$$\sum_i \dot{\mathbf{p}}_i \cdot \delta \mathbf{r}_1 = \sum_k \left[\frac{d}{dt} \left(\frac{\partial T}{\partial \dot{q}_k} \right) - \frac{\partial T}{\partial q_k} \right] \qquad ...(2.16)$$

Using Eqs. (2.7) and (2.16) in Eq.(2.6) we have

$$\sum_k \left\{ \left[\frac{d}{dt} \left(\frac{\partial T}{\partial \dot{q}_k} \right) - \frac{\partial T}{\partial q_k} \right] - Q_k \right\} \delta q_k = 0 \qquad ...(2.17)$$

The equation (2.17) contains only the quantities δq_k but not δr_i. The displacements δq_k are independent. Therefore, every term of Eq.(2.17) must vanish independently. Thus, we obtain a set of n equations

$$\frac{d}{dt} \left(\frac{\partial T}{\partial \dot{q}_k} \right) - \frac{\partial T}{\partial q_k} = Q_k \quad (k = 1, 2, ..., n) \qquad ...(2.18)$$

This is the fundamental holonomic form of Lagrange's equation. It results in n second-order differential equations. The Q's are generalized applied forces from any source.

The Eq.(2.18) takes a simple form if the forces f_i are derivable from a potential function. In this case

$$\mathbf{f}_i = -\nabla_i V \qquad ...(2.19)$$

and from Eq.(2.8)

$$Q_k = -\sum_i \nabla_i V(\mathbf{r}_1, \mathbf{r}_2, ..., \mathbf{r}_N) \frac{\partial \mathbf{r}_i}{\partial q_k} = -\frac{\partial}{\partial t} V(q_1, q_2, ..., q_n, t) \qquad ...(2.20)$$

Substituting the form of Q_k from Eq.(2.20) into Eq.(2.17)

$$\frac{d}{dt} \left(\frac{\partial T}{\partial \dot{q}_k} \right) - \frac{\partial T}{\partial q_k} = -\frac{\partial V}{\partial q_k} \qquad ...(2.21)$$

as V does not depend on $\dot{q}_k$, T and V can be combined to

$$L(q_k, \dot{q}_k, t) = T(q_k, \dot{q}_k) - V(q_k, t) \qquad ...(2.22)$$

L is called Lagrangian function. This form of Lagrangian function is called natural form. Eq.(2.21) can be written as

$$\frac{d}{dt}\left(\frac{\partial(T-V)}{\partial \dot{q}_k}\right)-\frac{\partial(T-V)}{\partial q_k}=0 \qquad ...(2.23)$$

Eq. (2.23) with the help of Eq.(2.22) takes the simple form

$$\frac{d}{dt}\left(\frac{\partial L}{\partial \dot{q}_k}\right)-\frac{\partial L}{\partial q_k}=0 \quad (k=1,2,........,n) \qquad ...(2.24)$$

The Eq.(2.24) is called Lagrange's equation. They contain the function L with

$$V(q_1,q_2,......,q_n,t)=V\left[\mathbf{r}_1(q_1,q_2,....,q_n,t),........,\mathbf{r}_N(q_1,q_2,......,q_n,t)\right]$$

There are n of Lagrange's equations and together with α equations of constraints and the $2n$ initial conditions (since there are n second order differential equations) that are imposed provide a complete description of the motion of the system. The Lagrange's equations follow only if the forces are potential forces. The Eq.(2.24) is not valid for frictional forces.

The validity of Lagrange's equations requires that

(*i*) the force acting on the system (apart from any force of constraint) must be derivable from a potential or several potentials.

(*ii*) the equations of constraints must be relations that connect the coordinates of the particle and may be function of time *i.e.* we must have constraint relation given by the Eq. (2.1).

In contrast the D'Alembert's equations hold if the constraints are formulated in differential form that cannot be integrated to holonomic equations. Therefore, D'Alembert's equations are more general.

The Lagrangian function L has dimension of energy. To obtain the Lagrangian we need to know only the kinetic and potential energies of the system. The explicit knowledge of the external force and the forces of constrain acting on the system is not necessary. The value of L is independent of coordinates in which it is expressed, though the functional form may change with the choice of coordinates. The Lagrangian function expresses generalized acceleration $\ddot{q}_k$ in terms of generalized positions q_k and velocities $\dot{q}_k$. In principle these quantities can be integrated to yield $q_k(t)$ the path of the system. Therefore, once the initial conditions $q_k(0)$ and $\dot{q}_k(0)$ (at $t=0$) have been specified, the function $q_k(t)$ and hence the motion of the system is determined for all later times. In Newtonian approach, the equations of motion directly express the acceleration in terms of the force that are functions of the position and velocities. In solving a problem by using the Newtonian approach, it is necessary to know all the forces acting on the body as appears in equation $m\ddot{\mathbf{r}}=\mathbf{F}$. However, in Lagrange's formulation, nowhere the concept of force enters. Lagrangian formulation is advantageous over Newtonian approach in the sense that in certain situation it may not even be possible to state explicitly all the forces acting on the body (as is sometimes the forces of constraints) whereas it is still possible to obtain kinetic and potential energies.

2.2 VELOCITY DEPENDENT POTENTIALS

If the forces acting on a dynamical system depend upon the velocities, it may be possible to obtain a function

$$U\,(q_1, q_{2,} \ldots\ldots, q_n, \dot{q}_1, \dot{q}_2, \ldots\ldots\ldots\ldots, \dot{q}_n, t)$$

such that

$$Q_k \quad = \quad \frac{d}{dt}\left(\frac{\partial U}{\partial \dot{q}_k}\right) - \frac{\partial U}{\partial q_k} \quad (k = 1,2,\ldots\ldots\ldots\ldots, n)$$

If such a function $U\,(q_k, \dot{q}_k, t)$ is obtained then Lagrangian function is defined as $L = T - U$ and the Lagrange's equation (2.18) can be written in the form (2.24)

$$\frac{d}{dt}\left(\frac{\partial L}{\partial \dot{q}_k}\right) - \frac{\partial L}{\partial q_k} = 0 \quad (k=1, 2, \ldots\ldots\ldots, n) \qquad \ldots(2.25)$$

The function U is called generalized potential or velocity dependent potential or external potential function. If there are forces derivable from the potential function $V\,(q_1, q_2, \ldots, q_n)$ then V may be included in U. As an example consider a particle of charge e esubject to an external electric field **E** and magnetic induction **B**. The force acting on the particle called Lorentz force is

$$\mathbf{F} = e\left(\mathbf{E} + \frac{\mathbf{v}\times\mathbf{B}}{c}\right) \qquad \ldots(2.26)$$

where **v** is the velocity of the charged particle. The Maxwell's equations are

$$\nabla \cdot \mathbf{D} = 4\pi\rho \qquad \ldots(2.27)$$

$$\nabla \cdot \mathbf{B} = 0 \qquad \ldots(2.28)$$

$$\nabla\times\mathbf{E} = -\frac{1}{c}\frac{\partial \mathbf{B}}{\partial t} \qquad \ldots(2.29)$$

$$\nabla\times\mathbf{H} = \frac{4\pi}{c}\mathbf{J} + \frac{1}{c}\frac{\partial \mathbf{D}}{\partial t} \qquad \ldots(2.30)$$

According to Eq.(2.29)

$$\nabla\times\mathbf{E} \neq 0$$

therefore **E** cannot be written as gradient of some scalar function. Further, according to Eq.(2.28)

$$\nabla \cdot \mathbf{B} = 0$$

therefore

$$\mathbf{B} = \nabla\times\mathbf{A} \qquad ...(2.31)$$

as $\nabla\cdot(\nabla\times\mathbf{A}) = 0$ and $A(x,y,z,t)$ is called magnetic vector potential

From Eqs.(2.29) and (2.31)

$$\nabla\times\mathbf{E} + \frac{1}{c}\frac{\partial\mathbf{B}}{\partial t} = \nabla\times\left[\mathbf{E} + \frac{1}{c}\frac{\partial\mathbf{A}}{\partial t}\right] = 0 \qquad ...(2.32)$$

Since $\nabla\times(\nabla f) = 0$, where f is a scalar function, therefore from Eq.(2.32), we have

$$\mathbf{E} + \frac{1}{c}\frac{\partial\mathbf{A}}{\partial t} = -\nabla\varphi$$

$$\mathbf{E} = -\frac{1}{c}\frac{\partial\mathbf{A}}{\partial t} - \nabla\varphi \qquad ...(2.33)$$

where $\varphi\,(x,y,z,t)$ is a scalar function.

Using equations (2.31) and (2.33) in (2.26)

$$\mathbf{F} = e\left[-\nabla\varphi - \frac{1}{c}\frac{\partial\mathbf{A}}{\partial t} + \frac{1}{c}\,\mathbf{v}\times(\nabla\times\mathbf{A})\right] \qquad ...(2.34)$$

consider x component of force

$$F_x = e\left[-(\nabla\varphi)_x - \frac{1}{c}\frac{\partial\mathbf{A}_x}{\partial t} + \frac{1}{c}[\mathbf{v}\times(\nabla\times\mathbf{A})]_x\right] \qquad ...(2.35)$$

Hence

$$\mathbf{v}\times(\nabla\times\mathbf{A}) = \begin{vmatrix} \mathbf{i} & \mathbf{j} & \mathbf{k} \\ v_x & v_y & v_z \\ \frac{\partial A_z}{\partial y} - \frac{\partial A_y}{\partial z} & \frac{\partial A_x}{\partial z} - \frac{\partial A_z}{\partial x} & \frac{\partial A_y}{\partial x} - \frac{\partial A_x}{\partial y} \end{vmatrix}$$

and

$$[\mathbf{v}\times(\nabla\times A)]_x = v_y\frac{\partial A_y}{\partial x} + v_z\frac{\partial A_z}{\partial x} - v_y\frac{\partial A_x}{\partial y} - v_z\frac{\partial A_x}{\partial z} \qquad ...(2.36)$$

Adding and subtracting $v_x(\partial A_x/\partial x)$ on the right hand side of the Eq. (2.36)

$$[\mathbf{v}\times(\nabla\times A)]_x = v_y\frac{\partial A_y}{\partial x} + v_z\frac{\partial A_z}{\partial x} - v_y\frac{\partial A_x}{\partial y} - v_z\frac{\partial A_x}{\partial z} + v_x\frac{\partial A_x}{\partial x} - v_x\frac{\partial A_x}{\partial x}$$

$$= \frac{\partial}{\partial x}(\mathrm{v_x} A_x + \mathrm{v_y} A_y + \mathrm{v_z} A_z)$$

$$- A_x \frac{\partial \mathrm{v_x}}{\partial x} - A_y \frac{\partial \mathrm{v_y}}{\partial x} - A_z \frac{\partial \mathrm{v_z}}{\partial x} - \mathrm{v_x} \frac{\partial \mathrm{A_x}}{\partial x} - \mathrm{v_y} \frac{\partial \mathrm{A}_x}{\partial y} - \mathrm{v_z} \frac{\partial \mathrm{A_x}}{\partial z} \qquad ...(2.37)$$

consider

$$\frac{dA_x}{dt} = \frac{\partial A_x}{\partial t} + \frac{\partial A_x}{\partial x}\dot{x} + \frac{\partial A_x}{\partial y}\dot{y} + \frac{\partial A_x}{\partial z}\dot{z} = \frac{\partial A_x}{\partial t} + \frac{\partial A_x}{\partial x}\mathrm{v_x} + \frac{\partial A_x}{\partial y}\mathrm{v_y} + \frac{\partial A_x}{\partial z}\mathrm{v_z}$$

$$\frac{dA_x}{dt} - \frac{\partial A_x}{\partial t} = \frac{\partial A_x}{\partial x}\mathrm{v_x} + \frac{\partial A_x}{\partial y}\mathrm{v_y} + \frac{\partial A_x}{\partial z}\mathrm{v_z} \qquad ...(2.38)$$

Substituting (2.38) in (2.37)

$$[\mathbf{v}\times(\mathbf{v}\times\mathbf{A})]_x = \frac{\partial}{\partial x}(\mathbf{v}\cdot\mathbf{A}) - A_x \frac{\partial \mathrm{v_x}}{\partial x} - A_y \frac{\partial \mathrm{v_y}}{\partial x} - A_z \frac{\partial \mathrm{v_z}}{\partial x} + \frac{\partial \mathrm{A_x}}{\partial \mathrm{t}} - \frac{d\mathrm{A_x}}{dt}$$

$$...(2.39)$$

the components of **v** ($\mathrm{v_x}, \mathrm{v_y}, \mathrm{v_z}$) are constant and are independent of *x, y* and *z* so that **v** is not differentiable by the operation ∇, therefore

$$\frac{\partial \mathrm{v_x}}{\partial x} = \frac{\partial \mathrm{v_y}}{\partial x} = \frac{\partial \mathrm{v_z}}{\partial x} = 0 \qquad ...(2.40)$$

From Eqs.(2.38) and (2.39)

$$[\mathbf{v}\times(\mathbf{v}\times\mathbf{A})]_x = \frac{\partial}{\partial x}(\mathbf{v}\cdot\mathbf{A}) + \frac{\partial A_\mathrm{x}}{\partial \mathrm{t}} - \frac{dA_\mathrm{x}}{dt} \qquad ...(2.41)$$

From Eqs.(2.35) and (2.41)

$$\mathrm{F_x} = e\left[-(\nabla\varphi)_x - \frac{1}{c}\frac{\partial A_x}{\partial t} + \frac{1}{c}\left(\frac{\partial}{\partial x}(\mathbf{v}\cdot\mathbf{A}) + \frac{\partial A_\mathrm{x}}{\partial \mathrm{t}} - \frac{dA_\mathrm{x}}{dt}\right)\right]$$

$$\mathrm{F_x} = e\left[-(\nabla\varphi)_x - \frac{1}{c}\frac{dA_x}{dt} + \frac{1}{c}\frac{\partial}{\partial x}(\mathbf{v}\cdot\mathbf{A})\right]$$

$$\mathrm{F_x} = -e\frac{\partial}{\partial x}\left[\varphi - \frac{1}{c}(\mathbf{v}\cdot\mathbf{A})\right] - \frac{e}{c}\frac{d\mathrm{A_x}}{\mathrm{dt}} \qquad ...(2.42)$$

The scalar potential φ is independent of velocity and Eq. (2.42) can be written in the form

$$\mathrm{F_x} = -\frac{\partial U}{\partial x} + \frac{d}{dt}\frac{\partial U}{\partial \mathrm{v_x}} \qquad ...(2.43)$$

where generalized potential *U* is

$$U = e\varphi - \frac{e}{c}\mathbf{A}\cdot\mathbf{v} \qquad ...(2.44)$$

The Lagrangian is therefore

$$L = T - U = T - e\varphi + \frac{e}{c}\mathbf{A}\cdot\mathbf{v} \qquad ...(2.45)$$

if **A** and φ are independent of time t, then L is independent of t in a fixed coordinate system.

2.3 RAYLEIGH FUNCTION

We have dealt with systems which are conservative; there was no loss of energy. In many cases the force acting on the system is such that, its one part is derivable from potential function, that is, conservative. The other part is dissipative like a frictional force and is not conservative unless we include heat energy. The heat energy cannot be defined in terms of coordinates and velocities. The force of friction is nearly constant for a given pair of surfaces with a given normal force between them. The force depends on the velocity only in that its direction is always opposed to the velocity, therefore does negative work, that is, absorbs energy from the system.

The frictional forces cannot be expressed in the form

$$Q_k = \frac{d}{dt}\left(\frac{\partial U}{\partial \dot{q}_k}\right) - \frac{\partial U}{\partial q_k} \quad (k = 1, 2, \ldots\ldots\ldots., n)$$

Therefore, if only some of the forces acting on the system are derivable from a potential then Lagrange's equation can be written as

$$\frac{d}{dt}\left(\frac{\partial L}{\partial \dot{q}_k}\right) - \frac{\partial L}{\partial q_k} = Q \quad (k=1,2,\ldots\ldots., n) \qquad ...(2.46)$$

where L contains the potential of conservative forces, Q represents the force not arising from a potential.

We assume that the force of friction is given by

$$\mathbf{F_f} = -b\,\mathbf{v} \qquad ...(2.47)$$

the component of frictional force has the form

$$\begin{aligned} F_{f_x} &= -b_x\, v_x \\ F_{f_y} &= -b_y\, v_y \\ F_{f_z} &= -b_z\, v_z \end{aligned} \qquad ...(2.48)$$

Such frictional or dissipative forces may be derived in terms of Rayleigh's dissipation function F defined as

$$F = \frac{1}{2}\sum_i \left(b_x\, v_{ix}^2 + b_y\, v_{iy}^2 + b_z\, v_{iz}^2\right) \qquad ...(2.49)$$

The summation is over the particles of the system. The components of F_f are obtained by differentiation of Eq. (2.49) with respect to v_x. v_y and v_z , that is,

$$F_{f_x} = -\frac{\partial F}{\partial v_x} = -b_x v_x$$

$$F_{f_y} = -\frac{\partial F}{\partial v_y} = -b_y v_y \qquad ...(2.50)$$

$$F_{f_z} = -\frac{\partial F}{\partial v_z} = -b_z v_z$$

or

$$\mathbf{F_f} = -\nabla_v F \qquad ...(2.51)$$

where ∇_v is gradient operator in velocity space ,that is,

$$\nabla_v = \frac{\partial}{\partial v_x}\mathbf{i} + \frac{\partial}{\partial v_y}\mathbf{j} + \frac{\partial}{\partial v_z}\mathbf{k} \qquad ...(2.52)$$

The work done by the system against the friction is

$$dW_f = -\mathbf{F_f} \cdot d\mathbf{r} = -\mathbf{F_f} \cdot \dot{\mathbf{r}}\, dt = -\mathbf{F_f} \cdot \mathbf{v}\, dt = -(b_x v_x^2 + b_y v_y^2 + b_z v_z^2) \qquad ...(2.53)$$

Rate of change of energy dissipation

$$\frac{dW_f}{dt} = -(b_x v_x^2 + b_y v_y^2 + b_z v_z^2) = -2F \qquad ...(2.54)$$

The component of generalized force resulting from the force of friction is obtained by using the Eq. (2.8)

$$Q_k = \sum_i \mathbf{F_{if}} \cdot \frac{\partial \mathbf{r}_i}{\partial q_k} = -\sum \nabla_{v_i} F \cdot \frac{\partial \mathbf{r}_i}{\partial q_k} \qquad ...(2.55)$$

Using Eq.(2.4)

$$Q_k = -\sum \nabla_{v_i} F \cdot \frac{\partial \mathbf{v}_i}{\partial \dot{q}_k} = -\sum \frac{\partial F}{\partial \mathbf{v}_i} \frac{\partial \mathbf{v}_i}{\partial \dot{q}_k} \qquad ...(2.56)$$

$$Q_k = -\frac{\partial F}{\partial \dot{q}_k} \qquad ...(2.57)$$

The Eq.(2.46) is written as

$$\frac{d}{dt}\left(\frac{\partial L}{\partial \dot{q}_k}\right) - \frac{\partial L}{\partial q_k} + \frac{\partial F}{\partial \dot{q}_k} \quad (k=1,2,........,n) \qquad ...(2.58)$$

Thus, to obtain the equation of motion when a dissipative force is proportional to velocity, we must know the Lagrangian L and dissipative function F.

2.4 INVARIANCE OF LAGRANGIAN UNDER GALILEAN TRANSFORMATION

Inertial reference frames are defined as the ones in which Newton's first law is true. Consider two inertial reference frames called S and S' with S' moving with a constant velocity. Galilean transformation relates space and time coordinates and other physical quantities in S and S' when relative speed v of the two frame of references is much small than the speed of light. Further, all the clocks distributed in S and S' tick at the same rate once synchronized can be arranged to indicate the same time, that is $t = t'$.

Let the origin of S and S' coincide at $t = t' = 0$ and S' is moving with velocity v along the x-axis. Therefore the particle position x' in S' has the coordinate x in S where

$$x = x' + \text{v}t \qquad ...(2.59)$$

$$y = y',\ z = z' \qquad ...(2.60)$$

Let the particle is moving in S' along the x' direction with velocity component

$$u'_x = \frac{dx'}{dt'}$$

The velocity component u_x of the particle from the viewpoint of S is from Eq.(2.59)

$$u_x = \frac{dx}{dt} = \frac{d(x' + \text{v}t)}{dt} = \frac{dx'}{dt} + \text{v}$$

$$u_x = \frac{dx'}{dt} + \text{v} = \frac{dx'}{dt'} + \text{v} = u'_x + \text{v}$$

as $t = t'$. And

$$u_x = u'_y,\ u_z = u'_z$$

The acceleration

$$a'_x = \frac{d^2x'}{dt'^2}$$

$$a_x = \frac{d^2(x' + \text{v}t)}{dt^2} = \frac{d^2x'}{dt^2} = \frac{d^2x'}{dt'^2} = a'_x \qquad ...(2.61)$$

Similarly, from Eq.(2.60)

$$a'_y = a_y,\ a'_z = a_z \qquad ...(2.62)$$

For a particle of mass m, we have from Eqs. (2.61) and (2.62) the force $\boldsymbol{F}$

$$m\frac{d^2\boldsymbol{r}}{dt^2} = m\frac{d^2\boldsymbol{r}'}{dt^2} = \boldsymbol{F} \qquad ...(2.63)$$

where $\boldsymbol{r}$ and $\boldsymbol{r}'$ are the position vector of the particle in S and S' respectively. For ith particle, the Eq.(2.63) is

$$m_i\frac{d^2\boldsymbol{r}_i}{dt^2} = m_i\frac{d^2\boldsymbol{r}'_i}{dt^2} = \boldsymbol{F}_i \qquad ...(2.64)$$

$$m_i \frac{d^2(\boldsymbol{r}_i - \boldsymbol{r}_i')}{dt^2} = 0$$

The Lagrangian in S' is given by

$$L' = \frac{1}{2} m\, \mathbf{u}'^2 - V = \frac{1}{2} m\, (\mathbf{u} - \mathbf{v})^2 - V$$

$$L' = \frac{1}{2} m\, (\mathbf{u}^2 + \mathbf{v}^2 - 2\,\mathbf{u}\cdot\mathbf{v}) - V = \frac{1}{2} m\mathbf{u}^2 - V + \frac{1}{2} m\,\mathbf{v}^2 - m\,\mathbf{u}\cdot\mathbf{v}$$

$$L' = L + \frac{1}{2} m\,\mathbf{v}^2 - m\,\mathbf{u}\cdot\mathbf{v} = L + \frac{d}{dt}\left(\frac{1}{2} m\,\mathbf{v}^2 t - m\,\mathbf{v}\cdot\mathbf{r}\right) = L + \frac{d\,G(\mathbf{r},t)}{dt}$$

...(2.65)

where

$$G(\boldsymbol{r},t) = \frac{1}{2} m v^2 t - m \boldsymbol{v}\cdot\boldsymbol{r} \qquad ...(2.66)$$

Since V is normally a function of $\boldsymbol{r}_2 - \boldsymbol{r}_1$ and $\boldsymbol{r}_2 - \boldsymbol{r}_1 = \boldsymbol{r}_2' - \boldsymbol{r}_1'$ at all instance

Putting L' in place of L in Eq.(2.24)

$$\frac{d}{dt}\left(\frac{\partial L'}{\partial \dot{q}_k}\right) - \frac{\partial L'}{\partial q_k} = 0 \quad (k=1,2,........,n) \qquad ...(2.67)$$

Substituting the value of L' from Eq. (2.65) in Eq.(2.67)

$$\frac{d}{dt}\left(\frac{\partial L}{\partial \dot{q}_k}\right) - \frac{\partial L}{\partial q_k} + \frac{d}{dt}\left(\frac{\partial}{\partial \dot{q}_k}\left(\frac{dG}{dt}\right)\right) - \frac{\partial}{\partial q_k}\left(\frac{dG}{dt}\right) = 0 \quad (k=1,2,........,n)$$

$$\frac{d}{dt}\left(\frac{\partial}{\partial \dot{q}_k}\left(\frac{dG}{dt}\right)\right) - \frac{\partial}{\partial q_k}\left(\frac{dG}{dt}\right) = 0 \qquad ...(2.68)$$

$$\frac{d}{dt}\left(\frac{\partial}{\partial \dot{q}_k}\left(\frac{\partial G}{\partial t} + \frac{\partial G}{\partial q_k}\dot{q}_k\right)\right) - \frac{\partial}{\partial q_k}\left(\frac{\partial G}{\partial t} + \frac{\partial G}{\partial q_k}\dot{q}_k\right) = 0 \qquad ...(2.69)$$

For our case $q_k = \mathrm{r}$

$$\frac{d}{dt}\left(\frac{\partial}{\partial \dot{\mathrm{r}}}\left(\frac{\partial G}{\partial t} + \frac{\partial G}{\partial \mathrm{r}}\dot{\mathrm{r}}\right)\right) - \frac{\partial}{\partial \mathrm{r}}\left(\frac{\partial G}{\partial t} + \frac{\partial G}{\partial \mathrm{r}}\dot{\mathrm{r}}\right) = 0$$

$$\frac{d}{dt}\left(\frac{\partial}{\partial \dot{\mathrm{r}}}\left(\frac{1}{2} m\mathbf{v}^2 + m\,\mathbf{v}\cdot\dot{\mathrm{r}}\right)\right) - \frac{\partial}{\partial \mathrm{r}}\left(\frac{1}{2} m\mathbf{v}^2 + m\,\mathbf{v}\dot{\mathrm{r}}\right) = 0 \qquad ...(2.70)$$

So the coordinate transformation corresponding to any Galilean transformation can be viewed as Lagrangian gauss transformation.

Solved Examples

Example 1. *Show that kinetic energy is a quadratic function of generalized velocities.*

Solution: Let at time t the position vector of the ith particle (mass m_i) of a holonomic system is r_i. The kinetic energy is

$$T = \frac{1}{2}\sum_{i=1}^{N} m_i\, \dot{\mathbf{r}}_i^2$$

where N is the number of particles. Let the system is specified by the n generalized coordinates $q_k\ (k=1,..,n)$. The position coordinate $\boldsymbol{r}_i$ is

$$\boldsymbol{r}_i = \boldsymbol{r}_i(q_1, q_2, ..., q_n, t)$$

$$\dot{\mathbf{r}}_i = \frac{\partial \mathbf{r}_i}{\partial \dot{q}_1}\dot{q}_1 + \frac{\partial \mathbf{r}_i}{\partial \dot{q}_2}\dot{q}_2 + ... + \frac{\partial \mathbf{r}_i}{\partial \dot{q}_n}\dot{q}_n + \frac{\partial \mathbf{r}_i}{\partial t}$$

$$T = \frac{1}{2}\sum m_i\left(\frac{\partial \mathbf{r}_i}{\partial \dot{q}_1}\dot{q}_1 + \frac{\partial \mathbf{r}_i}{\partial \dot{q}_2}\dot{q}_2 + ... + \frac{\partial \mathbf{r}_i}{\partial \dot{q}_n}\dot{q}_n + \frac{\partial \mathbf{r}_i}{\partial t}\right)^2$$

$$T = \frac{1}{2}\sum m_i\left(\frac{\partial \mathbf{r}_i}{\partial \dot{q}_1}\cdot\frac{\partial \mathbf{r}_i}{\partial \dot{q}_1}\dot{q}_1^2 + \frac{\partial \mathbf{r}_i}{\partial \dot{q}_2}\cdot\frac{\partial \mathbf{r}_i}{\partial \dot{q}_2}\dot{q}_2^2 + ... + \frac{\partial \mathbf{r}_i}{\partial \dot{q}_n}\cdot\frac{\partial \mathbf{r}_i}{\partial \dot{q}_n}\dot{q}_n^2\right) + \frac{1}{2}\sum m_i\left(\frac{\partial \mathbf{r}_i}{\partial t}\right)^2 +$$

$$+\frac{1}{2}\sum 2m_i\left(\frac{\partial \mathbf{r}_i}{\partial \dot{q}_1}\cdot\frac{\partial \mathbf{r}_i}{\partial \dot{q}_2}\dot{q}_1\dot{q}_2 + ... + \frac{\partial \mathbf{r}_i}{\partial \dot{q}_1}\cdot\frac{\partial \mathbf{r}_i}{\partial \dot{q}_n}\dot{q}_1\dot{q}_n + \frac{\partial \mathbf{r}_i}{\partial \dot{q}_2}\cdot\frac{\partial \mathbf{r}_i}{\partial \dot{q}_n}\dot{q}_2\dot{q}_n + ...\right)^2$$

$$T = a + \sum_k b_k\,\dot{q}_k + \sum_k\sum_l C_{kl}\,\dot{q}_k\,\dot{q}_l \qquad ...(2.72)$$

where

$$a = \sum_i m_i\left(\frac{\partial r_i}{\partial t}\right)^2 \qquad ...(2.73)$$

$$b_k = \sum_i m_i\,\frac{\partial \boldsymbol{r}_i}{\partial \dot{q}_k}\cdot\frac{\partial \boldsymbol{r}_i}{\partial t}\dot{q}_k \qquad ...(2.74)$$

$$C_{kl} = \frac{1}{2}\sum_i m_i\,\frac{\partial \mathbf{r}_i}{\partial \dot{q}_k}\cdot\frac{\partial \mathbf{r}_i}{\partial \dot{q}_l} \qquad ...(2.75)$$

The case where time is not explicitly involved we have $\partial \mathbf{r}_i / \partial t = 0$ and

$$T = \sum_k\sum_l C_{kl}\,\dot{q}_k\,\dot{q}_l \qquad ...(2.76)$$

and kinetic energy is a homogeneous quadratic form in the generalized velocities.

Example 2. *Show the equivalence of Lagrange's and Newton's equation.*

Solution: Consider the generalized coordinates to be the rectangular coordinates. The Lagrange's equation for a single particle is

$$\frac{d}{dt}\left(\frac{\partial[T-V]}{\partial\dot{x}_i}\right)-\frac{\partial[T-V]}{\partial x_i}=0 \ (i=1,2,3)$$

with $x_1 = x, x_2 = y, x_3 = z$

For a conservative system

$$T=T(\dot{x}_i),V=V(x_i)$$

Therefore,

$$\frac{\partial T}{\partial x_i}=0, \ \frac{\partial V}{\partial \dot{x}_i}=0$$

The Lagrange's equation of motion becomes

$$\frac{d}{dt}\left(\frac{\partial T}{\partial\dot{x}_i}\right)-\frac{\partial V}{\partial x_i}=0 \ (i=1,2,3)$$

For a conservative system

$$F_i=-\frac{\partial V}{\partial x_i}$$

$$F_i=\frac{d}{dt}\left(\frac{\partial T}{\partial\dot{x}_i}\right)=\frac{d}{dt}\frac{\partial}{\partial\dot{x}_i}\left(\sum_{j=1}^{3}\frac{1}{2}m\dot{x}_j^2\right)=\frac{d}{dt}(m\dot{x}_i)=\frac{dp_i}{dt}=\dot{p}_i$$

Thus, the Lagrange's and Newton's equations are identical.

Example 3. *Obtain Lagrange's equation of motion for a Simple Harmonic Oscillator.*

Solution: The generalized coordinate is x. The kinetic energy is

$$T=\frac{1}{2}m\dot{x}^2$$

The potential energy is

$$V=\frac{1}{2}kx^2$$

where k is spring constant. The Lagrangian is

$$L=T-V=\frac{1}{2}m\dot{x}^2-\frac{1}{2}kx^2$$

The Lagrange's equation of motion is

$$\frac{d}{dt}\left(\frac{\partial L}{\partial\dot{x}}\right)-\frac{\partial L}{\partial x}=0$$

$$\frac{d}{dt}(m\dot{x}) + kx = 0$$

$$m\ddot{x} + kx = 0$$

$$\ddot{x} + \frac{k}{m}x = 0$$

$$\ddot{x} + w^2 x = 0$$

where $w = \sqrt{k/m}$ is the frequency of the oscillator.

Example 4. *Simple pendulum: Consider a particle of mass m suspended from a weightless cord of length l. The motion of the particle takes place in a plane. Obtain the Lagrangian and equation of motion.*

Solution: Choose generalized coordinate angle θ made by the string *OB* of the pendulum and the vertical *OA* (Fig. 2.1). Let the coordinate of *m* are (x,y). If l is the length of *OB*,

$$x = l\sin\theta,\ y = l\cos\theta$$

the kinetic energy is

$$T = \frac{1}{2}m(\dot{x}^2 + \dot{y}^2) = \frac{1}{2}m(l^2\cos^2\theta\dot{\theta}^2 + l^2\sin^2\theta\dot{\theta}^2) = \frac{1}{2}ml^2\dot{\theta}^2$$

The potential energy of mass *m* (taking a reference level, a horizontal plane through the lowest point A) is given by

$$V = mg(OA - OC) = mg(l - l\cos\theta) = mgl(1 - \cos\theta)$$

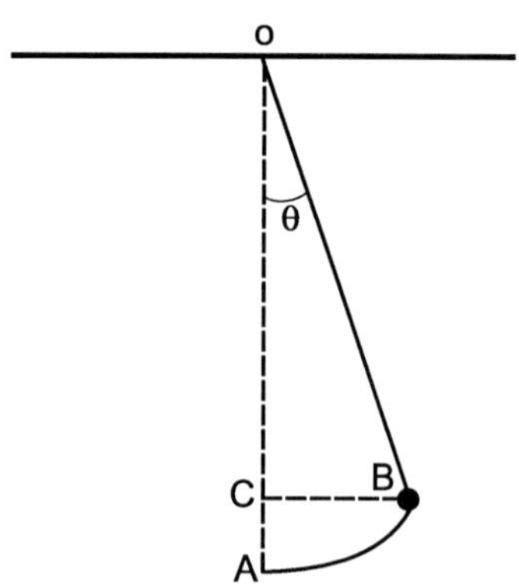

Fig. 2.1 Simple pendulum

The Lagrangian is

$$L = T - V = \frac{1}{2}ml^2\dot{\theta}^2 - mgl(1 - \cos\theta)$$

The equation of motion is

$$\frac{d}{dt}\left(\frac{\partial L}{\partial \dot{\theta}}\right) - \frac{\partial L}{\partial \theta} = 0$$

$$\frac{d}{dt}\left(ml^2\,\dot{\theta}\right) + m\,g\,l\sin\theta = 0$$

$$ml^2\,\ddot{\theta} + m\,g\,l\sin\theta = 0$$

$$\ddot{\theta} + \frac{g}{l}\sin\theta = 0$$

For small θ , $\sin\theta = 0$

$$\ddot{\theta} + \frac{g}{l}\,\theta = 0$$

Example 5. *The Atwood's Machine: Two point like masses m_1 and m_2 are connected by a massless thread which rests on a wheel (Fig. 2.2). The motion is assumed to be frictionless. Obtain Lagrangian and equation of motion.*

Solution: Let the length of the thread is l. The position of the mass m_1 is given by the coordinate x. Since m_1 and m_2 are connected by a thread of constant length l therefore the position of m_2 is located by $l-x$. Therefore, the generalized coordinate is x. The kinetic energy is

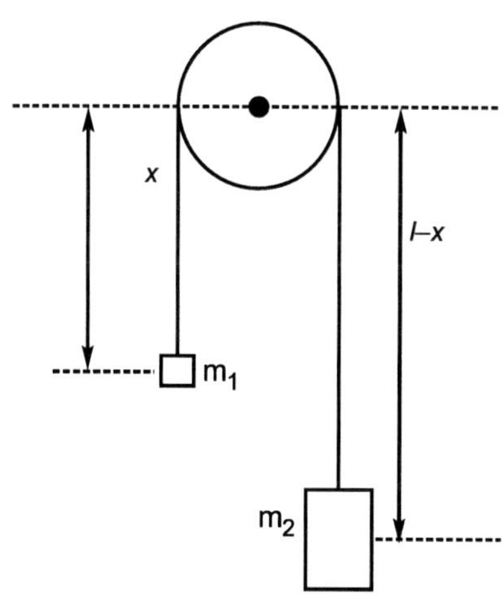

Fig. 2.2 Atwood's Machine

$$T = \frac{1}{2}m_1\dot{x}^2 + \frac{1}{2}m_2(\dot{l} - \dot{x})^2 = \frac{1}{2}(m_1 + m_2)\dot{x}^2$$

The potential energy is

$$V = -m_1 g x - m_2 g(l - x)$$

The Lagrangian is

$$L = T - V = \frac{1}{2}(m_1 + m_2)\dot{x}^2 + m_1 g x + m_2 g(l - x) \qquad ...(2.77)$$

The equation of motion is

$$\frac{d}{dt}\left(\frac{\partial L}{\partial \dot{x}}\right) - \frac{\partial L}{\partial x} = 0 \qquad ...(2.78)$$

From Eqs.(2.77) and (2.78)

$$\frac{d}{dt}(m_1 + m_2)\dot{x} - (m_1 - m_2)g = 0$$

$$\ddot{x} = \frac{(m_1 - m_2)}{(m_1 + m_2)} g \qquad ...(2.79)$$

Example 6. *A bead is sliding on a uniformly rotating wire in a force free space. Obtain Lagrangian and equation of motion.*

Solution: The wire is straight, and is rotating with angular velocity ω about some fixed axis perpendicular to the wire (Fig. 2.3). Hence constraint is time dependent. The generalized coordinate is r.

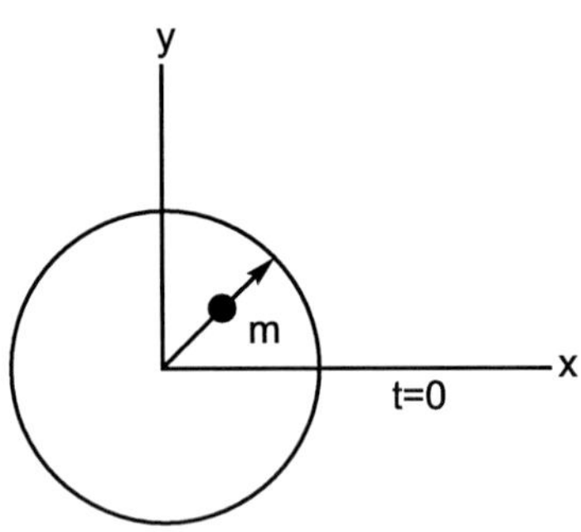

Fig. 2.3 A bead sliding on a uniformly rotating wire in a force free space.

The position of the bead at any time t is specified by coordinates (x,y) such that

$$x = r\cos\omega t,\ y = r\sin\omega t$$

The kinetic energy is

$$T = \frac{1}{2}m(\dot{x}^2 + \dot{y}^2) = \frac{1}{2}m(\dot{r}^2 + r^2\omega^2)$$

Since bead is moving in force free space, that is, there is no gravity, therefore the potential energy $V = 0$.

The Lagrangian L is therefore,

$$L = T - V = \frac{1}{2} m (\dot{\text{r}}^2 + \text{r}^2 \omega^2) \qquad ...(2.80)$$

The Lagrange equation of motion is

$$\frac{d}{dt}\left(\frac{\partial L}{\partial \dot{\text{r}}}\right) - \frac{\partial L}{\partial \text{r}} = 0 \qquad ...(2.81)$$

$$\frac{d}{dt}(m\dot{\text{r}}) - m r \omega^2 = 0$$

$$\ddot{\text{r}} = \omega^2 \text{r} \qquad ...(2.82)$$

This is nothing but centrifugal acceleration.

Example 7. *Spherical pendulum: Obtain Lagrange's equation of motion for a spherical pendulum, that is, a mass point suspended by a rigid weightless rod.*

Solution: The pendulum bob is constraint to move on a spherical surface of radius R. We locate the bob by the spherical coordinates θ and φ (Fig. 2.4). From the Fig. 2.4

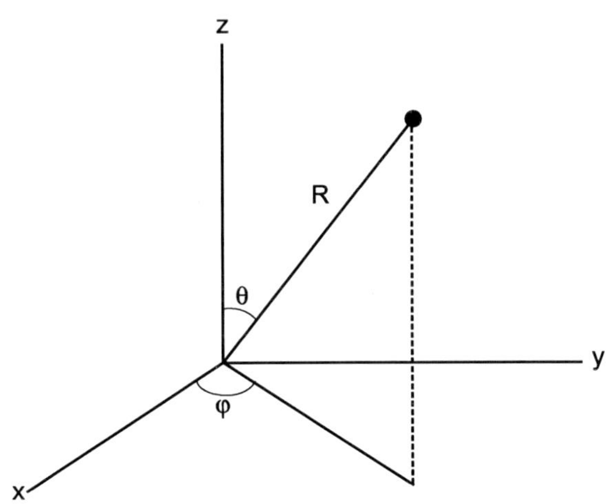

Fig. 2.4 Spherical Pendulum.

$$x = R\sin\theta\cos\varphi,\ \ y = R\sin\theta\sin\varphi,\ z = R\cos\theta$$

$$\dot{x} = R\cos\theta\cos\varphi\dot{\theta} - R\sin\theta\sin\varphi\dot{\varphi}$$

$$\dot{y} = R\cos\theta\sin\varphi\dot{\theta} + R\sin\theta\cos\varphi\dot{\varphi}$$

$$\dot{z} = -R\sin\theta\dot{\theta}$$

The kinetic energy of the mass point m

$$T = \frac{1}{2} m(\dot{x}^2 + \dot{y}^2 + \dot{z}^2)$$

$$T = \frac{1}{2} m[(R \cos\theta \cos\varphi \dot{\theta} - R \sin\theta \sin\varphi \dot{\varphi})^2 + (R \cos\theta \sin\varphi \dot{\theta} + R \sin\theta \cos\varphi \dot{\varphi})^2 + (-R \sin\theta \dot{\theta})^2]$$

$$T = \frac{1}{2} m \, (R^2 \cos^2\theta \dot{\theta}^2 + R^2 \sin^2\theta \, \dot{\varphi}^2 + R^2 \sin^2\theta \dot{\theta}^2)$$

$$= \frac{1}{2} m \, (R^2 \; \dot{\theta}^2 + R^2 \sin^2\theta \, \dot{\varphi}^2) \qquad ...(2.83)$$

The potential energy due to gravity relative to horizontal plane is

$$V = m g z = m g R \cos\theta \qquad ...(2.84)$$

The Lagrangian is

$$L = T - V = \frac{1}{2} m \, (R^2 \dot{\theta}^2 + R^2 \sin^2\theta \, \dot{\varphi}^2) - m g R \cos\theta \qquad ...(2.85)$$

The equations of motions are

$$\frac{d}{dt}\left(\frac{\partial L}{\partial \dot{\theta}} \right) - \frac{\partial L}{\partial \theta} = 0 \qquad ...(2.86)$$

$$\frac{d}{dt}\left(\frac{\partial L}{\partial \dot{\varphi}} \right) - \frac{\partial L}{\partial \varphi} = 0 \qquad ...(2.87)$$

From Eqs. (2.85) and (2.86)

$$\frac{d}{dt}\left(m R^2 \dot{\theta} \right) - mgR \sin\theta - m R^2 \sin\theta \cos\theta \, \dot{\varphi}^2 = 0$$

$$\ddot{\theta} - \frac{g}{R} \sin\theta - \sin\theta \cos\theta \, \dot{\varphi}^2 = 0 \qquad ...(2.88)$$

From Eqs.(2.85) and (2.87)

$$\frac{d}{dt}\left(mR^2 \sin^2\theta \, \dot{\varphi} \right) = 0$$

$$mR^2 \sin^2\theta \, \dot{\varphi} = \text{constant} = p_{\varphi} \qquad ...(2.89)$$

Example 8. *Double Pendulum: Find the Lagrangian and equations of motion for the double pendulum shown in the Fig. 2.5 where the lengths of the pendulum are l_1 and l_2 with corresponding masses m_1 and m_2.*

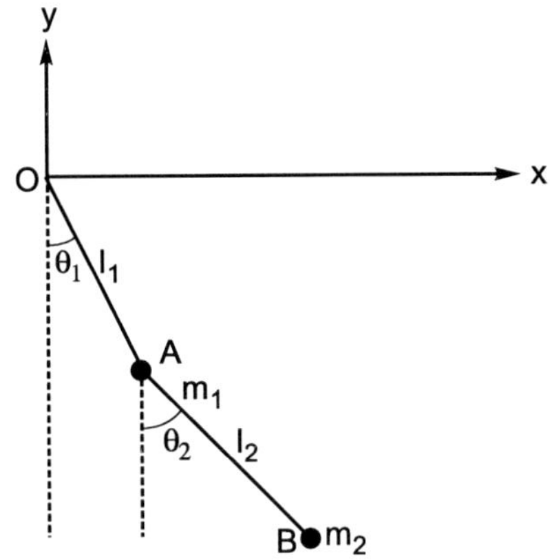

Fig. 2.5 Double pendulum.

Solution: Choose the generalized coordinates θ_1 and θ_2 made by the string OA and AB with the vertical. The motion takes place in a plane. Let the coordinates of m_1 are (x_1, y_1) and that of m_2 (x_2, y_2) where

$$x_1 = l_1 \cos\theta_1 \,,\; y_1 = l_1 \sin\theta_1 \,, x_2 = l_1 \cos\theta_1 + l_2 \cos\theta_2 \,,\; y_2 = l_1 \sin\theta_1 + l_2 \sin\theta_2$$

and

$$\dot{x}_1 = -l_1 \sin\theta_1 \,\dot{\theta}_1, \qquad \dot{y}_1 = l_1 \cos\theta_1 \,\dot{\theta}_1$$

$$\dot{x}_2 = -l_1 \sin\theta_1 \,\dot{\theta}_1 - l_2 \sin\theta_2 \,\dot{\theta}_2 \,, \qquad \dot{y}_2 = l_1 \cos\theta_1 \,\dot{\theta}_1 + l_2 \cos\theta_2 \,\dot{\theta}_2$$

The kinetic energy of the system is

$$T = \frac{1}{2} m_1 (\dot{x}_1^2 + \dot{y}_1^2) + \frac{1}{2} m_2 (\dot{x}_2^2 + \dot{y}_2^2)$$

$$T = \frac{1}{2} m_1 (l_1^2 \sin^2\theta_1 \,\dot{\theta}_1^2 + l_1^2 \cos^2\theta_1 \,\dot{\theta}_1^2)$$
$$+ \frac{1}{2} m_2 (l_1^2 \sin^2\theta_1 \,\dot{\theta}_1^2 + l_2^2 \sin^2\theta_2 \,\dot{\theta}_2^2 + 2 l_1 l_2 \sin\theta_1 \sin\theta_2 \,\dot{\theta}_1 \dot{\theta}_2)$$
$$+ \frac{1}{2} m_2 (l_1^2 \cos^2\theta_1 \,\dot{\theta}_1^2 + l_2^2 \cos^2\theta_2 \,\dot{\theta}_2^2 + 2 l_1 l_2 \cos\theta_1 \cos\theta_2 \,\dot{\theta}_1 \dot{\theta}_2)$$

$$T = \frac{1}{2} m_1 l_1^2 \dot{\theta}_1^2 + \frac{1}{2} m_2 (l_1^2 \dot{\theta}_1^2 + l_2^2 \dot{\theta}_2^2 + 2 l_1 l_2 \cos(\theta_1 - \theta_2) \dot{\theta}_1 \dot{\theta}_2) \qquad ...(2.90)$$

Potential energy of the system (taking reference level a plane at distance $l_1 + l_2$ below the point of suspension)

$$V = m_1 g (l_1 + l_2 - l_1 \cos\theta_1) + m_2 g (l_1 + l_2 - l_1 \cos\theta_1 - l_2 \cos\theta_2) ...(2.91)$$

The Lagrangian is

$$L=\frac{1}{2}m_1 l_1^2\dot{\theta}_1^2+\frac{1}{2}m_2(\,l_1^2\dot{\theta}_1^2+l_2^2\dot{\theta}_2^2+2l_1l_2\,cos(\,\theta_1-\theta_2\,)\dot{\theta}_1\dot{\theta}_2\,)-$$
$$-m_1 g\,(\,l_1+l_2-l_1\,cos\,\theta_1\,)+m_2 g\,(\,l_1+l_2-l_1\,cos\,\theta_1-l_2\,cos\,\theta_2\,) \quad ...(2.92)$$

Equations of motions are

$$\frac{d}{dt}\left(\frac{\partial L}{\partial\dot{\theta}_1}\right)-\frac{\partial L}{\partial\theta_1}=0 \quad ...(2.93)$$

$$\frac{d}{dt}\left(\frac{\partial L}{\partial\dot{\theta}_2}\right)-\frac{\partial L}{\partial\theta_2}=0 \quad ...(2.94)$$

From Eqs. (2.92) and (2.93)

$$\frac{d}{dt}[(\,m_1+m_2\,)l_1^2\,\dot{\theta}_1+m_2l_1l_2\dot{\theta}_2\,cos(\,\theta_1-\theta_2\,)]$$
$$+m_2l_1l_2\dot{\theta}_1\dot{\theta}_2\,sin(\,\theta_1-\theta_2\,)+(\,m_1+m_2\,)gl_1\,sin\,\theta_1+=0$$

on simplification

$$(m_1+m_2)\,l_1^2\,\ddot{\theta}_1+m_2l_1l_2\ddot{\theta}_2\cos(\theta_1-\theta_2)-m_2l_1l_2\dot{\theta}_2\sin(\theta_1-\theta_2)(\dot{\theta}_1-\dot{\theta}_2)$$
$$+m_2l_1l_2\dot{\theta}_1\dot{\theta}_2\sin(\theta_1-\theta_2)+(m_1+m_2)gl_1\sin\theta_1+=0 \quad ...(2.95)$$

From Eqs. (2.92) and (2.94)

$$m_2\,l_2^2\,\ddot{\theta}_2+m_2\,l_1\,l_2\,\ddot{\theta}_1\,cos\,(\,\theta_1-\theta_2\,)-m_2\,l_1\,l_2\,\dot{\theta}_1^2\,sin\,(\,\theta_1-\theta_2\,)+m_2\,g\,l_2\,sin\,\theta_2=0 \quad ...(2.96)$$

If $m_1=m_2=m$, and $l_1=l_2=l$, Eq.(2.95) is

$$2\,l\,\ddot{\theta}_1+l\ddot{\theta}_2\,cos(\,\theta_1-\theta_2\,)+l\dot{\theta}_2^2\,sin(\,\theta_1-\theta_2\,)+2g\,sin\,\theta_1=0 \quad ...(2.97)$$

and Eq. (2.96)

$$l\ddot{\theta}_2+l\ddot{\theta}_1\,cos\,(\,\theta_1-\theta_2\,)-l\dot{\theta}_1^2\,sin\,(\,\theta_1-\theta_2\,)+g\,sin\,\theta_2=0 \quad ...(2.98)$$

For small oscillation cos $\theta \simeq 1$, sin $\theta \simeq \theta$, Eqs. (2.97) and (2.98) are

$$2l\ddot{\theta}_1+l\ddot{\theta}_2+l\dot{\theta}_2^2\,(\,\theta_1-\theta_2\,)+2g\theta_1=0 \quad ...(2.99)$$

$$l\ddot{\theta}_2+l\ddot{\theta}_1\;-l\dot{\theta}_1^2\;(\,\theta_1-\theta_2\,)+g\theta_2=0 \quad ...(2.100)$$

Neglected the product $\theta\,\dot{\theta}$ in Eqs(2.99) and (2.100)

$$2l\ddot{\theta}_1+l\ddot{\theta}_2+2g\theta_1=0 \quad ...(2.101)$$

$$l\ddot{\theta}_2+l\ddot{\theta}_1\;+g\theta_2=0 \quad ...(2.102)$$

Example 9. *Find the Lagrangian for a disk rolling without slipping on an inclined plane.*

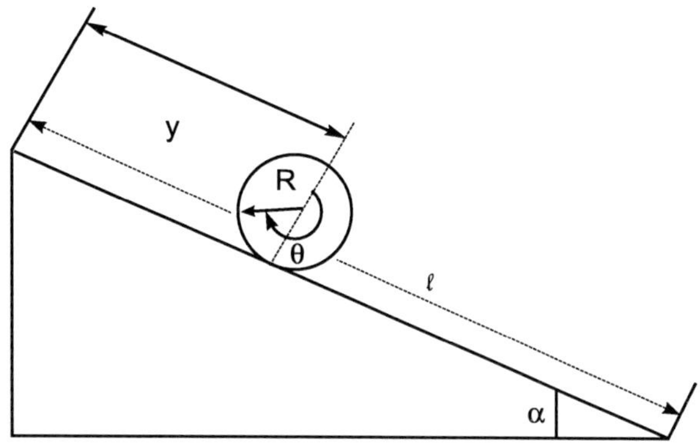

Fig. 2.6 A disk rolling on an inclined plane without slipping.

Solution: Consider a disk of mass M and radius R rolling without slipping on an inclined plane (Fig. 2.6). of length l. The configuration of this system can be described by the generalized coordinates y and θ. During the rolling of the disk down the inclined plane a translational as well as rotational motion takes place. Therefore, kinetic energy is sum of translational energy and rotational energy, that is,

$$T = \frac{1}{2} M \dot{y}^2 + \frac{1}{2} I \dot{\theta}^2$$

where I is the moment of inertia of the disk about an axis passes through its centre. The potential energy is

$$V = M g(z_2 - z_1)$$

where

$$z_2 = l \sin\alpha$$

$$z_1 = y \sin\alpha$$

$$V = M g(l - y) \sin\alpha$$

The Lagrangian is therefore

$$L = \frac{1}{2} M \dot{y}^2 + \frac{1}{2} I \dot{\theta}^2 - M g(l - y) \sin\alpha = \frac{1}{2} M \dot{y}^2 + \frac{1}{4} MR^2 \dot{\theta}^2 - M g(l - y) \sin\alpha$$

...(2.103)

Example 10. *A massless spring of unstretched length l_0 has a point mass m connected to one end and the other end fixed so the spring hangs in the gravity field (Fig.2.7). The motion of the spring is in the vertical plane. Obtain Lagrangian and equation of motion.*

Solution: The coordinates of the particle of mass m are (x,y). The kinetic energy is

$$T = \frac{1}{2} m(\dot{x}^2 + \dot{y}^2)$$

From the Fig.2.7

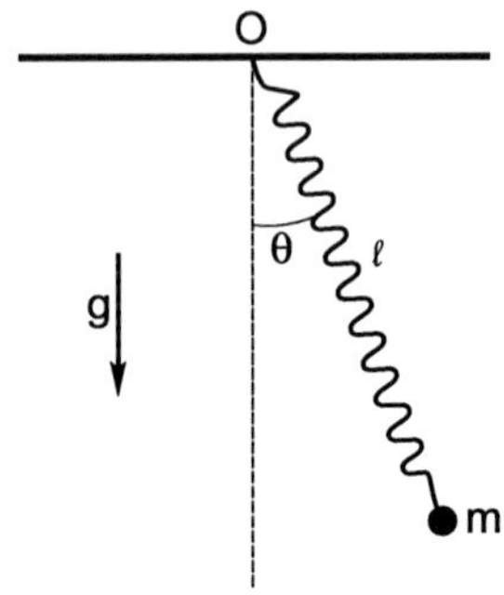

Fig. 2.7

$$x = l \sin\theta, \; y = -l\cos\theta$$

$$\dot{x} = \dot{l}\sin\theta + l\cos\theta\,\dot{\theta}, \; \dot{y} = -\dot{l}\cos\theta + l\sin\theta\,\dot{\theta}$$

$$\dot{x}^2 + \dot{y}^2 = \dot{l}^2 + l^2\dot{\theta}^2$$

$$T = \frac{1}{2} m\left(\dot{l}^2 + l^2\dot{\theta}^2\right)$$

The potential energy is

$$V = -m g l\cos\theta + \frac{1}{2}k(l - l_0)^2$$

where k is the spring constant. The Lagrangian is

$$L = T - V = \frac{1}{2}m(\dot{l}^2 + l^2\dot{\theta}^2) + m g l\cos\theta - \frac{1}{2}k(l - l_0)^2 \qquad ...(2.104)$$

The equations of motion are

$$\frac{d}{dt}\left(\frac{\partial L}{\partial \dot{l}}\right) - \frac{\partial L}{\partial l} = 0 \qquad ...(2.105)$$

$$\frac{d}{dt}\left(\frac{\partial L}{\partial \dot{\theta}}\right) - \frac{\partial L}{\partial \theta} = 0 \qquad ...(2.106)$$

From Eqs. (2.104) and (2.105)

$$\frac{d}{dt}\left(m\dot{l}\right) - m l\dot{\theta}^2 - mg\cos\theta + k(l - l_0) = 0$$

$$m\ddot{l} - m l\dot{\theta}^2 - mg\cos\theta + k(l - l_0) = 0 \qquad ...(2.107)$$

and from Eqs. (2.104) and (2.106)

$$\frac{d}{dt}\left(ml^2\,\dot{\theta}\right) + mg\,l\,sin\,\theta\;=0$$

$$ml^2\,\ddot{\theta} + 2ml\dot{l}\dot{\theta}\;+mg\,l\,sin\,\theta\;=0$$

$$l\ddot{\theta} + 2\;\dot{l}\dot{\theta}\;+g\,sin\,\theta\;=0 \qquad ...(2.108)$$

Example 11. *Two mass points m_1 and m_2 (m_1 m_2) are connected by a string of length l passing through a hole in a horizontal table. The mass m_1 is on the table while m_2 is free to move in a vertical line. What initial velocity m_1 be given so that m_2 will remain stationary at distance d below the surface of the table (Fig. 2.8). If m_2 is slightly displaced in a vertical direction, obtain Lagrangian.*

Solution: The mass m_1 must have velocity v perpendicular to the string such that centripetal force on it is equal to the gravitational force on m_2, that is,

$$\frac{m_1\,\mathrm{v}^2}{l-d} = m_2\,g$$

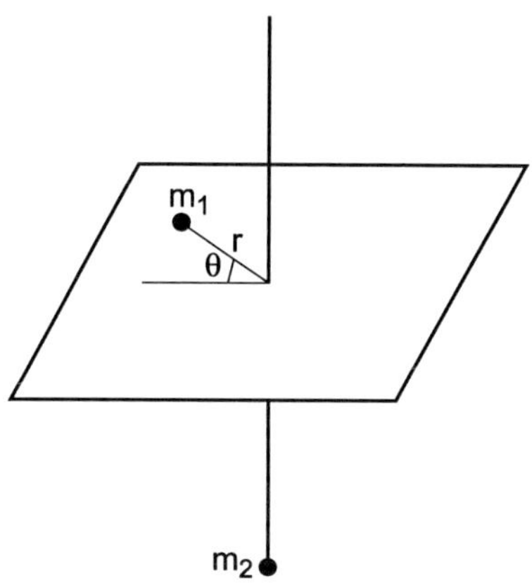

Fig. 2.8

$$\mathrm{v} = \sqrt{\frac{m_2(l-d)\,g}{m_1}} \qquad ...(2.109)$$

Let the surface of the table is xy plane and the position of mass m_1 is given by (x,y). In plane polar coordinates

$$x = (l-d\,)cos\,\theta = \mathrm{r}\cos\theta$$

$$y = (l-d\,)sin\,\theta = \mathrm{r}\,sin\,\theta$$

The kinetic energy of mass m_1 is

$$\frac{1}{2}m_1\,(\,\dot{x}^2+\dot{y}^2\,) = \frac{1}{2}m_1\,(\,\dot{\mathrm{r}}^2+\mathrm{r}^2\,\dot{\theta}^2\,)$$

The mass m_2 can move in vertical or z direction, therefore kinetic energy of m_2 is

$$\frac{1}{2} m_2 \dot{r}^2$$

Total kinetic energy is therefore

$$T = \frac{1}{2} m_1 (\dot{r}^2 + r^2 \dot{\theta}^2) + \frac{1}{2} m_2 \dot{r}^2$$

Potential energy of m_1 is zero while the potential energy of m_2 is

$$V = -m_2 g (l - r)$$

Lagrangian is

$$L = T - V = \frac{1}{2} m_1 (\dot{r}^2 + r^2 \dot{\theta}^2) + \frac{1}{2} m_2 \dot{r}^2 + m_2 g (l - r) \quad \text{...(2.110)}$$

The equations of motion are

$$\frac{d}{dt}\left(\frac{\partial L}{\partial \dot{r}}\right) - \frac{\partial L}{\partial r} = 0 \quad \text{...(2.111)}$$

$$\frac{d}{dt}\left(\frac{\partial L}{\partial \dot{\theta}}\right) - \frac{\partial L}{\partial \theta} = 0 \quad \text{...(2.112)}$$

From Eqs.(2.110) and (2.111)

$$\frac{d}{dt}(m_1 \dot{r} + m_2 \dot{r}) - m_1 r \dot{\theta}^2 + m_2 g = 0$$

$$(m_1 + m_2)\ddot{r} - m_1 r \dot{\theta}^2 + m_2 g = 0 \quad \text{...(2.113)}$$

From Eqs. (2.110) and (2.112)

$$m_1 r^2 \ddot{\theta} = 0$$

$$m_1 r^2 \dot{\theta} = \text{constant} \quad \text{...(2.114)}$$

Example 12. *A mass M is constrained to slide without friction on the path AB as shown in the Fig. 2.9. A mass m is connected to M by a massless inextensible string. Obtain the Lagrangian and equation of motion.*

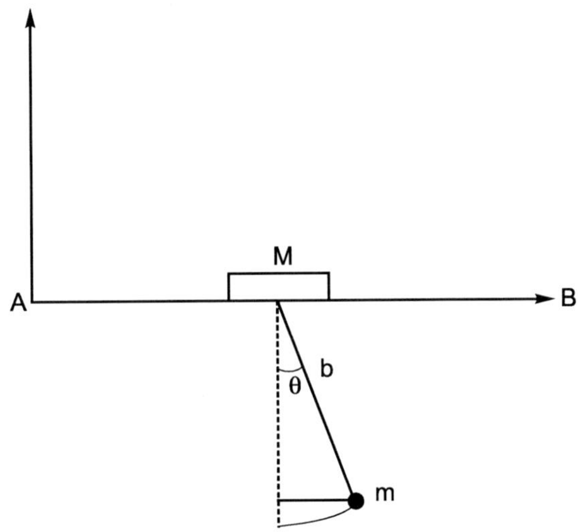

Fig. 2.9

Solution : The coordinates of M are $(x,0)$. The coordinates of m are $(x + b \sin\theta, -b\cos\theta)$. The potential energy of m is $-mgb \cos\theta$ while the potential energy of M can be taken to be zero. The Kinetic energy of M is

$$\frac{1}{2}M\dot{x}^2$$

The kinetic energy of m is

$$\frac{1}{2}m(\dot{x}^2 + b^2\dot{\theta}^2 + 2b\dot{x}\dot{\theta}\cos\theta)$$

Total kinetic energy is

$$T = \frac{1}{2}(M+m)\dot{x}^2 + \frac{1}{2}m(b^2\dot{\theta}^2 + 2b\dot{x}\dot{\theta}\cos\theta)$$

The Lagrangian is

$$L = T - V = \frac{1}{2}(M+m)\dot{x}^2 + \frac{1}{2}m(b^2\dot{\theta}^2 + 2b\dot{x}\dot{\theta}\cos\theta) + mgb\cos\theta \quad ...(2.115)$$

For small θ and $\dot{\theta}$

$$L = T - V = \frac{1}{2}(M+m)\dot{x}^2 + \frac{1}{2}m(b^2\dot{\theta}^2 + 2b\dot{x}\dot{\theta}) + mgb(1 - \frac{\theta^2}{2} + ...) \quad ...(2.116)$$

The equations of motion are

$$\frac{d}{dt}\left(\frac{\partial L}{\partial \dot{\theta}}\right)-\frac{\partial L}{\partial \theta}=0 \qquad ...(2.117)$$

$$\frac{d}{dt}\left(\frac{\partial L}{\partial \dot{x}}\right)-\frac{\partial L}{\partial x}=0 \qquad ...(2.118)$$

From Eqs.(2.116) and (2.117)

$$\frac{d}{dt}\left(m b^2 \dot{\theta}+m b \dot{x}\right)+m g b \theta=0$$

$$m b^2 \ddot{\theta}+m b \ddot{x}+m g b \theta=0$$

$$b \ddot{\theta}+\ddot{x}+g \theta=0 \qquad ...(2.119)$$

From Eqs. (2.116) and (2.118)

$$\frac{d}{dt}(M+m) \dot{x}+m b \dot{\theta}=0$$

$$(M+m) \ddot{x}+m b \dot{\theta}=0 \qquad ...(2.120)$$

Example 13. *A simple pendulum consisting of a mass m and weightless string of length l is mounted on a support of mass M which is attached to a horizontal spring with force constant k (Fig. 2.10). Obtain Lagrangian and equation of motion.*

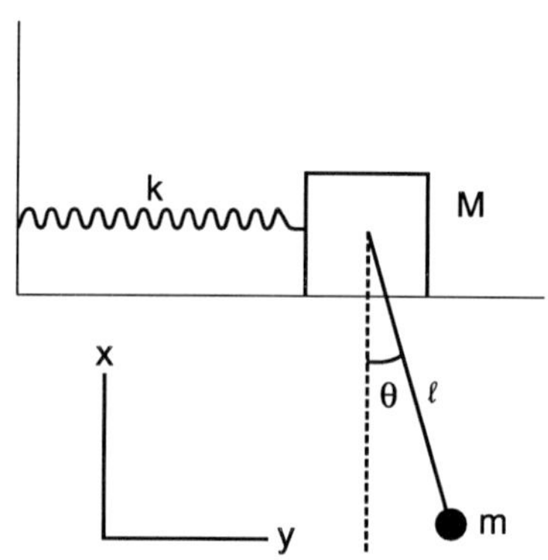

Fig. 2.10

Solution: Consider O as the origin of the coordinate system. With respect to O the coordinate of the mass point m are (x', y') with

$$x'=x+l \sin \theta,\ y'=l-l \cos \theta$$

The coordinates of M are (x, l). The kinetic energy is

$$T=\frac{1}{2}m(\dot{x}^2+l^2\cos^2\theta\,\dot{\theta}^2+2l\,\dot{x}\dot{\theta}\cos\theta+l^2\sin^2\theta\,\dot{\theta}^2)+\frac{1}{2}M\,\dot{x}^2$$

$$T=\frac{1}{2}(m+M)\dot{x}^2+\frac{1}{2}m(l^2\,\dot{\theta}^2+2l\,\dot{x}\dot{\theta}\cos\theta)$$

Potential energy is

$$V=-m\,g\,y'+M\,g\,l+\frac{1}{2}kx^2=-mg(l-l\cos\theta)+M\,g\,l+\frac{1}{2}kx^2$$

The Lagrangian is

$$L=T-V=\frac{1}{2}(m+M)\dot{x}^2+\frac{1}{2}m(l^2\,\dot{\theta}^2+2l\,\dot{x}\dot{\theta}\cos\theta)-mg(l-l\cos\theta)-M\,g\,l-\frac{1}{2}kx^2 \quad ...(2.121)$$

equations of motion are

$$\frac{d}{dt}\left(\frac{\partial L}{\partial\dot{\theta}}\right)-\frac{\partial L}{\partial\theta}=0 \quad ...(2.122)$$

$$\frac{d}{dt}\left(\frac{\partial L}{\partial\dot{x}}\right)-\frac{\partial L}{\partial x}=0 \quad ...(2.123)$$

From Eqs.(2.121) and (2.122)

$$\frac{d}{dt}\left(ml^2\dot{\theta}+m\,l\dot{x}\cos\theta\right)+ml\dot{x}\dot{\theta}\sin\theta+mgl\sin\theta=0$$

$$ml^2\ddot{\theta}+m\,l\ddot{x}\cos\theta-m\,l\,\dot{x}\dot{\theta}\sin\theta+m\,l\dot{x}\dot{\theta}\sin\theta+mgl\sin\theta=0$$

$$l\ddot{\theta}+\ddot{x}\cos\theta+g\sin\theta=0 \quad ...(2.124)$$

From Eqs.(2.121) and (2.123)

$$\frac{d}{dt}\left([m+M]\,\dot{x}+ml\dot{\theta}\cos\theta\right)+k\,x=0$$

$$[m+M]\,\ddot{x}+ml\,\ddot{\theta}\cos\theta-ml\dot{\theta}^2\sin\theta+k\,x=0 \quad ...(2.125)$$

Example 14. *Prove the invariance of the Lagrange's equation of motion under the coordinate transformation*

$$q_k=q_k(Q_1,Q_2,........,Q_n,t)$$

Solution: Let $q_1,q_2,...,q_n$ be the old set of generalized coordinates and $Q_1,Q_2,........,Q_n$ be the new set, hence

$$q_k = q_k(Q_1, Q_2, ..., Q_n, t)$$

Let the Lagrangian in new set of coordinates is represented by L'

$$L'(Q,\dot{Q},t) = L[q(Q,t),\dot{q}(Q,\dot{Q},t),t] = L\left[q(Q,t),\frac{\partial q}{\partial Q}\dot{Q}+\frac{\partial q}{\partial t},t\right]$$

as $q = q(Q,t)$

$$\dot{q} = \frac{\partial q}{\partial t} + \frac{\partial q}{\partial Q}\dot{Q}$$

$$\frac{\partial \dot{q}}{\partial \dot{Q}} = \frac{\partial q}{\partial Q}$$

Therefore,

$$\frac{d}{dt}\left(\frac{\partial L'}{\partial \dot{Q}}\right) = \frac{d}{dt}\left(\frac{\partial L}{\partial q}\frac{\partial q}{\partial \dot{Q}} + \frac{\partial L}{\partial \dot{q}}\frac{\partial \dot{q}}{\partial \dot{Q}}\right) = \frac{d}{dt}\left(\frac{\partial L}{\partial \dot{q}}\frac{\partial \dot{q}}{\partial \dot{Q}}\right) = \frac{d}{dt}\left(\frac{\partial L}{\partial \dot{q}}\frac{\partial q}{\partial Q}\right)$$

$$\frac{d}{dt}\left(\frac{\partial L'}{\partial \dot{Q}}\right) = \frac{d}{dt}\left(\frac{\partial L}{\partial \dot{q}}\right)\frac{\partial q}{\partial Q} + \frac{\partial L}{\partial \dot{q}}\frac{d}{dt}\left(\frac{\partial q}{\partial Q}\right)$$

$$\frac{\partial L'}{\partial Q} = \frac{\partial L}{\partial q}\frac{\partial q}{\partial Q} + \frac{\partial L}{\partial \dot{q}}\frac{\partial \dot{q}}{\partial Q}$$

$$\frac{d}{dt}\left(\frac{\partial L'}{\partial \dot{Q}}\right) - \frac{\partial L'}{\partial Q} = \left[\frac{d}{dt}\left(\frac{\partial L}{\partial \dot{q}}\right) - \frac{\partial L}{\partial q}\right]\frac{\partial q}{\partial Q} + \frac{\partial L}{\partial \dot{q}}\frac{d}{dt}\left(\frac{\partial q}{\partial Q}\right) - \frac{\partial L}{\partial \dot{q}}\frac{\partial \dot{q}}{\partial Q}$$

$$\frac{d}{dt}\left(\frac{\partial L'}{\partial \dot{Q}}\right) - \frac{\partial L'}{\partial Q} = \left[\frac{d}{dt}\left(\frac{\partial L}{\partial \dot{q}}\right) - \frac{\partial L}{\partial q}\right]\frac{\partial q}{\partial Q}$$

The validity of the equation

$$\frac{d}{dt}\left(\frac{\partial L}{\partial \dot{q}}\right) - \frac{\partial L}{\partial q} = 0$$

leads to

$$\frac{d}{dt}\left(\frac{\partial L'}{\partial \dot{Q}}\right) - \frac{\partial L'}{\partial Q} = 0 \qquad ...(2.126)$$

If there are several degrees of freedom, we obtain instead of Eq. (2.126), the following

$$\frac{d}{dt}\left(\frac{\partial L'}{\partial \dot{Q}_k}\right) - \frac{\partial L'}{\partial Q_k} = \sum_i \left[\frac{d}{dt}\left(\frac{\partial L}{\partial \dot{q}_i}\right) - \frac{\partial L}{\partial q_i}\right]\frac{\partial q_i}{\partial Q_k} \qquad ...(2.127)$$

Example 15. *Two masses, 2m and m are suspended from a fixed frame by elastic spring of spring constant k (Fig.2.11). Obtain Lagrangian and equation of motion assuming only vertical motion.*

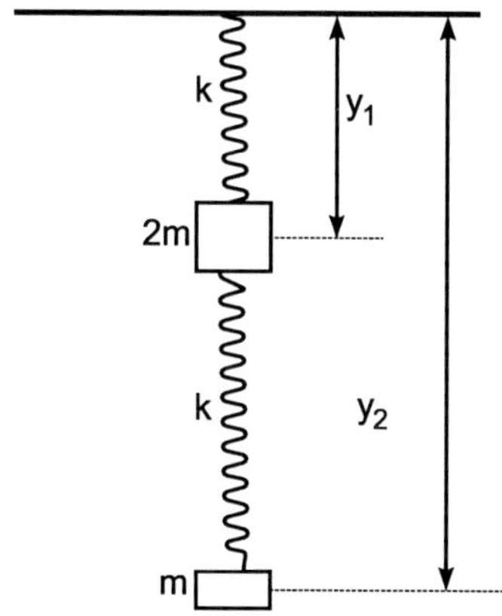

Fig. 2.11

Solution: Let the unstretched length of upper and lower spring be d_1 and d_2. The point coordinate of mass *2m* are $(0,y_1)$ and that of m is $(0,y_2)$. The generalized coordinates are y_1 and y_2. The kinetic energy is

$$T = \frac{1}{2}(2m\,\dot{y}_1^2 + m\,\dot{y}_2^2) = m(\dot{y}_1^2 + \frac{1}{2}\dot{y}_2^2)$$

The potential energy of 2*m* is

$$= -2mgy_1$$

The potential energy of *m* is

$$= -mgy_2$$

Potential energy of spring is

$$\frac{1}{2}k(y_1 - d_1^2) + \frac{1}{2}k(y_2 - y_1 - d_2^2)$$

Total potential energy *V* is

$$V = -\,2mgy_1 - mgy_2 + \frac{1}{2}k(y_1 - d_1^2) + \frac{1}{2}k(y_2 - y_1 - d_2^2)$$

The Lagrangian is

$$L = T - V = m(\dot{y}_1^2 + \frac{1}{2}\dot{y}_2^2) + mg(2y_1 + y_2) - \frac{1}{2}k(y_1 - d_1^2) - \frac{1}{2}k(y_2 - y_1 - d_2^2)$$

...(2.128)

The equations of motions are

$$\frac{d}{dt}\left(\frac{\partial L}{\partial \dot{y}_1}\right)-\frac{\partial L}{\partial y_1}=0 \qquad ...(2.129)$$

$$\frac{d}{dt}\left(\frac{\partial L}{\partial \dot{y}_2}\right)-\frac{\partial L}{\partial y_2}=0 \qquad ...(2.130)$$

$$\frac{\partial L}{\partial \dot{y}_1}=2m\dot{y}_1, \frac{\partial L}{\partial \dot{y}^2}=m\dot{y}_2, \frac{\partial L}{\partial y^1}=2mg-k(y_1-d_1)-k(y_2-y_1-d_2),$$

$$\frac{\partial L}{\partial y_2}=mg+k(y_2-y_1-d_2) \qquad ...(2.131)$$

From Eqs. (2.129) and (2.131)

$$2m\ddot{y}_1-2mg+k(d_2-d_1)-k(y_2-2y_1)=0 \qquad ...(2.132)$$

From Eqs. (2.130) and (2.131)

$$m\ddot{y}_2-mg-kd_2+k(y_2-y_1)=0 \qquad ...(2.133)$$

Example 16. *A long thin tube of negligible mass is pivoted so that it may rotate in a horizontal plane. A thin rod of mass m and length l slides in the tube. Obtain Lagrange's equation of motion for the system ignoring friction.*

Solution: Let r is the distance of centre of mass of rod from the pivot and θ is the angle between the tube and fixed horizontal line passing through pivot (Fig. 2.12.).

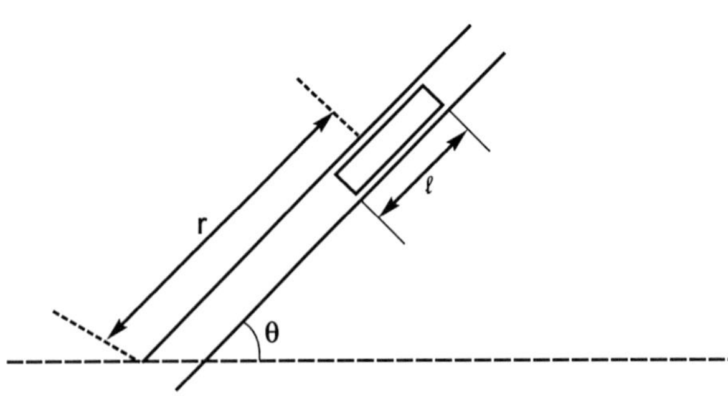

Fig. 2.12

The generalized coordinates are r and θ. The coordinates of centre of mass are (x,y)

$$x = \mathrm{r}\cos\theta,\ y = \mathrm{r}\sin\theta$$

$$\dot{x} = \dot{\mathrm{r}}\cos\theta - \mathrm{r}\sin\theta\,\dot{\theta},\quad \dot{y} = \dot{\mathrm{r}}\sin\theta + \mathrm{r}\cos\theta\,\dot{\theta},$$

Kinetic energy is

$$\frac{1}{2}m(\dot{x}^2 + \dot{y}^2) = \frac{1}{2}m(\dot{\mathrm{r}}^2 + r^2\dot{\theta}^2)$$

Kinetic energy of rotation is

$$\frac{1}{2}I\dot{\theta}^2 = \frac{ml^2}{24}\dot{\theta}^2$$

where the moment of inertia I through the centre of mass is $\dfrac{ml^2}{12}$.

Total kinetic energy is

$$T = \frac{1}{2}m(\dot{\mathrm{r}}^2 + r^2\dot{\theta}^2) + \frac{ml^2}{24}\dot{\theta}^2$$

Since the rod moves in horizontal plane, therefore the potential energy $V = 0$. The Lagrangian, is therefore

$$L = T - V = \frac{1}{2}m(\dot{\mathrm{r}}^2 + r^2\dot{\theta}^2) + \frac{ml^2}{24}\dot{\theta}^2 \qquad \text{...(2.134)}$$

$$\frac{d}{dt}\left(\frac{\partial L}{\partial\dot{\theta}}\right) - \frac{\partial L}{\partial\theta} = 0 \qquad \text{...(2.135)}$$

$$\frac{d}{dt}\left(\frac{\partial L}{\partial\dot{\mathrm{r}}}\right) - \frac{\partial L}{\partial\mathrm{r}} = 0 \qquad \text{...(2.136)}$$

From Eqs. (2.134) and (2.135)

$$m(\mathrm{r}^2 + \frac{l^2}{12})\dot{\theta} = \text{constant} \qquad \text{...(2.137)}$$

From Eqs.(2.134) and (2.136)

$$\ddot{\mathrm{r}} = \mathrm{r}\dot{\theta}^2 \qquad \text{...(2.138)}$$

Example 17. *A particle of mass m is constrained to move on the surface of a cylinder of radius R under a force* $\mathbf{F} = -\mathrm{k}\,\mathbf{r}$ *(Fig. 2.13). Obtain the Lagrangian for a particle of mass m moving on a cylindrical surface.*

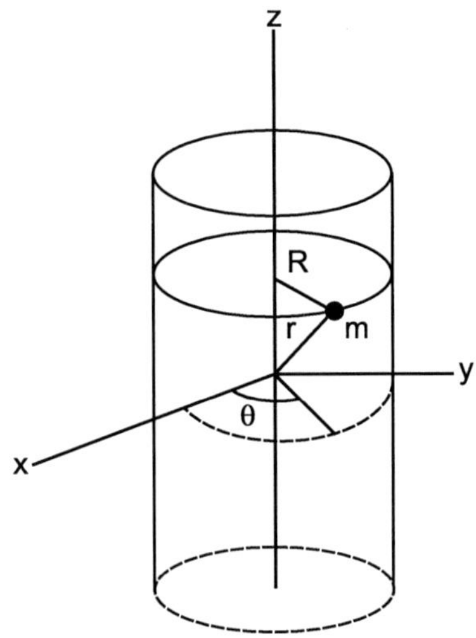

Fig. 2.13

Solution: Consider a particle of mass m that is constrained to move on the surface of a cylinder (Fig. 2.13) such that

$$x^2 + y^2 = R^2$$

The particle having coordinates (x,y,z) is subjected to a force directed toward the origin and proportional to the distance of the particle from the origin, that is,

$$\mathbf{F} = -k\mathbf{r}$$

$$V = -\int \mathbf{F} \cdot d\mathbf{r} = \int k\,\mathbf{r} \cdot d\mathbf{r} = \frac{1}{2}kr^2 = \frac{1}{2}k(x^2 + y^2 + z^2) = \frac{1}{2}k(R^2 + z^2) \quad ...(2.139)$$

The coordinates x,y,z are

$$x = r\cos\theta,\ y = r\sin\theta, z = z$$

$$\dot{x} = \dot{r}\cos\theta - r\sin\theta\dot{\theta},\quad \dot{y} = \dot{r}\sin\theta + r\cos\theta\dot{\theta},\quad \dot{z} = \dot{z}$$

The kinetic energy T is

$$T = \frac{1}{2}m(\dot{r}^2 + r^2\dot{\theta}^2 + \dot{z}^2) = \frac{1}{2}m(R^2\dot{\theta}^2 + \dot{z}^2) \quad ...(2.140)$$

as $r = R =$ constant. From Eq. (2.139) and (2.140) the Lagrangian is

$$L = T - V = \frac{1}{2}m(R^2\dot{\theta}^2 + \dot{z}^2) - \frac{1}{2}k(R^2 + z^2) \quad ...(2.141)$$

OBJECTIVE TYPE QUESTIONS

1. The Lagrangian of a simple pendulum is

(*a*) $\frac{1}{2}ml^2\dot{\theta}^2 - mgl(1-\cos\theta)$

(*b*) $\frac{1}{2}ml^2\dot{\theta}^2 - mgl(1+\cos\theta)$

(*c*) $\frac{1}{2}ml\dot{\theta}^2 - mgl(1-\cos\theta)$

(*d*) $\frac{1}{2}ml^2\dot{\theta}^2 - mg(1-\cos\theta)$

2. The Lagrangian of a cylinder rolling on inclined plane is

(*a*) $\frac{1}{2}m\dot{x}^2 + \frac{1}{4}\mathrm{mr}^2\dot{\theta}^2 + mg(l-x)\sin\varphi$

(*b*) $m\ddot{x} - mg\sin\varphi$

(*c*) $\frac{1}{2}m\dot{x}^2 + \frac{1}{4}mx^2\dot{\theta}^2 + mg\,x\cos\theta$

(*d*) none of these

3. The Lagrangian for compound pendulum is

(*a*) $\frac{1}{2}I\dot{\theta}^2 + mgl\cos\theta$

(*b*) $\frac{1}{2}I\dot{\theta}^2 - mgl\cos\theta$

(*c*) $\frac{1}{2}m(\dot{\mathbf{r}}^2 + \mathbf{r}^2\dot{\theta}^2) + \frac{1}{2}[\dot{\theta}^2 - mg]\cos\theta$

(*d*) $\frac{1}{2}m(\dot{\mathbf{r}}^2 + \mathbf{r}^2\dot{\theta}^2) + \frac{1}{2}[\dot{\theta}^2 + mg]\cos\theta$

4. Which of the following Lagrangian gives the correct equation of motion for simple harmonic oscillator?

(*a*) $\frac{1}{2}m\dot{q}^2 - \frac{1}{2}kq^2$

(b) $\frac{1}{2}m\dot{q}^2 - \frac{1}{2}k\,x^2$

(c) $\frac{1}{2}m\dot{x}^2 - \frac{1}{2}k\,q^2$

(d) $\frac{1}{2}m\dot{x}^2 + \frac{1}{2}k\,x^2$

5. Two Lagrangian functions give the same equation of motion if

(a) The two Lagrangian functions differ by the total time derivative of a function which depends on the coordinates only.

(b) The two Lagrangian function differ by the total time derivative of a function which depends on velocities only.

(c) both (a) and (b).
(d) none of these.

6. A bead of mass m slides without friction on a rotating wire hoop of radius a whose axis of rotation is through a vertical diameter. The angular velocity ω of the hoop is constant. The Lagrangian is

(a) $\frac{1}{2}ma^2\dot{\theta}^2 - mg\cos\theta - \frac{1}{2}ma^2\omega^2\sin^2\theta$

(b) $\frac{1}{2}ma^2\dot{\theta}^2 - mga\sin\theta$

(c) $\frac{1}{2}ma^2\dot{\theta}^2 + \frac{1}{2}ma^2\omega^2\sin^2\theta$

(d) $\frac{1}{2}ma^2\dot{\theta}^2 + mg\cos\theta + \frac{1}{2}ma^2\omega^2\sin^2\theta$

7. A particle of mass m is constrained to move in a vertical plane along a trajectory given by $x = a\cos\theta$, $y = a\sin\theta$ where a is constant. The Lagrangian of the particle is

(a) $\frac{1}{2}ma^2\dot{\theta}^2 - mga\cos\theta$

(b) $\frac{1}{2}ma^2\dot{\theta}^2 - mga\sin\theta$

(c) $\frac{1}{2}ma^2\dot{\theta}^2 + mga\sin\theta$

(*d*) $\frac{1}{2}ma^2\dot{\theta}^2 + mga(1-\cos\theta)$

8. Which of the following Lagrangian gives the correct equation of motion for simple harmonic oscillator?

(*a*) $\frac{1}{2}\left[\left(\frac{dz_1}{dt}\right)^2 - z_1^2\right]$

(*b*) $\frac{1}{2}\left[\left(\frac{dz_1}{dt}\right)^2 - z_1^2\right] + z_1\frac{dz_1}{dt}$

(*c*) both (a) and (b)

(*d*) none of these

9. The Lagrangian for a charged particle of charge e in an electromagnetic field is given by

(*a*) $T - e\varphi + \frac{e}{c}\mathbf{A}\cdot\mathbf{v}$

(*b*) $T + e\varphi + \frac{e}{c}\mathbf{A}\cdot\mathbf{v}$

(*c*) $T + e\varphi - \frac{e}{c}\mathbf{A}\cdot\mathbf{v}$

(*d*) $T - e\varphi - \frac{e}{c}\mathbf{A}\cdot\mathbf{v}$

10. The Lagrangian of a system is $L = \frac{1}{2}m(x^2 - \omega^2 x^2)\exp(\gamma t)$ in which m, γ and ω are real and positive constants. The equation of motion is

(*a*) $\ddot{x} + \omega^2 x = -\gamma\dot{x}$

(*b*) $\ddot{x} + \omega^2 x - \gamma\dot{x} = 0$

(*c*) $\ddot{x} + \omega^2 x = 0$

(*d*) $\ddot{x} - \omega^2 x = 0$

11. The Lagrangian of the two coupled oscillator of mass m each is

$$L = \frac{1}{2}m(\dot{q}_1^2 + \dot{q}_2^2) - \frac{1}{2}m\omega^2(q_1^2 + q_2^2) + m\omega^2\mu q_1 q_2$$

The equation of motion is

(a) $\ddot{q}_1 + \omega^2 q_1 = \omega^2 \mu q_1; \quad \ddot{q}_2 + \omega^2 q_2 = \omega^2 \mu q_2$

(b) $\ddot{q}_1 + \omega^2 q_1 = \omega^2 \mu q_2; \quad \ddot{q}_2 + \omega^2 q_2 = \omega^2 \mu q_1$

(c) $\ddot{q}_1 + \omega^2 q_1 = \omega^2 \mu q_1; \quad \ddot{q}_2 + \omega^2 q_2 = -\omega^2 \mu q_2$

(d) $\ddot{q}_1 + \omega^2 q_1 = \omega^2 \mu q_1; \quad \ddot{q}_2 + \omega^2 q_2 = \omega^2 \mu q_1$

12. The Lagrangian is a function of

(a) q_k, p_k

(b) $\dot{q}_k, q_k$

(c) $q_k, \dot{p}_k$

(d) $p_k, \dot{p}_k$

PROBLEMS

1. A ring of mass M and radius R is supported from a pivot at one point of the ring about which it is free to rotate in its own vertical plane. A bead of mass m slides without friction about the ring. Obtain the Lagrangian and equation of motion.

2. Three massless springs of natural length d and spring constant k are attached to a point particle of mass m and to fixed points $(-1,1)$, $(1,1)$ and $(-1,-1)$. The mass point is allowed to move in the xy plane. Obtain the Lagrangian.

3. A planar pendulum is suspended such that its point of suspension glides without friction along a horizontal axis. Obtain Lagrangian.

4. Particles A and B, each of mass m, are connected by a rigid massless rod of length d. Particle A can move on the horizontal axis, while particle B can move on the vertical y axis. Ignore the friction and obtain the Lagrangian.

5. Two pendulum of equal length l and equal mass m are coupled by a massless spring of constant k. The unstretched length of the spring is equal to the distance between the supports. Find the Lagrangian.

6. A particle of mass m slides on the inside of a smooth paraboloid of revolution $r^2 = a\,z$. Set up the Lagrangian.

7. A sphere of mass M and radius r rolls without slipping down a triangular block of mass m that is free to move on a frictionless horizontal surface. Obtain the Lagrangian and equations of motion.

8. Three particles of equal mass m moves in one dimension. Two of the particles are each connected to the third by a massless spring of spring constant k. Obtain Lagrangian and equation of motion. Ignore friction.

9. A thin uniform rod of mass m and length $(3l/2)$ is suspended by a massless string of length l. The motion of the rod takes place in a plane. Obtain the Lagrangian and equation of motion.

10. In a spherical pendulum a particle of mass m moves on the surface of a sphere of radius R in a gravitational field. Show that the equation of motion of the particle may be written as

$$\ddot{\theta} - \frac{g}{R} \sin\theta + \frac{\cos\theta \, p_{\varphi}^2}{m^2 R^4 \sin^3\theta} = 0$$

❑❑❑

CHAPTER 3

Hamilton's Equations

3.1 LEGENDRE TRANSFORMATION

The generalized momenta is defined as

$$p_k = \frac{\partial L}{\partial \dot{q}_k} \quad (k = 1, 2, ..., n) \qquad ...(3.1)$$

The Eq.(3.1) defined p's as a function of generalized coordinates q_k, generalized velocities $\dot{q}_k$ and time t. Differentiating Eq. (3.1)

$$\dot{p}_k = \frac{dp_k}{dt} = \frac{d}{dt}\left(\frac{\partial L}{\partial \dot{q}_k}\right) = \frac{\partial L}{\partial q_k} \quad (k = 1, 2, ..., n) \qquad ...(3.2)$$

The Eq. (3.2) specifies the acceleration of the system.

In the Lagrange's form of the equation we take the partial derivative of Lagrangian function L with respect to a certain generalized coordinate q_k, keeping remaining q's and all generalized velocities fixed. Conversely, to differentiate with respect to a particular generalized velocity $\dot{q}_k$, we keep the remaining generalized velocities and all generalized coordinates fixed. We can change from the scheme in which q and $\dot{q}$ are variables to one in which q_k and p_k are fundamental variables, by making use of Eq. (3.1). Legendre transformation can be used to go from the formulation in which q_k and $\dot{q}_k$ are variables to a formulation in which q_k and p_k are variables.

Consider a function F of two kinds of variables x_k and y_k

$$F = F(x_1, x_2, \ldots\ldots, x_n, y_1, y_2, \ldots\ldots, y_n, t) \qquad \ldots(3.3)$$

where t is a parameter, F is differentiable

$$dF = \sum_{k=1}^{n} \frac{\partial F}{\partial x_k} dx_k + \sum_{k=1}^{n} \frac{\partial F}{\partial y_k} dy_k + \frac{\partial F}{\partial t} dt = \sum_k (u_k dx_k + \mathrm{v}_k dy_k) + \frac{\partial F}{\partial t} dt \qquad \ldots(3.4)$$

where

$$u_k = \frac{\partial F}{\partial x_k}, \quad \mathrm{v}_k = \frac{\partial F}{\partial y_k} \qquad \ldots(3.5)$$

The Legendre transformation F is defined as

$$G(u_1, u_2, \ldots\ldots\ldots, u_n; y_1, y_2, \ldots\ldots, y_n) = \sum_k u_k x_k - F \qquad \ldots(3.6)$$

$$dG = \sum_k u_k dx_k + \sum_k x_k du_k - dF$$

Using Eq. (3.4) in the above equation

$$dG = \sum_k (u_k dx_k + x_k du_k) - \sum_k (u_k dx_k + \mathrm{v}_k dy_k) + \frac{\partial F}{\partial t} dt$$

$$dG = \sum (x_k du_k - \mathrm{v}_k dy_k) - \frac{\partial F}{\partial t} dt \qquad \ldots(3.7)$$

Now

$$x_k = \frac{dG}{du_k}, \mathrm{v}_k = -\frac{dG}{dy_k}, \frac{\partial G}{\partial t} = -\frac{\partial F}{\partial t} \qquad \ldots(3.8)$$

The quantities x_k and v_k are now functions of variables u_k and y_k.

3.2 HAMILTON'S EQUATION OF MOTION

If we identify the variables $(x_1, \ldots, x_n)$ with $(\dot{q}_1, \ldots., \dot{q}_n)$ and $(u_1, \ldots., u_n)$ with $(q_1, \ldots, q_n)$, the generalized momenta is

$$p_k = \frac{\partial L(q, \dot{q}, t)}{\partial \dot{q}_k} \quad (k = 1, 2, \ldots\ldots., n)$$

The Legendre transform denoted by H is (identifying G by H and F by L)

$$H(q, p, t) = \sum_k p_k \dot{q}_k - L(q, \dot{q}, t) \qquad \ldots(3.9)$$

Differential of H is

$$dH = \sum_k (dp_k \dot{q}_k + p_k d\dot{q}_k) - \sum_k \left(\frac{\partial L}{\partial q_k} dq_k + \frac{\partial L}{\partial \dot{q}_k} d\dot{q}_k \right) - \frac{\partial L}{\partial t} dt \quad ...(3.10)$$

$$dH = \sum_k (dp_k \dot{q}_k + p_k d\dot{q}_k) - \sum_k \left(\frac{\partial L}{\partial q_k} dq_k + p_k d\dot{q}_k \right) - \frac{\partial L}{\partial t} dt \quad ...(3.11)$$

$$dH = \sum_k \left(\frac{\partial H}{\partial q_k} dq_k + \frac{\partial H}{\partial p_k} dp_k \right) + \frac{\partial H}{\partial t} dt = \sum_k dp_k \dot{q}_k - \sum_k \left(\frac{\partial L}{\partial q_k} dq_k \right) - \frac{\partial L}{\partial t} dt \quad ...(3.12)$$

From Eq. (3.12)

$$\dot{q}_k = \frac{\partial H}{\partial p_k} \quad (k = 1,2,...,n) \quad ...(3.13)$$

$$\dot{p}_k = -\frac{\partial H}{\partial q_k} \quad (k = 1,2,...,n) \quad ...(3.14)$$

$$\frac{\partial H}{\partial t} = -\frac{\partial L}{\partial t} \quad ...(3.15)$$

The Eqs.(3.13) and (3.14) are called the Hamilton's equations of motion and are also known as canonical equations of Hamilton. They contain only the Hamiltonian function $H(q,p,t)$ and the variables q, p and t. The Eqs. (3.13) and (3.14) form a system of $2n$ ordinary differential equations of first order replacing the n differential equations of second order obtained in the Lagrangian formalism. The Hamilton's formalism find application in many branches of physics. It is used in old quantum mechanics, matrix mechanics, development of perturbation theory for those system where exact solution is not obtainable. Hamiltonian approach is also used in statistical mechanics; $2n$ dimension p, q space is called phase space. The phase space of the system is a real space whose points are labeled by the generalized coordinates q's and generalized momenta p's. The range of each q and each p is again determined by the physical meaning of the relevant variable. Any given configuration of the system at time t together with any given momenta at that time t collectively determine the phase of the system at that instant and correspond to a point in phase space. When the system is in motion, the representative point in phase space performs a curve called phase trajectory. On the other hand, Lagrangian formalism is useful in development of field theory.

3.3 PHYSICAL INTERPRETATION OF HAMILTONIAN

The Hamiltonian function H is a function of q's, p's and t, that is,

$$H = H(q,p,t) \quad ...(3.16)$$

From Eq.(3.9)

$$H(q,p,t) = \sum_k p_k \dot{q}_k - L(q,\dot{q},t)$$

The Lagrangian $L = T - V$. Using Eq.(3.1)

$$\sum_k \dot{q}_k p_k = \sum_k \frac{\partial L}{\partial \dot{q}_k} \dot{q}_k \qquad ...(3.17)$$

If V is independent of velocity dependent forces, that is, $V = V(q)$ and therefore

$$\frac{\partial V}{\partial \dot{q}_k} = 0$$

Eq.(3.17) is written as

$$\sum_k \dot{q}_k p_k = \sum_k \frac{\partial (T-V)}{\partial \dot{q}_k} \dot{q}_k = \sum_k \frac{\partial T}{\partial \dot{q}_k} \dot{q}_k \qquad ...(3.18)$$

The kinetic energy is quadratic function of generalized velocity given by Eq.(2.72)

$$T = a + \sum_k b_k \dot{q}_k + \sum_k \sum_l c_{kl} \dot{q}_k \dot{q}_l$$

For a particular case of a scleronomic system first two terms of the above expression are zero and

$$T = \sum_k \sum_l c_{kl} \dot{q}_k \dot{q}_l \qquad ...(3.19)$$

Differentiating with respect to $\dot{q}_i$

$$\frac{\partial T}{\partial \dot{q}_i} = \sum_k c_{ki} \dot{q}_k + \sum_l c_{il} \dot{q}_l \qquad ...(3.20)$$

Multiplying this equation by $\dot{q}_i$ and summing over i

$$\sum_i \dot{q}_i \frac{\partial T}{\partial \dot{q}_i} = \sum_{i,k} c_{ki} \dot{q}_i \dot{q}_k + \sum_{i,l} c_{i,l} \dot{q}_i \dot{q}_l \qquad ...(3.21)$$

Now all the indices are dummies, so that both terms on the right hand sides of Eq.(3.21) are identical.

The Eq.(3.21) is

$$\sum \dot{q}_i \frac{\partial T}{\partial \dot{q}_i} = 2 \sum_{k,l} c_{kl} \dot{q}_k \dot{q}_l \qquad ... (3.22)$$

Using Euler's theorem which states that if f is homogeneous function of degree n in the variable x_i, then

$$\sum_i x_i \frac{\partial f}{\partial x_i} = n f \qquad ...(3.23)$$

Since T is a homogeneous function of degree 2 in $\dot{q}_k$'s, the equation (3.22) with the help of (3.23) gives

$$\sum_i \dot{q}_i \frac{\partial T}{\partial \dot{q}_i} = 2T \qquad ...(3.24)$$

Using Eqs. (3.18) and (3.24) we have Hamiltonian function H

$$H = 2T - L = 2T - (T - V) = T + V \qquad ...(3.25)$$

Thus H is total mechanical energy. Total time derivative of H (q, p, t) is

$$\frac{dH}{dt} = \sum_k \frac{\partial H}{\partial q_k} \dot{q}_k + \sum_k \frac{\partial H}{\partial p_k} \dot{p}_k + \frac{\partial H}{\partial t} \qquad ...(3.26)$$

Using Eqs. (3.15) and (3.26)

$$\frac{dH}{dt} = \frac{\partial H}{\partial t} = -\frac{\partial L}{\partial t} \qquad ...(3.27)$$

Thus, if t does not appear explicitly in L then

$$\frac{dH}{dt} = 0$$

$$H = \text{constant}$$

3.4 IGNORABLE COORDINATES

Consider the Lagrange's equation (2.24)

$$\frac{d}{dt}\left(\frac{\partial L}{\partial \dot{q}_k}\right) = \frac{\partial L}{\partial q_k} \quad (k=1, 2, ..., n) \qquad ...(3.28)$$

Consider the Lagrangian function in which some coordinate q_k does not occur explicitly. The corresponding Lagrange's equation (3.28) is

$$\frac{d}{dt}\left(\frac{\partial L}{\partial \dot{q}_k}\right) = 0 \quad (k=1, 2, ..., n) \qquad ...(3.29)$$

as

$$\frac{\partial L}{\partial q_k} = 0$$

on integrating Eq. (3.29)

$$\frac{\partial L}{\partial \dot{q}_k} = p_k = \alpha_k = a \text{ constant} \qquad ...(3.30)$$

where α_k is a constant of integration. Thus whenever a coordinate q_k does not occur explicitly in the Lagrangian function, the corresponding momentum p_k is a constant of motion. Such coordinates q_k which are absent from Lagrangian are said to be ignorable or cyclic. The term cyclic refer to the fact that such coordinates are very often angles. Consider Eq.(3.14)

$$\dot{p}_k = -\frac{\partial H}{\partial q_k} = \frac{\partial L}{\partial q_k} \qquad ...(3.31)$$

Hence if a certain coordinate is missing from the Lagrangian function *L*, it will also be missing from the Hamiltonian function *H*. The Hamiltonian function can now be written in the form

$$H(q_1,\ldots\ldots,q_{k-1},q_{k+1},\ldots,q_n,p_1,\ldots,p_{k-1},p_{k+1},\ldots\ldots,p_n,\alpha_k,t) \qquad ...(3.32)$$

The Hamiltonian now describes a problem involving only $n-1$ coordinates and there are $2(n-1)$ first order differential equations. On the other hand, there are still *n* second order Lagrange's equations for the system. The motion of the ignorable coordinate is by using Eq. (3.13) is

$$\dot{q}_k = \frac{\partial H}{\partial \alpha_k} \qquad ...(3.33)$$

If q_k is ignorable the Lagrangian function is

$$L(q_1,\ldots\ldots,q_{k-1},q_{k+1},\ldots,q_n,\dot{q}_1,\ldots,\ldots\ldots,\dot{q}_n,t) \qquad ...(3.34)$$

In the Lagrangian function q_k is missing although the corresponding velocity $\dot{q}_k$ is contained. Since q_k is ignorable, the Eq.(3.30) can be solved for $\dot{q}_k$ in terms of the other coordinates, velocities and of constant momentum given by Eq.(3.30), that is,

$$\dot{q}_k = \dot{q}_k(q_1,\ldots\ldots,q_{k-1},q_{k+1},\ldots,q_n,\dot{q}_1,\ldots,q_{k-1},q_{k+1},\ldots,\dot{q}_n,\alpha_k,t) \qquad ...(3.35)$$

The Eq.(3.35) expresses the velocity $\dot{q}_k$ corresponding to ignorable coordinate q_k in terms of

$$q_1,\ldots\ldots,q_{k-1},q_{k+1},\ldots,q_n,\dot{q}_1,\ldots,q_{k-1},q_{k+1},\ldots,\dot{q}_n,\alpha_k.$$

If a system contains a large number of ignorable coordinates and hence of constant of momentum, it is sometimes convenient to modify Lagrange's equations using the method developed by Routh. In this method a transformation is carried for $q, \dot{q}$ basis to *q* and *p* basis only for ignorable coordinates obtaining their equations of motion in the Hamiltonian form. The remaining coordinates which are not ignorable is described by the modified Lagrange's equation. The modified Lagrangian function is known as Routhian and is denoted by the symbol *R*. If first *k* *q*'s are ignorable, the Routhian *R* will be a function of

$$q_{k+1},\ldots,q_n,\dot{q}_{k+1},\ldots,\dot{q}_n,\alpha_1,\ldots\ldots,\alpha_k,t$$

and is

$$R = L - \sum_{i=1}^{k} \alpha_i \dot{q}_i \qquad ...(3.36)$$

where the ignorable $\dot{q}^s$ have been eliminated by solving the *k* equations of the form (3.30) for $(\dot{q}_1,\ldots,\dot{q}_k)$ in terms of $(q_{k+1},\ldots\ldots,q_n,\alpha_1,\ldots\ldots,\alpha_k,t)$. To find the equation of motion in terms of R we make an arbitrary variation to the right hand side of the Eq. (3.36)

$$\delta\,(L-\sum_{i=1}^{k}\alpha_i\,\dot{q}_i)=\delta L-\sum_{i=1}^{k}\alpha_i\,\delta\dot{q}_i-\sum_{i=1}^{k}\dot{q}_i\,\delta\alpha_i \qquad ...(3.37)$$

$$\delta L=\sum_{i=k+1}^{n}\frac{\partial L}{\partial q_i}\delta q_i+\sum_{i=k+1}^{n}\frac{\partial L}{\partial \dot{q}_i}\delta\dot{q}_i+\sum_{i=1}^{k}\frac{\partial L}{\partial \dot{q}_i}\delta\dot{q}_i+\frac{\partial L}{\partial t}$$

$$\delta L=\sum_{i=k+1}^{n}\frac{\partial L}{\partial q_i}\delta q_i+\sum_{i=k+1}^{n}\frac{\partial L}{\partial \dot{q}_i}\delta\dot{q}_i+\sum_{i=1}^{k}\alpha_i\,\delta\dot{q}_i+\frac{\partial L}{\partial t} \qquad ...(3.38)$$

Substituting Eq.(3.38) in Eq. (3.37)

$$\delta\,(L-\sum_{i=1}^{k}\alpha_i\,\dot{q}_i)=\sum_{i=k+1}^{n}\frac{\partial L}{\partial q_i}\delta q_i+\sum_{i=k+1}^{n}\frac{\partial L}{\partial \dot{q}_i}\delta\dot{q}_i++\frac{\partial L}{\partial t}--\sum_{i=1}^{k}\dot{q}_i\,\delta\alpha_i \qquad ...(3.39)$$

Making arbitrary variation to the left hand side of Eq. (3.36)

$$\delta R=\sum_{i=k+1}^{n}\frac{\partial R}{\partial q_i}\delta q_i+\sum_{i=k+1}^{n}\frac{\partial R}{\partial \dot{q}_i}\delta\dot{q}_i+\sum_{i=1}^{k}\frac{\partial R}{\partial \alpha_i}\delta\alpha_i+\frac{\partial R}{\partial t}\delta t \qquad ...(3.40)$$

From Eqs.(3.36), (3.39) and Eq.(3.40)

$$\sum_{i=k+1}^{n}\left(\frac{\partial L}{\partial q_i}-\frac{\partial L}{\partial q_i}\right)\delta q_i+\sum_{i=k+1}^{n}\left(\frac{\partial R}{\partial \dot{q}_i}-\frac{\partial L}{\partial \dot{q}_i}\right)\delta\dot{q}_i+\sum_{i=1}^{k}\left(\frac{\partial R}{\partial \alpha_i}-\dot{q}_i\right)\delta\alpha_i+\left(\frac{\partial R}{\partial t}-\frac{\partial L}{\partial t}\right)\delta t=0 \qquad ...(3.41)$$

Assuming that variation in quantities are independent and therefore the corresponding coefficients must vanish in Eq. (3.41) we have

$$\frac{\partial R}{\partial q_i}=\frac{\partial L}{\partial q_i}\quad (i=k+1,.........,n) \qquad ...(3.42)$$

$$\frac{\partial R}{\partial \dot{q}_i}=\frac{\partial L}{\partial \dot{q}_i}\quad (i=k+1,.........,n) \qquad ...(3.43)$$

$$\frac{\partial R}{\partial \alpha_i}=-\dot{q}_i\quad (i=1,.........,k) \qquad ...(3.44)$$

$$\frac{\partial R}{\partial t}=\frac{\partial L}{\partial t}\quad (i=k+1,.........,n) \qquad ...(3.45)$$

Substituting Eqs. (3.42) and (3.43) in (3.28) we have

$$\frac{d}{dt}\left(\frac{\partial R}{\partial \dot{q}_k}\right)=\frac{\partial R}{\partial q_k} \qquad (i=k+1,........,n) \qquad ...(3.46)$$

The Eqs. (3.42) & (3.43) are of the form of Lagrange's equations with the Routhian function R replacing the Lagrangian function L. There are $(n-k)$ second-order differential equations in the coordinates which are not ignorable, that is, $(q_{k+1}....q_n)$ and new Lagrangian is R. The dynamical system which is obtained after the ignoration of coordinates, the function R cannot be divided into two parts, that is, kinetic energy and potential energy.

By solving Eq. (3.45) one can obtain the value of non-ignorable coordinates $(q_{k+1.....}q_n)$ in terms of time t. The remainder of the original coordinates $(q_1 \cdots q_k)$ can be obtained from the Eq.(3.44). Thus a dynamical problem with n degrees of freedom which has k ignorable coordinates can be reduced to a dynamical problem which has $(n-k)$ degrees of freedom.

Solved Examples

Example 1. *The Lagrangian for a simple harmonic oscillator is* $L=\frac{1}{2}m\dot{q}^2-\frac{1}{2}kq^2$. *Obtain the Hamiltonian and Hamilton equation of motion.*

Solution: We have

$$p=\frac{\partial L}{\partial \dot{q}}=m\dot{q}$$

We have

$$H=p\dot{q}-L=\frac{p^2}{m}-\frac{p^2}{2m}+\frac{1}{2}kq^2=\frac{p^2}{2m}+\frac{1}{2}kq^2$$

Hamilton's equation of motion

$$\dot{q}=\frac{\partial H}{\partial P}=\frac{p}{m},\ \dot{p}=-\frac{\partial H}{\partial q}=-kq$$

$$\ddot{q}=\frac{\dot{p}}{m}=-\frac{kq}{m}$$

$$\ddot{q}+\frac{kq}{m}=\ddot{q}+\omega^2 q=0$$

where $\omega^2 = k/m$.

Example 2. *Lagrangian is given by* $L=T-e\phi+\frac{e}{c}\mathrm{A.v}$ *if* **A** *and* φ *are independent of time t. Obtain the Hamiltonian.*

Solution:

$$L = T - e\phi + \frac{e}{c}\mathbf{A}\cdot\mathbf{v} = \frac{1}{2}m\mathrm{v}^2 - e\phi + \frac{e}{c}\mathbf{A}\cdot\mathbf{v}$$

$$p = \frac{\partial L}{\partial \mathrm{v}} = m\mathrm{v} + \frac{\mathrm{e}}{\mathrm{c}}A$$

$$\mathrm{v} = \frac{1}{m}\left(p - \frac{\mathrm{e}}{\mathrm{c}}A\right)$$

$$H = \sum p\dot{q} - L = \frac{1}{m}\left(p - \frac{e}{c}A\right)p - \frac{1}{2}m\left(p - \frac{e}{c}A\right)^2 + e\phi - \frac{e}{mc}A\left(p - \frac{e}{c}A\right)$$

$$H = \frac{p^2}{m} - \frac{eAp}{mc} - \frac{1}{2m}\left(p^2 + \frac{\mathrm{e}^2}{\mathrm{c}^2}A^2 - \frac{2eAp}{c}\right) + \frac{e^2}{mc^2}A^2 - \frac{eAp}{mc} + e\phi$$

$$H = \frac{p^2}{2m} + \frac{1}{2m}\frac{e^2}{c^2}A^2 - \frac{eAp}{mc} + e\phi = \frac{1}{2m}\left(p - \frac{\mathrm{e}}{\mathrm{c}}A\right)^2 + e\phi$$

Example 3. *For the Lagrangian* $L = \frac{1}{2}m(\dot{x}^2 + \dot{y}^2 + \dot{z}^2) + \frac{\omega}{2}L_z$, *where* L_z *is the z component of angular momentum. Obtain the Hamiltonian.*

Solution: The z component of angular momentum is

$$L_z = m(x\dot{y} - y\dot{x})$$

The Lagrangian is therefore,

$$L = \frac{1}{2}m(\dot{x}^2 + \dot{y}^2 + \dot{z}^2) + \frac{\omega}{2}m(x\dot{y} - y\dot{x})$$

we have

$$p_x = \frac{\partial L}{\partial \dot{x}} = m\dot{x} - \frac{m\omega y}{2}$$

$$\dot{x} = \frac{p_x}{m} + \frac{\omega y}{2} \qquad ...(3.47)$$

$$p_y = \frac{\partial L}{\partial \dot{y}} = m\dot{y} + \frac{m\omega x}{2}$$

$$\dot{y} = \frac{p_y}{m} - \frac{\omega x}{2} \qquad ...(3.48)$$

$$p_z = \frac{\partial L}{\partial \dot{z}} = m\dot{z} \qquad ...(3.49)$$

The Hamiltonian is

$$H = \sum_k p_k \dot{q}_k - L = (p_x \dot{x} + p_y \dot{y} + P_z \dot{z}) - \frac{1}{2} m(\dot{x}^2 + \dot{y}^2 + \dot{z}^2) + \frac{\omega}{2} m(x\dot{y} - y\dot{x}) \qquad ...(3.50)$$

Substituting the values of $\dot{x}, \dot{y}, \dot{z}$ from Eqs. (3.47)-(3.49) in Eq. (3.50)

$$H = \frac{p_x^2}{2m} + \frac{p_y^2}{2m} + \frac{p_z^2}{2m} - \frac{m\omega^2 y^2}{8} - \frac{m\omega^2 x^2}{8} - \frac{x\omega p_y}{2} + \frac{m\omega^2 x^2}{4} + \frac{y\omega p_x}{2}$$

$$H = \frac{1}{2m}\left[p_x^2 + p_y^2 + p_z^2 + \frac{m^2\omega^2 y^2}{4} + \frac{m^2\omega^2 x^2}{4} - m\omega x p_y + m\omega y p_x\right]$$

$$H = \frac{1}{2m}\left[\left(p_x + \frac{m\omega y}{2}\right)^2 + \left(p_y - \frac{m\omega x}{2}\right)^2 + p_z^2\right]$$

Example 4. *Obtain the Hamiltonian, if Lagrangian is*

$$L = \sum_{i,k=1}^{2} c_{ik}\dot{q}_i\dot{q}_k + \sum_{k=1}^{2} b_k \dot{q}_k + a$$

Solution: The Lagrangian is

$$L = c_{11}\dot{q}_1^2 + c_{22}\dot{q}_2^2 + (c_{12} + c_{21})\dot{q}_1 \dot{q}_2 + b_1 \dot{q}_1 + b_2 \dot{q}_2 + a$$

and

$$p_1 = \frac{\partial L}{\partial \dot{q}_1} = 2c_{11}\dot{q}_1 + (c_{12} + c_{21})\dot{q}_2 + b_1$$

$$p_2 = \frac{\partial L}{\partial \dot{q}_2} = 2c_{22}\dot{q}_2 + (c_{12} + c_{21})\dot{q}_1 + b_2$$

Let

$$2c_{11} = \alpha_{11}, \quad 2c_{22} = \alpha_{22}, \quad c_{12} + c_{21} = \alpha_{12} = \alpha_{21}$$

and

$$p_1 - b_1 = \beta_1, \quad p_2 - b_2 = \beta_2$$

$$\beta_1 = \alpha_{11}\dot{q}_1 + \alpha_{12}\dot{q}_2$$

$$\beta_2 = \alpha_{22}\dot{q}_2 + \alpha_{12}\dot{q}_1$$

Multiplying β_1 by α_{22} and β_2 by α_{12} and subtracting

$$\alpha_{22}\beta_1 - \alpha_{12}\beta_2 = (\alpha_{11}\alpha_{22} - \alpha_{12}\alpha_{21})\dot{q}_1$$

$$\dot{q}_1 = \frac{\alpha_{22}\,\beta_1 - \alpha_{12}\,\beta_2}{\alpha_{11}\,\alpha_{22} - \alpha_{12}\,\alpha_{21}} = \frac{\alpha_{22}\,\beta_1 - \alpha_{12}\,\beta_2}{D}$$

Similarly

$$\dot{q}_2 = -\frac{\alpha_{21}\,\beta_1 + \alpha_{11}\,\beta_2}{D}$$

where

$$D = \alpha_{11}\,\alpha_{22} - \alpha_{12}\,\alpha_{21}$$

The Hamiltonian is

$$H = p_1\,\dot{q}_1 + p_2\,\dot{q}_2 - L$$

On substituting the values of $\dot{q}_1$ and $\dot{q}_2$ in the expression for H we have

$$H = \frac{1}{D}[\,c22\beta_1^2 - (c_{12} + c_{21})\beta_1\beta_2 + c_{11}\,\beta_2^2\,] - a + V$$

Example 5. *Consider a dynamical system whose Lagrangian is*

$$L = \frac{1}{2}\frac{\dot{q}_1^2}{a + b\,q_2^2} + \frac{1}{2}\dot{q}_2^2 - c - d\,q_2^2$$ *, where a,b,c, d are given constants.*

Using the Routhian, obtain equation of motion.

Solution: In the Lagrangian q_1 is ignorable coordinate as it does not occur in L. We have

$$\frac{\partial L}{\partial \dot{q}_1} = \frac{\dot{q}_1}{a + b\,q_2^2} = \alpha$$

where α is a constant, whose value is determined by the initial condition of the motion. The Routhian of the system is

$$R = L - \dot{q}_1\,\frac{\partial L}{\partial \dot{q}_1}$$

$$R = \frac{1}{2}\frac{\dot{q}_1^2}{a + b\,q_2^2} + \frac{1}{2}\dot{q}_2^2 - c - d\,q_2^2 - \alpha^2(a + b\,q_2^2)$$

$$R = \frac{1}{2}\frac{\alpha^2(a + b\,q_2^2)^2}{a + b\,q_2^2} + \frac{1}{2}\dot{q}_2^2 - c - d\,q_2^2 - \alpha^2(a + b\,q_2^2)$$

$$R = \frac{1}{2}\dot{q}_2^2 - c - d\,q_2^2 - \frac{1}{2}\alpha^2(a + b\,q_2^2)$$

The equation of motion is

$$\frac{d}{dt}\left(\frac{\partial R}{\partial \dot{q}_2}\right) - \frac{\partial R}{\partial q_2} = 0 \qquad ...(3.51)$$

$$\frac{\partial R}{\partial \dot{q}_2} = \dot{q}_2, \quad \frac{\partial R}{\partial q_2} = -2dq_2 - \alpha^2 bq_2 \qquad ...(3.52)$$

Substituting Eq. (3.52) in (3.51)

$$\frac{d}{dt}(\dot{q}_2) + (2d + \alpha^2 b)q_2 = 0$$

$$\ddot{q}_2 + \omega^2 q_2 = 0 \qquad ...(3.53)$$

where $\omega^2 = 2d + \alpha^2 b$

The solution of the Eq. (3.53) is of the form

$$q_2 = A\, sin\{ (2d + \alpha^2 b)^{\frac{1}{2}} t + \beta \}$$

where A and β are constants of integration to be determined by the initial condition of the motion. The equation gives q_2 in term of t.

The value of q_1 in terms of t is by Eq. (3.44)

$$\dot{q}_1 = -\int \frac{\partial R}{\partial \alpha}$$

$$q_1 = -\int \frac{\partial R}{\partial \alpha} dt = \int \alpha (a + bq_2^2) dt$$

$$q_1 = (\alpha a + \frac{1}{2}\alpha b A^2)t - \frac{\alpha b A^2}{\sqrt{4(2d + b\alpha^2)}} \sin 2\{\sqrt{(2d + b\alpha^2)}\, t + \beta\}$$

OBJECTIVE TYPE QUESTIONS

1. If Hamiltonian does not involve a particular coordinate q_k, such coordinate is called

   (*a*) cyclic or ignorable
   (*b*) fictious coordinate
   (*c*) both (a) and (b)
   (*d*) none of these

2. For the Hamiltonian, $H = \frac{p^2}{2m} + \frac{1}{2}kq^2$ the Lagrangian is

   (*a*) $L = \frac{1}{2}m\dot{q}^2 + \frac{1}{2}kq^2$
   (*b*) $L = \frac{1}{2}m\dot{q}^2 - \frac{p^2}{2m} - \frac{1}{2}kq^2$
   (c) $L = \frac{p^2}{2m} - \frac{1}{2}kq^2$
   (*d*) $L = \frac{1}{2}m\dot{q}^2 - \frac{1}{2}kq^2$

3. For a charged particle in electromagnetic field, the Hamiltonian is

(a) $\frac{m}{2}\left(\frac{p}{m}-\frac{e}{mc}A\right)^2+e\phi$ (b) $\frac{1}{2m}\left(p+\frac{e}{c}A\right)^2+e\phi$

(c) $\frac{m}{2}\left(p-\frac{e}{c}A\right)^2-e\phi$ (d) $\frac{1}{2m}\left(p-\frac{e}{c}A\right)^2-e\phi$

4. The product $p_k q_k$ has the dimension of

(a) energy (b) linear momentum
(c) action (d) none of these

5. Hamilton's canonical equations of motion are

(a) $\dot{q}_k=\frac{\partial H}{\partial p_k}, \dot{p}_k=-\frac{\partial H}{\partial q_k}$ (b) $\dot{q}_k=\frac{\partial H}{\partial \dot{p}_k}, \dot{p}_k=-\frac{\partial H}{\partial q_k}$

(c) $\dot{q}_k=-\frac{\partial H}{\partial p_k}, \dot{p}_k=+\frac{\partial H}{\partial q_k}$ (d) $\dot{q}_k=-\frac{\partial H}{\partial p_k}, \dot{p}_k=-\frac{\partial H}{\partial q_k}$

6. The number of differential equations of motion in

(a) Hamiltonian form is $2n$ of first order, in Lagrangian form is n of second order

(b) Hamiltonian form is n of second order, in Lagrangian form is $2n$ of first order

(c) Hamiltonian form is n of first order, in Lagrangian form is n of second order

(d) Hamiltonian form is $2n$ of first order, in Lagrangian form is $2n$ of second order

7. If a coordinate is cyclic, Hamiltonian would reduce the number of variables in new formulation by

(a) four (b) three
(c) two (d) one

8. For a charged particle in an electromagnetic field the canonical momenta are

(a) $\frac{m}{2}\text{v}^2-\frac{e}{c}A$ (c) $\frac{m}{2}\text{v}^2+\frac{e}{c}A$

(b) $m\text{v}-\frac{e}{c}A$ (d) $m\text{v}+\frac{e}{c}A$

9. The Hamiltonian corresponding to the Lagrangian $L = a\dot{x}^2 + b\dot{y}^2 - k\,x\,y$ is

(a) $\dfrac{p_x^2}{2a} + \dfrac{p_y^2}{2b} + k\,x\,y$ (b) $\dfrac{p_x^2}{2a} + \dfrac{p_y^2}{2b} - k\,x\,y$

(c) $\dfrac{p_x^2}{4a} + \dfrac{p_y^2}{4b} + k\,x\,y$ (d) $\dfrac{p_x^2 + p_y^2}{4ab} + k\,x\,y$

PROBLEMS

1. A particle of mass m is moving on the plane xy which is rotating about the z axis with angular velocity ω. The Hamiltonian is given by

$$H = \frac{p_x^2 + p_y^2}{2m} + p_x \omega\, y - p_y \omega\, x + V$$

Obtain the Lagrangian.

2. The Hamiltonian of a simple harmonic oscillator is given by

$$H = \frac{p^2}{2m} + \frac{1}{2} k\, q^2$$

Obtain the Lagrangian.

3. Consider a particle moving in central field of force and the Lagrangian is

$$L = \frac{m}{2}(\dot{r}^2 + r^2\dot{\theta}^2 + r^2 \sin^2\theta\, \dot{\varphi}^2) - V(r)$$

Obtain the Hamiltonian.

4. Lagrangian is given by

$$L = \frac{m}{2} R^2(\dot{\theta}^2 + \dot{\varphi}^2 \sin^2\theta)$$

Obtain the Hamiltonian. Is Hamiltonian conserved?

5. Obtain the Hamiltonian from the Lagrangian

$$L = \frac{m}{2}(1 + 4A^2 r^2)\dot{r}^2 + \frac{1}{2} m r^2 \dot{\varphi}^2 - A\,m\,g\,r^3$$

where A is a positive constant.

6. A particle of mass m is moving on a plane xy which is rotating about the z axis with angular velocity ω. Obtain the Hamiltonian if the Lagrangian is

$$L = \frac{m}{2}[(\dot{x} - \omega y)^2 + (\dot{y} + \omega x)^2] - V(x, y)$$

7. Reverse the Legendre transformation to derive the $L(q.\dot{q},t)$ from $H(q, p, t)$ treating the $\dot{q}$ as independent quanties and show that it leads to Lagrange equation of motion.

8. A particle of mass m moves in a force field having potential $V(\rho, \varphi, z)$ where ρ, φ, z are cylindrical coordinates. Obtain Hamiltonian and Hamilton's equation of motion.

9. Obtain Hamilton's equation of motion for a free particle.

10. Obtain Hamilton's equation of motion for a particle in central force field.

❑❑❑

CHAPTER 4

Symmetry and Conservation Laws

4.1 SYMMETRY AND CONSERVATION LAWS

The relationship between the accelerations, velocities and coordinates is called the equation of motion. For the laws of motion to have a meaning, a reference frame must be chosen with respect to which the motion of the bodies can be measured. Inertial frame is such a frame of reference. In this, no external force is acting on an object and the object is found to be moving in straight line with constant velocity (or is at rest).

For description of motion of an object, let us consider a coordinate system in an inertial frame. The equation of motion of the object should be independent of position of the origin of the coordinate system and on its orientation in space. Therefore, the space must have the properties of homogeneity and isotropy. Further, if the object is moving with constant velocity, its velocity should remain the same irrespective of the various time intervals used to measure it. It means that time is homogeneous.

These symmetry properties of the space and time are related to conservation of linear momentum, angular momentum and total energy of a closed system. A closed system is defined as one that is not acted upon by any field of force whose source is external to the system.

4.2 CONSERVATION OF ENERGY

Consider a conservative system and we assume that constraints are independent of time. Let $q_1, q_2, \ldots.., q_n$ be the coordinates and Lagrangian L is a function of

$q_2, \ldots.., q_{n,,}$ $\dot{q}_1, \dot{q}_2, \ldots\ldots.., \dot{q}_n$ only not involving the time explicitly, that is,

$$\frac{\partial L}{\partial t} = 0 \qquad ...(4.1)$$

The total time derivative of L is therefore

$$\frac{dL}{dt} = \sum_{k=1}^{n} \frac{\partial L}{\partial q_k}\frac{\partial q_k}{\partial t} + \sum_{k=1}^{n} \frac{\partial L}{\partial \dot{q}_k}\frac{d\dot{q}_k}{dt} \qquad ...(4.2)$$

From Lagrange's equation

$$\frac{d}{dt}\left(\frac{\partial L}{\partial \dot{q}_k}\right) = \frac{\partial L}{\partial q_k} \qquad ...(4.3)$$

The Eq.(4.2) is therefore

$$\frac{dL}{dt} = \sum_k \frac{d}{dt}\left(\frac{\partial L}{\partial \dot{q}_k}\right)\dot{q}_k + \sum_k \frac{\partial L}{\partial \dot{q}_k}\ddot{q}_k = \sum_k \frac{d}{dt}\left(\dot{q}_k \frac{\partial L}{\partial \dot{q}_k}\right)$$

$$\frac{d}{dt}\left(L - \sum_k \dot{q}_k \frac{\partial L}{\partial \dot{q}_k}\right) = 0 \qquad ...(4.4)$$

indicating that the expression in parenthesis must be some constant, which we shall denote by $-H$, that is,

$$L - \sum_k \dot{q}_k \frac{\partial L}{\partial \dot{q}_k} = -H = \text{constant}$$

$$H = \sum_k \dot{q}_k \frac{\partial L}{\partial \dot{q}_k} - L \qquad ...(4.5)$$

Right hand side remains constant during the motion of the closed system. For conservative system, the potential energy V does not depend explicitly on the velocity or time t. Thus, we have

$$p_k = \frac{\partial L}{\partial \dot{q}_k} = \frac{\partial (T - V)}{\partial \dot{q}_k} = \frac{\partial T}{\partial \dot{q}_k} \qquad ...(4.6)$$

$$\sum_k \dot{q}_k \frac{\partial L}{\partial \dot{q}_k} = \sum_k \dot{q}_k \frac{\partial T}{\partial \dot{q}_k} \qquad ...(4.7)$$

The Eq. (4.5) is thus

$$H = \sum_k \dot{q}_k \frac{\partial T}{\partial \dot{q}_k} - (T - V) \qquad ...(4.8)$$

As constraints do not involve time t and kinetic energy is quadratic function of generalized velocities, then from Euler's theorem

$$\sum_k \dot{q}_k \frac{\partial T}{\partial \dot{q}_k} = 2T \qquad ...(4.9)$$

Substituting Eq. (4.9) in Eq.(4.8)

$$H = 2T - (T - V) = T + V \qquad ...(4.10)$$

which is the total energy of the system. The Hamiltonian H is equal to total energy if (a) the potential energy is velocity independent (b) kinetic energy is independent of time that is, quadratic function of the generalized velocities only. The law of conservation is valid not only for closed systems, but also for those in constant external field (the one that is independent of time).

4.3 CONSERVATION OF LINEAR MOMENTUM

If space is homogeneous, mechanical properties of a closed system are unchanged by any parallel displacement of the entire system in the space. Consider a conservative system. Let $q_1, q_2, ..., q_n$ be the generalized coordinates. Consider the generalized coordinate q_k which is changed by an amount dq_k. Since T is independent of q_k, therefore,

$$\frac{\partial T}{\partial q_k} = 0 \qquad ...(4.11)$$

The Lagrange's equation of motion is written as

$$\frac{d}{dt}\left(\frac{\partial T}{\partial \dot{q}_k}\right) = -\frac{\partial V}{\partial q_k} = \dot{p}_k = Q_k \qquad ...(4.12)$$

Q_k is the component of the total generalized force along the direction of the translation of q_k. p_k is the component of the total momentum along this direction

$$Q_k = \sum_{i=1}^{N} \mathbf{f}_i \cdot \frac{\partial \mathbf{r}_i}{\partial q_k} \qquad ...(4.13)$$

dq_k corresponds to a translation of the system along some axis. The relation between $\mathbf{r}_i(q_k)$ and $\mathbf{r}_i(q_k+dq_k)$ is shown in the Fig. 4.1. The derivative of r_i relative to q_k is defined as

$$\frac{\partial \mathbf{r}_i}{\partial q_k} = \lim_{dq_k \to 0} \frac{\mathbf{r}_i(q_k + dq_k) - \mathbf{r}_i(q_k)}{dq_k} = \frac{dq_k}{dq_k}\mathbf{n} = \mathbf{n} \qquad ...(4.14)$$

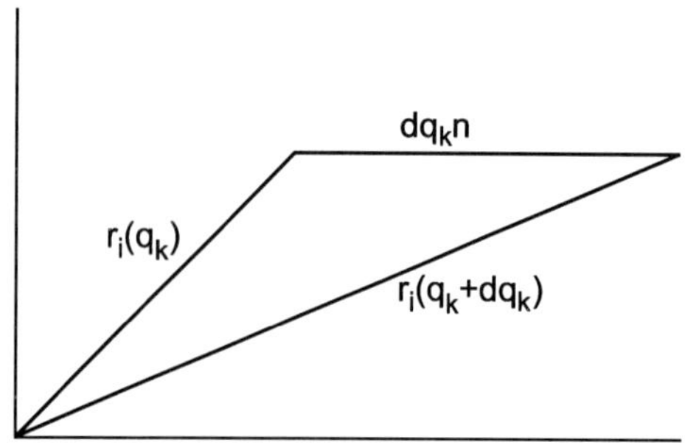

Fig. 4.1 Change in a position vector under translation of the system.

where **n** is a unit vector along the direction of translation. Thus

$$Q_k = \sum_i \mathbf{f}_i \cdot \mathbf{n} = \mathbf{n} \cdot \mathbf{F} \qquad \text{...(4.15)}$$

which is the component of the total force along the direction **n.** The kinetic energy is

$$T = \frac{1}{2}\sum_i m_i \mathbf{r}_i^2 \qquad \text{...(4.16)}$$

$$p_k = \frac{\partial T}{\partial \dot{q}_k} = \sum m_i \dot{\mathbf{r}}_i \cdot \frac{\partial \dot{\mathbf{r}}_i}{\partial \dot{q}_k} = \sum m_i \mathbf{v}_i \cdot \frac{\partial \mathbf{r}_i}{\partial q_k} \qquad \text{...(4.17)}$$

Since from Eq. (2.4)

$$\frac{\partial \mathbf{r}_i}{\partial q_k} = \frac{\partial \dot{\mathbf{r}}_i}{\partial \dot{q}_k}$$

Using Eq. (4.14) in Eq. (4.17)

$$p_k = \mathbf{n} \cdot \sum_i m_i \mathbf{v}_i \qquad \text{...(4.18)}$$

This is the component of momentum along **n**. In Cartesian coordinate system, the three components of the momentum are conserved if the external field is absent. The individual components may be conserved in the presence of the field, however, if the potential energy in the field does not depend on all the Cartesian coordinates. A particular component of the momentum of the system is unchanged by a displacement along particular axis of the coordinate system which does not appear in the potential energy V. For example, in a uniform field in the z direction the x and y components of momentum are conserved.

4.4 CONSERVATION OF ANGULAR MOMENTUM

It was stated in Sect. 4.1 that space is isotropic, that is, the mechanical properties of a closed system are unaffected by the orientation of the system. Thus, the Lagrangian of the closed system will not change if the system is rotated through an infinitesimal angle dq_k. Let the system is rotated about an axis by infinitesimal angle dq_k (Fig. 4.2). As a result of this, coordinates of the constituent of the system change by dr_i and their velocities by $d\dot{r}_i$. However, the Lagrangian will not change. From the Fig. 4.2

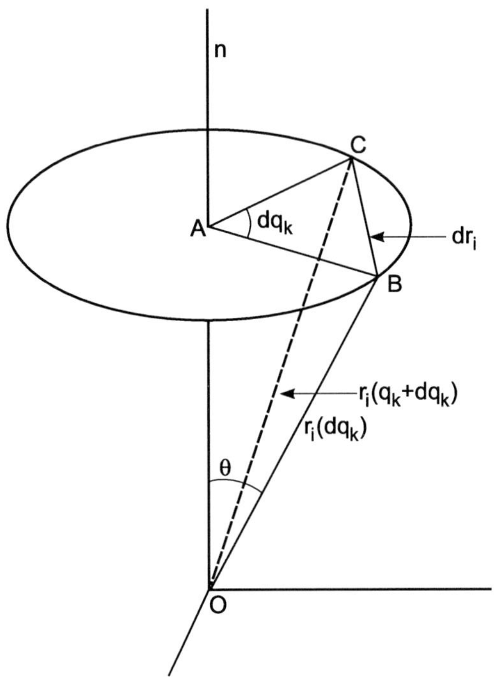

Fig. 4.2 Change of position vector under rotation of the system

$$AB = r_i \, sin\theta$$

$$\frac{BC}{AB} = sin\, dq_k$$

$$BC = |d\mathbf{r}_i| = r_i \, sin\theta \; sin\, dq_k = r_i \, sin\theta \; dq_k$$

$$\left|\frac{\partial \mathbf{r}_i}{\partial q_k}\right| = r_i \, sin\theta \qquad ...(4.19)$$

and its direction is perpendicular to both $\mathbf{r}_i$ and $\mathbf{n}$. Thus

$$\left|\frac{\partial \mathbf{r}_i}{\partial q_k}\right| = \mathbf{n} \times \mathbf{r}_i \qquad ...(4.20)$$

Substituting Eq. (4.20) in Eq. (4.13)

$$Q_k = \sum_i \mathbf{f}_i \cdot \mathbf{n} \times \mathbf{r}_i \qquad ...(4.21)$$

Using vector identity

$$\mathbf{A} \cdot (\mathbf{B} \times \mathbf{C}) = \mathbf{B} \cdot (\mathbf{C} \times \mathbf{A})$$

Eq. (4.21) is

$$Q_k = \sum_i \mathbf{n} \cdot (\mathbf{r}_i \times \mathbf{f}_i) = \mathbf{n} \cdot \mathbf{N} \qquad ...(4.22)$$

where torque N is

$$\mathbf{N} = \sum_i \mathbf{r}_i \times \mathbf{f}_i \qquad ...(4.23)$$

If $\mathbf{Q_k} = \mathbf{n.N}$ is zero, then consider

$$p_k = \frac{\partial L}{\partial \dot{q}_k} = \frac{\partial T}{\partial \dot{q}_k} = \sum_i m_i \mathbf{v}_i \cdot \frac{\partial \mathbf{r}_i}{\partial q_k} = \sum_i m_i \mathbf{v}_i \cdot \frac{\partial \mathbf{r}_i}{\partial q_k} = \sum_i m_i \mathbf{v_i} \cdot \mathbf{n} \times \mathbf{r}_i$$

$$p_k = \sum_i \mathbf{n} \cdot (\mathbf{r}_i \times m_i \mathbf{v}_i) = \sum_i \mathbf{n} \times (\mathbf{r}_i \times \mathbf{p}_i) = \sum_i \mathbf{n} \cdot \mathbf{L}_i = \mathbf{n} \cdot \mathbf{L}$$

Thus, p_k is the component of angular momentum along the axis of rotation n. From Lagrange's equation if q_k is cyclic *i.e.*

$$\frac{\partial L}{\partial q_k} = 0 \qquad ...(4.24)$$

and

$$\frac{d}{dt} \frac{\partial T}{\partial \dot{q}_k} = Q_k = \dot{p}_k = 0 \qquad ...(4.25)$$

Thus, if $\mathbf{n.N} = 0$, then $\mathbf{n.L}$ = constant *i.e.* component of $\mathbf{L}$ along the direction of $\mathbf{n}$ is constant for example for the Cartesian coordinate system, all the three components of the angular momentum (relative to arbitrary origin) are conserved for a closed system. The law of conservation may also hold in a more restricted form in the presence of external field. In such a case the component of the angular momentum along the axis about which field is symmetrical is conserved. For centrally symmetric field or central field (one in which potential energy depends only on the distance from a particular point), component of angular momentum along any axis passing through the center is conserved. Thus, if the field possesses an axis of symmetry, then the angular momentum about the axis of symmetry is conserved.

The conservation of linear momentum, angular momentum and total energy of a closed system is a result of symmetry properties of space and time.

Solved Examples

Example 1. *From the Lagrangian*

$$L=\frac{1}{2}m(\dot{r}^2+r^2\dot{\theta}^2)-\frac{1}{2}k(r-r_0)^2$$

obtain the conserved quantities.

Solution: Since $\frac{\partial L}{\partial t}=0$, therefore energy is conserved. Further

$$\frac{\partial L}{\partial \theta}=0, \quad \frac{\partial L}{\partial \dot{\theta}}=m\,r^2\dot{\theta}$$

From Lagrange equation

$$\frac{d}{dt}\left(\frac{\partial L}{\partial \dot{q}_k}\right)=\frac{\partial L}{\partial q_k}$$

we have

$$\frac{d}{dt}\left(\frac{\partial L}{\partial \dot{\theta}}\right)-\frac{\partial L}{\partial \theta}=0=\frac{d}{dt}\left(m\,r^2\dot{\theta}\right)=0$$

$$m\,r^2\dot{\theta}=\text{constant}$$

or angular momentum is conserved

Example 2. *From the Lagrangian*

$$L=\frac{1}{2}m(\dot{r}^2+r^2\dot{\theta}^2+r^2\sin^2\theta\,\dot{\varphi}^2)-\mu\,r\sin\theta\sin\varphi$$

Find the conserved quantities.

Solution: The relation between spherical polar coordinates and Cartesian coordinate system is

$$\begin{aligned} x&=r\sin\theta\cos\varphi \\ y&=r\sin\theta\sin\varphi \\ z&=r\cos\theta \end{aligned} \qquad ...(4.26)$$

Converting the Lagrangian from spherical polar coordinates to Cartesian coordinate system by using Eq. (4.26), we have

$$L=\frac{1}{2}m(\dot{x}^2+\dot{y}^2+\dot{z}^2)-\mu\,y$$

From the Lagrangian

$$\frac{\partial L}{\partial x}=0, \quad \frac{\partial L}{\partial y}=-\mu, \quad \frac{\partial L}{\partial z}=0$$

The coordinates x and z are cyclic. From Lagrange's equation

$$\frac{d}{dt}\left(\frac{\partial L}{\partial \dot{q}_k}\right)=\frac{\partial L}{\partial q_k}$$

we have

$$\frac{d}{dt}\left(\frac{\partial L}{\partial \dot{x}}\right)=\frac{d}{dt}(p_x)=\frac{\partial L}{\partial x}=0$$

$p_x =$ constant

$$\frac{d}{dt}\left(\frac{\partial L}{\partial \dot{y}}\right)=\frac{d}{dt}(p_y)=\frac{\partial L}{\partial y}=-\mu$$

p_y is not constant

$$\frac{d}{dt}\left(\frac{\partial L}{\partial \dot{z}}\right)=\frac{d}{dt}(p_z)=\frac{\partial L}{\partial z}=0$$

$p_z =$ constant

Consider x component of angular momentum

$$L_x = y\,p_z - z\,p_y$$

$$\frac{dL_x}{dt}=\dot{y}\,p_z + y\,\dot{p}_z - \dot{z}\,p_y - z\,\dot{p}_y = \frac{p_y}{m}\,p_z + y\,\dot{p}_z - \frac{p_z}{m}\,p_y - z\,\dot{p}_y = -z\,\dot{p}_y$$

Therefore, L_x is not conserved.

Consider y component of angular momentum

$$L_y = z\,p_x - x\,p_z$$

$$\frac{dL_y}{dt}=\dot{z}\,p_x + z\,\dot{p}_x - \dot{x}\,p_z - x\,\dot{p}_z = \frac{p_z}{m}\,p_x + z\,\dot{p}_x - \frac{p_x}{m}\,p_z - x\,\dot{p}_z = 0$$

Thus, L_y is conserved.

Consider z component of angular momentum

$$L_z = x\,p_y - y\,p_x$$

$$\frac{dL_z}{dt}=\dot{x}\,p_y + x\,\dot{p}_y - \dot{y}\,p_x - y\,\dot{p}_x = \frac{p_x}{m}\,p_y + x\,\dot{p}_y - \frac{p_y}{m}\,p_x - x\,\dot{p}_z = -\mu\,x$$

Therefore, L_z is not conserved.

OBJECTIVE TYPE QUESTIONS

1. Imagine a particle is moving in the gravitational field of an infinite homogeneous *xy* plane, which of the following is conserved

(*a*) L_x (*b*) L_y
(*c*) L_z (*d*) p_z

2. Which component of momentum and angular momentum are conserved in the field of an infinite homogeneous cylinder with *z* axis taken as symmetry axis.

(*a*) L_x, p_x (*b*) L_z, p_x
(*c*) L_x, L_y (*d*) L_z, p_z

3. Which is conserved in the field of a homogeneous cone if the axis of the cone is z axis?

(*a*) L_z (*b*) L_x
(*c*) L_y (*d*) none of these

4. If the Lagrangian is

$$L = \frac{1}{2}m(R^2\dot{\theta}^2 + \dot{z}^2) - \frac{1}{2}k(R^2 + z^2)$$

where R is constant. What is conserved?

(*a*) L_x (*b*) L_z
(*c*) L_y (*d*) none of these

5. A physical system is invariant under rotation about a fixed axis, then the following is conserved:

(*a*) total angular momentum the axis of rotation (*b*) angular momentum along
(*c*) linear momentum along (*d*) total angular momentum the axis of rotation

6. If the Lagrangian is invariant under translation, then the following is conserved:

(*a*) linear momentum (*b*) energy
(*c*) angular momentum (*d*) none of these

7. Conservation of energy is due to

(*a*) isotropy of space (*b*) homogeneity of space
(*c*) homogeneity of time (*d*) none of these

8. If a coordinate corresponding to a rotation is cyclic, rotation of the system about given axis remains invariant then the following is conserved:
(*a*) linear momentum (*b*) kinetic energy
(*c*) angular momentum (*d*) none of these

9. Conservation of linear momentum is due to
(*a*) isotropy of space (*b*) homogeneity of space
(*c*) homogeneity of time (*d*) none of these

10. Conservation of angular momentum is due to
(*a*) isotropy of space (*b*) homogeneity of space
(*c*) homogeneity of time (*d*) none of these

11. A physical system is invariant under translation along *x*-axis, then the following is conserved:
(*a*) total angular momentum (*b*) total linear momentum
(*c*) *x* component of angular momentum (*d*) *x* component of linear momentum

PROBLEMS

1. Obtain the conserved quantities from the Lagrangian

$$L = \frac{1}{2} m (\dot{r}^2 + r^2 \dot{\theta}^2 + r^2 \sin^2 \theta \dot{\phi}^2) - m g r \cos \theta$$

2. For the Lagrangian

$$L = \dot{\mathbf{r}}^2 + \mathbf{r}^2 + \mathbf{r} \cdot \dot{\mathbf{r}}$$

determine whether angular momentum is conserved. Is it invariant under translation?

3. If Lagrangian is

$$L = \frac{1}{2} m v^2 - \frac{k t}{y^2 + z^2}$$

Determine the conserved quantities.

❑❑❑

CHAPTER 5

Small Oscillation

5.1 STABLE AND UNSTABLE EQUILIBRIUM

Some of the principal features of the motion that takes place when a particle is acted upon by the conservative forces can be easily understood by considering a graph of potential energy function *V(x)*. Consider the motion in one dimension say *x*. Fig. 5.1 shows a graph of *V(x)* versus *x*. Consider a case where all the forces are conservative and are included in the given potential energy. In such a case, total mechanical energy is conserved and is

$$E = \frac{1}{2} m \mathrm{v}^2 + V(x)$$

$$\mathrm{v} = \frac{dx}{dt} = \sqrt{\frac{2}{m}[E - V(x)]}$$

$$\int \frac{dx}{\sqrt{\frac{2}{m}[E - V(x)]}} = \int dt$$

In many cases, this integral is too difficult to solve. In such cases , the study of potential energy diagrams are of much use. In these diagrams total energy can also be depicted. The plot of total energy and potential energy is called energy diagram. Its main features are (*a*) at any point, kinetic energy can be determined by using the relation that kinetic energy is equal to total energy minus potential energy, (*b*) can locate the turning points, that is points where potential energy equals total energy. Between these points, the system oscillates. (*c*) if total energy is increased, then the turning points are farther points, (*d*) from the minimum or maximum of the potential energy curve, the stability of the equilibrium of the system can be understood.

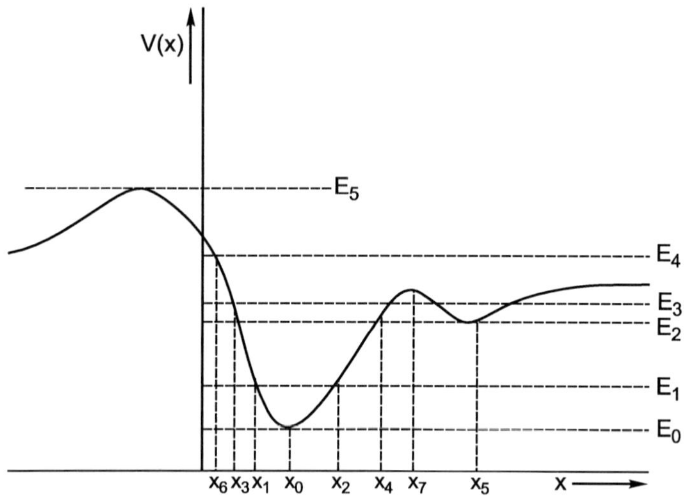

Fig. 5.1

Consider the potential energy diagram shown in Fig. 5.1. The total energy is conserved and is represented by a horizontal line on the diagram. Six different values of E are shown. It is clear that $V(x)$ must be less than or equal to E for velocity not to be imaginary. Consider the case when total energy is equal to the minimum of potential energy. This energy is labeled as E_0. For this value of E, the particle can only be at rest at $x = x_0$. It has potential energy but no kinetic energy and the particle can only be at rest.

If $E>E_0$, say E_1, particle can have both kinetic and potential energy. Since curve of Fig. 5.1 represents $V(x)$ at each x, therefore kinetic energy at any value of x is represented by the distance between E line and curve $V(x)$ at that value of x. A particle with energy E_1 can oscillate between points x_1 and x_2. If $x<x_1$ or $x>x_2$, potential energy would be greater than E. At x_1 and x_2 the velocity is zero as potential energy equals total energy. As particle approaches x_1 or x_2 , its velocity decreases and it stops and reverses its direction when it reaches either x_1 or x_2 which is called turning points of the motion. At $E = E_2$, there are two turning points x_3 and x_4 and oscillate between them or remain at rest at x_5. For $E = E_3$ there are four turning points and particle may oscillate in either of the two potential valley depending on where it is initially. It cannot go from one valley to the other because of barrier between them. For E_4, there is only one turning point since $V(x)<E_4$ for all $x>x_6$, it then proceeds to the right indefinitely never to return. At energy E_5 there is no turning point and particle will move only in one direction.

The particle reverses the direction at the turning points because of the force exerted on it. F and $V(x)$ are related by

$$F = -\frac{dV}{dx}$$

Force F equals to the negative of the slope of V versus x curve at any point x. At $x = x_2$ the slope is positive, so force is negative, that is it acts to the left or to the decreasing value of x. At x_1, the slope is negative and therefore force is positive and it will act towards the right. In both the cases force acts to reverse the direction of the particle motion.

At x_0, the slope is zero and hence force is zero. At such points the particle is said to be in equilibrium. If the particle is initially at rest, it remains at rest. If the particle is moved slightly to the left or right , a non-zero force would then act on it and the direction of force move the particle back to equilibrium position. A particle which returns towards its equilibrium point when displaced slightly is said to be in stable equilibrium. Any minimum of potential energy curve represents a point of stable equilibrium.

A particle at $x = x_7$ would also be in equilibrium since $F = 0$. A particle at rest in this position remains at rest, since the force is zero. If the particle is displaced slightly to either side of x_7, a force would act to pull the particle away from the equilibrium position. Point like x_7 where V has a maximum are points of unstable equilibrium. The particle will not return to equilibrium if displaced slightly but moves further away. When a particle is in a region where V is constant, the force is zero over the region. The particle is in equilibrium and if displaced slightly to one side is still zero (constancy of V) . The particle is said to be in neutral equilibrium in the region.

5.2 FORMULATION OF THE PROBLEM

Consider a conservative system having generalized coordinates q_k $(k = 1,2,...,n)$ and time t. Let q_{k0} the values that these coordinates have in equilibrium. In such a configuration, Lagrangian equations will be satisfied by

$$q_k = q_{k0}\, , \dot{q}_k = 0, \ \ddot{q}_k = 0 \ (k = 1,2,...,n) \qquad ...(5.1)$$

For $\frac{d}{dt}\left(\frac{\partial L}{\partial \dot{q}_k}\right)$ to be non-zero, it must contain at least either $\dot{q}_k$ or $\ddot{q}_k$.

Therefore, at equilibrium the term vanishes and from Lagrangian Equation

$$\left.\frac{\partial L}{\partial q_k}\right|_{k=0} = \left.\frac{\partial T}{\partial q_k}\right|_{k=0} - \left.\frac{\partial V}{\partial q_k}\right|_{k=0} = 0 \qquad ...(5.2)$$

The kinetic energy is a homogeneous quadratic function of the generalized velocities [Eq. (2.76)]

$$T = \sum_{k,l} C_{kl}\, \dot{q}_k\, \dot{q}_l \qquad ...(5.3)$$

In general

$$\left.\frac{\partial T}{\partial q_k}\right|_{k=0} = 0 \qquad \text{...(5.4)}$$

From Eq.(5.2)

$$\left.\frac{\partial V}{\partial q_k}\right|_{k=0} = 0 \qquad \text{...(5.5)}$$

Let the general configuration of the system is given by

$$q_k = q_{k0} + u_k \text{ ...} \qquad (5.6)$$

The expansion of the potential energy in a Taylor series about the equilibrium

$$V(q_1, q_2, \ldots, q_n) = V(q_{10} q_{20}, \ldots q_{n0}) + \sum_k \left.\frac{\partial V}{\partial q_k}\right|_0 u_k + \frac{1}{2!}\sum_{k,l} \left.\frac{\partial^2 V}{\partial q_k ql}\right|_0 u_k u_l + \ldots \quad (5.7)$$

At equilibrium $\left.\frac{\partial V}{\partial q_k}\right|_{k=0} = 0$ and we may choose to measure V in such a way that $V(q_{10}, q_{20}, \ldots, q_{n0}) = 0$. Assuming that departure from equilibrium is small, we can ignore terms containing products of the u_k of degree higher than second. This is equivalent to restricting to simple harmonic oscillations, in which case only terms quadratic in the coordinates appear. The Eq. (5.7) is

$$V(q_1, q_2, \ldots\ldots, q_n) = \frac{1}{2!}\sum_{k,l} \left.\frac{\partial^2 V}{\partial q_k q_l}\right|_0 u_k u_l = \frac{1}{2}\sum_{k,l} A_{kl}\, u_k\, u_l \quad (k, l = 1, 2, \ldots, n)$$

...(5.8)

where

$$A_{k,l} = \sum_{k,l} \left.\frac{\partial^2 V}{\partial q_k q_l}\right|_0 \qquad \text{...(5.9)}$$

Since the order of differential in immaterial (if V has continuous second partial derivative), the quantity A_{kl} is real symmetric, that is,

$$A_{kl} = A_{lk} = A_{kl}^{*} \qquad \text{...(5.10)}$$

The form of kinetic energy given by Eq. (5.3) is same as that of potential energy V given by Eq. (5.8). The C_{kl} are given by [Eq. (2.75)]

$$C_{kl} = \frac{1}{2}\sum_{i=1}^{N} m_i \frac{\partial \mathbf{r}_i}{\partial q_k}\cdot\frac{\partial \mathbf{r}_i}{\partial q_l} \qquad ..(5.11)$$

The quantities A_{kl} are just numbers. On the other hand m_i may be functionof the coordinates. Expanding C_{kl} about the equilibrium position

$$C_{kl}(q_1, q_2, ..., q_n) = C(q_{10}, q_{20}, ..., q_{n0}) + \sum_j \left.\frac{\partial C_{kl}}{\partial q_j}\right|_o u_j + ...(5.12)$$

The constant $C_{kl} \neq 0$, therefore the leading term is the constant value of C_{kl} in this approximation. This is the same order of approximation as that used for V since the next higher order term in T would involve the cubic quantity $\dot{u}_k\dot{u}_l u_j$. Denoting constant value of C_{kl} function at equilibrium by T_{kl}, we can write kinetic energy, using Eq. (5.6) as

$$T = \frac{1}{2}\sum_{k,l} T_{kl}\, \dot{u}_k\, \dot{u}_l \qquad ...(5.13)$$

The constant T_{kl} is symmetric, since the individual terms in the Eq. (5.13) are unaffected by the interchange of indices.

If $T_{kl} \neq 0$ for $k \neq l$, then the kinetic energy will contain a term proportional to $\dot{u}_k\, \dot{u}_l$ and a coupling exists between kth and ith coordinate. If on the other hand T_{kl} is diagonal so that $T_{kl} \neq 0$ for $k = l$ and $T_{kl} = 0$ for $k \neq l$, then the kinetic energy is of the form

$$T = \frac{1}{2}\sum_k T_{kk}\, \dot{u}_k^2 \qquad ..(5.14)$$

Thus kinetic energy is a simple sum of the kinetic energy associated with various coordinates.

The Lagrangian is therefore given by

$$L = \frac{1}{2}\sum_{k,l} (T_{kl}\, \dot{u}_k\, \dot{u}_l - A_{kl}\, u_k\, u_l) \qquad ...(5.15)$$

The Lagrangian equation of motion is

$$\frac{d}{dt}\left(\frac{\partial L}{\partial \dot{q}_k}\right) - \frac{\partial L}{\partial q_k} = 0$$

or

$$\frac{d}{dt}\left(\frac{\partial T}{\partial \dot{q}_k}\right) + \frac{\partial V}{\partial q_k} = 0$$

gives

$$\sum_l (T_{kl}\ddot{u}_l + A_{kl}u_l) = 0 \qquad \text{...(5.16)}$$

This is a set of n second-order linear homogeneous differential equations with constant coefficients. Let the solution of the Eq. (5.16) is of the form

$$u_l(t) = a_l \exp[i(\omega t - \delta)] \qquad \text{...(5.17)}$$

where a_l are real amplitude and δ is a phase constant. The ω and δ is to be determined by the equation of motion. If ω is real then the above equation represents n oscillator solution. Suppose ω is complex. The imaginary part gives rise to terms of the form *exp* $(-\omega\ t)$ and *exp* $(\omega\ t)$ in the expression for u_l. The total energy will contain factors which increases or decreases monotonically with time, but this violates our assumption that system is conservative. Therefore, ω is real.

From Eq. (5.17)

$$\dot{u}_l = i\omega u_l \qquad \text{...(5.18)}$$

$$\ddot{u}_l = -\omega^2 u_l \qquad \text{...(5.19)}$$

Substituting Eqs. (5.17) and (5.19) in Eq. (5.16)

$$\sum(-\omega^2 T_{kl} + A_{kl})\, u_l = 0$$

$$\sum(A_{kl} - \omega^2 T_{kl})\, a_l = 0 \qquad \text{...(5.20)}$$

The common factor $exp[i(\omega t - \delta)]$ has been cancelled. This is a set of n linear homogeneous algebraic equations which the a_l must satisfy. This has non-trivial solution if and only if the determinant of its coefficients vanishes, that is,

$$\left| A_{kl} - \omega^2 T_{kl} \right| = 0 \qquad \text{...(5.21)}$$

or

$$\begin{vmatrix} A_{11} - \omega^2 T_{11} & A_{12} - \omega^2 T_{12} & \cdots & A_{1n} - \omega^2 T_{1n} \\ A_{21} - \omega^2 T_{21} & A_{22} - \omega^2 T_{22} & \vdots & A_{2n} - \omega^2 T_{2n} \\ \vdots & \vdots & \vdots & \vdots \\ A_{n1} - \omega^2 T_{n1} & A_{11} - \omega^2 T_{n2} & \cdots & A_{nn} - \omega^2 T_{nn} \end{vmatrix} = 0 \qquad \text{...(5.22)}$$

The Eq. (5.22) is called the characteristic equation or secular equation of the system and is an equation of degree n in ω^2. There are in general n roots which may be label ω_i. The ω_i are called characteristic frequencies $(i = 1,2,\ldots,n)$

or eigen frequencies of the system. For each of these values of ω_i^2 the Eq. (5.20) may be solved for the amplitude of a_l in terms of the remaining $(n-1)$ amplitude. By determining the frequencies from Eq. (5.22) and inserting these values one by one into Eq. (5.21). On solving this system the eigen vectors $a_1, a_2, \ldots, a_n$ pertain to eigenvalue ω_i^2. We designate by a_{li} the the lth component of the ith eigenvector. The Eq. (5.17) can be written as a linear combination of the solution for each of the n values of i.

$$u_l(t) = \sum_i a_{li} \exp[i(\omega_i t - \delta_i)] \qquad \ldots(5.23)$$

However, only the real part of u_l is physically meaningful.

5.3 THE ORTHOGONALITY OF THE EIGEN VECTORS

Let the eigenvalues are different and eigenvectors are uniquely determined. The Eq. (5.21) for the eigenvalues ω_i^2 and ω_j^2 are

$$\sum_l \omega_i^2 T_{kl} a_{li} = \sum_l A_{kl} a_{li} \qquad \ldots(5.24)$$

$$\sum_k \omega_j^2 T_{kl} a_{kj} = \sum_k A_{kl} a_{kj} \qquad \ldots(5.25)$$

Multiply Eq.(5.24) by a_{kj} and sum over k and Eq. (5.25) by a_{li} and sum over l

$$\omega_i^2 \sum_{k,l} T_{kl} a_{li} a_{kj} = \sum_{k,l} A_{kl} a_{li} a_{kj} \qquad \ldots(5.26)$$

$$\omega_j^2 \sum_{k,l} T_{kl} a_{li} a_{kj} = \sum_{k,l} A_{kl} a_{li} a_{kj} \qquad \ldots(5.27)$$

The right hand side of Eqs. (5.25) and (5.26) are now equal. On subtracting Eqs. (5.25) and (5.26)

$$(\omega_j^2 - \omega_i^2) \sum_{k,l} T_{kl} a_{li} a_{kj} = 0 \qquad \ldots(5.28)$$

As $\omega_j^2 \neq \omega_i^2$, the double sum must vanish if $i \neq j$, that is,

$$\sum_{k,l} T_{kl} a_{li} a_{kj} = 0 \text{ for } i \neq j \qquad \ldots(5.29)$$

For $i = j$, the term $\omega_j^2 - \omega_i^2$ vanishes and the sum is indeterminate. Consider the Eq. (5.13) and substitute the expression for $\dot{u}_k$ and $\dot{u}_l$ using Eq. (5.23)

$$T = \frac{1}{2}\sum_{k,l} T_{kl} \left[\sum \omega_i a_{li} \, sin(\omega_i t - \delta_i) \right] \left[\sum [\omega_j a_{kj} \, sin(\omega_j t - \delta_j) \right] \quad ...(5.30)$$

$$T = \frac{1}{2}\sum_{i,j} \omega_i \omega_j \, sin(\omega_i t - \delta_i) \, sin(\omega_j t - \delta_j) \sum_{k,l} T_{kl} a_{li} a_{kj} \quad ...(5.31)$$

Kinetic energy for $i = j$ is

$$T = \frac{1}{2}\sum_{i} \omega_i^2 \, sin^2(\omega_i t - \delta_i) \sum_{k,l} T_{kl} a_{li} a_{ki} \quad ...(5.32)$$

since $\omega_i^2 \sin^2(\omega_i t - \delta_i)$ is always greater or equal to zero and kinetic energy is positive , therefore T can become zero only if all of the velocities vanish, that is, the system is not in motion. Therefore

$$\sum_{k,l} T_{kl} a_{li} a_{ki} \geq 0 \quad ...(5.33)$$

If a_{kj} are normalised

$$\sum_{k,l} T_{kl} a_{li} a_{ki} = 1 \quad ...(5.34)$$

Combining Eqs. (5.29) and (5.34)

$$\sum_{kl} T_{kl} \, a_{li} a_{kj} = \delta_{ij} \quad (\delta_{ij} = 0 \text{ for } i \neq j, \text{and 1 for } i = j) \quad ...(5.35)$$

5.4 NORMAL COORDINATES

Both V and T may simultaneously diagonalized by transforming to normal coordinates. The normal coordinates are defined through the relation

$$u_l = \sum_i a_{li} Q_i \quad (i = 1,2,...,n) \quad ...(5.36)$$

Q_i are quantities which undergo oscillation at only one frequency. They may be called normal coordinates for the system. Differentiating Eq. (5.36)

$$\dot{u}_l = \sum_i a_{li} \dot{Q}_i \quad (i = 1,2,...,n) \quad ...(5.37)$$

The kinetic energy is obtained by using Eqs. (5.37) and (5.13)

$$T = \frac{1}{2}\sum_{k,l} T_{kl} \left(\sum_i a_{li} \dot{Q}_i \right) \left(\sum_j a_{kj} \dot{Q}_j \right)$$

$$T = \frac{1}{2}\sum_{i,j}\left(\sum_{k,l} T_{kl}\, a_{li}\, a_{kj}\right)\dot{Q}_i \dot{Q}_j \qquad ...(5.38)$$

The sum in the parentheses is just δ_{ij} according to the orthonormality condition (5.35). Therefore,

$$T = \frac{1}{2}\sum_{i,j}\dot{Q}_i \dot{Q}_j\, \delta_{ij} = \frac{1}{2}\sum_i \dot{Q}_i^2 \qquad ...(5.39)$$

From Eqs. (5.8) and (5.36) the potential energy V is

$$V = \frac{1}{2}\sum_{i,j}\left(\sum_{k,l} A_{kl}\, a_{li}\, a_{kj}\right) Q_i Q_j \qquad ...(5.40)$$

From Eqs. (5.26) and (5.35)

$$\omega_i^2\, \delta_{ij} = \sum_{kl} A_{kl}\, a_{li}\, a_{kj} \qquad ...(5.41)$$

From Eqs.(5.40) and (5.41)

$$V = \frac{1}{2}\sum_{i,j}\omega_i^2\, \delta_{ij}\, Q_i Q_j = \frac{1}{2}\sum_i \omega_i^2\, Q_i^2 \qquad ...(5.42)$$

The Lagrangian is therefore from Eqs. (5.39) and (5.42)

$$L = T - V = \frac{1}{2}\sum_i \left(\dot{Q}_i^2 - \omega_i^2 Q_i^2\right) \qquad ...(5.43)$$

and

$$\frac{\partial L}{\partial \dot{Q}_i} = \dot{Q}_i\, , \quad \frac{\partial L}{\partial Q_i} = -\,\omega_i^2\, Q_i$$

The Lagrange's equation of motion are

$$\frac{d}{dt}\left(\dot{Q}_i\right) + \omega_i^2\, Q_i = 0$$

$$\ddot{Q}_i + \omega_i^2\, Q_i = 0 \quad (i = 1, 2, ..., n) \qquad ...(5.44)$$

The potential energy and kinetic energy become simultaneously diagonal when the configuration of the system is expressed in normal coordinates. The off diagonal elements of T and A give rise to the coupling of the particles. Thus, by transforming to normal coordinates all the modes have been decoupled. This is a consequence of removing coupling term from T and V.

The solution of the Eq. (5.44) is

$$Q_i = C_i \cos(\omega_i t + \delta_i) \qquad ...(5.45)$$

are the normal modes of the system. C_i and δ_i are derived from the initial conditions when a_{li} and ω_i are respectively, the eigen vectors and eigen values.

Solved Examples

Example 1. *The potential energy function between two atoms of a diatomic molecule is given by*

$$V = ax^{-12} - bx^{-6}$$

where a and b are positive constants. x is the separation between atoms. Find the equilibrium position.

Solution: For V to be minimum

$$\frac{dV}{dx} = -12ax^{-13} + 6bx^{-7} = 0$$

$$x = \pm\sqrt{\left(\frac{2a}{b}\right)}$$

$$\left.\frac{d^2V}{dx^2}\right|_0 = 156ax^{-14} - 42bx^{-8}\Big|_0 > 0$$

$$\left.\frac{d^2V}{dx^2}\right|_0 = 156ax_0^{-14} - 42bx_0^{-8} = 156a\left(\frac{2a}{b}\right)^{-14/6} - 42b\left(\frac{2a}{b}\right)^{-8/6} > 0$$

$$\left.\frac{d^2V}{dx^2}\right|_0 = [156a - 84a]\left(\frac{2a}{b}\right)^{-14/6} > 0$$

The equilibrium is stable.

Example 2. *A particle of mass m moves along the x axis under the influence of the potential energy*

$$V(x) = -kx\exp(-\beta x)$$

where k and b are constants. Find the equilibrium position.

Solution: We have

$$\frac{dV}{dx} = k\beta x\exp(-\beta x) - k\exp(-\beta x) = 0$$

$$x_0 = \frac{1}{\beta}$$

$$\left.\frac{d^2V}{dx^2}\right|_0 = 2k\,\beta\,exp(-\beta\,x) - k\beta^2 x\,exp(-\beta\,x)\big|_0 > 0$$

$$\left.\frac{d^2V}{dx^2}\right|_0 = 2k\,\beta(2-\beta\,x_0)exp(-\beta\,x_0) = 2k\,\beta(2-\frac{\beta}{\beta})exp(-\beta\,x_0) > 0$$

$$\left.\frac{d^2V}{dx^2}\right|_0 = \frac{k\,\beta}{e} > 0$$

The equilibrium is stable.

Example 3. *The kinetic energy of a system is*

$$T = \frac{1}{2}m(\dot{x}^2 + \dot{y}^2 + \dot{z}^2)$$

and the potential energy is

$$V = \frac{1}{2}(k_1x^2 + k_2y^2 + k_3z^2)$$

Obtain the eigen frequencies.

Solution: From Eq. (5.9)

$$A_{11} = \left.\frac{\partial^2V}{\partial x^2}\right|_0 = k_1,\ A_{22} = \left.\frac{\partial^2V}{\partial y^2}\right|_0 = k_2,\ A_{33} = \left.\frac{\partial^2V}{\partial z^2}\right|_0 = k_3,\ A_{21} = \left.\frac{\partial^2V}{\partial x\partial y}\right|_0 = A_{12} = 0$$

The other off diagonal elements are also zero. From kinetic energy expression we have by using Eq. (5.14)

$$T_{11} = T_{22} = T_{33} = m,\ T_{12} = T_{21} = T_{13} = T_{31} = T_{23} = T_{32} = 0$$

The secular determinant (5.22) is

$$\begin{vmatrix} k_1 - m\omega^2 & 0 & 0 \\ 0 & k_2 - m\omega^2 & 0 \\ 0 & 0 & k_3 - m\omega^2 \end{vmatrix} = 0$$

On solving

$$(k_1 - m\omega^2)(k_2 - m\omega^2)(k_3 - m\omega^2) = 0$$

or

$$\omega_1 = \sqrt{\frac{k_1}{m}},\quad \omega_2 = \sqrt{\frac{k_2}{m}},\quad \omega_3 = \sqrt{\frac{k_3}{m}},$$

Example 4. *The kinetic energy of a system is*

$$T = \frac{1}{2} m(\dot{x}^2 + \dot{y}^2)$$

and the potential energy is

$$V = \frac{1}{2} \omega_0^2 (x^2 + y^2) - \alpha x y$$

Obtain eigen frequencies and eigen vectors.

Solution: From Eq. (5.9)

$$A_{11} = \left.\frac{\partial^2 V}{\partial x^2}\right|_0 = \omega_0^2, \; A_{22} = \left.\frac{\partial^2 V}{\partial y^2}\right|_0 = \omega_0^2, \quad A_{21} = \left.\frac{\partial^2 V}{\partial x \partial y}\right|_0 = A_{21} = -\alpha$$

From kinetic energy expression we have by using Eq. (5.14)

$$T_{11} = T_{22} = 1 \quad T_{12} = T_{21} = 0$$

The secular determinant (5.22) is

$$\begin{vmatrix} \omega_0^2 - \omega^2 & -\alpha \\ -\alpha & \omega_0^2 - \omega^2 \end{vmatrix} = 0$$

On solving

$$(\omega_0^2 - \omega^2)^2 - \alpha^2 = 0$$

$$[(\omega_0^2 - \omega^2) - \alpha][(\omega_0^2 - \omega^2) - \alpha] = 0$$

$$\omega^2 = \omega_0^2 - \alpha, \quad \omega^2 = \omega_0^2 + \alpha$$

Consider the equation of motion (5.26)

$$\sum_k (A_{kl} - \omega_i^2 T_{kl})a_{ki} = 0$$

To determine the eigen vector component a_{ki}, we have two equations for each value of *i*, but since we can determine only the ratio a_{1i}/a_{2i}, one equation for each *I* is sufficient. For $i = 1$, $l = 1$ we have

$$(\omega_0^2 - \omega_0^2 + \alpha)a_{11} + (-\alpha - 0)a_{21} = 0$$

$$a_{11} = a_{21}$$

Putting $i = 2, l = 1$

$$(\omega_0^2 - \omega_0^2 - \alpha)a_{12} + (-\alpha - 0)a_{22} = 0$$

$$a_{12} = -a_{22}$$

From orthonormality condition (5.35)

$$\sum_{kl} T_{kl}\, a_{ki} a_{lj} = \delta_{ij}$$

T is diagonal with each element equal to 1, therefore the orthogonality condition becomes after summing over k

$$\sum_{l} a_{li} a_{lj} = \delta_{ij}$$

For $i = j = 1$, we have

$$a_{11}^2 + a_{21}^2 = 1$$

But $a_{11} = a_{21}$, therefore,

$$2a_{11}^2 = 1, \quad \text{hence} \quad a_{11} = a_{21} = \sqrt{\frac{1}{2}}$$

For $i = j = 2$

$$a_{12}^2 + a_{22}^2 = 1$$

but $a_{12} = -a_{22}$, therefore

$$2a_{12}^2 = 1, \text{ hence } a_{12} = \sqrt{\frac{1}{2}} = -a_{22}$$

Thus, we have

$$\begin{pmatrix} x \\ y \end{pmatrix} = \begin{pmatrix} \sqrt{1/2} & \sqrt{1/2} \\ \sqrt{1/2} & -\sqrt{1/2} \end{pmatrix} \begin{pmatrix} Q_1 \\ Q_2 \end{pmatrix}$$

$$x = \frac{1}{\sqrt{2}}(Q_1 + Q_2), \quad y = \frac{1}{\sqrt{2}}(Q_1 - Q_2)$$

$$L = \frac{1}{2}\left[(\dot{Q}_1 + \dot{Q}_2)^2 (\dot{Q}_1 + \dot{Q}_2)\right] - \frac{1}{4}\omega_0^2 \left[(Q_1 + Q_2)^2 + (Q_1 - Q_2)^2\right]$$
$$+ \frac{\alpha}{2}((Q_1 + Q_2)(Q_1 - Q_2) \;]$$

$$L = \frac{1}{2}(\dot{Q}_1^2 + \dot{Q}_2^2) - \frac{1}{2}\omega_0^2 (Q_1^2 + Q_2^2) + \frac{\alpha}{2}(Q_1^2 - Q_2^2)$$

Example 5. *Bonds between the atoms of molecule may be likened to springs and a linear triatomic molecule like carbon dioxide may be represented as in Fig. 5.2 Obtain the Lagrangian of the system. Find the eigen frequencies and eigen vectors of the system.*

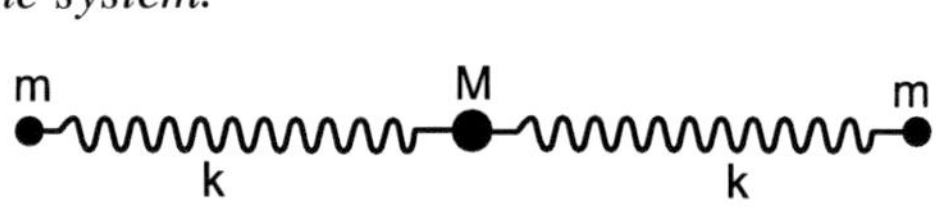

Fig. 5.2

Solution: Let the equilibrium distance between the two masses is b. The force constants of the spring is k. The position of the three masses are given by the coordinates x_1, x_2 and x_3.

The potential energy of the system is

$$V = \frac{1}{2}k(x_2 - x_1 - b)^2 + \frac{1}{2}k(x_3 - x_2 - b)^2$$

The equilibrium distance b is given by

$$b = x_{02} - x_{01} = x_{03} - x_{02}$$

The potential energy is therefore

$$V = \frac{1}{2}k(x_2 - x_1 - x_{02} + x_{01})^2 + \frac{1}{2}k(x_3 - x_2 - x_{03} + x_{02})^2$$

Putting

$$\eta_1 = x_1 - x_{01}, \quad \eta_2 = x_2 - x_{02}, \quad \eta_3 = x_3 - x_{03}$$

we have

$$V = \frac{1}{2}k(\eta_2 - \eta_1)^2 + \frac{1}{2}k(\eta_3 - \eta_2)^2$$

$$V = \frac{1}{2}k(\eta_1^2 + 2\eta_2^2 + \eta_3^2 - 2\eta_1\eta_2 - 2\eta_2\eta_3)$$

The kinetic energy is

$$T = \frac{1}{2}m\dot{\eta}_1^2 + \frac{1}{2}M\dot{\eta}_2^2 + \frac{1}{2}m\dot{\eta}_3^2$$

The Lagrangian is

$$L = T - V = \frac{1}{2}m\dot{\eta}_1^2 + \frac{1}{2}M\dot{\eta}_2^2 + \frac{1}{2}m\dot{\eta}_3^2 - \frac{1}{2}k(\eta_1^2 + 2\eta_2^2 + \eta_3^2 - 2\eta_1\eta_2 - 2\eta_2\eta_3)$$

From Eq. (5.9)

$$A_{11} = \left.\frac{\partial^2 V}{\partial \eta_1^2}\right|_0 = k, \; A_{22} = \left.\frac{\partial^2 V}{\partial \eta_2^2}\right|_0 = 2k, \; A_{33} = \left.\frac{\partial^2 V}{\partial \eta_3^2}\right|_0$$

$$= k, \; A_{21} = \left.\frac{\partial^2 V}{\partial \eta_2 \partial \eta_1}\right|_0 = A_{12} = -k$$

$$A_{23} = \left.\frac{\partial^2 V}{\partial\eta_2 \partial\eta_3}\right|_0 = A_{32} = -k, \quad A_{13} = \left.\frac{\partial^2 V}{\partial\eta_1 \partial\eta_3}\right|_0 = A_{31} = 0$$

From kinetic energy expression, we have by using Eq. (5.14)

$T_{11} = m,\ T_{22} = M,\ T_{33} = m, \quad T_{12} = T_{21} = T_{13} = T_{31} = T_{12} = T_{21} = 0$

The secular determinant (5.22) is

$$\left| A_{kl} - \omega^2 T_{kl} \right| = \begin{vmatrix} k - m\omega^2 & -k & 0 \\ -k & 2k - M\omega^2 & -k \\ 0 & -k & k - m\omega^2 \end{vmatrix} = 0$$

The value of determinant is

$$(k - m\omega^2)\{[(2k - M\omega^2)(k - m\omega^2) - k^2] + k[-k(k - m\omega^2)]\} = 0$$

$$\omega^2 (k - m\omega)[k(M + 2m) - M m\omega^2] = 0$$

The solutions are

$$\omega_1 = 0, \quad \omega_2 = \sqrt{\frac{k}{m}}, \quad \omega_3 = \pm\sqrt{\frac{k(M + 2m)}{M m}} = \pm\sqrt{\frac{k}{m}\left(1 + \frac{2m}{M}\right)}$$

Hence the system has three normal-mode (angular) frequencies

$$\omega_1 = 0, \quad \omega_2 = \sqrt{\frac{k}{m}}, \quad \omega_3 = \sqrt{\frac{k}{m}\left(1 + \frac{2m}{M}\right)}$$

$\omega_1 = 0$ does not correspond to an oscillatory motion. The vanishing frequency arises from the fact that the system may be translated rigidly along its axis without any change in the potential energy an example of neutral equilibrium (Fig. 5.3). ω_2 is the frequency of oscillator for a mass m suspended by the spring of force constant k. Thus, only end atoms take part in the oscillations and the centre mass M remains stationary (Fig. 5.4). The value of ω_3 indicates that mass M also take part in the oscillation (Fig. 5.5). Figs. (5.3-5.5) shows the longitudinal normal modes of the symmetric triatomic molecule.

Fig. 5.3

Fig. 5.4

Fig. 5.5

Consider the equation of motion (5.26)

$$\sum_k (A_{kl} - \omega_i^2 T_{kl})a_{ki} = 0$$

For $i = 1$, $l = 1$, we have

$$(A_{11} - \omega_1^2 T_{11})\, a_{11} + (A_{21} - \omega_1^2 T_{21})a_{21} + (A_{31} - \omega_1^2 T_{31})a_{31} = 0$$

putting the value of T's, A's and ω_1^2 we have

$$k\, a_{11} - k\, a_{21} = 0$$

$$a_{11} = a_{21}$$

For $i = 1$, $l = 2$, we have

$$(A_{12} - \omega_1^2 T_{12})\, a_{11} + (A_{22} - \omega_1^2 T_{22})a_{21} + (A_{32} - \omega_1^2 T_{32})a_{31} = 0$$

putting the value of T's, A's and ω_1^2 we have

$$-k\, a_{11} + 2k\, a_{21} - k\, a_{31} = 0$$

$$a_{11} = a_{31}$$

Thus, we have

$$a_{11} = a_{21} = a_{31}$$

From orthonormality condition (5.35)

$$\sum_{k,l} T_{kl}\, a_{ki} a_{lj} = \delta_{ij}$$

T is diagonal, therefore the orthogonality condition becomes after summing over k

$$m\, a_{11}^2 + M\, a_{21}^2 + m a_{31}^2 = 1$$

$$m\,(a_{11}^2 + a_{31}^2) + M\, a_{21}^2 = 1$$

$$a_{11} = a_{21} = a_{31} = \sqrt{\frac{1}{(2m + M)}}$$

Putting $i = 2$ and $l = 1$ in Eq. (5.26)

$$(A_{11} - \omega_2^2 T_{11})\, a_{12} + (A_{21} - \omega_2^2 T_{21})a_{22} + (A_{31} - \omega_2^2 T_{31})a_{32} = 0$$

Putting the value of T's, A's and ω_2^2 we have

$$(k - \frac{k}{m} m)\, a_{12} + (-k - 0)a_{22} + (0 - 0)a_{32} = 0$$

$$a_{22} = 0$$

Putting $i = 2$ and $l = 2$ in Eq. (5.26)

$$(A_{12} - \omega_2^2 T_{12})\, a_{12} + (A_{22} - \omega_2^2 T_{22})\, a_{22} + (A_{32} - \omega_2^2 T_{32})\, a_{32} = 0$$

Putting the value of T's, A's and ω_2^2 we have

$$(-k - 0)\, a_{12} + (2k - \frac{k}{m} M)\, a_{22} + (-k - 0)\, a_{32} = 0$$

$$-a_{12} = a_{32}$$

T is diagonal, therefore the orthogonality condition becomes after summing over k

$$m\,(a_{12}^2 + a_{32}^2) + M\, a_{22}^2 = 1$$

$$2m\, a_{12}^2 = 1 \quad \text{or} \quad a_{12} = \sqrt{\frac{1}{2m}} = -a_{32}$$

In this mode the centre atom is at rest, while the two outer ones vibrate exactly out of phase (Fig.5.4).

Putting $i = 3$ and $l = 1$ in Eq.(5.26)

$$(A_{11} - \omega_3^2 T_{11})\, a_{13} + (A_{21} - \omega_3^2 T_{21})\, a_{23} + (A_{31} - \omega_3^2 T_{31})\, a_{33} = 0$$

Putting the value of T's, A's and ω_3^2 we have

$$\left[k - \frac{k}{m}\left(1 + \frac{2m}{M}\right)m\right] a_{13} + \left[-K - \frac{k}{m}\left(1 + \frac{2m}{M}\right)0\right] a_{23} + \left[0 - \frac{k}{m}\left(1 + \frac{2m}{M}\right)0\right] a_{33} = 0$$

$$\left[-\frac{2km}{M}\right] a_{13} + [-k]\, a_{23} = 0$$

$$a_{23} = \left[-\frac{2m}{M}\right] a_{13}$$

Putting $i = 3$ and $l = 2$ in Eq.(5.26)

$$(A_{12} - \omega_3^2 T_{12})\, a_{13} + (A_{22} - \omega_3^2 T_{22})\, a_{23} + (A_{32} - \omega_3^2 T_{32})\, a_{33} = 0$$

Putting the value of T's, A's and ω_3^2 we have

$$(-k - \omega_3^2 0)\, a_{13} + \left[2k - \frac{k}{m}\left(1 + \frac{2m}{M}\right)M\right] a_{23} + (-k - \omega_3^2 0)\, a_{33} = 0$$

$$a_{13} + \left[\frac{M}{m}\right] a_{23} + a_{33} = 0$$

$$-\frac{M}{2m} a_{23} + \frac{M}{m} a_{23} + a_{33} = 0$$

$$a_{23} = -\frac{2m}{M} a_{33}$$

$$a_{13} = a_{33}$$

T is diagonal , therefore the orthogonality condition becomes after summing over k

$$m\,(a_{13}^2 + a_{33}^2) + M\,a_{23}^2 = 1$$

$$2m\,a_{13}^2 + M\,a_{23}^2 = 1$$

$$2m\,a_{13}^2 + M\frac{4m^2}{M^2} a_{13}^2 = \left(2m + \frac{4m^2}{M}\right) a_{13}^2 = 1$$

$$a_{13} = \frac{1}{\sqrt{2m\left(1 + \frac{2m}{M}\right)}} = a_{33}$$

$$a_{23} = \left[-\frac{2\,m}{M}\right] a_{13} = \left[-\frac{2\,m}{M}\right] \frac{1}{\sqrt{2m\left(1 + \frac{2m}{M}\right)}} = \frac{-2}{\sqrt{2M\left(2 + \frac{M}{m}\right)}}$$

Here, the two outer masses oscillate with the same amplitude and phase while the inner one oscillate out of phase and with a different amplitude (Fig.5.5).

OBJECTIVE TYPE QUESTIONS

1. Oscillatory motion occurs when the system is displaced from the position of

(*a*) stable equilibrium (*b*) unstable equilibrium
(*c*) neutral equilibrium (*d*) both (*a*) and (*b*)

2. Egg standing on end is an example of

(*a*) stable equilibrium (*b*) unstable equilibrium
(*c*) neutral equilibrium (*d*) none of these

3. The potential function of a system is given by

$$V = k(x^3 - 2x^2 + x)$$

the position of stable equilibrium is

(*a*) $x = 1$, (*b*) $x = (1/3)$,
(*c*) both (*a*) and (*b*) (*d*) none of these

4. The potential function of a system is given by

$$V = k(x^3 - 2x^2 + x)$$

the frequency of small oscillation about the stable equilibrium point is

(*a*) $\sqrt{\frac{k}{m}}$ (*b*) $\sqrt{\frac{2k}{m}}$

(*c*) $\sqrt{\frac{k}{2m}}$ (*d*) none of these

5. Which one is not correct?

(*a*) Potential function has extremum at equilibrium.
(*b*) Lagrangian in the normal coordinate is sum of Lagrangian for har monic oscillator of frequency ω_k.
(*c*) In oscillations with small amplitudes, only the fundamental frequencies are excited and none of the harmonics.
(*d*) When configuration of a system is expressed in normal coordinates both kinetic and potential energies are not diagonalized.

6. Which one is not correct?

(*a*) Eigen vectors are orthogonal.
(*b*) Harmonics of the fundamental frequencies are absent in oscillations of small amplitude.
(*c*) For conservative systems V is a function of position only and time dependent constraints are to be excluded.
(*d*) Components of eigen vectors are not all real.

7. All the particles of a system in a normal mode

(*a*) vibrate with different frequencies and different phase.
(*b*) vibrate with different frequencies but in same phase.
(*c*) vibrate with same frequency and in same phase.
(*d*) vibrate with same frequency but in different phase.

8. Normal coordinates are coordinate transformation under which

(*a*) only V is diagonalized
(*b*) only T is diagonalized
(*c*) both T and V are diagonalized
(*d*) none of these

9. When configuration of a system is expressed in normal coordinates, then

(*a*) only V is diagonalized
(*b*) only T is diagonalized
(*c*) both T and V are diagonalized
(*d*) T and V are not diagonalized

10. Two pendulum of equal length l and mass m are coupled by a mass less spring of spring constant k. The normal frequencies are

(*a*) $\omega_1 = \sqrt{\frac{g}{l}}$, $\omega_2 = \sqrt{\frac{2k}{m}}$

(*b*) $\omega_1 = \sqrt{\frac{g}{l}}$, $\omega_2 = \sqrt{\frac{g}{l} + \frac{2k}{m}}$

(*c*) $\omega_1 = \sqrt{\frac{g}{l}}$, $\omega_2 = \sqrt{\frac{k}{m}}$

(*d*) $\omega_1 = 0$, $\omega_2 = \sqrt{\frac{g}{l} + \frac{k}{m}}$

11. Three particles of equal mass m move without friction in one dimension. Two of the particles are each connected to the third by a mass less spring of spring constant k. The normal frequencies are

(*a*) $\omega_1 = 0$, $\omega_2 = \sqrt{\frac{k}{m}}$, $\omega_3 = \sqrt{\frac{2k}{m}}$

(*b*) $\omega_1 = 0$, $\omega_2 = \sqrt{\frac{k}{m}}$, $\omega_3 = \sqrt{\frac{k}{2m}}$

(*c*) $\omega_1 = 0$, $\omega_2 = \sqrt{\frac{k}{m}}$, $\omega_3 = \sqrt{\frac{3k}{m}}$

(*d*) $\omega_1 = 0$, $\omega_2 = \sqrt{\frac{2k}{m}}$, $\omega_3 = \sqrt{\frac{2k}{m}}$

12. For a linear triatomic molecule like CO_2 (where C atom of mass M is at the centre and O atom of mass m are at the end of a linear chain and bonds between the atoms are like spring of spring constant k) the frequency $\omega_1 = 0$ corresponds to

(*a*) central atom is at rest while outer atoms vibrate with same amplitude and are exactly out of phase.
(*b*) central atom takes part in oscillation but outer atoms are stationary.
(*c*) uniform translation motion of the molecule.
(*d*) two outer atoms vibrating with same amplitude and phase while the central atom vibrates out of phase with them and has a different amplitude.

13. For a linear triatomic molecule like CO_2 (where C atom of mass M is at the centre and O atom of mass m are at the end of a linear chain and bonds between the atoms are like spring of spring constant k) the frequency $\omega_2 = \sqrt{\frac{k}{m}}$ corresponds to

(*a*) central atom is at rest while outer atoms vibrate with same amplitude and are exactly out of phase.
(*b*) two outer atoms vibrating with same amplitude and phase while the central atom vibrates out of phase with them and has a different amplitude.
(*c*) uniform translation motion of the molecule.
(*d*) two outer atoms vibrating with same amplitude and phase while the central atom vibrates out of phase with them and has a different amplitude.

14. For a linear triatomic molecule like CO_2 (where C atom of mass M is at the centre and O atom of mass m are at the end of a linear chain and bonds between the atoms are like spring of spring constant k) the frequency $\omega_3 = \sqrt{\frac{k}{m}\left(1+\frac{2m}{M}\right)}$ corresponds to

(*a*) central atom is at rest while outer atoms vibrate with same amplitude and are exactly out of phase.
(*b*) two outer atoms vibrating with same amplitude and phase while the central atom vibrates out of phase with them and has a different amplitude.
(*c*) uniform translation motion of the molecule.
(*d*) two outer atoms vibrating with same amplitude and phase while the central atom vibrates out of phase with them and has a different amplitude.

PROBLEMS

1. A particle of mass m is constrained to move on the curve $z = (x^2/a)$ in a plane, where a is a constant. The potential energy is given by

$$V = \frac{mgx^2}{a}$$

Obtain the equilibrium position.

2. Consider a particle of mass m moving in the potential

$$V(x,y) = -\frac{1}{2}kx^2 + \frac{1}{2}Ax^2y^2 + \frac{1}{4}Bx^4$$

at what points (x_0, y_0) is the particle in a stable equilibrium.

3. The kinetic energy of a system is

$$T = \frac{1}{2}m(\dot{x}^2 + \dot{y}^2)$$

and the potential energy V is

$$V = \frac{1}{4}k(3x^2 + 2xy + 3y^2)$$

where k and m are constants. Calculate the frequencies of the normal modes of oscillation of this system.

4. The kinetic energy of a system is

$$T = \frac{1}{2}m(2\dot{x}_1^2 + \dot{x}_2^2)$$

and the potential energy V is

$$V = \frac{1}{4}k\,[(x_1 - l_1)^2 + (x_2 - x_1 - l)^2] - \frac{1}{2}mg(2x_1 + x_2)$$

where k, l, g and m are constants. Calculate the frequencies of the normal modes of oscillation of this system.

5. The kinetic energy of a system is

$$T = \frac{1}{2}m(\dot{x}_1^2 + \dot{x}_2^2)$$

and the potential energy V is

$$V = \frac{1}{2}mw_0^2(x_1^2 + x_2^2) + \frac{1}{2}mw_1^2(x_1 - x_2)^2$$

Obtain the eigen frequencies of the system.

6. A particle of mass m moves under gravity on a smooth surface, the equation of which is

$$z = x^2 + y^2 - x y$$

the z axis being vertical, pointing upward. Determine the frequencies of the normal modes of small oscillation about the position of stable equilibrium.

7. A thin uniform bar of mass m and length $(3\, l\, /\, 2)$ is suspended by a string of length l and negligible mass (Fig.5.6). Obtain the normal frequencies and normal modes for small oscillations in the plane.

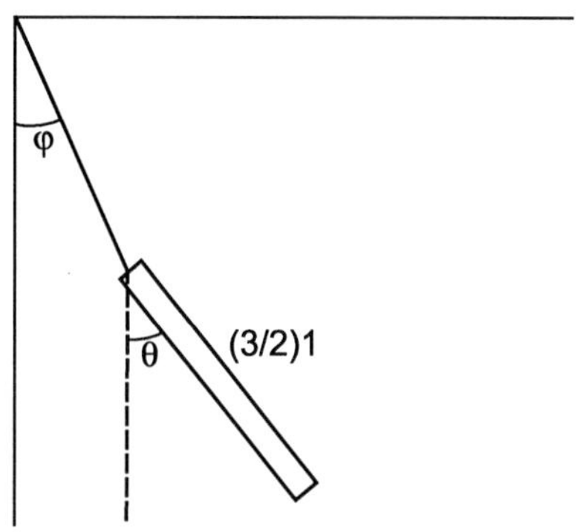

Fig. 5.6

8. A block of mass m is attached to a wedge of mass M by a spring with spring constant k. The wedge is free to oscillate on the horizontal frictionless surface as shown in the Fig. 5.7. Obtain the natural frequencies of the vibration.

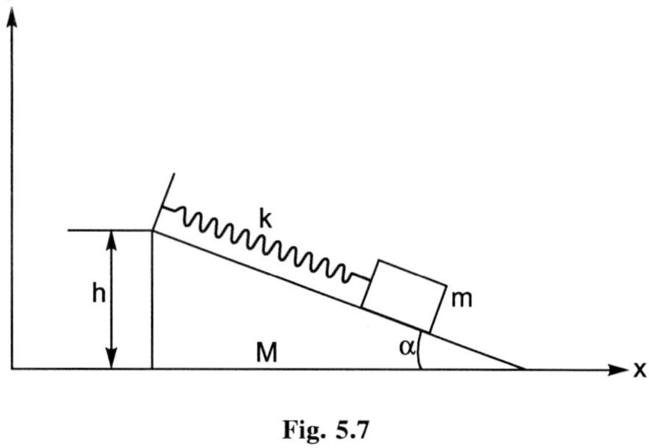

Fig. 5.7

9. One simple pendulum is hung from another, that is string of the lower pendulum is tied to the bob of the upper one. Obtain the frequencies of the system assuming identical pendulums.

10. Three particles of equal mass m move without friction in one dimension. Two of the particles are each connected to the third by a mass-less spring constant k (Fig. 5.8). Find normal modes of oscillations and their corresponding frequencies.

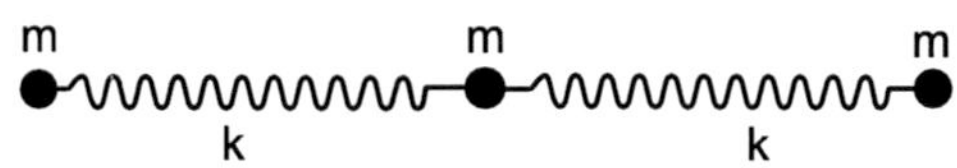

Fig. 5.8

11. The Parallel pendulum: The system consists of two identical pendula each of mass m, length l coupled by a mass-less spring of force constant k (Fig. 5.9). They move in vertical plane. Find the normal mode frequencies for the small oscillations

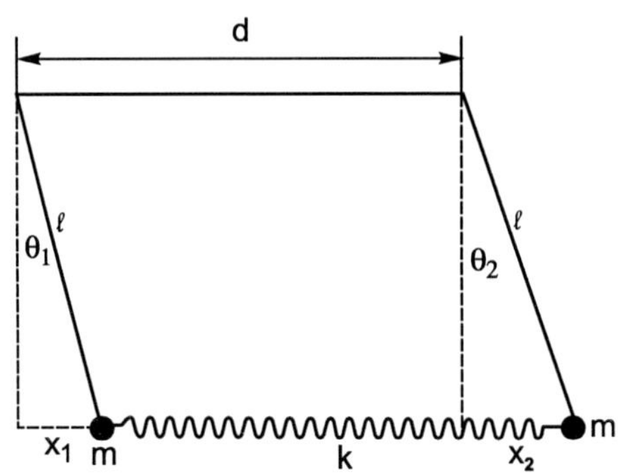

Fig. 5.9

12. Obtain the normal modes of vibration for the double pendulum assuming equal lengths and masses.

❑❑❑

CHAPTER 6

Variational Basis of Mechanics-Hamilton's Principle

6.1 VARIATION TECHNIQUES

Consider a real function $y(x)$ of a real variable x such that a given function $I(y)$ of this function assume an extremum (minimum or maximum). Let

$$I(y) = \int_{x_1}^{x_2} f\{y(x), y'(x); x\}dx \qquad ...(6.1)$$

In Eq. (6.1), $y' = dy/dx$, and the semicolon in f separates the independent variable x from the dependent variable $y(x)$ and its derivative y', x_1 and x_2 are arbitrary but fixed end points. The function $y(x)$ takes the values $y_1 = y(x_1)$ and $y_2 = y(x_2)$ at the end points. $I(y)$ is extremum at these points.

Let $y = y(x)$ is function for which I is minimum. Thus, I is increased when $y(x)$ is replaced by any function of the form

$$y(\alpha, x) = y(0, x) + \alpha\eta(x) \qquad ...(6.2)$$

here a is independent of $x.\eta(x)$ called variation of the function $y(x)$ is a function of x. It has a continuous first derivative and vanishes at x_1 and x_2. The varied function $y(a,x)$ (Fig. 6.1) be identical with $y(x)$ at the end points x_1 and x_2 of the path, that is,

$$\eta(x_1) = \eta(x_2) = 0 \qquad ...(6.3)$$

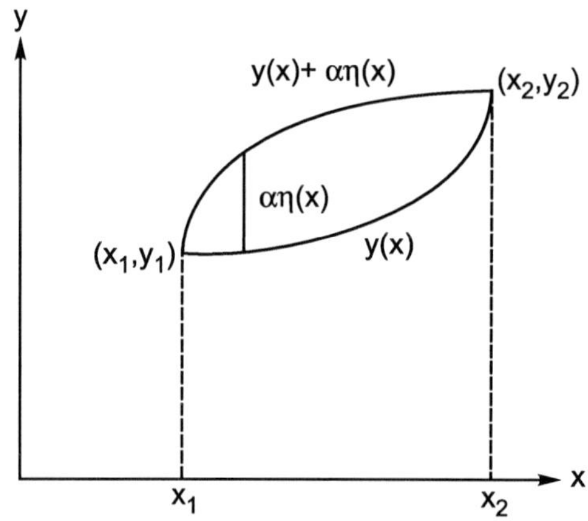

Fig. 6.1

If the function (6.2) are considered, the integral I becomes a function of parameter α . The value of I for the neighbouring curve is

$$I(\alpha)=\int_{x_1}^{x_2} f\{ y(\alpha,x), y'(\alpha,x); x\}dx \qquad ...(6.4)$$

This is an extremum for $\alpha = 0$. The condition that the integral (6.4) have an extremum is that I is independent of α in first order or equivalently

$$\left.\frac{\partial I}{\partial \alpha}\right|_{\alpha=0} = 0$$

for all functions $\eta(x)$.

Consider

$$\delta I = \frac{dI}{d\alpha} d\alpha$$

and

$$\delta I(\alpha) = \delta \int_{x_1}^{x_2} f\{ y(\alpha,x), y'(\alpha,x); x\}dx$$

Since the limits of integration are fixed, the differential operator effects only the integrands hence taking the variation symbol inside the integral (by hypothesis the limit of integration are not affected by the variation)

$$\delta I(\alpha)=\int_{x_1}^{x_2} \delta f\{ y(\alpha,x), y'(\alpha,x); x\}dx$$

$$\delta I(\alpha)=\int_{x_1}^{x_2}\frac{d}{d\alpha}[f\{y(\alpha,x),y'(\alpha,x);x\}dx]\,d\alpha$$

$$\delta I(\alpha)=\int_{x_1}^{x_2}dx\left\{\frac{\partial f}{\partial y}\frac{dy}{d\alpha}+\frac{\partial f}{\partial y'}\frac{dy'}{d\alpha}\right\}d\alpha \qquad ...(6.5)$$

where

$$\frac{dy'}{d\alpha}=\frac{d}{dx}\left(\frac{dy}{d\alpha}\right) \qquad ...(6.6)$$

Eq. (6.5) is

$$\delta I(\alpha)=\int_{x_1}^{x_2}dx\left\{\frac{\partial f}{\partial y}\frac{dy}{d\alpha}+\frac{\partial f}{\partial y'}\frac{d}{dx}\left(\frac{dy}{d\alpha}\right)\right\}d\alpha \qquad ...(6.7)$$

Integrating by parts the second term on the right hand side of the Eq.(6.7)

$$\int_{x_1}^{x_2}\frac{\partial f}{\partial y'}\frac{d}{dx}\left(\frac{dy}{d\alpha}\right)dx=\int_{x_1}^{x_2}\frac{\partial f}{\partial y'}d\left(\frac{dy}{d\alpha}\right)=\frac{\partial f}{\partial y'}\frac{dy}{d\alpha}\Bigg|_{x_1}^{x_2}-\int_{x_1}^{x_2}\frac{dy}{d\alpha}\frac{d}{dx}\left(\frac{\partial f}{\partial y'}\right)dx \qquad ...(6.8)$$

From Eq. (6.2)

$$\frac{dy}{d\alpha}=\eta(x)$$

and $\eta(x)$ vanishes at x_1 and x_2. Therefore, Eq. (6.8) is

$$\int_{x_1}^{x_2}\frac{\partial f}{\partial y'}\frac{d}{dx}\left(\frac{dy}{d\alpha}\right)dx=-\int_{x_1}^{x_2}\frac{dy}{d\alpha}\frac{d}{dx}\left(\frac{\partial f}{\partial y'}\right)dx \qquad ...(6.9)$$

Substituting Eq. (6.9) in (6.7)

$$\delta I=\int_{x_1}^{x_2}dx\left\{\frac{\partial f}{\partial y}-\frac{d}{dx}\left(\frac{\partial f}{\partial y'}\right)\right\}\frac{dy}{d\alpha}d\alpha \qquad ...(6.10)$$

$$\delta I=\int_{x_1}^{x_2}dx\left\{\frac{\partial f}{\partial y}-\frac{d}{dx}\left(\frac{\partial f}{\partial y'}\right)\right\}\eta(x)d\alpha$$

Introducing

$$\delta y = \frac{dy}{d\alpha} d\alpha \qquad ...(6.11)$$

where δy is an infinitesimal variation of the varied path from the correct path *y(x)*. From relations (6.10) and (6.11)

$$\delta I = \int_{x_1}^{x_2} dx \left\{ \frac{\partial f}{\partial y} - \frac{d}{dx}\left(\frac{\partial f}{\partial y'} \right) \right\} \delta y \qquad ...(6.12)$$

$I(\alpha)$ assume an extreme value, that is $\delta I = 0$. This must hold for an arbitrary variation δy, and integrand in Eq. (6.12) must vanish for $\alpha = 0$, that is,

$$\left\{ \frac{\partial f}{\partial y} - \frac{d}{dx}\left(\frac{\partial f}{\partial y'} \right) \right\} = 0 \qquad ...(6.13)$$

This is Euler's differential equation of variational calculus.

Let us now assume that *f* is a function of many independent variables y_k and their derivative, that is,

This is Euler's differential equation of variational calculus.

Let us now assume that *f* is a function of many independent variables y_k and their derivatives y'_k, that is,

$$f = f\{ y_1(x), y'_1(x), y_2(x), y'_2(x), ...; x \}$$

$$f = f\{ y_k(x), y'_k(x); x \} \quad (k = 1,2,....,n) \qquad ...(6.14)$$

The relation (6.2) takes the form

$$y_k(\alpha, x) = y_k(0, x) + \alpha\, \eta_k(x) \qquad ... (6.15)$$

that is,

$$\begin{aligned} y_1(\alpha, x) &= y_1(0, x) + \alpha\, \eta_1(x) \\ y_2(\alpha, x) &= y_2(0, x) + \alpha\, \eta_2(x) \\ &\ldots\ldots\ldots\ldots\ldots\ldots \\ &\ldots\ldots\ldots\ldots\ldots\ldots \\ y_n(\alpha, x) &= y_n(0, x) + \alpha\, \eta_n(x) \end{aligned} \qquad ...(6.16)$$

The Eq. (6.7) takes the form

$$\delta I(\alpha)=\int_{x_1}^{x_2} dx\left\{\frac{\partial f}{\partial y_k}\frac{dy_k}{d\alpha}+\frac{\partial f}{\partial y_k'}\frac{d}{dx}\left(\frac{dy_k}{d\alpha}\right)\right\}d\alpha \qquad ...(6.17)$$

Integrating by parts the second term on the right hand side of the Eq. (6.17)

$$\int_{x_1}^{x_2}\frac{\partial f}{\partial y_k'}\frac{d}{dx}\left(\frac{dy_k}{d\alpha}\right)dx=\left.\frac{\partial f}{\partial y_k'}\frac{dy_k}{d\alpha}\right|_{x_1}^{x_2}-\int_{x_1}^{x_2}\frac{dy_k}{d\alpha}\frac{d}{dx}\left(\frac{\partial f}{\partial y_k'}\right)dx \qquad ...(6.18)$$

The first term on the right hand side of Eq. (6.18) vanishes at the end points. The Eq. (6.17) is then

$$\delta I=\int_{x_1}^{x_2} dx\left\{\frac{\partial f}{\partial y_k}-\frac{d}{dx}\left(\frac{\partial f}{\partial y_k'}\right)\right\}\frac{dy_k}{d\alpha}d\alpha$$

$$\delta I=\int_{x_1}^{x_2} dx\left\{\frac{\partial f}{\partial y_k}-\frac{d}{dx}\left(\frac{\partial f}{\partial y_k'}\right)\right\}\delta y_k \qquad ...(6.19)$$

Since y variables are independent, the variation δy_k are independent, that is, $\eta_k(x)$ are independent of each other. Vanishing of Eq.(6.19) when evaluated at $\alpha=0$ requires the separate vanishing of each expression in the bracket

$$\left\{\frac{\partial f}{\partial y_k}-\frac{d}{dx}\left(\frac{\partial f}{\partial y_k'}\right)\right\}=0 \quad (k=1,2,....,n) \qquad ...(6.20)$$

The Eq. (6.20) is known as Euler-Lagrange equation.

6.2 HAMILTON'S PRINCIPLE

Hamilton's principle in terms of the calculus of variation, can be stated

$$\delta I=\delta\int_{t_1}^{t_2}(T-V)\,dt=0 \qquad ...(6.21)$$

that is, the motion of a dynamical system from one point to another within a specified time interval $t_2 - t_1$ (consistent with any constraint) is such as to extremize the time integral of the difference between the kinetic energy T and the potential energy V. The extremum is usually a minimum.

The kinetic energy is a function of velocities $\dot{q}_k$ and for conservative forces, the potential energy is a function of position q_k and

$$L=T-V=L(q_k,\dot{q}_k) \qquad ...(6.22)$$

in terms of which Hamilton's principle becomes

$$\delta I = \delta \int_{t_1}^{t_2} L(q_k, \dot{q}_k, t)\, dt = 0 \qquad ...(6.23)$$

6.3 LAGRANGE'S EQUATION

The function L appearing in Eq. (6.23) may be identified with the function f of the variation integral

$$\delta \int_{x_1}^{x_2} f\{ y_k(x), y_k'(x); x \}\, dx \qquad ...(6.24)$$

If we make the transformation

$$\begin{aligned} x &\to t \\ y(x) &\to q(t) \\ y'(x) &\to \dot{q}(t) \end{aligned} \qquad ...(6.25)$$

$$f\{ y_k(x), y_k'(x); x \} = L(q_k, \dot{q}_k, t) \qquad ...(6.26)$$

The Euler-Lagrange Eq. (6.22) corresponding to (6.23) are

$$\frac{\partial L}{\partial q_k} - \frac{d}{dt}\frac{\partial L}{\partial \dot{q}_k} = 0 \quad (k = 1, 2, ..., n) \qquad ...(6.27)$$

These are the Lagrange's equation of motion for the system of particles.

6.4 HAMILTON'S EQUATION OF MOTION

The Lagrangian function L from Eq. (3.9) is

$$L = \sum_k \dot{q}_k p_k - H(q_k, p_k, t) \qquad ...(6.28)$$

The Hamiltonian principle (6.23) is modified to

$$\delta I = \delta \int_{t_1}^{t_2} \left(\sum_k \dot{q}_k p_k - H \right) dt = 0 \qquad ...(6.29)$$

Since the end point times are not varied hence are not function of α, therefore the variation symbol can be taken inside the integral

$$\delta I = \int_{t_1}^{t_2} \sum_k \left(\delta \dot{q}_k p_k + \dot{q}_k \delta p_k - \frac{\partial H}{\partial q_k} \delta q_k - \frac{\partial H}{\partial p_k} \delta p_k \right) dt = 0 \qquad ...(6.30)$$

In the Hamiltonian formalism q_k and p_k are treated independent. However, $\dot{q}_k$ are not independent of q_k. Therefore,

$$\int_{t_1}^{t_2} \sum p_k \, \delta \dot{q}_k \, dt = \int_{t_1}^{t_2} \sum p_k \frac{d}{dt}(\delta q_k) dt \qquad ...(6.31)$$

On integration by parts

$$\int_{t_1}^{t_2} \sum p_k \frac{d}{dt}(\delta q_k) dt = \delta q_k \, p_k \Big|_{t_1}^{t_2} - \int_{t_1}^{t_2} \sum \dot{p}_k \, \delta q_k \, dt = -\int_{t_1}^{t_2} \sum \dot{p}_k \, \delta q_k dt \qquad ...(6.32)$$

From relations (6.30) and (6.32)

$$\int_{t_1}^{t_2} \sum \left\{ \left(\dot{q}_k - \frac{\partial H}{\partial p_k} \right) \delta p_k - \left(\dot{p}_k + \frac{\partial H}{\partial q_k} \right) \delta q_k \right\} dt = 0 \qquad ...(6.33)$$

Since δq_k and δp_k represent independent variation, therefore the terms in the parentheses must separately vanish and therefore,

$$\dot{q}_k = \frac{\partial H}{\partial p_k}$$

$$\dot{p}_k = -\frac{\partial H}{\partial q_k} \qquad ...(6.34)$$

6.5 PRINCIPLE OF LEAST ACTION

The development of Hamilton's principle proceeds on the assumption that the variations δq_k of the generalized coordinates of a point ($q_k + \delta q_k$) on the varied path corresponds to a point ($q_k t$) on the actual path. The variation occurs without the passage of time.

Let us consider a more general type of variation in which the varied points occus in general at a different time then the corresponding point on the actual path. With the introduction of variation in time as well as position, a new notation is needed. Suppose a system is described in terms of n generalized coordinates q_k (k = 1,2,…., n). When a point on the varied motion is compared with the corresponding point on the actual path, the difference in the coordinate value may be denoted by Δq_k and the difference in time by Δt .

Consider any conservative holonomic system whose configuration at any instant is specified by n independent coordinates $q_1, q_2, \ldots, q_n$. Suppose A and B are two points over the path C in the configuration space. Let D is another path connecting the points E and F which are infinitesimally close to A and B (Fig. 6.2).

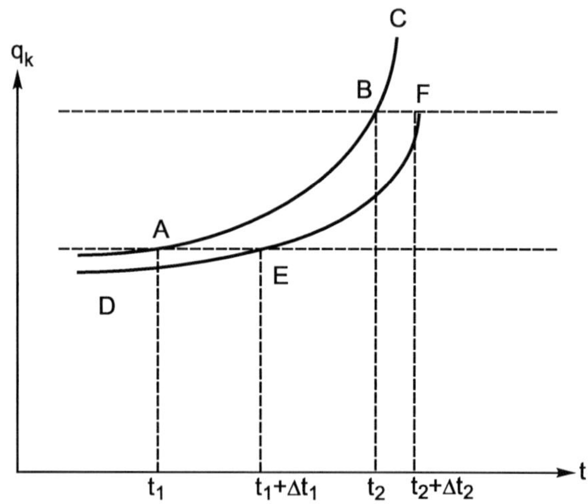

Fig. 6.2

The system starting from point A at time t_1 travelling along path C at variable velocities reaches B at time t_2. The coordinates of the point A and B are q_k and q_k'

$$q_k(t_1) = q_k \qquad\qquad ...(6.35)$$
$$q_k'(t_2) = q_k'$$

The velocity is

$$\dot{q}_k = \frac{d}{dt} q_k(t) \qquad\qquad ...(6.36)$$

The action along the path C is defined as

$$A[C] = \int_{t_1}^{t_2} L(q_k, \dot{q}_k, t)\, dt$$

$$\Delta A[C] = \Delta \int_{t_1}^{t_2} L(q_k, \dot{q}_k, t)\, dt \qquad\qquad ...(6.37)$$

Along the path D

$$A[D] = \int_{t_1+\Delta t_2}^{t_2+\Delta t_2} L(q_k'(t), \dot{q}_k'(t), t)\, dt \qquad\qquad ...(6.38)$$

The time difference Δt_i are small quantities of the first order. The coordinates of points E are given by the function $q_k(t)$

$$q'_k(t)=q_k(t)+\delta q_k(t)$$
$$\dot{q}'_k(t)=\dot{q}_k+\frac{d}{dt}(\delta q_k(t)) \qquad ...(6.39)$$

The first order change in action A in going from C to D is

$$\Delta A=A[D]-A[C]=\int_{t_1+\Delta t_1}^{t_2+\Delta t_2} L\{q'_k(t),\dot{q}'_k(t),t\}dt-\int_{t_1}^{t_2} L\{q_k(t),\dot{q}_k(t),t\}dt \qquad ...(6.40)$$

The right hand side of the Eq. (6.40) is

$$\int_{t_1}^{t_2}[L(q'_k,\dot{q}'_k,t)-L(q_k,\dot{q}_k,t)]dt+\int_{t_2}^{t_2+\Delta t_2} L(q'_k,\dot{q}'_k,t)dt-\int_{t_1}^{t_1+\Delta t_1} L(q'_k,\dot{q}'_k,t)dt \qquad ...(6.41)$$

$$\Delta A=\int_{t_1}^{t_2}[L(q'_k,\dot{q}'_k,t)-L(q_k,\dot{q}_k,t)]dt+[L\Delta t]\Big|_{t_1}^{t_2} \qquad ...(6.42)$$

The first term of the right hand side of the Eq. (6.42) is

$$=\int_{t_1}^{t_2}\sum_k\left[L(q_k,\dot{q}_k(t))+\frac{\partial L}{\partial_k}\delta q_k+\frac{\partial L}{\partial \dot{q}_k}\frac{d}{dt}(\delta q_k)+..-L(q_k,\dot{q}_k,t)\right]dt$$

$$=\int_{t_1}^{t_2}\sum_k\left[\frac{\partial L}{\partial_k}\delta q_k+\frac{\partial L}{\partial \dot{q}_k}\frac{d}{dt}\delta q_k\right]dt \qquad ...(6.43)$$

and

$$\frac{d}{dt}\left(\frac{\partial L}{\partial \dot{q}_k}\delta q_k\right)=\frac{d}{dt}\left(\frac{\partial L}{\partial \dot{q}_k}\right)\delta q_k+\frac{\partial L}{\partial \dot{q}_k}\frac{d}{dt}\delta q_k \qquad ...(6.44)$$

Using relation (6.44) in relation (6.43) we have

$$\int_{t_1}^{t_2}[L(q'_k,\dot{q}'_k,t)-L(q_k,\dot{q}_k,t)]dt=\int_{t_1}^{t_2}dt\sum_k\left[\frac{\partial L}{\partial q_k}-\frac{d}{dt}\frac{\partial L}{\partial \dot{q}_k}\right]\delta q_k+\sum_k\frac{\partial L}{\partial \dot{q}_k}\delta q_k\Big|_{t_1}^{t_2} \qquad ...(6.45)$$

From Eqs. (6.45) and (6.42)

$$\Delta A = \int_{t_1}^{t_2} dt \left[\frac{\partial L}{\partial q_k} - \frac{d}{dt}\frac{\partial L}{\partial \dot{q}_k} \right] \delta q_k + \left[L\,\Delta t + \sum_k \frac{\partial L}{\partial \dot{q}_k} \delta q_k \right] \Bigg|_{t_1}^{t_2} \qquad ...(6.46)$$

The total variance Δq_k in the coordinates q_k at the end points of the path C is the differences in the coordinates $E(F)$ and $A(B)$

$$\Delta q_k(t_i) = q_k'(t_i') - q_k(t_i) = q_k'(t_i + \Delta t_i) - q_k(t_i) \qquad ...(6.47)$$

Using Taylor series , the right hand side of Eq. (6.47) is

$$= q_k'(t_i) + \frac{\partial q_k'}{\partial t_i} \Delta t_i + ... \quad - q_k(t_i)$$

Using Eq. (6.)

$$= q_k(t_i) + \delta q_k(t) + \frac{\partial (q_k + \delta q_k)}{\partial t} \Delta t_i \quad - q_k(t_i)$$

Ignoring the smaller term

$$\frac{\partial (\delta q_k)}{\partial t} \Delta t_i$$

we have

$$\Delta q_k(t_i) = \delta q_k(t) + \frac{\partial q_k}{\partial t} \Delta t_i = \delta q_k(t) + \dot{q}_k\, \Delta t_i \qquad ...(6.48)$$

Putting

$$L = \sum_k p_k \dot{q}_k - H \quad and \quad p_k = \frac{\partial L}{\partial \dot{q}_k} \qquad ...(6.49)$$

in Eq. (6.39)

$$\Delta A = \int_{t_1}^{t_2} dt \left[\frac{\partial L}{\partial q_k} - \frac{d}{dt}\frac{\partial L}{\partial \dot{q}_k} \right] \delta q_k + \left[\sum_k p_k \dot{q}_k \Delta t - H\,\Delta t + \sum_k p_k \delta q_k \right] \Bigg|_{t_1}^{t_2}$$

...(6.50)

Using Eq. (6.48) in Eq. (6.50)

$$\Delta A = \int_{t_1}^{t_2} dt \left[\frac{\partial l}{\partial q_k} - \frac{d}{dt}\frac{\partial L}{\partial \dot{q}_k} \right] \delta q_k + \left[\sum_k p_k \dot{q}_k \Delta t - H\,\Delta t + \sum_k p_k (\Delta q_k - \dot{q}_k \Delta t) \right]_{t_1}^{t_2}$$

$$\Delta A = \int_{t_1}^{t_2} dt \left[\frac{\partial L}{\partial q_k} - \frac{d}{dt}\frac{\partial L}{\partial \dot{q}_k} \right] \delta q_k + \left[\sum_k p_k \Delta q_k - H\,\Delta t \right] \Bigg|_{t_1}^{t_2} \qquad ...(6.51)$$

If the path C is that on which the Lagrangian equation of motion are satisfied then the integral on the right hand side of Eq. (6.51) vanishes and

$$\Delta A[C] = \left[\sum_k p_k \Delta q_k - H\,\Delta t \right]\Bigg|_{t_1}^{t_2} \qquad ...(6.52)$$

The variation ΔA in the action receive contribution only from the end points of path C.

To obtain principle of least action, it is assumed that there are no variation in the position of the system at the initial and final times, then Δq_k vanishes at end points. This implies that the actual and varied motions are between the same initial and final configuration. However, the time at which they are in these states may be varied slightly. Further, the Lagrangian function L should not depend on time explicitly. It is further assumed that varied motion is such that the energy is conserved.

Since H is constant therefore from Eq. (6.52)

$$\Delta A = [0 - H\,\Delta t]\Big|_{t_1}^{t_2} = -H(\Delta t_2 - \Delta t_1) = -\Delta \int_{t_1}^{t_2} H\,dt \qquad ...(6.53)$$

Consider the configuration A and B at times t_1 and t_2 ($t_2 > t_1$), the actual dynamical path C followed by the system is that for which action A is stationary or C is that path about which infinitesimal variation produce no change in A, that is,

$$\Delta A[C] = \Delta \int_{t_1}^{t_2} L(q_k(t), \dot{q}_k(t), t)\,dt = 0 \qquad ...(6.54)$$

From Eqs. (6.52)-(6.54)

$$\Delta \int_{t_1}^{t_2} L(q_k(t), \dot{q}_k(t), t)\,dt = -\Delta \int_{t_1}^{t_2} H\,dt \qquad ...(6.55)$$

$$\Delta \int_{t_1}^{t_2} (L + H)\,dt = \Delta \int_{t_1}^{t_2} p_k \dot{q}_k\,dt = \Delta \int_{t_1}^{t_2} W\,dt = 0 \qquad ...(6.56)$$

The function $W = p_k\,\dot{q}_k$ is called the Hamilton's characteristic function. Eq. (6.56) is known as Maupertuis' principle of least action. For scleronomous system $p_k\,\dot{q}_k = 2T$ and Eq.(6.56) becomes

$$\Delta \int_{t_1}^{t_2} 2T\,dt = 0$$

$$\Delta \int_{t_1}^{t_2} T\,dt = 0 \qquad \text{...(6.57)}$$

If there are no external forces on the system, for example, a rigid body with no net applied force, then T is constant and Eq. (6.57) is then

$$T\,\Delta \int_{t_1}^{t_2} dt = 0$$

$$\Delta(t_2 - t_1) = 0 \qquad \text{...(6.58)}$$

Thus, for all possible paths between two points, consistent with conservation of energy, the system moves along the path for which the time of transit is an extremum. In this form the principle of least action is called Fermat's principle in geometrical optics.

Solved Examples

Example 1. *Show that the curve of minimum length joining a pair of points in the plane is a straight line.*

Solution: An element of arc length ds in a plane is given by

$$ds = \sqrt{(dx)^2 + (dy)^2}$$

Total length of any curve going between point 1 and 2 is

$$I = \int_1^2 ds = \int_{x_1}^{x_2} \sqrt{(dx)^2 + (dy)^2} = \int_{x_1}^{x_2} \sqrt{1 + (dy/dx)^2}\,dx$$

The condition that curve to be the shortest path is that I be a minimum. The function f in this problem is

$$f = \sqrt{1 + (dy/dx)^2} = \sqrt{1 + y'^2}$$

where $y' = dy/dx$. The condition for minimum is given by the Eq. (6.13)

$$\left\{\frac{\partial f}{\partial y} - \frac{d}{dx}\left(\frac{\partial f}{\partial y'}\right)\right\} = 0 \qquad \text{...(6.59)}$$

we have

$$\frac{\partial f}{\partial y} = 0, \quad \frac{\partial f}{\partial y'} = \frac{1}{2}(1 + y'^2)^{-\frac{1}{2}}(2y') = \frac{y'}{\sqrt{1 + y'^2}}$$

The Eq. (6.59) is therefore

$$-\frac{d}{dx}\left(\frac{y'}{\sqrt{1+y'^2}}\right)=0$$

$$\frac{y'}{\sqrt{1+y'^2}}=\text{constant}=\text{c}$$

$$y'^2=c^2(1+y'^2)$$

$$y'=\frac{c}{\sqrt{1-c^2}}=a$$

On integration

$$y=ax+b \qquad ...(6.60)$$

where b is a constant. Eq. (6.60) is an equation of straight line. The constants of integration a and b are determined by the condition that the curve passes through the two end points (x_1,y_1) and (x_2,y_2).

Example 2. *Find the curve which gives minimum surface of revolution about y-axis.*

Solution: Suppose we form a surface of revolution by taking some curve passing between two fixed end points (x_1,y_1) and (x_2,y_2) and revolving it about the y-axis (Fig. 6.3).

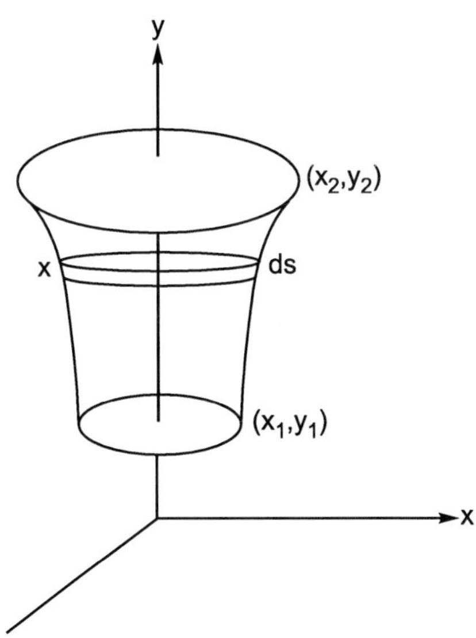

Fig. 6.3

Consider a strip of the surface of length *ds*. The area of the strip of the surface is $2\pi x\, ds$ and

$$ds^2 = dx^2 + dy^2$$

$$ds = dx\sqrt{1+(dy/dx)^2} = dx\sqrt{1+y'^2}$$

where $y' = dy/dx$. Area of strip of surface is

$$2\pi x\, dx\sqrt{1+y'^2}$$

Total area is

$$= 2\pi \int_1^2 x\sqrt{1+y'^2}\, dx$$

The function *f* in this problem is

$$f = x\sqrt{1+y'^2}$$

$$\frac{\partial f}{\partial y} = 0, \quad \frac{\partial f}{\partial y'} = \frac{x}{2}(1+y'^2)^{-\frac{1}{2}}(2y') = \frac{xy'}{\sqrt{1+y'^2}} \qquad ...(6.61)$$

Substituting Eq. (6.61) in the condition for minimum (6.13) we have

$$\frac{d}{dx}\left(\frac{xy'}{\sqrt{1+y'^2}}\right) = 0$$

$$\left(\frac{xy'}{\sqrt{1+y'^2}}\right) = a$$

a is constant of integration clearly smaller than the minimum value of *x*. Squaring the above equation

$$x^2 y'^2 = a^2(1+y'^2)$$

$$y'^2 = \frac{a^2}{x^2 - a^2}$$

$$\frac{dy}{dx} = \frac{a}{\sqrt{x^2 - a^2}}$$

On integration

$$y = a\int \frac{dx}{\sqrt{x^2 - a^2}} + b$$

we know

$$\int \frac{dx}{\sqrt{x^2 - a^2}} = \text{arc}\,cosh\frac{x}{a}$$

Thus,

$$y = a\,\text{arc}\,cosh\frac{x}{a} + b$$

$$x = a\,cosh\frac{y-b}{a}$$

which is the equation of a catenary. The constants a and b are determined by the requirement that curve passes through to two given end points.

Example 3. T*he Brachistochrone between two points: determine the equation of the plane curve down which a particle acted upon by the gravity alone would descend from one fixed point to another in the shortest possible time.*

Solution: Let A be the upper point and B the lower one. Assume the x axis of a Cartesian reference frame to be measured vertically downward, and let A be the origin of the coordinate as shown in the Fig. 6.4

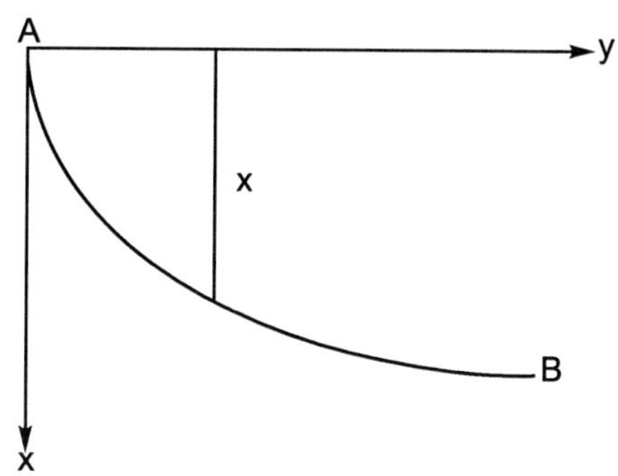

Fig. 6.4

Let s be the length of the required curve at any point measured from A. Let v be the velocity of the particle at the same point and t its time of descent from A to that point. We want to determine the curve that will make T a minimum, where T is the total time of descent from A to B. Thus

ds/dt = v or $dt = ds/$v where

$$ds = \sqrt{dx^2 + dy^2} = \sqrt{1 + y'^2}\,dx \qquad ...(6.62)$$

where $y' = dy/dx$. From conservation of energy

$$mgx = \frac{1}{2}m\text{v}^2$$

$$\mathrm{v} = \frac{ds}{dt} = \sqrt{2gx} \qquad ...(6.63)$$

g is acceleration due to gravity.

From Eqs. (6.62) and (6.63)

$$dt = \frac{ds}{\sqrt{2gx}} = \frac{\sqrt{1+y'^2}}{\sqrt{2gx}}$$

on integration

$$T = \frac{1}{\sqrt{2g}} \int_{x=0}^{x_0} \frac{\sqrt{1+y'^2}}{\sqrt{x}}\, dx$$

The function f in this problem is

$$f = \frac{\sqrt{1+y'^2}}{\sqrt{x}}$$

$$\frac{\partial f}{\partial y} = 0, \frac{\partial f}{\partial y'} = \frac{1}{\sqrt{x}}\left(\frac{1}{2}(1+y'^2)^{-\frac{1}{2}} 2y'\right) = \frac{y'}{\sqrt{x(1+y'^2)}}$$

Substituting for $\partial f/\partial y$ and $\partial f/\partial y'$ in the condition for minimum (6.13) we have

$$\frac{d}{dx}\left(\frac{y'}{\sqrt{x(1+y'^2)}}\right) = 0$$

$$\frac{y'}{\sqrt{x(1+y'^2)}} = c_1 \qquad ...(6.64)$$

where c_1 is an arbitrary constant. For simplicity let $c_1 = 1/\sqrt{a}$. The Eq. (6.64) is then

$$\frac{y'}{\sqrt{x(1+y'^2)}} = \frac{1}{\sqrt{a}}$$

$$y'^2 = \frac{1}{a}(x + xy'^2)$$

$$y'^2\left(\frac{a-x}{a}\right)=\frac{x}{a}$$

$$y'^2=\frac{x}{a-x} \text{ or } y'=\frac{dy}{dx}=\sqrt{\frac{x}{a-x}}$$

On integration

$$y=\int\frac{\sqrt{x}}{\sqrt{a-x}}dx+c_2 \qquad ...(6.65)$$

Let

$$x=a\sin^2\theta, dx=2a\sin\theta\cos\theta\, d\theta \qquad ...(6.66)$$

Substituting Eq. (6.66) in Eq. (6.65)

$$y=\int\frac{2a^{\frac{3}{2}}\sin^2\theta\cos\theta\, d\theta}{\sqrt{a(1-\sin^2\theta)}}+c_2=2a\int\sin^2\theta\, d\theta+c_2$$

$$y=a\int(1-\cos 2\theta)d\theta+c_2=a\left(\theta-\frac{\sin 2\theta}{2}\right)+c_2$$

$$y=a\left(\theta-\frac{2\sin\theta\cos\theta}{2}\right)+c_2=a\left(\theta-\frac{2\sin\theta\sqrt{1-\sin^2\theta}}{2}\right)+c_2$$

$$y=a\left(\sin^{-1}\sqrt{\frac{x}{a}}-\frac{2\sqrt{(x/a)}\sqrt{1-(x/a)}}{2}\right)+c_2$$

$$y=a\sin^{-1}\sqrt{\frac{x}{a}}-\sqrt{ax-x^2}+c_2$$

The arbitrary constant c_2 is zero since we have $x = 0$ at $y = 0$. Hence, the equation of the curve is

$$y=a\sin^{-1}\sqrt{\frac{x}{a}}-\sqrt{ax-x^2}$$

which is the equation of a cycloid, where a is the diameter of the generating circle. A is determined by the condition that cycloid must pass through point (x_0,y_0)

Example 4. *For a linear harmonic oscillator, potential energy is (1/2) k x^2. Using Hamilton principle obtain the equation of motion.*

Solution: The Lagrangian is

$$L = T - V = \frac{1}{2} m \dot{x}^2 - \frac{1}{2} k x^2$$

From Hamilton's principle (Eq. 6.23) we have

$$\delta \int \left(\frac{1}{2} m \dot{x}^2 - \frac{1}{2} k x^2 \right) dt$$

$$f = \frac{1}{2} m \dot{x}^2 - \frac{1}{2} k x^2$$

$$\frac{\partial f}{\partial x} = -k x; \frac{\partial f}{\partial \dot{x}} = m \dot{x}$$

From Eq. (6.13)

$$m \ddot{x} + k x = 0$$

which is equation of motion for simple harmonic oscillator.

Example: 5. *If in the integral*

$$I = \int_{x_1}^{x_2} f(y, y') dx$$

f does not depend explicitly on x, show that

$$y' \frac{\partial f}{\partial y'} - f(y, y') = \text{constant}$$

Solution: The Euler- Lagrange equation (6.13) is

$$\frac{\partial f}{\partial y} = \frac{d}{dx}\left(\frac{\partial f}{\partial y'} \right)$$

Multiplying the above equation by y' and adding the term $y'' \frac{\partial f}{\partial y'}$ on both sides

$$y' \frac{\partial f}{\partial y} + y'' \frac{\partial f}{\partial y'} = y' \frac{d}{dx}\left(\frac{\partial f}{\partial y'} \right) + y'' \frac{\partial f}{\partial y'} = \frac{d}{dx}\left(y' \frac{\partial f}{\partial y'} \right)$$

If f does not depend explicitly on x, then the left hand side is $\dfrac{d f(y, y')}{dx}$.

Thus

$$\frac{d f(y,y')}{dx}=\frac{d}{dx}\left(y'\frac{\partial f}{\partial y'}\right)$$

Example 6. *Obtain Newton's second law from Hamilton's principle.*

Solution: Consider a particle of mass m moving with a velocity $\dot{\mathbf{r}}$ under the action of force **F.** The kinetic energy T is

$$T=\frac{1}{2}m\dot{\mathbf{r}}^2$$

variation of work done

$$\delta W=\mathbf{F}\cdot\delta\mathbf{r}=-\delta V$$

From Hamilton's principle (6.23)

$$\delta\int L\,dt=\delta\int(T-V)\,dt=\int\delta T\,dt-\int\delta V\,dt$$

$$=\int_{t_1}^{t_2}\delta\left(\frac{1}{2}m\dot{\mathbf{r}}^2\right)dt+\int_{t_1}^{t_2}(\mathbf{F}\cdot\delta\mathbf{r})\,dt$$

$$=\int_{t_1}^{t_2}(m\dot{\mathbf{r}}\,\delta\dot{\mathbf{r}})\,dt+\int_{t_1}^{t_2}(\mathbf{F}\cdot\delta\mathbf{r})\,dt$$

$$=\int_{t_1}^{t_2}m\dot{\mathbf{r}}\,\delta\left(\frac{d\mathbf{r}}{dt}\right)dt+\int_{t_1}^{t_2}(\mathbf{F}\cdot\delta\mathbf{r})\,dt$$

$$=\int_{t_1}^{t_2}m\dot{\mathbf{r}}\frac{d}{dt}(\delta\mathbf{r})\,dt+\int_{t_1}^{t_2}(\mathbf{F}\cdot\delta\mathbf{r})\,dt$$

Integrating by parts

$$=m\dot{\mathbf{r}}\,\delta\mathbf{r}\Big|_{t_1}^{t_2}-\int_{t_1}^{t_2}\delta\mathbf{r}\,m\ddot{\mathbf{r}}\,dt+\int_{t_1}^{t_2}(\mathbf{F}\cdot\delta\mathbf{r})\,dt$$

$$0=\int_{t_1}^{t_2}(\mathbf{F}-m\ddot{\mathbf{r}})\cdot\delta\mathbf{r}\,dt$$

The above equation is true for every virtual displacement $\delta\mathbf{r}$. Hence, integrand must vanish, that is,

$$\mathbf{F}=m\ddot{\mathbf{r}}$$

OBJECTIVE TYPE QUESTIONS

1. The shortest distance between two points in a plane is

(*a*) a straight line (*b*) cycloid
(*c*) parabola (*d*) geodesic

2. A line which represents the shortest path between any two points, when the path is restricted to be on the surface is

(*a*) a straight line (*b*) geodesic
(*c*) cycloid (*d*) none of these

3. The path followed by a particle in sliding from one point to another in the absence of friction in the shortest time is

(*a*) sphere (*b*) cycloid
(*c*) catenary (*d*) straight line

4. The shortest distance between two points on the surface of the sphere is

(*a*) a straight line (*b*) sphere
(*c*) catenary (*d*) geodesic

5. Equation of line which yields the shortest distance between the points $(x_1, y_1) = (0,0)$ and $(x_2, y_2) = (1,0)$ is

(*a*) x-axis (*b*) y-axis
(*c*) $x = y + c$ (*d*) $y = x$

6. The necessary condition that I have an extreme value is $[y' = (dy/dx)]$

(*a*) $\frac{d}{dx}\left(\frac{\partial f}{\partial y'}\right) + \frac{\partial f}{\partial y} = 0$ (*b*) $\frac{d}{dx}\left(\frac{\partial f}{\partial y}\right) - \frac{\partial f}{\partial y'} = 0$

(*c*) $\frac{d}{dx}\left(\frac{\partial f}{\partial y'}\right) - \frac{\partial f}{\partial y} = 0$ (*d*) $\frac{d}{dx}\left(\frac{\partial f}{\partial y}\right) + \frac{\partial f}{\partial y'} = 0$

7. Modified Hamilton's principle is

(*a*) $\delta \int L\, dt = 0$ (*b*) $\delta \int \left(\sum_k p_k \dot{q}_k - H \right) dt = 0$

(*c*) $\delta \int \left(\sum_k p_k \dot{q}_k + L \right) dt = 0$ (*d*) $\delta \int \left(\sum_k \dot{p}_k q_k - L \right) dt = 0$

8. In Hamilton's principle expression, L has dimension of

(*a*) energy (*b*) action
(*c*) angular momentum (*d*) none of these

9. I has the dimension of

(*a*) energy (*b*) action
(*c*) angular momentum (*d*) none of these

10. The shortest line between any two points on a cylinder is

(*a*) a straight line (*b*) catenary
(*c*) cycloid (*d*) helix

PROBLEMS

1. Find the curve which gives minimum surface of revolution about x axis.

2. Show that Δ-variation applied to any function

$$f(q,\dot{q},t) \text{ gives } \Delta f = \delta f + \dot{f}\,\Delta t$$

3. Consider the path of a particle of unit mass in a uniform gravitational field. Its displacement is given by $x = ut + gt^2/2$ and Lagrangian is $(\dot{x}^2/2) + gx$. Show that the action is smallest for the actual path x.

4. Show that the shortest distance between two points in space is a straight line passing through them.

5. Show that the geodesic (shortest distance between two points on a surface) of a sphere is a great circle.

6. If $L' = L + \dfrac{df(q,t)}{dt}$ show that $\delta \int_{t_1}^{t_2} L'\,dt = \delta \int_{t_1}^{t_2} L\,dt.$

7. A particle moves along a curve from one point to another point. If the rate of motion is $v = x$, find the curve, so that time spent is minimum.

8. A particle of mass m falls a given distance z_0 in time $t_0 = \sqrt{(2z_0/g)}$ and the distance travelled in time t is given by $z = \alpha t + \beta t^2$, where α and

β are such that time t_o is always the same. Find the condition under which $\int_0^{t_0} L\,dt$ is an extremum.

9. Show that the shortest line between any two points on a cylinder is a helix.

10. For a pendulum bob suspended from a spring (Fig. 2.7), find the equation of motion by a direct application of Hamilton's principle.

11. Obtain Hamilton's principle from D'Alembert principle.

❑❑❑

CHAPTER 7

Motion in Non-Inertial Frame

7.1 ROTATING COORDINATE SYSTEM

Consider a point P in space as shown in Fig. 7.1. The point is located by vector r and r' with respect to two origin of coordinates O and O'. The point O' is at $\boldsymbol{R}$ relative to O. The vectors $\mathbf{r}, \mathbf{r}'$ and R are related by

$$\mathbf{r} = \mathbf{R} + \mathbf{r}' \qquad ...(7.\ 1)$$

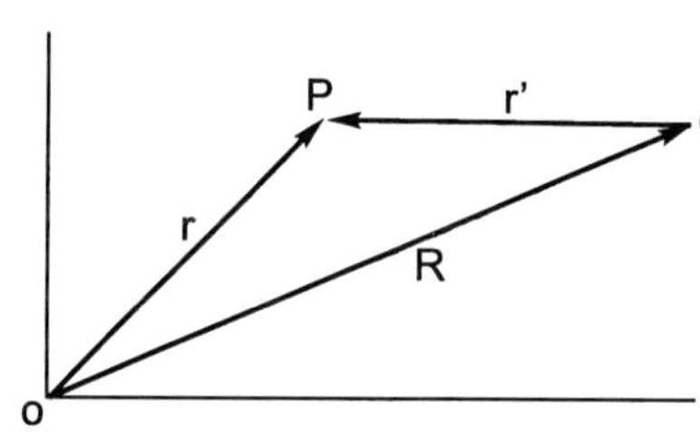

Fig. 7.1 Change of origin of coordinates.

If the origin O' is moving with respect to O which we regard as fixed, the relationship between the velocities is obtained by differentiating Eq. (7.1)

$$\frac{d\mathbf{r}}{dt} = \frac{d\mathbf{R}}{dt} + \frac{d\mathbf{r}'}{dt} \qquad ...(7.2)$$

$$\mathbf{v} = \mathbf{V} + \mathbf{v}'$$

where $\mathbf{v}$ and $\mathbf{v}'$ are the velocities of the point P relative to O and O' respectively, and $\mathbf{V}$ is the velocity of O' relative to O.

Consider coordinate systems $S(x,y,z)$ and $S'(x',y',z')$ whose axes are related relative to one another as shown in Fig. 7.2 . We assume that their origin O and O' coincide. The unit vector associated with the S coordinate system are **i, j** and **k** and **i′**, **j′**,**k′** are the unit vectors associated with the coordinate system S'. The position vector r of point P in coordinate system S' is

$$\mathbf{r} = x\mathbf{i} + y\mathbf{j} + z\mathbf{k} \qquad ...(7.3)$$

and in coordinate system S' is

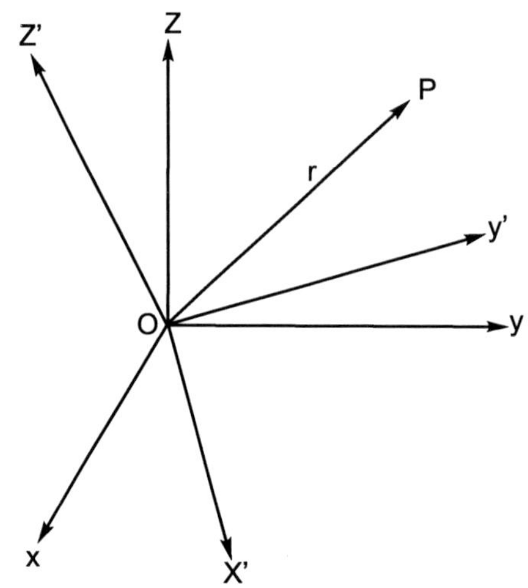

Fig. 7.2 Rotation of coordinate axes.

$$\mathbf{r} = x'\mathbf{i}' + y'\mathbf{j}' + z'\mathbf{k}' \qquad ...(7.4)$$

There is no special property of the position vector **r**, it can as well apply for some general vector **B**. The vector **B** in coordinate systems S and S' is

$$\mathbf{B} = B_x\mathbf{i} + B_y\mathbf{j} + B_z\mathbf{k} \qquad ...(7.5)$$

$$\mathbf{B} = B'_x\mathbf{i}' + B'_y\mathbf{j}' + B'_z\mathbf{k}' \qquad ...(7.6)$$

Let S be a fixed frame of reference. As S' rotates unit vectors **i′**, **j′** and **k′** are function of time. Taking time derivative of Eqs. (7.5) and (7.6)

$$\frac{d\mathbf{B}}{dt} = \frac{dB_x}{dt}\mathbf{i} + \frac{dB_y}{dt}\mathbf{j} + \frac{dB_z}{dt}\mathbf{k} \qquad ...(7.7)$$

$$\frac{d'\mathbf{B}}{dt} = \frac{d'B'_x}{dt}\mathbf{i}' + \frac{d'B'_y}{dt}\mathbf{j}' + \frac{d'B'_z}{dt}\mathbf{k}' \qquad ...(7.8)$$

If vector **B** is at rest in the primed coordinate system then its primed derivative is zero.

Let the unit vectors $\mathbf{i}'$, $\mathbf{j}'$ and $\mathbf{k}'$are rotating relative to **i, j** and **k** with angular velocity ω, therefore the time derivative in primed components can be written by taking unprimed derivative of Eq. (7.6)

$$\frac{d\mathbf{B}}{dt} = \frac{d'B_x'}{dt}\mathbf{i}' + \frac{d'B_y'}{dt}\mathbf{j}' + \frac{d'B_z'}{dt}\mathbf{k}' + B_x'\frac{d\mathbf{i}'}{dt} + B_y'\frac{d\mathbf{j}'}{dt} + B_z'\frac{d\mathbf{k}'}{dt} \qquad ...(7.9)$$

Consider the vector **B** with its tail at O and let it rotate about OC with angular velocity ω as shown in Fig. 7.3. The position of vector **B** at time t and $(t + \Delta t)$ is shown in the Fig. 7.3. The magnitude of **B** and **B** $(t + \Delta t)$ is same but

$$\mathbf{B}(t + \Delta t) = \mathbf{B}(t) + \Delta\mathbf{B}(t)$$

From the Fig. (7.3)

$$CE = B \sin\theta \qquad ...(7.10)$$

$$\Delta B = CE \sin\omega\Delta t \qquad ...(7.11)$$

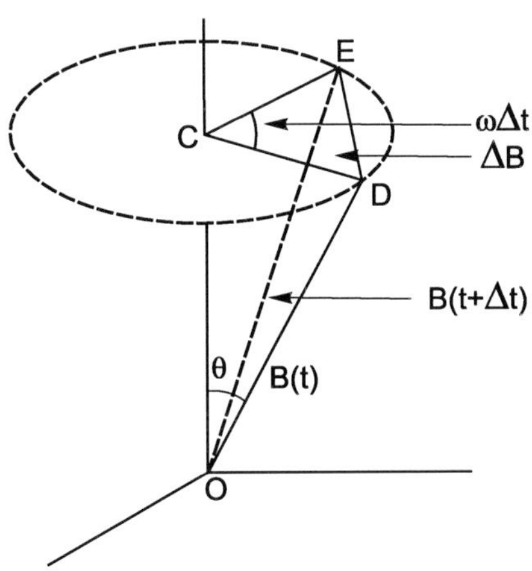

Fig. 7.3 Time derivative of a rotating vector

as $\Delta t \rightarrow 0, \sin\omega\Delta t \rightarrow \omega\Delta t$. Therefore Eq. (7.11) is

$$\Delta B = CE \sin\omega\,\Delta t \qquad ...(7.12)$$

From Eqs. (7.10) and (7.12)

$$\Delta B = B \sin\theta\ \omega\,\Delta t = \omega \times \boldsymbol{B}\,\Delta t \qquad ...(7.13)$$

Now

$$\frac{d\mathbf{B}}{dt} = \lim \Delta t \to 0 \frac{\mathbf{B}(t+\Delta t) - \mathbf{B}(t)}{\Delta t} = \frac{\mathbf{B}(t) + \Delta \mathbf{B}(t) - \mathbf{B}(t)}{\Delta t} = \omega \times \mathbf{B} \qquad ...(7.14)$$

From Eqs. (7.8),(7.9) an (7.14)

$$\frac{d\mathbf{B}}{dt} = \frac{d'\mathbf{B}}{dt} + B'_x(\omega \times \mathbf{i}') + B'_y(\omega \times \mathbf{j}') + B'_z(\omega \times \mathbf{k}')$$

$$\frac{d\mathbf{B}}{dt} = \frac{d'\mathbf{B}}{dt} + \omega \times (B'_x\,\mathbf{i}' + B'_y\,\mathbf{j}' + B'_z\,\mathbf{k}')$$

$$\frac{d\mathbf{B}}{dt} = \frac{d'\mathbf{B}}{dt} + \omega \times \mathbf{B} \qquad ...(7.15)$$

Thus, the time derivative of any vector in the unprimed coordinate system is its derivative in the primed system plus the unprimed derivative it would have it were at rest in the primed system. If the vector **B** is position vector **r**, the Eq. (7.15) is

$$\frac{d\mathbf{r}}{dt} = \frac{d'\mathbf{r}}{dt} + \omega \times \mathbf{r} \qquad ...(7.16)$$

For the case when origin of S and S' do not coincide, Eq. (7.2) with the use of Eq. (7.16) is

$$\frac{d\mathbf{r}}{dt} = \frac{d\mathbf{R}}{dt} + \frac{d'\mathbf{r}'}{dt} + \omega \times \mathbf{r}' \qquad ...(7.17)$$

$$\mathbf{v} = \mathbf{V} + \mathbf{v}' + \omega \times \mathbf{r}' \qquad ...(7.18)$$

where **v** is velocity relative to the fixed axes, **V** is linear velocity of the moving origin, **v′** is velocity relative to rotating axes, $\omega \times \mathbf{r}$ is velocity due to rotation of the moving axes.

Time derivative of Eq. (7.15)

$$\frac{d^2\mathbf{B}}{dt^2} = \frac{d}{dt}\left(\frac{d\mathbf{B}}{dt}\right) = \frac{d}{dt}\left(\frac{d'\mathbf{B}}{dt} + \omega \times \mathbf{B}\right) \qquad ...(7.19)$$

From Eq. (7.15)

$$\frac{d}{dt} = \frac{d'}{dt} + \omega \times \qquad ...(7.20)$$

Substituting Eq. (7.20) in Eq. (7.19)

$$\frac{d^2\mathbf{B}}{dt^2} = \left(\frac{d'}{dt} + \omega\times\right)\left(\frac{d'\mathbf{B}}{dt} + \omega\times\mathbf{B}\right) \qquad ...(7.21)$$

$$\frac{d^2\mathbf{B}}{dt^2} = \frac{d'^2\mathbf{B}}{dt^2} + 2\omega\times\frac{d'\mathbf{B}}{dt} + \omega\times(\omega\times\mathbf{B}) + \frac{d\omega}{dt}\times\mathbf{B} \qquad ...(7.22)$$

as from Eq. (7.16)

$$\frac{d\omega}{dt} = \frac{d'\omega}{dt}$$

7.2 CORIOLIS FORCE

If vector **B** is a position vector , then Eq. (7.22) is

$$\frac{d^2\mathbf{r}}{dt^2} = \frac{d'^2\mathbf{r}}{dt^2} + 2\omega\times\frac{d'\mathbf{r}}{dt} + \omega\times(\omega\times\mathbf{r}) + \frac{d\omega}{dt}\times\mathbf{r} \qquad ...(7.23)$$

Eq. (7.23) is called Coriolis theorem. In the expression (7.23)

$\frac{d'^2 r}{dt^2}$ is acceleration relative to the primed system

$2\omega\times\frac{d'\mathbf{r}}{dt}$ is Coriolis acceleration and is present when the point **r** is moving in the primed system

$\omega\times(\omega\times\mathbf{r})$ is centripetal acceleration

$\frac{d\omega}{dt}\times\mathbf{r}$ is present when angular velocity is not constant and vanishes for a constant angular velocity about a fixed axis.

We can treat coordinate systems in simultaneous translation and rotation relative to each other by using Eq. (7.1) to represent relation between the coordinate vector **r** and **r′** relative to origin O and O' not necessarily coincident. The position and velocity are given by Eqs. (7.1) and (7.17), respectively. The acceleration is then

$$\frac{d^2\mathbf{r}}{dt^2} = \frac{d^2\mathbf{R}}{dt^2} + \frac{d}{dt}\left(\frac{d'\mathbf{r}'}{dt} + \omega\times\mathbf{r}'\right)$$

Using Eq. (7.20)

$$\frac{d^2\mathbf{r}}{dt^2} = \frac{d^2\mathbf{R}}{dt^2} + \left(\frac{d'}{dt} + \omega\times\right)\left(\frac{d'\mathbf{r}'}{dt} + \omega\times\mathbf{r}'\right)$$

$$\frac{d^2\mathbf{r}}{dt^2} = \frac{d^2\mathbf{R}}{dt^2} + \frac{d'^2\mathbf{r}'}{dt^2} + 2\omega\times\frac{d'\mathbf{r}'}{dt} + \frac{d'\omega}{dt}\times\mathbf{r}' + \omega\times(\omega\times\mathbf{r})$$

where $\ddot{\mathbf{R}}$ is the acceleration of the origin of moving coordinate system relative to the fixed system. If the origin O' of the rotating coordinate system do not have significant acceleration with respect to O of the fixed coordinate system, then $\ddot{\mathbf{R}} = 0$

Suppose that Newton's law of motion $\mathbf{F} = m\mathbf{a}$ holds in the unprimed coordinate system, then from Eq. (7.23)

$$\mathbf{F} = m\mathbf{a} = m\frac{d^2\mathbf{r}}{dt^2} = m\frac{d'^2\mathbf{r}}{dt^2} + 2m\omega\times\frac{d'\mathbf{r}}{dt} + m\omega\times(\omega\times\mathbf{r}) + m\frac{d\omega}{dt}\times\mathbf{r}$$

$$m\frac{d'^2\mathbf{r}}{dt^2} = \mathbf{F} - 2m\omega\times\frac{d'\mathbf{r}}{dt} - m\omega\times(\omega\times\mathbf{r}) - m\frac{d\omega}{dt}\times\mathbf{r} \quad ...(7.24)$$

The first term on the right hand side of the Eq. (7.24) is the force as given by Newton's second law in an inertial frame. The second term is called Coriolis force. This term arises from the motion of the particle since the force is proportional to **v** and hence vanishes if there is no motion. The third term is centrifugal term and if ω is normal to radius its value is $-m\omega^2 r$ .The minus sign indicates that the centrifugal force is directed outwards from the centre of rotation. The last term appears only for the case where ω is not constant.

The centrifugal and Coriolis forces are not forces in the usual sense. They are not present if we refer to fixed coordinate system in space. Rotating coordinate system can be treated as fixed by introducing the centrifugal and Coriolis forces. For a particle moving in a circle, has no centrifugal force acting on it but only a force towards the centre which produces its centripetal acceleration. An observer moving with the rotating particle, however measures this central force and observes that the particle does not fall toward the force centre. In order to explain this the observer must assume an additional force, the centrifugal force. The same applies for the Coriolis force.

7.3 MOTION RELATIVE TO EARTH

The earth rotates counter clockwise about the north pole with an angular velocity

$$\omega = \frac{2\pi}{24\times 60\times 60}\sec^{-1} = 7.29\times 10^{-5}\sec^{-1}$$

the radius **r** of the earth is

$$\mathbf{r} = 6.37\times 10^6\, m$$

The centripetal acceleration

$$|\omega\times(\omega\times\mathbf{r})| \approx \omega^2 \mathrm{r} = (7.29\times10^{-5}\,\mathrm{sec}^{-1})^2 \times 6.37\times10^6 m = 3.38\,cm\,\mathrm{sec.}^{-2}$$

Suppose the earth is not rotating then acceleration due to gravity at point A (Fig. 7.4) is denoted by g_0. The acceleration measured by an observer rotating with the earth is from Eq. (7.23) is (assuming that the angular velocity of earth is uniform)

$$\frac{d'^2\mathbf{r}}{dt^2} = \frac{d^2\mathbf{r}}{dt^2} - 2\omega\times\frac{d'\mathbf{r}}{dt} - \omega\times(\omega\times\mathbf{r})$$

$$a = g_0 - 2\omega\times\frac{d'\mathbf{r}}{dt} - \omega\times(\omega\times\mathbf{r}) \qquad ...(7.25)$$

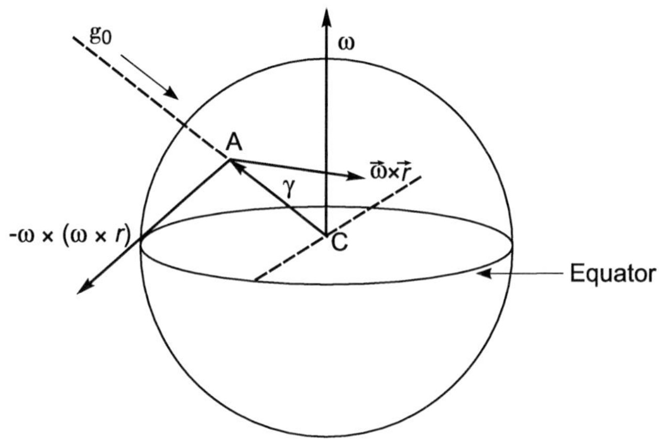

Fig. 7.4 Acceleration of gravity on the rotating earth

where a is $\frac{d^2\mathbf{r}}{dt^2}$

For a body which is stationary or moving very slowly relative to the earth surface, the Coriolis term

$$2\omega\times\frac{d'\mathbf{r}}{dt} \approx 0$$

The acceleration measured in this case is called effective acceleration of gravity $\boldsymbol{g}$

$$g = g_0 - \omega\times(\omega\times\mathbf{r}) \qquad ...(7.26)$$

Suppose that the earth is spherical and there are no local anomalies. The direction of g_0 is then toward the centre of earth. The second term of Eq. (7.26) points in the outward direction. The second term decreases from equator to the poles as the earth is not spherical, its radius is maximum at equator and least at the poles. The g is the sum of the gravitational acceleration directed towards the centre of the earth and centrifugal acceleration directed away from it. The direction of g is called the vertical and it deviates slightly from the radial direction. The vertical is determined by a plumb line.

The effect of centrifugal acceleration on a freely falling body is to displace the body slightly from the radial direction towards south in the Northern hemisphere and towards the north in Southern hemisphere.

The Coriolis term has no effect if the velocity of body relative to the earth is zero or negligibly small. The Coriolis force on a moving particle is perpendicular to both ω and $\mathbf{v}'$. For a falling body the velocity v' points vertically downward, therefore, $\omega \times \mathbf{v}'$ points towards the west. The Coriolis term $-2\ \omega \times \mathbf{v}'$ is pointing east and the falling body deviates in the eastern direction. In the Southern hemisphere the deviation is in the western direction

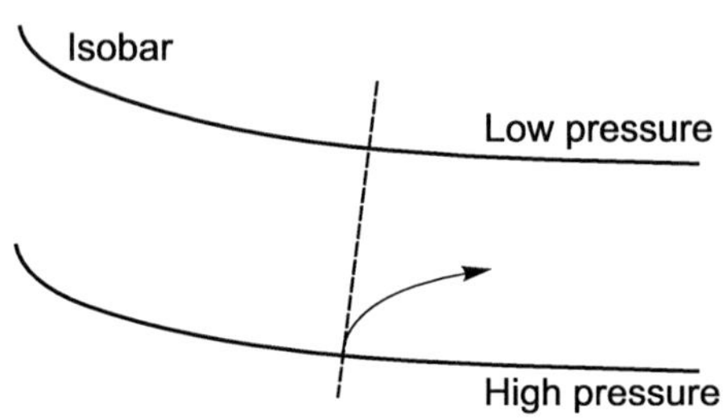

Fig. 7.5 Deflection of wind from the direction of the pressure gradient by the Coriolis force in the Northern Hemisphere.

Masses of air tend to move from high pressure regions into low pressure region. In the vertical direction the pressure gradient is roughly balanced by gravitational forces. Therefore, in the horizontal plane there are persistent long range motion of air masses which we perceive as winds. The wind is expected to flow normal to lines of equal pressure called isobars from high pressure to low pressure. However, the Coriolis force deviates the air molecules to the right of their path in the Northern hemisphere (Fig. 7.4). The deflection to the right continues until the wind vector is parallel to the isobar and the Coriolis force is in opposite direction to the pressure gradient force. The wind then continues parallel to the isobar and circulates counterclockwise in the northern hemisphere. In the southern hemisphere the motion is in clockwise direction.

In the northern hemisphere ω has a component ω_z directed outward along the local vertical. If particle is projected in a horizontal plane (in the local coordinate system at the surface of the earth) with a velocity $\mathbf{v}'$ then the Coriolis force $-2m\omega \times \mathbf{v}'$ will have a component in the plane of magnitude $-2m\omega_z v_z'$ which will be directed towards the right of the particle's motion and a deflection from the original direction of motion result. Since the magnitude of the horizontal component of the Coriolis force is proportional to the vertical component of ω, the position of the Coriolis force which is effective in producing deflection depends upon the latitude being a maximum at the north pole and zero at the equator. In the Southern hemisphere, the component ω_z is directed inward along the local vertical and hence all deflections are in the opposite sense from those in Northern hemisphere.

Solved Examples

Example 1. *Deviation from Vertical of free falling body due to Coriolis acceleration.*

Solution: The velocity $\mathbf{v}'$ of a falling body makes an angle θ with ω. Thus, the magnitude of the Coriolis acceleration is

$$-2\omega \times \mathbf{v}' = -2\omega\, v' \sin\theta \qquad ...(7.27)$$

Let the direction of the vertical is z axis and $v' = v_z$. Coriolis acceleration is

$$-2\omega\, v_z \sin\theta$$

This term gives the acceleration d^2x/dt^2 of the falling body when eastern direction is taken as x axis.

$$\frac{d^2x}{dt^2} = -2\omega\, v_z \sin\theta \qquad ...(7.28)$$

Since the particle velocity is almost vertical, w lies in the north south vertical plane, the deflection force $2m\,\mathbf{v}' \times \omega$ is in the east west direction.

$$m\frac{d^2x}{dt^2} = -2m\omega\, v_z \sin\theta \qquad ...(7.29)$$

As Coriolis forces are small, we can compute $\mathbf{v}_z$ as

$$v_z = g\,t \qquad ...(7.30)$$

$$\frac{dz}{dt} = g\,t$$

On integration

$$z = \frac{1}{2} g\,t^2$$

$$t = \sqrt{\frac{2z}{g}} \qquad ...(7.31)$$

Substituting Eq. (7.30) in (7.29)

$$\frac{d^2x}{dt^2} = -2\,\omega\, g\, t \sin\theta \qquad ...(7.32)$$

On integration of Eq. (7.32)

$$\frac{dx}{dt} = -\,\omega\, g\, t^2 \sin\theta + A \qquad ...(7.33)$$

$dx/dt = 0$ at $t = 0$, hence $A = 0$. Eq. (7.33) is therefore

$$\frac{dx}{dt} = -\,\omega\, g\, t^2 \sin\theta \qquad ...(7.34)$$

On integration of Eq. (7.34)

$$x = -\omega\, g \sin\theta \frac{t^3}{3} + B \qquad ...(7.35)$$

$x = 0$ at $t = 0$. Therefore, $B = 0$ and Eq. (7.35) is

$$x = -\omega g \sin\theta \frac{t^3}{3} \qquad ...(7.36)$$

Substituting the value of t from Eq. (7.31) in Eq. (7.36)

$$x = -\frac{1}{3}\omega\, g \left(\frac{2z}{g}\right)^{\frac{3}{2}} \sin\theta \;=\; -\frac{1}{3}\omega \left(\frac{(2z)^3}{g}\right)^{\frac{1}{2}} \sin\theta \qquad ...(7.37)$$

If θ is measured from equator, that is, it is latitude then replacing θ by $(\pi/2)-\theta$ in Eq.(7.37)

$$x \;=\; -\frac{1}{3}\omega \left(\frac{(2z)^3}{g}\right)^{\frac{1}{2}} \cos\theta \qquad ...(7.38)$$

Example 2. *A merry-go-round starts from rest and accelerates with constant* $\omega = 0.02$ *rev./sec. A person sitting 6m from the axis of revolution holds a 2 Kg ball. Obtain the force, the person must exert to hold the ball 5 seconds after the merry-go-round begin, to rotate.*

Solution: In the rotating frame attached to merry-go-round, the equation of motion is given by Eq. (7.24) with $\mathbf{F} = m(d^2\theta/dt^2)$. As angular velocity is perpendicular to radius vector, the centrifugal term is $-\omega^2 r$. Since the ball is held stationary relative to merry-go-round, we have $\mathbf{a}' = 0$ and $\mathbf{v}' = 0$. The Eq. (7.24) is thus

$$\mathbf{F} = \;-\; m\omega^2 \mathrm{r} - \; m\frac{d\omega}{dt} \times \mathbf{r} \qquad ...(7.39)$$

For rotating frame of reference, take z axis along the axis of rotation and the x axis from the centre to the person. Then

$$\dot{\omega} = \dot{\omega}\,\mathbf{k},\ \ \mathbf{r} = \mathrm{r}\,\mathbf{i}$$

The force acting on the ball is the sum of gravity of the earth and the force **f** exerted by the person:

$$\mathbf{F} = \mathbf{f} - mg\,\mathbf{k}$$

$$\mathbf{f} = -\,m\omega^2 r\mathbf{i} + m\omega\,\mathrm{r}(\mathbf{k}\times\mathbf{i}) + mg\,\mathbf{k}$$

$$\mathbf{f} = -\,m\omega^2 r\mathbf{i} + m\omega\,\mathrm{r}\,\mathbf{j} + mg\,\mathbf{k}$$

with

$$\omega = 0.02\times 2\pi\ rad/s^2\ ,\ \dot{\omega} = 5\omega = 5\times 0.02 = 0.1,\ \mathrm{r}=6\,\mathrm{m},\ m=2\,\mathrm{Kg}$$

$$f = -\,4.74\mathbf{i} + 1.51\mathbf{j} + 19.6\mathbf{k}\ N$$

magnitude = 20.2 N

Example 3. *A Cartesian coordinate system S (x, y, z) is rotating relative to an inertial frame with constant angular velocity ω about the z axis. The origins of S and inertial frame of reference coincide. A particle of mass m moves in S frame of reference under a force whose potential is V(x, y, z). Obtain the Lagrangian equation of motion in the rotating coordinate system. Show that their equations are the same as those or a particle in fixed frame of reference acted on by the force -∇V and a force derivative from a velocity potential U.*

Solution: From Eq. (7.16)

$$\mathbf{v}' = \mathbf{v} + \omega\times\mathbf{r}$$

$$\mathrm{v}'^2 = (\mathbf{v}+\omega\times\mathbf{r})\cdot(\mathbf{v}+\omega\times\mathbf{r}) = \mathrm{v}^2 + (\omega\times\mathbf{r})^2 + 2\mathbf{v}\cdot(\omega\times\mathbf{r})$$

$$\mathrm{v}'^2 = \dot{x}^2 + \dot{y}^2 + \dot{z}^2 + \omega^2(x^2+y^2) + 2\omega(x\dot{y} - y\dot{x})$$

The Lagrangian L is

$$L = T - V = \frac{m}{2}[\dot{x}^2 + \dot{y}^2 + \dot{z}^2 + \omega^2(x^2+y^2) + 2\omega(x\dot{y} - y\dot{x})] - V(x,y,z) \qquad ...(7.40)$$

The equations of motion are

$$\frac{d}{dt}\left(\frac{\partial L}{\partial \dot{x}}\right) - \frac{\partial L}{\partial x} = 0 \qquad ...(7.41)$$

$$\frac{d}{dt}\left(\frac{\partial L}{\partial \dot{y}}\right) - \frac{\partial L}{\partial y} = 0 \qquad ...(7.42)$$

$$\frac{d}{dt}\left(\frac{\partial L}{\partial \dot{z}}\right)-\frac{\partial L}{\partial z}=0 \qquad \text{...(7.43)}$$

Eqs. (7.40) and (7.41) give

$$m\,\ddot{x}-2m\omega\,\dot{y}-m\omega^2\,x+\frac{\partial V}{\partial x}=0 \qquad \text{...(7.44)}$$

From Eqs. (7.40) and (7.42)

$$m\,\ddot{y}+2m\omega\dot{x}-m\omega^2 y+\frac{\partial V}{\partial y}=0 \qquad \text{...(7.45)}$$

From Eqs. (7.40) and (7.43)

$$m\,\ddot{z}\;+\frac{\partial V}{\partial z}=0 \qquad \text{...(7.46)}$$

The Lagrangian for a particle of mass m moving in a fixed frame (x, y, z) under a force -∇V and an additional velocity dependent potential U.

$$L=T-V=\frac{m}{2}[\dot{x}^2+\dot{y}^2+\dot{z}^2\,)\,-V(\,x,y,z\,)-U \qquad \text{...(7.47)}$$

A comparison of Eq. (7.40) and Eq.(7.47) gives

$$U=T-V=-\frac{m}{2}[\,\omega^2\,(x^2+y^2)+2\omega\,(x\,\dot{y}-y\,\dot{x})] \qquad \text{...(7.48)}$$

OBJECTIVE TYPE QUESTIONS

1. A body subjected to no force moves with constant velocity in a frame of reference. The frame of reference is called

   (*a*) inertial (*b*) non-inertial
   (*c*) accelerated (*d*) none of these

2. The frame of reference attached to the earth is

   (*a*) inertial (*b*) non-inertial
   (*c*) accelerated (*d*) fixed

3. Rotating coordinate system is

   (*a*) inertial (*b*) accelerated
   (*c*) non-inertial (*d*) fixed

4. The formula for centripetal acceleration is

   (*a*) $\omega\times(\omega\times\mathbf{r})$ (*b*) $\omega.\mathbf{r}$

   (*c*) $2\omega\times\mathbf{v}'$ (*d*) $(d\omega/dt\times\mathbf{v}')$

5. The formula for Coriolis acceleration is

(*a*) $\omega \times (\omega \times \mathbf{r})$ (*b*) $\omega.\mathbf{r}$
(*c*) $2\omega \times \mathbf{v'}$ (d) $(d\omega / dt) \times \mathbf{v'}$

6. The plumb bob will be along the radius vector at

(*a*) Equator (*b*) south pole
(*c*) north pole (*d*) 45 degree north of equator

7. The ratio of the centrifugal force arising from the earth's revolution to the centrifugal force due to its rotation is

(*a*) 0.02 (*b*) 0.05
(*b*) 0.2 (*d*) 0.5

8. An ocean current circulating counter-clockwise when viewed directly overhead was discovered. In which hemisphere was the current detected ?

(*a*) northern hemisphere (*b*) southern hemisphere
(*c*) eastern hemisphere (*d*) western hemisphere

9. In the northern hemisphere, the direction of the Coriolis force on a body moving vertically upward is

(*a*) east (*b*) west
(*c*) north (*d*) south

10. In the northern hemisphere, the direction of the Coriolis force on a body moving eastward is

(*a*) east (*b*) west
(*c*) north (*d*) south

11. The Coriolis force is zero at

(*a*) Equator (*b*) north pole
(*c*) south pole (*d*) 45 degree south of equator

12. A body of mass *m* is dropped from rest at a height *h* above the surface of the earth. The Coriolis force as a function of time is

(*a*) $m\omega g$ t $\sin\theta$ (*b*) $m\omega g$ t $\cos\theta$
(*c*) 2 $m\omega g$ t $\cos\theta$ (*d*) 2 $m\omega g$ t $\sin\theta$

PROBLEMS

1. A body is dropped from rest at a height h above the surface of the earth and a latitude 40° N. For $h = 100$m, calculate the lateral displacement of the point of impact due to the Coriolis force.

2. An ocean current circulating counter-clockwise when viewed from directly overhead was discovered. The period of rotation was 14 hours. At what latitude and in which hemisphere was the current detected.?

3. Obtain the ratio of the centrifugal force arising from the earth's revolution to the centrifugal force due to its rotation.

4. Obtain the direction of the Coriolis force on a body moving vertically upward in the northern hemisphere.

❑❑❑

CHAPTER 8

Canonical Transformations

8.1 CANONICAL TRANSFORMATION

In dealing with a given dynamical system defined physically, the choice of a set of generalized coordinates $q_1, q_2, ..., q_n$ is not unique. There may be any n quantities which uniquely defined the position of the system in space. The appearance of the Lagrange's equation does not depend on the choice of the generalized coordinates. In that sense equation may be said to be invariant under the transformation from coordinates $q_1, q_2, ..., q_n$ to another set of coordinates $Q_1, Q_2, ..., Q_n$. The new coordinates Q' *s* are functions of q's, that is,

$$Q_k = Q_k(q,t) \quad (k = 1,2,...,n) \qquad ...(8.1)$$

It is assumed that Q's may explicitly depend on the time t. The transformation of the type (6.1) are called point transformation.

Since Lagrange's equation remains invariant under the transformation $q \to Q$, the Hamilton's equations are also unchanged. In Hamilton's theory, the momenta p and coordinate q are independent variable and are on equal footing. Therefore, we make a change

$$(q, p) \to (Q, P)$$

The transformation (8.1) can be expanded to include $2n$ variables q and p.

$$Q_k = Q_k(q, p, t); \quad P_k = P_k(q, p, t) \quad (k = 1,2,...,n) \qquad ...(8.2)$$

The Eq.(8.2) expresses the q's and p's in terms of Q's and P's. The Eq. (8.2) provide a new set of label for the points of phase space, which were originally labeled by the q's and p's.

Under the general transformation of the form (8.2), the canonical form of the equation of motion (3.13) and (3.14) may be lost and the Hamilton's method no longer apply. Therefore, the transformation is restricted to those which retain the form of canonical equations and satisfy the condition

$$\dot{Q}_k = -\frac{\partial \hat{H}}{\partial P_k} \qquad ...(8.3)$$

$$\dot{P}_k = \frac{\partial \hat{H}}{\partial Q_k} \qquad ...(8.4)$$

with some Hamiltonian $\hat{H}(Q, P)$. Such transformations are called canonical or contact transformation. In such canonical transformation, the Hamiltonian remains unchanged in value, although it is changed in the form.

The transformations (8.1) and (8.2) are useful only whenever one succeeds in making some or all the new coordinates cyclic. If a particular new coordinate Q_k is cyclic then from Eq. (3.29)

$$\frac{d}{dt}\left(\frac{\partial L}{\partial \dot{Q}_k}\right) = \dot{P}_k = \frac{\partial L}{\partial Q_k} = 0$$

also from Hamilton equations

$$\dot{P}_k = -\frac{\partial \hat{H}}{\partial Q_k}$$

or

$$P_k = \alpha_k = \text{constant}$$

The Hamiltonian of the system is

$$H(Q_1,...,Q_{k-1},Q_{k+1},.....,Q_n,P_1,...,P_{k-1},\alpha_k,P_{k+1},..,P_n,t)$$

is reduced to a system of $n-1$ degree's of freedom. In case when all the coordinates are cyclic, the Hamiltonian is

$$H(\alpha_1,.......,\alpha_n,t)$$

and

$$\dot{Q}_k = \left.\frac{\partial H}{\partial P_k}\right|_{P_k=\alpha_k} = \omega_k$$

$$Q_k = \omega_k t + \beta_k \qquad ...(8.5)$$

The $2n$ parameters (α_k, β_k) are constant of integration. Let the Lagrangian in the coordinate system $(q, \dot{q}, t)$ is $L(q, \dot{q}, t)$ and in the coordinate system

$(Q,\dot{Q},t)$ is $\hat{L}(Q,\dot{Q},t)$. They are related to the Hamiltonian $H\ (q,p,t)$ and $\hat{H}(Q,P,t)$ by the equation

$$H = \sum_{k=1}^{n} p_k \dot{q}_k - L, \quad \hat{H} = \sum_{k=1}^{n} P_k \dot{Q}_k - \hat{L}$$

If the Q_k and P_k are to be canonical coordinates satisfying the Eqs. (8.3) and (8.4), then by Hamilton's principle they must satisfy the transformation (8.2) must satisfy the condition that $\delta \int L\,dt$ and $\delta \int \hat{L}\,dt$ are both extrema at the end points

$$\delta \int_{t_1}^{t_2} L\,dt = \delta \int_{t_1}^{t_2} \{\sum_k p_k \dot{q}_k - H(q,p,t)\}dt = 0 \qquad ...(8.6)$$

$$\delta \int_{t_1}^{t_2} \hat{L}\,dt = \delta \int_{t_1}^{t_2} \{\sum_k P_k \dot{Q}_k - \hat{H}(Q,P,t)\}dt = 0 \qquad ...(8.7)$$

The simultaneous validity of Eqs. (8.6) and (8.7) does not mean that the integrands of the two integrals are equal, but that then can differ at most by the total time derivative of a function F

$$\sum_k p_k \dot{q}_k - H(q,p,t) = \sum_k P_k \dot{Q}_k - \hat{H}(Q,P,t) + \frac{dF}{dt} \qquad ...(8.8)$$

where F depends on old and new variables but not on their time derivatives and, possibly, time.

To get the transformation F must be a function of old and new variables. F is called generating function. There are four ways of choosing F, corresponding to the possible choice of old coordinates/momenta and new coordinates/ momenta. These four classes can be obtained from one another by Legendre transformation

1. The choice $F = F_1(q,Q,t)$

The Eq. (6.8) is then

$$\sum_k p_k \dot{q}_k - H(q,p,t) = \sum_k P_k \dot{Q}_k - \hat{H}(Q,P,t) + \frac{dF_1(q,Q,t)}{dt} \qquad ...(8.9)$$

$$\frac{dF_1}{dt} = \frac{\partial F_1}{\partial t} + \sum_k \left[\frac{\partial F_1}{\partial q_k}\dot{q}_k + \frac{\partial F_1}{\partial Q_k}\dot{Q}_k\right] \qquad ...(8.10)$$

As q and Q are Independent variables, Eq. (8.9) is fulfilled if the coefficients of $\dot{q}$ and $\dot{Q}$ separately vanishes, that is,

$$p_k = \frac{\partial F_1}{\partial q_k} \quad \text{...(8.11)}$$

$$P_k = -\frac{\partial F_1}{\partial Q_k} \quad \text{...(8.12)}$$

finally leaving

$$\hat{H} = H + \frac{\partial F_1}{\partial t} \quad \text{...(8.13)}$$

If the generating function does not depend explicitly on t then there is no change in the Hamiltonian, though it may be expressed in terms of the new variables.

2. The choice $F = F_2(q,P,t)$
The Eq. (8.8) is then

$$\sum_k p_k \dot{q}_k - H(q,p,t) = \sum_k P_k \dot{Q}_k - \hat{H}(Q,P,t) + \frac{dF_2(q,P,t)}{dt} \quad \text{...(8.14)}$$

From Legendre transformation (3.6), by putting ($x_k = Q_k$)

$$G = F_2,\ F = F_1,\ u_k = \frac{\partial F_1}{\partial q_k} = -P_k$$

$$F_2(q,P,t) = F_1(q,Q,t) + \sum_k P_k Q_k$$

$$F_1(q,Q,t) = F_2(q,P,t) - \sum_k P_k Q_k \quad \text{...(8.15)}$$

Substituting Eq. (8.15) in Eq.(8.9)

$$\sum_k p_k \dot{q}_k - H(q,p,t) = \sum_k P_k \dot{Q}_k - \hat{H}(Q,P,t) + \frac{d}{dt}[F_2(q,P,t) - \sum_k P_k Q_k]$$

$$\sum_k p_k \dot{q}_k - H(q,p,t) = \sum_k P_k \dot{Q}_k - \hat{H}(Q,P,t) + \frac{dF_2}{dt} + \sum_k \left(\frac{\partial F_2}{\partial q_k}\dot{q}_k + \frac{\partial F_2}{\partial P_k}\dot{P}_k \right) - \sum_k \dot{P}_k Q_k - \sum_k P_k \dot{Q}_k$$

$$\sum_k \left(p_k - \frac{\partial F_2}{\partial q_k} \right)\dot{q}_k + \sum_k \left(-Q_k + \frac{\partial F_2}{\partial P_k} \right)\dot{P}_k + \left(H + \frac{\partial F_2}{\partial t} - \hat{H} \right) = 0 \quad \text{... (8.16)}$$

As q and P are independent variables, the condition (8.16) is fulfilled if the coefficients of $\dot{q}_k$ and $\dot{P}_k$ separately vanishes, that is,

$$p_k = \frac{\partial F_2}{\partial q_k} \qquad \text{...(8.17)}$$

$$Q_k = \frac{\partial F_2}{\partial P_k} \qquad \text{...(8.18)}$$

and Eq. (8.16) is satisfied if

$$\hat{H} = H + \frac{\partial F_2}{\partial t} \qquad \text{...(8.19)}$$

3. The choice $F = F_3(p,Q,t)$

Now

$$p_k = \frac{\partial F_1}{\partial q_k}$$

using

$$F = F_1(q,Q,t) \text{ and } G = F_3(p,Q,t)$$

in the Legendre transformation (3.6)

$$F_3(p,Q,t) = F_1(q,Q,t) - \sum_k \frac{\partial F_1}{\partial q_k} q_k$$

$$F_1(q,Q,t) = \sum_k q_k p_k + F_3(p,Q,t) \qquad \text{...(8.20)}$$

Substituting Eq. (8.20) in Eq. (3.6)

$$\sum_k p_k \dot{q}_k - H(q,p,t) = \sum_k P_k \dot{Q}_k - \hat{H}\ (Q,P,t) + \frac{d}{dt}\left[F_3(p,Q,t) + \sum_k q_k P_k\right]$$

$$\sum_k p_k \dot{q}_k - H(q,p,t) = \sum_k P_k \dot{Q}_k - \hat{H}(Q,P,t) + \frac{dF_3}{dt} + \sum_k \left(\frac{\partial F_3}{\partial Q_k}\dot{Q}_k + \frac{\partial F_3}{\partial p_k}\dot{p}_k\right) + \sum_k \dot{q}_k p_k + \sum_k q_k \dot{p}_k$$

$$\sum_k \left(P_k + \frac{\partial F_3}{\partial Q_k}\right)\dot{Q}_k + \sum_k \left(q_k + \frac{\partial F_3}{\partial p_k}\right)\dot{p}_k + \left(H + \frac{\partial F_3}{\partial t} - \hat{H}\right) = 0 \qquad \text{...(8.21)}$$

As Q and p are independent variables, the equation (8.21) is satisfied if the coefficients of $\dot{Q}_k$ and $\dot{p}_k$ separately vanish, that is

$$P_k = -\frac{\partial F_3}{\partial Q_k} \qquad \text{...(8.22)}$$

$$q_k = -\frac{\partial F_3}{\partial p_k} \qquad \text{...(8.23)}$$

$$\hat{H} = H + \frac{\partial F_3}{\partial t} \qquad \text{...(8.24)}$$

4. The choice $F = F_4(p,P,t)$

The $F_4(p,P,t)$ can be related to $F_1(q,Q,t)$ by a double Legendre transformation. Let $F_4 = G$ and $F_3 = F$, then from Eq. (3.6)

$$F_4(p,P,t) = F_3(p,Q,t) - \sum_k \frac{\partial F_3}{\partial Q_k} Q_k = F_3 + \sum_k P_k Q_k \qquad \text{...(8.25)}$$

Substituting the value of F_1 from Eq. (8.20) in Eq. (8.25)

$$F_4 = F_1 + \sum_k P_k Q_k - \sum_k q_k p_k$$

$$F_1 = F_4 - \sum_k P_k Q_k + \sum_k q_k p_k \qquad \text{...(8.26)}$$

Substituting the values of F_1 from Eq. (8.26) in Eq. (8.9)

$$\sum_k p_k \dot{q}_k - H(q,p,t) = \sum_k P_k \dot{Q}_k - \hat{H}(Q,P,t) + \frac{d}{dt}\left[F_4(P,Q,t) + \sum_k (q_k P_k - P_k Q_k)\right]$$

$$\sum_k p_k \dot{q}_k - H(q,p,t) = \sum_k P_k \dot{Q}_k - \hat{H}(Q,P,t) + \frac{\partial F_4}{\partial t} + \sum_k \left(\frac{\partial F_4}{\partial P_k}\dot{P}_k + \frac{\partial F_4}{\partial P_k}\dot{P}k\right) + \sum_k \dot{q}_k p_k + \sum_k q_k \dot{p}_k - \sum_k (\dot{P}_k Q_k + P_k \dot{Q}_k)$$

...(8.27)

on simplifying Eq. (8.27)

$$\sum_k\left(-Q_k+\frac{\partial F_4}{\partial P_k}\right)\dot{P}_k+\sum_k\left(q_k+\frac{\partial F_4}{\partial p_k}\right)\dot{p}_k+\left(H+\frac{\partial F_4}{\partial t}-\hat{H}\right)=0 \qquad ...(8.28)$$

For Eq.(8.28) to vanish, the coefficients of $\dot{p}_k$ and $\dot{P}_k$ must be zero, that is,

$$q_k=-\frac{\partial F_4}{\partial p_k} \qquad ...(8.29)$$

$$Q_k=\frac{\partial F_4}{\partial P_k} \qquad ...(8.30)$$

$$\hat{H}=H+\frac{\partial F_4}{\partial t} \qquad ...(8.31)$$

In all these transformations, time remains an untransformed quantity. From Eq. (8.8)

$$\sum_k p_k\,dq_k-H(q,p,t)\,dt \;=\; \sum_k P_k\,dQ_k-\hat{H}(Q,P,t)\,dt+dF$$

Since t does not appear directly except in

$$\hat{H}=H+\frac{\partial F}{\partial t}$$

we will set time $dt = 0$. Thus, at every instant of time, a transformation generated by the function F is canonical if the differential dF is exact and equals

$$\sum_k p_k\,dq_k-\sum_k P_k\,dQ_k=dF$$

The above equation is a simple criterion to check that the transformation is canonical.

8.2 POISSON BRACKET

Let $f(q,p)$ and $g(q,p)$ be functions of coordinate and momenta. We define a quantity

$$[f,g]_{q,p}=\sum_{k=1}^{n}\left(\frac{\partial f}{\partial q_k}\frac{\partial g}{\partial p_k}-\frac{\partial g}{\partial q_k}\frac{\partial f}{\partial p_k}\right) \qquad ...(8.33)$$

This is called the Poisson bracket of f and g. Poisson bracket find it analog in quantum mechanics; the commutator in quantum mechanics, dynamical variables are represented by the operators. The commutator of two operator contains the information whether or not the corresponding observables can be measured simultaneously.

8.3 PROPERTIES OF POISSON BRACKET

1. The Poisson bracket does not obey the commutation law of algebra.

$$[f,g]_{q,p}=\sum_{k=1}^{n}\left(\frac{\partial f}{\partial q_k}\frac{\partial g}{\partial p_k}-\frac{\partial g}{\partial q_k}\frac{\partial f}{\partial p_k}\right)=-\sum_{k=1}^{n}\left(\frac{\partial g}{\partial q_k}\frac{\partial f}{\partial p_k}-\frac{\partial f}{\partial q_k}\frac{\partial g}{\partial p_k}\right)=-[g,f]_{q,p} \quad ...(8.34)$$

2. If one of the functions is a constant c, the Poisson bracket is zero

$$[c,g]_{q,p}=\sum_{k=1}^{n}\left(\frac{\partial c}{\partial q_k}\frac{\partial g}{\partial p_k}-\frac{\partial g}{\partial q_k}\frac{\partial c}{\partial p_k}\right)=0 \quad ...(8.35)$$

as

$$\frac{\partial c}{\partial q_k}=\frac{\partial c}{\partial p_k}=0$$

3. Poisson bracket obeys the distributive law of algebra

$$[f+g,h]=[f,h]+[g,h]$$

$$[f+g,h]=\sum_k\left(\frac{\partial}{\partial q_k}(f+g)\frac{\partial h}{\partial p_k}-\frac{\partial h}{\partial q_k}\frac{\partial}{\partial p_k}(f+g)\right)$$

$$=\sum_k\left(\frac{\partial f}{\partial q_k}\frac{\partial h}{\partial p_k}-\frac{\partial h}{\partial q_k}\frac{\partial f}{\partial p_k}\right)+\sum_k\left(\frac{\partial g}{\partial q_k}\frac{\partial h}{\partial p_k}-\frac{\partial h}{\partial q_k}\frac{\partial g}{\partial p_k}\right) \quad ...(8.36)$$

$$=[f,h]+[g,h]$$

4. $[fg,h]=[f,h]g+f[g,h]$ ...(8.37)

$$[fg,h]=\sum_k\left(\frac{\partial}{\partial q_k}(fg)\frac{\partial h}{\partial p_k}-\frac{\partial h}{\partial q_k}\frac{\partial}{\partial p_k}(fg)\right)$$

$$=\sum_k\left(\frac{\partial f}{\partial q_k}\frac{\partial h}{\partial p_k}g-\frac{\partial h}{\partial q_k}\frac{\partial f}{\partial p_k}g\right)+\sum_k\left(f\frac{\partial g}{\partial q_k}\frac{\partial h}{\partial p_k}-f\frac{\partial h}{\partial q_k}\frac{\partial g}{\partial p_k}\right)$$

$$=[f,h]g+f[g,h]$$

5. $\frac{d}{dt}[f,g]=\left[\frac{df}{dt},g\right]+\left[f,\frac{dg}{dt}\right]$ ...(8.38)

we have

$$\frac{d}{dt}\left(\frac{\partial f(q,p,t)}{\partial p_k}\right)=\frac{\partial^2 f}{\partial t\partial p_k}+\sum_i\left(\frac{\partial^2 f}{\partial p_k\partial p_i}\dot{p}_i+\frac{\partial^2 f}{\partial p_k\partial q_i}\dot{q}_i\right)=\frac{\partial^2 f}{\partial p_k\partial t}+\frac{\partial}{\partial p_k}[f,H]$$

$$\frac{d}{dt}\left(\frac{\partial f}{\partial p_k}\right)=\frac{\partial}{\partial p_k}\left(\frac{\partial f}{\partial t}+[f,H]\right)=\frac{\partial}{\partial p_k}\left(\frac{df}{dt}\right) \qquad ...(8.39)$$

Similarly

$$\frac{d}{dt}\left(\frac{\partial f}{\partial q_k}\right)=\frac{\partial}{\partial q_k}\left(\frac{\partial f}{\partial t}+[f,H]\right)=\frac{\partial}{\partial q_k}\left(\frac{df}{dt}\right)$$

$$\frac{d}{dt}\left(\frac{\partial g}{\partial q_k}\right)=\frac{\partial}{\partial q_k}\left(\frac{\partial g}{\partial t}+[g,H]\right)=\frac{\partial}{\partial q_k}\left(\frac{dg}{dt}\right) \qquad ...(8.40)$$

$$\frac{d}{dt}\left(\frac{\partial g}{\partial p_k}\right)=\frac{\partial}{\partial p_k}\left(\frac{\partial g}{\partial t}+[f,H]\right)=\frac{\partial}{\partial p_k}\left(\frac{dg}{dt}\right)$$

Eq. (8.38) is

$$\frac{d}{dt}[f,g]=\frac{d}{dt}\sum_k\left(\frac{\partial f}{\partial q_k}\frac{\partial g}{\partial p_k}-\frac{\partial f}{\partial p_k}\frac{\partial g}{\partial q_k}\right)$$

$$\frac{d}{dt}[f,g]=\sum_k\left[\frac{d}{dt}\left(\frac{\partial f}{\partial q_k}\right)\frac{\partial g}{\partial p_k}+\frac{\partial f}{\partial q_k}\frac{d}{dt}\left(\frac{\partial g}{\partial p_k}\right)-\frac{d}{dt}\left(\frac{\partial f}{\partial p_k}\right)\frac{\partial g}{\partial q_k}-\frac{\partial f}{\partial p_k}\frac{d}{dt}\left(\frac{\partial g}{\partial q_k}\right)\right] \qquad ...(8.41)$$

Substituting Eqs. (8.39) and (8.40) in Eq. (8.41)

$$\frac{d}{dt}[f,g]=\sum_k\left[\frac{\partial}{\partial q_k}\left(\frac{df}{dt}\right)\frac{\partial g}{\partial p_k}+\frac{\partial f}{\partial q_k}\frac{d}{dp_k}\left(\frac{\partial g}{\partial t}\right)-\frac{d}{dp_k}\left(\frac{\partial f}{\partial t}\right)\frac{\partial g}{\partial q_k}-\frac{\partial f}{\partial p_k}\frac{d}{dp_k}\left(\frac{\partial g}{\partial t}\right)\right]$$

$$\frac{d}{dt}[f,g]=\left[\frac{df}{dt},g\right]+\left[f,\frac{dg}{dt}\right]$$

6.
$$\frac{\partial}{\partial t}[f,g]=\left[\frac{\partial f}{\partial t},g\right]+\left[f,\frac{\partial g}{\partial t}\right] \qquad ...(8.42)$$

7. Jacobi's identity: It states that if *f*, *g* and *h* are three functions of *q*'s and *p*'s then

$$[f,[g,h]]+[h,[f,g]]+[g,[h,f]]=0 \qquad ...(8.43)$$

The Poisson bracket $[g,h]$ can be considered as a linear differential operator D_g acting on h, where

$$D_g = \sum_{k=1}^{n}\left(\frac{\partial g}{\partial q_k}\frac{\partial}{\partial p_k} - \frac{\partial g}{\partial p_k}\frac{\partial}{\partial q_k}\right) \qquad ...(8.44)$$

or

$$D_g = \sum_{k=1}^{2n}\alpha_k \frac{\partial}{\partial \lambda_k}$$

where

$$\alpha_k = \frac{\partial g}{\partial q_k} \qquad (k = 1,......,n)$$
$$= -\frac{\partial g}{\partial p_k} \qquad (k = n+1,........,2n) \qquad ...(8.45)$$

$$\frac{\partial}{\partial \lambda_k} = \frac{\partial}{\partial p_k} \qquad (k = 1,......,n)$$
$$= \frac{\partial}{\partial q_k} \qquad (k = n+1,........,2n) \qquad ...(8.46)$$

The first and third terms of the Eq. (8.43)

$$[f,[g,h]] + [g,[h,f]] = [f,[g,h]] - [g,[f,h]]$$
$$= [f, D_g h] - [g, D_f h] = D_f D_g h - D_g D_f h \qquad ...(8.47)$$

$$[f,[g,h]] - [g,[f,h]] = \sum_{i,k}\left[\beta_k \frac{\partial}{\partial \eta_k}\left(\alpha_i \frac{\partial h}{\partial \lambda_i}\right) - \alpha_i \frac{\partial}{\partial \lambda_i}\left(\beta_k \frac{\partial h}{\partial \eta_k}\right)\right]$$

$$= \sum_{i,k}\left[\beta_k \frac{\partial \alpha_i}{\partial \eta_k}\left(\frac{\partial h}{\partial \lambda_i}\right) + \alpha_i\beta_k\left(\frac{\partial^2 h}{\partial \eta_k \partial \lambda_i}\right) - \alpha_i \frac{\partial \beta_k}{\partial \lambda_i}\left(\frac{\partial h}{\partial \eta_k}\right) - \alpha_i\beta_k\left(\frac{\partial^2 h}{\partial \lambda_i \partial \eta_k}\right)\right]$$

where

$$D_f = \sum_k \beta_k \frac{\partial}{\partial \eta_k}, \quad D_g = \sum_i \alpha_i \frac{\partial}{\partial \lambda_i} \qquad ...(8.48)$$

The terms involving the second derivative of h vanishes, therefore, $[f,[g,h]] - [g,[f,h]]$ can involve only first derivative of h and must have the form

$$[f,[g,h]]-[g,[f,h]] \;=\; \sum_i \left(A_i \frac{\partial h}{\partial p_i} + B_i \frac{\partial h}{\partial q_i} \right) \qquad ...(8.49)$$

Putting $h = p_k$ in Eq. (8.49)

$$[f,[g,p_k]]-[g,[f,p_k]] \;=\; \sum_i \left(A_i \frac{\partial p_i}{\partial p_i} + B_i \frac{\partial p_i}{\partial q_i} \right) = A_k$$

$$\left[f, \frac{\partial g}{\partial q_k}\frac{\partial p_k}{\partial p_k} - \frac{\partial g}{\partial p_k}\frac{\partial p_k}{\partial q_k} \right] - \left[g, \frac{\partial f}{\partial q_k}\frac{\partial p_k}{\partial p_k} - \frac{\partial f}{\partial p_k}\frac{\partial p_k}{\partial q_k} \right] = A_k$$

$$\left[f, \frac{\partial g}{\partial q_k} \right] - \left[g, \frac{\partial f}{\partial q_k} \right] = \left[f, \frac{\partial g}{\partial q_k} \right] + \left[\frac{\partial f}{\partial q_k}, g \right] \;=\; \frac{\partial}{\partial q_k}[f,g] = A_k$$

$$...(8.50)$$

similarly by putting $h = q_k$ in Eq. (8.49) we have

$$[f,[g,q_k]]-[g,[f,q_k]] = -\left[f, \frac{\partial g}{\partial q_k} \right] - \left[\frac{\partial f}{\partial q_k}; g \right] = \sum_i \left(A_i \frac{\partial q_i}{\partial p_i} + B_i \frac{\partial q_i}{\partial q_i} \right) = B_k$$

$$-\left[f, \frac{\partial g}{\partial p_k} \right] - \left[\frac{\partial f}{\partial p_k}, g \right] \;=\; -\frac{\partial}{\partial p_k}[f,g] = B_k \qquad ...(8.51)$$

Substituting Eqs. (8.50) and (8.51) in Eq. (8.49)

$$[f,[g,h]]+[g,[h,f]] \;=\; \sum_k \left(\frac{\partial}{\partial q_k}[f,g]\frac{\partial h}{\partial p_k} - \frac{\partial}{\partial p_k}[f,g]\frac{\partial h}{\partial q_k} \right)$$

$$[f,[g,h]]+[g,[h,f]] \;=\; [[f,g],h] = -[h,[f,g]] \qquad ...(8.52)$$

Substituting Eq. (8.52) in Eq. (8.43)

$$[h,[f,g]] \;-[h,[f,g]] = 0 \qquad ...(8.53)$$

This proves the Jacobi's identity.

8.4 INTEGRAL OF MOTION

Let $f(q,p,t)$ be some function of coordinate, momenta and time. Its total time derivative is

$$\frac{df}{dt} = \frac{\partial f}{\partial t} + \sum_k \left(\frac{\partial f}{\partial q_k}\dot{q}_k + \frac{\partial f}{\partial p_k}\dot{p}_k \right) = \frac{\partial f}{\partial t} + \sum_k \left(\frac{\partial f}{\partial q_k}\frac{\partial H}{\partial p_k} - \frac{\partial f}{\partial p_k}\frac{\partial H}{\partial q_k} \right)$$

$$\frac{df}{dt} = \frac{\partial f}{\partial t} + [f, H] \qquad \text{...(8.54)}$$

Those functions of the dynamical variable which remain constant during the motion of the system are called integral of the motion. The condition for quantity f to be integral of motion $(df/dt) = 0$ is

$$\frac{\partial f}{\partial t} + [f, H] = 0 \qquad \text{...(8.55)}$$

if f does not explicitly dependent on time

$$[f, H] = 0 \qquad \text{...(8.56)}$$

that is Poisson bracket of the integral and the Hamiltonian must be zero.

8.5 POISSON'S THEOREM

It states that the Poisson bracket of two integrals of the motion is again an integral of motion. Let us consider a function $h = h(q,p,t)$. The total time derivative of h is given by Eq. (8.54)

$$\frac{dh}{dt} = \frac{\partial h}{\partial t} + [h, H] \qquad \text{...(8.57)}$$

Putting $h = [f, g]$ in the Eq. (8.57)

$$\frac{d}{dt}[f, g] = \frac{\partial}{\partial t}[f, g] + [[f, g], H] \qquad \text{...(8.58)}$$

From Jacobi's identity (8.43)

$$[f,[g,h]] + [g,[h,f]] = -[h,[f,g]] = [[f,g],h] \qquad \text{...(8.59)}$$

Putting $h = H$ in the Eq. (8.59)

$$[f,[g,H]] + [g,[H,f]] = [[f,g],H]$$

$$[f,[g,H]] + [[f,H],g] = [[f,g],H] \qquad \text{...(8.60)}$$

Substituting Eq. (8.60) in Eq. (8.58)

$$\frac{d}{dt}[f,g] = \frac{\partial}{\partial t}[f,g] + [f,[g,H]] + [[f,H],g]$$

$$\frac{d}{dt}[f,g] = \left[\frac{\partial f}{\partial t} + [f,H], g\right] + \left[f, \frac{\partial g}{\partial t} + [g,H]\right] = \left[\frac{df}{dt}, g\right] + \left[f, \frac{dg}{dt}\right] \qquad \text{...(8.61)}$$

Since

$$\frac{df}{dt} = \frac{dg}{dt} = 0 \qquad ...(8.62)$$

f and g being the constant of motion. We have

$$\frac{d}{dt}[f, g] = 0 \qquad ...(8.63)$$

$[f, g]$ is a constant of motion.

$$[f, q_k] = \sum_l \left(\frac{\partial f}{\partial q_l}\frac{\partial q_k}{\partial p_l} - \frac{\partial f}{\partial p_l}\frac{\partial q_k}{\partial q_l} \right) = -\sum_l \left(\frac{\partial f}{\partial p_l}\frac{\partial q_k}{\partial q_l} \right) = -\frac{\partial f}{\partial p_k} \qquad ...(8.64)$$

since

$$\frac{\partial q_k}{\partial q_l} = 1 \text{ for } \quad k=l, \quad \text{and 0 for } k \neq l \qquad ...(8.65)$$

and

$$\frac{\partial q_k}{\partial p_l} = 0 \text{ for all } l \qquad ...(8.66)$$

Substituting $f = q_i$ in Eq.(8.64)

$$[q_i, q_k] = -\frac{\partial q_i}{\partial p_k} = 0 \qquad ...(8.67)$$

Substituting $f = p_i$ in Eq.(8.64)

$$[P_i, q_k] = \sum_i \left(\frac{\partial P_i \partial q_k}{\partial q_i \partial P_l} - \frac{\partial p_i}{\partial p_l}\frac{\partial q_k}{\partial ql} \right) = -\sum_l \left(\frac{\partial p_i}{\partial p_l}\frac{\partial p_k}{\partial q_l} \right) = -\sum_l \delta_{i,l}\delta_k, l = -\delta_{i,k} \qquad ...(8.68)$$

$$[p_k, q_k] = -1 \qquad \text{for } i = k \qquad ...(8.69)$$

$$[p_i, q_k] = 0 \quad \text{if } i \neq k \qquad ...(8.70)$$

8.6 INVARIANCE OF POISSON BRACKET UNDER CANONICAL TRANSFORMATION

$$[f, g]_{q,p} = \sum_k \left(\frac{\partial f}{\partial q_k}\frac{\partial g}{\partial p_k} - \frac{\partial f}{\partial p_k}\frac{\partial g}{\partial q_k} \right)$$

$$= \sum_{k,l} \left\{ \frac{\partial f}{\partial q_k}\left(\frac{\partial g}{\partial Q_l}\frac{\partial Q_l}{\partial p_k} + \frac{\partial g}{\partial P_l}\frac{\partial P_l}{\partial p_k} \right) - \frac{\partial f}{\partial p_k}\left(\frac{\partial g}{\partial Q_l}\frac{\partial Q_l}{\partial q_k} + \frac{\partial g}{\partial P_l}\frac{\partial P_l}{\partial q_k} \right) \right\}$$

$$[f,g]_{q,p} = \sum_l \left\{ \frac{\partial g}{\partial Q_l} \sum_k \left(\frac{\partial f}{\partial q_k}\frac{\partial Q_l}{\partial p_k} - \frac{\partial f}{\partial p_k}\frac{\partial Q_l}{\partial q_k} \right) + \frac{\partial g}{\partial P_l} \sum_k \left(\frac{\partial f}{\partial q_k}\frac{\partial P_l}{\partial p_k} - \frac{\partial f}{\partial p_k}\frac{\partial P_l}{\partial q_k} \right) \right\}$$

$$[f,g]_{q,p} = \sum_l \left\{ \frac{\partial g}{\partial Q_l}[f,Q_k]_{q,p} + \frac{\partial g}{\partial P_l}[f,P_k]_{q,p} \right\} \qquad ...(8.71)$$

Let $f = Q_l$ and $g = f$

$$[Q_l, f]_{q,p} = \sum_l \left\{ \frac{\partial f}{\partial Q_l}[Q_l,Q_k] + \frac{\partial f}{\partial P_l}[Q_l,P_k] \right\} = \sum_k \frac{\partial f}{\partial P_l}\delta_{k,l}$$

$$[f,Q_k]_{q,p} = -\frac{\partial f}{\partial P_l} \qquad ...(8.72)$$

Let $f = P_l$ and $g = f$

$$[P_l, f]_{q,p} = \sum_l \left\{ \frac{\partial f}{\partial Q_l}[P_l,Q_k] + \frac{\partial f}{\partial P_l}[P_l,P_k] \right\} = -\sum_l \frac{\partial f}{\partial Q_l}\delta_{k,l}$$

$$[f,P_k]_{q,p} = \frac{\partial f}{\partial Q_l} \qquad ...(8.73)$$

Substituting Eqs (8.72) and (8.73) in Eq. (8.71)

$$[f,g]_{q,p} = \sum_l \left\{ -\frac{\partial g}{\partial Q_l}\frac{\partial f}{\partial P_l} + \frac{\partial g}{\partial P_l}\frac{\partial f}{\partial Q_l} \right\} = [f,g]_{Q,P} \qquad ...(8.74)$$

The property of the invariance gives

$$[Q_i, Q_k] = 0, \quad [P_i, P_k] = 0, \quad [Q_i, P_k] = \delta_{ik} \qquad ...(8.75)$$

For a transformation to be canonical, the Eq. (8.75) must be satisfied.

8.7 LAGRANGE BRACKETS

The Lagrange brackets of two dynamical variables f and g is defined as

$$\{f,g\}_{q,p} = \{f,g\} = \sum_k \left(\frac{\partial q_k}{\partial f}\frac{\partial p_k}{\partial g} - \frac{\partial p_k}{\partial f}\frac{\partial q_k}{\partial g} \right) \qquad ...(8.76)$$

From Eq. (8.76)

$$\{f,g\} = -\{g,f\}$$

Putting $f = q_i, g = q_j$ in Eq.(8.76)

$$\{q_i, q_j\} = \sum_k \left(\frac{\partial q_k}{\partial q_1} \frac{\partial p_k}{\partial q_j} - \frac{\partial p_k}{\partial q_i} \frac{\partial q_k}{\partial q_j} \right) \qquad ...(8.77)$$

Since q's and p's are independent variables

$$\frac{\partial p_k}{\partial q_i} = 0, \quad \frac{\partial p_k}{\partial q_j} = 0 \qquad ...(8.78)$$

From Eqs. (8.77) and (8.78)

$$\{q_i, q_j\} = 0 \qquad ...(8.79)$$

Similarly putting $f = p_i, g = p_j$ in Eq. (8.77) we have

$$\{p_i, p_j\} = 0 \qquad ...(8.80)$$

Let $f = q_i, g = p_j$ in Eq. (8.77)

$$\{q_i, p_j\} = \sum_k \left(\frac{\partial q_k}{\partial q_1} \frac{\partial p_k}{\partial p_j} - \frac{\partial p_k}{\partial q_i} \frac{\partial q_k}{\partial p_j} \right) = \sum_k \frac{\partial q_k}{\partial q_1} \frac{\partial p_k}{\partial p_j} \qquad ...(8.81)$$

Now

$$\frac{\partial p_k}{\partial p_j} = \delta_{jk}, \quad \frac{\partial q_k}{\partial q_i} = \delta_{ki} \qquad ...(8.82)$$

From Eqs .(8.81) and (8.82)

$$\{q_i, p_j\} = \sum \delta_{jk} \delta_{ki} = \delta_{ij} \qquad ...(8.83)$$

The Lagrangian and Poisson brackets are related by

$$\sum_{l=1}^{2n} \{f_l, f_i\} [f_l, f_i] = \delta_{ij} \qquad ...(8.84)$$

8.8 INFINITESIMAL CONTACT TRANSFORMATION

Let us consider an infinitesimal contact transformation. In such a transformation, the new coordinates differ from the old coordinates by an infinitesimal amount. Let

$$Q_k = q_k + \delta q_k \qquad ...(8.85)$$

$$P_k = p_k + \delta p_k \qquad ...(8.86)$$

be the transformation equations wherein δq_k and δp_k are the infinitesimal changes in coordinates and momenta. Let ε be a parameter, taken to be infinitesimally small and $G(q,P)$ is a differentiable function of old coordinates and new momenta.

$$F_2 = \sum_k q_k P_k + \varepsilon G(q, P) \qquad \text{...(8.87)}$$

From Eqs. (8.17) and (8.87) we obtain

$$p_k = P_k + \varepsilon \frac{\partial G}{\partial q_k} \qquad \text{...(8.88)}$$

hence

$$\delta p_k = P_k - p_k = -\varepsilon \frac{\partial G}{\partial q_k} \qquad \text{...(8.89)}$$

From Eqs. (8.18) and (8.87) we obtain

$$Q_k = q_k + \varepsilon \frac{\partial G}{\partial P_k} \qquad \text{...(8.90)}$$

$$\delta q_k = Q_k - q_k = \varepsilon \frac{\partial G}{\partial P_k} \qquad \text{...(8.91)}$$

Here the derivatives $\frac{\partial G}{\partial P_k}$ and $\frac{\partial G}{\partial q_k}$ depends on the old new momenta and old coordinates. Since $P_k - p_k$ is very small hence P_k can be replaced by p_k. Hence

$$\varepsilon \frac{\partial G}{\partial P_k} = \varepsilon \frac{\partial G}{\partial p_k} \qquad \text{...(8.92)}$$

From Eqs. (8.91) and (8.92)

$$\delta q_k = Q_k - q_k = \varepsilon \frac{\partial G}{\partial p_k} \qquad \text{...(8.93)}$$

Let us consider the change in some function $f(q,p)$ under an infinitesimal transformation of the type (8.87)

$$\delta f = f(q_k + \delta q_k, p_k + \delta p_k) - f(q_k, p_k) \qquad \text{...(8.94)}$$

Using Taylor series

$$\delta f = \sum_k \left(f(q_k, p_k) + \frac{\partial f}{\partial q_k} \delta q_k + \frac{\partial f}{\partial p_k} \delta p_k + ... - f(q_k, p_k) \right) \qquad \text{...(8.95)}$$

$$\delta f = \sum_k \left(\frac{\partial f}{\partial q_k} \delta q_k + \frac{\partial f}{\partial p_k} \delta p_k \right) \quad ...(8.96)$$

Substituting Eqs. (8.89) and (8.93) in Eq. (8.96)

$$\delta f = \sum_k \left(\frac{\partial f}{\partial q_k} \frac{\partial G}{\partial p_k} - \frac{\partial f}{\partial p_k} \frac{\partial G}{\partial q_k} \right) \varepsilon \quad ...(8.97)$$

$$\delta f = \varepsilon \, [f, G]_{q,p} \quad ...(8.98)$$

If we take $f = H$

$$\delta H = \varepsilon \, [H, G]_{q,p} \quad ...(8.99)$$

If G is constant of motion then

$$[H, G]_{q,p} = 0 \quad ...(8.100)$$

The vanishing of the bracket $[H,G]$ means that it stays invariant under this transformation. Thus constants of the motion are the generating functions of those infinitesimal canonical transformation which leaves the Hamiltonian invariant.

8.9 THE ANGULAR MOMENTUM POISSON BRACKET RELATIONS

Consider any scalar function $\varphi = \varphi(\boldsymbol{r}, \boldsymbol{p})$ and its infinitesimal rotation about any arbitrary direction **n** passing through the origin by an angle $\delta\theta$ such that

$$\mathbf{r} \to \mathbf{r} + \delta\mathbf{r}; \ \mathbf{p} \to \mathbf{p} + \delta\mathbf{p}; \quad \phi(\mathbf{r} + \delta\mathbf{r}, \mathbf{p} + \delta\mathbf{p}) \to \phi(\mathbf{r}, \mathbf{p}) \quad ...(8.101)$$

where

$$\delta\mathbf{r} = \delta\theta \, \mathbf{n} \times \mathbf{r}; \quad \delta\mathbf{p} = \delta\theta \, \mathbf{n} \times \mathbf{p} \quad ...(8.102)$$

The scalar function φ remains invariant under rotation, therefore

$$\delta\varphi = 0 = \frac{\partial \varphi}{\partial x_i} \delta x_i + \frac{\partial \varphi}{\partial p_i} \delta p_i$$

Since

$$\delta x_i = \delta\theta (\mathbf{n} \times \mathbf{r})_i = \delta\theta (n_j x_k - n_k x_j) = \varepsilon_{ijk} n_j x_k + \varepsilon_{ikj} n_k x_j = \varepsilon_{ijk} n_j x_k \quad ...(8.103)$$

ε is Levi-Civita symbol with the properties

$$\varepsilon_{123} = \varepsilon_{231} = \varepsilon_{312} = 1$$

$$\varepsilon_{132} = \varepsilon_{213} = \varepsilon_{321} = -1$$

all others $\varepsilon_{ijk} = 0$, that is, when two indices are equal.

Similarly

$$\delta p_i = \delta\theta(\mathbf{n}\times\mathbf{p})_i = \varepsilon_{ijk} n_j p_k \qquad ...(8.104)$$

$$\delta\varphi = 0 = \delta\theta\, \varepsilon_{ijk}\left(\frac{\partial\varphi}{\partial x_i} x_k + \frac{\partial\varphi}{\partial p_i} p_k\right) n_j$$

$$\delta\varphi = 0 = \delta\theta\left(\frac{\partial\varphi}{\partial x_i}\frac{\partial(\varepsilon_{ijk} x_k p_i)}{\partial p_i} + \frac{\partial\varphi}{\partial p_i}\frac{\partial(\varepsilon_{jik} x_i p_k)}{\partial x_i}\right) n_j$$

Now $L_j = \varepsilon_{jki} x_k p_i = \varepsilon_{jki} x_k p_i + \varepsilon_{jik} x_i p_k$

$$\delta\varphi = 0 = \delta\theta\left(\frac{\partial\varphi}{\partial x_i}\frac{\partial L_j}{\partial p_i} + \frac{\partial\varphi}{\partial p_i}\frac{\partial L_j}{\partial x_i}\right) n_j = \delta\theta\,[\varphi, L_j n_j] \qquad ...(8.105)$$

Since δq is arbitrary

$$[\varphi, L_j n_j] = 0 \qquad ...(8.106)$$

In general

$$[\phi, \mathbf{L}\cdot\mathbf{n}] = 0 \qquad ...(8.107)$$

If **f** is a vector function, that is, **f = f (r, p)**

$$\delta\mathbf{f} = \delta\theta\,\mathbf{n}\times\mathbf{f} = \delta\theta[\mathbf{f}, \mathbf{L}\cdot\mathbf{n}] \qquad ...(8.108)$$

$$\mathbf{n}\times\mathbf{f} = [\mathbf{f}, \mathbf{L}\cdot\mathbf{n}]$$

$$[\mathbf{f}\cdot\mathbf{g}, \mathbf{L}\cdot\mathbf{n}] = \mathbf{f}\cdot[\mathbf{g}, \mathbf{L}\cdot\mathbf{n}] + \mathbf{g}\cdot[\mathbf{f}, \mathbf{L}\cdot\mathbf{n}] = \mathbf{f}\cdot\mathbf{n}\times\mathbf{g} + \mathbf{g}\cdot\mathbf{n}\times\mathbf{f} = \mathbf{f}\cdot\mathbf{n}\times\mathbf{g} + \mathbf{f}\cdot\mathbf{g}\times\mathbf{n} = 0 \qquad ...(8.109)$$

$$\begin{aligned}[L^2, \mathbf{L}\cdot\mathbf{n}] &= [\mathbf{L}\cdot\mathbf{L}, \mathbf{L}\cdot\mathbf{n}] = \mathbf{L}\cdot[\mathbf{L}, \mathbf{L}\cdot\mathbf{n}] + \mathbf{L}\cdot[\mathbf{L}, \mathbf{L}\cdot\mathbf{n}] \\ &= 2\mathbf{L}\cdot[\mathbf{L}, \mathbf{L}\cdot\mathbf{n}] \\ &= 2\mathbf{L}\cdot(\mathbf{n}\times\mathbf{L})\cdot = 0\end{aligned} \qquad ...(8.110)$$

as the vector which is perpendicular to both **n** and **L** is also perpendicular to **L.** In general

$$[F^2, \mathbf{L}\cdot\mathbf{n}] = 0$$

Solved Examples

Example 1. *Consider the generating function*

$$F_1(q, Q) = \sum_{k=1}^{n} q_k Q_k$$

Obtain canonical transformation

Solution: From Eqs. (8.11) and (8.12)

$$p_k = \frac{\partial F_1}{\partial q_k} = Q_k$$

$$P_k = -\frac{\partial F_1}{\partial Q_k} = -q_k$$

From Eq. (8.13)

$$\hat{H}(Q_k, P_k) = H(q_k, p_k) = H(-P_k, Q_k)$$

Example 2. *For the simple harmonic oscillator*

$$H = \frac{p^2}{2m} + \frac{1}{2} m\omega^2 q^2$$

The generating function is

$$F_1 = \frac{1}{2} m\omega q^2 \cot Q$$

Obtain canonical transformation.

Solution: From Eqs. (8.11) and (8.12)

$$p = \frac{\partial F_1}{\partial q} = m\omega q \cot Q \qquad \text{...(8.111)}$$

$$P = -\frac{\partial F_1}{\partial Q} = \frac{1}{2} m\omega q^2 \operatorname{cosec}^2 Q \qquad \text{...(8.112)}$$

From Eq. (8.112)

$$q^2 = \frac{2P \sin^2 Q}{m\omega}$$

$$q = \sqrt{\frac{2P}{m\omega}} \sin Q$$

Eq. (8.111) is

$$p = m\omega \sqrt{\frac{2P}{m\omega}} \sin Q \cot Q = \sqrt{2m\omega P} \cos Q$$

From Eqs. (8.13) and the Hamiltonian H we have

$$\hat{H} = H = \frac{2m\omega \mathrm{P}}{2m}\cos^2 Q + \frac{1}{2}m\omega^2 \frac{2P}{m\omega}\sin^2 Q = \omega P$$

Example 3. *Show that the following transformations are canonical*

$$Q = \frac{1}{p}, \; P = q\,p^2$$

Solution: Consider

$$\frac{\partial P}{\partial P} = 1 = \frac{\partial P}{\partial p}\frac{\partial p}{\partial P} + \frac{\partial P}{\partial q}\frac{\partial q}{\partial P}, \quad \frac{\partial Q}{\partial Q} = 1 = \frac{\partial Q}{\partial p}\frac{\partial p}{\partial Q} + \frac{\partial Q}{\partial q}\frac{\partial q}{\partial Q}$$

and

$$\frac{\partial P}{\partial Q} = 0 = \frac{\partial P}{\partial p}\frac{\partial p}{\partial Q} + \frac{\partial P}{\partial q}\frac{\partial q}{\partial Q}, \quad \frac{\partial Q}{\partial P} = 0 = \frac{\partial Q}{\partial p}\frac{\partial p}{\partial P} + \frac{\partial Q}{\partial q}\frac{\partial q}{\partial P}$$

Now

$$\frac{\partial P}{\partial p} = 2q\,p, \quad \frac{\partial P}{\partial q} = p^2, \quad \frac{\partial Q}{\partial p} = -\frac{1}{p^2}, \quad \frac{\partial Q}{\partial q} = 0$$

$$\frac{\partial P}{\partial P} = 1 = 2q\,p\frac{\partial p}{\partial P} + p^2\frac{\partial q}{\partial P}, \quad \frac{\partial Q}{\partial Q} = 1 = -\frac{1}{p^2}\frac{\partial p}{\partial Q} \qquad \text{...(8.113)}$$

$$\frac{\partial P}{\partial Q} = 0 = 2q\,p\frac{\partial p}{\partial Q} + p^2\frac{\partial q}{\partial Q}, \quad \frac{\partial Q}{\partial P} = 0 = -\frac{1}{p^2}\frac{\partial p}{\partial P} \qquad \text{...(8.114)}$$

From Eqs. (8.113) and (8.114) we have

$$\frac{\partial q}{\partial P} = \frac{1}{p^2}, \quad \frac{\partial q}{\partial Q} = 2\,p\,q, \quad \frac{\partial p}{\partial P} = 0, \quad \frac{\partial p}{\partial Q} = -p^2 \qquad \text{...(8.115)}$$

we have

$$\dot{p} = -\frac{\partial H}{\partial q} = -\frac{\partial \hat{H}}{\partial P}\frac{\partial P}{\partial q} - \frac{\partial \hat{H}}{\partial Q}\frac{\partial Q}{\partial q} = -p^2\frac{\partial \hat{H}}{\partial P} \qquad \text{...(8.116)}$$

Further,

$$\dot{p} = \frac{\partial p}{\partial P}\dot{P} + \frac{\partial p}{\partial Q}\dot{Q} = 0 - p^2\dot{Q} \qquad \text{...(8.117)}$$

Equating Eqs. (8.116) and (8.117)

$$\dot{Q} = \frac{\partial \hat{H}}{\partial P} \qquad \text{...(8.118)}$$

Now

$$\dot{q} = \frac{\partial H}{\partial p} = \frac{\partial \hat{H}}{\partial P}\frac{\partial P}{\partial p} + \frac{\partial \hat{H}}{\partial Q}\frac{\partial Q}{\partial p} = 2qp\frac{\partial \hat{H}}{\partial P} - p^2\frac{\partial \hat{H}}{\partial Q} \quad ...(8.119)$$

$$\dot{q} = \frac{\partial q}{\partial P}\dot{P} + \frac{\partial q}{\partial Q}\dot{Q} = \frac{1}{p^2}\dot{P} + 2pq\dot{Q} \quad ...(8.120)$$

On comparing Eqs. (8.119) and (8.120) and using Eq. (8.118)

$$2qp\frac{\partial \hat{H}}{\partial P} - p^2\frac{\partial \hat{H}}{\partial Q} = \frac{1}{p^2}\dot{P} + 2pq\dot{Q} = \frac{1}{p^2}\dot{P} + 2pq\frac{\partial \hat{H}}{\partial P}$$

$$\dot{P} = -\frac{\partial \hat{H}}{\partial Q} \quad ...(8.121)$$

Eqs. (8.118) and (8.121) show that the transformation is canonical.

Example 4. *Show that the following transformation is canonical*

$$Q = aq + bp,\ P = cq + dp$$

only if $ad - bc = 1$

Solution: For the transformation to be canonical the Poisson bracket of Q and P, that is, $[Q,P] = 1$

$$[Q,P] = \frac{\partial Q}{\partial q}\frac{\partial P}{\partial p} - \frac{\partial Q}{\partial p}\frac{\partial P}{\partial q} = ad - bc = 1$$

Thus for transformation to be canonical $ad - bc = 1$.

Example 5. *Show that the transformation*

$Q = \sqrt{2}\, q\, exp(k) \cos p,\ P = \sqrt{2}\, q\, exp(-k) \sin p$ is canonical.

Solution: For transformation to canonical $p\,dq - P\,dQ$ should be exact differential

$$PdQ = \sqrt{2}q\, exp(-k) \sin p[\sqrt{2}\frac{1}{2}q^{-1/2} \cos p dq - \sqrt{2}q^{1/2} \sin p dq]\, exp(k)$$

$$P\,dQ = \sin p \cos p\, dq - 2q \sin^2 p\, dp = \frac{1}{2}\sin 2p\ dq - q\,dp + q \cos 2p\, dp$$

$$p\,dq - P\,dQ = p\,dq - \frac{1}{2}\sin 2p\ dq + q\,dp - q\cos 2p\,dp = d(pq - \frac{1}{2}q\sin 2p)$$

which is exact differential

Example 6. *Show* $P = \dfrac{p^2 + q^2}{2},\ Q = \tan^{-1}\dfrac{q}{p}$ *is canonical.*

Solution: We have

$$\frac{\partial P}{\partial p} = p, \frac{\partial P}{\partial q} = q, \frac{\partial Q}{\partial q} = \frac{1}{1+(q^2/p^2)}\frac{1}{p} = \frac{p}{q^2+p^2}, \frac{\partial Q}{\partial p} =$$

$$-\frac{1}{1+(q^2/p^2)}\frac{q}{p^2} = -\frac{q}{q^2+p^2}$$

The Poisson bracket of Q and P is

$$[Q,P] = \frac{p}{q^2+p^2}p + \frac{q}{q^2+p^2}q = \frac{p^2+q^2}{p^2+q^2} = 1$$

Thus, the transformation is canonical.

Example 7. *Suppose we have transformation equation*

$$Q = \log\frac{\sin p}{q}, P = q\cot p.$$

Show that transformation is canonical and obtain the generating function.

Solution: For transformation to be canonical $[Q,P] = 1$. We have

$$\frac{\partial P}{\partial p} = -q\,\mathrm{cosec}^2 p, \quad \frac{\partial P}{\partial q} = \cot p, \quad \frac{\partial Q}{\partial q} = \frac{q}{\sin p}\frac{(-\sin p)}{q^2} = -\frac{1}{q}, \quad \frac{\partial Q}{\partial p} = -\frac{q}{\sin p}\frac{\cos p}{q} = \cot p$$

$$[Q,P] = -\frac{1}{q}(-q\,\mathrm{cosec}^2 p) - \cot p \cot p = (1+\cot^2 p) - \cot^2 p = 1$$

Hence, the transformation is canonical. Writing the given transformation as $q = \exp(-Q)\sin p, \quad P = \exp(-Q)\cos p$ that is, in terms of one old and one new variable. Since $P = -\frac{\partial F_3}{\partial Q}$ we have

$$F_3 = -\int P\,dQ + C = -\int \exp(-Q)\cos p\,dQ + C = \exp(-Q)\cos p + C$$

where C is independent of Q to be adjusted by using the condition that

$$\frac{\partial F_3}{\partial p} = -q = -\exp(-Q)\sin p$$

we find that $C = 0$. The required generating function is then

$$F_3 = \exp(-Q)\cos p$$

Example 8. *The motion of the particle of mass m is described by the Hamiltonian*

$$H = \frac{p_1^2}{2m} + \frac{p_2^2}{2m} + mAq_1$$

where A is a constant. Obtain the solution of the equation of motion using Poisson brackets.

Solution: From Eq. (8.54) we have

$$\dot{p}_1 = [\, p_1, H \,] = \frac{\partial p_1}{\partial q_1}\frac{\partial H}{\partial p_1} - \frac{\partial p_1}{\partial p_1}\frac{\partial H}{\partial q_1} + \frac{\partial p_1}{\partial q_2}\frac{\partial H}{\partial p_2} - \frac{\partial p_1}{\partial p_2}\frac{\partial H}{\partial q_2} = -mA$$

$$p_1 = -mA\,t + c_1$$

Let at $t = 0$ $p_1 = p_x$. Then $c_1 = p_x$ and above equation takes the form

$$p_1 = -mA\,t + p_x$$

Now consider

$$\dot{p}_2 = [\, p_2, H \,] = 0, \text{ or } p_2 = \text{constant} = \mathrm{p_y}$$

$$\dot{q}_1 = [\, q_1, H \,] = \frac{p_1}{m_1} \text{ or } \quad q_1 = \frac{p_1 t}{m} + c_2 = -\frac{mA\,t^2}{m} + \frac{p_x t}{m} + c_2$$

Let at $t = 0$, $q_1 = x_0$, then $c_2 = x_0$ and the above equation takes the form

$$q_1 = -A\,t^2 + \frac{p_x t}{m} + x_0$$

and

$$\dot{q}_2 = [\, q_2, H \,\} = \frac{p_2}{m} \text{ or } q_2 = \frac{p_2}{m} t + c_3 = \frac{p_y}{m} t + c_3$$

Let at $t = 0$, $q_2 = y_0$, then $c_3 = y_0$ and the above equation takes the form

$$q_2 = \frac{p_y}{m} t + y_0$$

Example 9. *Evaluate $[L_i, L_j]$*

Solution: We have

$$L_x = y p_z - z p_y = \varepsilon_{ijk} x_j p_k + \varepsilon_{ikj} x_k p_j$$

ε is Levi-Civita symbol with the properties

$$\varepsilon_{123} = \varepsilon_{231} = \varepsilon_{312} = 1$$

$$\varepsilon_{132} = \varepsilon_{213} = \varepsilon_{321} = -1$$

all others $\varepsilon_{ijk} = 0$, that is, when two indices are equal. For a fixed value of i

$$L_i = \varepsilon_{ijk} x_j p_k$$

Consider $[L_i, L_j]$

$$[\, L_i, L_j \,] = [\, \varepsilon_{ink} x_n, \varepsilon_{jlm} x_l P_m \,] = \varepsilon_{ink} \varepsilon_{jlm} [\, x_n p_k, x_l p_m \,] = \varepsilon_{ink} \varepsilon_{jlm} [\, x_n p_k, \alpha \,]$$

where

$$\alpha = x_l p_m$$

$$[\, L_i, L_j \,] = \varepsilon_{ink}\, \varepsilon_{jlm} \{\, x_n [\, p_k, \alpha \,] + [\, x_n, \alpha \,] p_k$$

$$= \varepsilon_{ink}\, \varepsilon_{jlm}\, \{x_n[p_k, x_l]p_m + x_n x_l[p_k, p_m] + x_l[x_n, p_m]p_k + [x_n, x_l]p_m p_k\}$$

$$= \varepsilon_{ink}\, \varepsilon_{jlm}\, \{-x_n\, \delta_{kl}\, p_m + 0 + x_l\, \delta_{nm}\, p_k + 0\}$$

$$= \varepsilon_{ink}\, \varepsilon_{jln}\, x_l\, p_k - \varepsilon_{ink}\, \varepsilon_{jkm} x_n\, p_m$$

$$= \varepsilon_{nki}\, \varepsilon_{jln}\, x_l\, p_k - \varepsilon_{nki}\, \varepsilon_{jkm} x_n\, p_m$$

Putting $k = m$ in the first term and $n = l$ in second term

$$= \varepsilon_{nmi}\, \varepsilon_{jln}\, x_l\, p_m - \varepsilon_{lki}\, \varepsilon_{jkm} x_l\, p_m$$

$$= (\varepsilon_{nmi}\, \varepsilon_{jln} - \varepsilon_{lki}\, \varepsilon_{jkm})x_l\, p_m$$

In $\varepsilon_{nmi}\varepsilon_{jln}$ for a given n implies $m \neq i$ for $\varepsilon_{nmi} \neq 0$. For $\varepsilon_{jln} \neq 0$ requires either $m = j$ and $i = l$ or $j = l$, then $m = l$.

$$\varepsilon_{nmi}\varepsilon_{jln} = \delta_{mj}\, \delta_{il} - \delta_{ml}\, \delta_{ij}$$

and

$$\varepsilon_{kil}\, \varepsilon_{kmj} = \delta_{im}\, \delta_{lj} - \delta_{ij}\, \delta_{lm} \quad \text{for a given } k$$

Thus

$$(\varepsilon_{nmi}\, \varepsilon_{jln} - \varepsilon_{lki}\, \varepsilon_{jkm})x_l\, p_m = (\delta_{mj}\, \delta_{il} - \delta_{ml}\, \delta_{ij} - \delta_{im}\, \delta_{lj} + \delta_{ij}\, \delta_{lm})\, x_l\, p_m$$

$$[L_i, L_j] = (\varepsilon_{nmi}\, \varepsilon_{jln} - \varepsilon_{lki}\, \varepsilon_{jkm})x_l\, p_m = (\delta_{mj}\, \delta_{il} - \delta_{im}\, \delta_{lj})\, x_l\, p_m$$

$$[L_i, L_j] = \varepsilon_{kij}\, \varepsilon_{klm}\, x_l\, p_m = \varepsilon_{ijk}\, \varepsilon_{klm}\, x_l\, p_m = \varepsilon_{ijk}\, L_k$$

Thus

$$[L_i, L_j] = \varepsilon_{ijk}\, L_k$$

for $i = j$, $\varepsilon_{iik} = 0$

$$[L_i, L_i] = 0$$

Therefore,

$$[L_x, L_x] = [L_y, L_y] = [L_z, L_z] = 0$$

$$[L_x, L_y] = L_z; \quad [L_y, L_z] = L_x; \quad [L_z, L_x] = L_y$$

Example 10. *Evaluate* $[L_i, x_j]$

Solution: $[L_i, x_j] = [\varepsilon_{ikl} x_k\, p_l, x_j] = \varepsilon_{ikl}\, [x_k\, p_l, x_j]$

$$[L_i, x_j] = \varepsilon_{ikl}\, \{x_k\, [p_l, x_j] + [x_k, x_j]\, p_l = -\varepsilon_{ikl}\, x_k \delta_{jl} = -\varepsilon_{ikj} x_k = \varepsilon_{ijk} x_k$$

putting $i = j$

$$[L_i, x_i] = [L_x, x] = \varepsilon_{iik} x_k = 0$$

Similarly

$$[L_y, y] = 0; \quad [L_z, z] = 0$$

for $i \neq j$

$$[L_i, x_j] = [L_x, y] = \varepsilon_{ijk} x_k = z; [L_y, z] = x; [L_z, x] = y$$

Example 11. *Evaluate* $[L_i, p_j]$

Solution:

$$[L_i, p_j] = [\varepsilon_{ikl} x_k p_l, p_j] = \varepsilon_{ikl}\{x_k [p_l, p_j] + [x_k, p_j] p_l\} = \varepsilon_{ikl}\, \delta_{jk} p_l$$

$$[L_i, p_j] = \varepsilon_{ijl}\; p_l$$

putting $i = j$

$$[L_i, p_i] = \varepsilon_{iil} p_l = 0$$

or

$$[L_x, p_x] = [L_y, p_y] = [L_y, p_y] = 0$$

if $i \neq j$

$$[L_y, p_y] = \varepsilon_{ijl}\; p_l \text{ or } [L_y, p_y] = p_z, [L_y, p_y] = p_x, [L_z, p_x] = p_y$$

OBJECTIVE TYPE QUESTIONS

1. The transformation is called canonical if *pdq - PdQ* is

   (*a*) a partial differential (*b*) an exact differential
   (*c*) both (*a*) and (*b*) (*d*) none of these

2. The Poisson bracket of two constants of the motion is itself a constant of motion. This is

   (*a*) Poisson's equation theorem (*b*) Canonical theorem
   (*c*) Poisson's theorem (*d*) Jacobi's

3. The Poisson brackets are defined by the equation

   (*a*) $[f, g]_{q,p} = \sum_{k=1}^{n}\left(\frac{\partial f}{\partial q_k}\frac{\partial g}{\partial p_k} - \frac{\partial g}{\partial q_k}\frac{\partial f}{\partial p_k}\right)$

   (*b*) $[f, g]_{q,p} = \sum_{k=1}^{n}\left(\frac{\partial f}{\partial q_k}\frac{\partial g}{\partial p_k} + \frac{\partial g}{\partial q_k}\frac{\partial f}{\partial p_k}\right)$

   (*c*) $[f, g]_{q,p} = \sum_{k=1}^{n}\left(\frac{\partial f}{\partial q_k}\frac{\partial g}{\partial q_k} - \frac{\partial g}{\partial p_k}\frac{\partial f}{\partial p_k}\right)$

$$(d)\ [f,g]_{q,p} = -\sum_{k=1}^{n}\left(\frac{\partial f}{\partial q_k}\frac{\partial g}{\partial p_k} - \frac{\partial g}{\partial q_k}\frac{\partial f}{\partial p_k}\right)$$

4. Poisson bracket have the relation

(*a*) $[f, g] = [g, f]$ (*b*) $[f, g] = [g, g]$

(*c*) $[f, g] = 0$ (*d*) $[f, g] = -[g, f]$

5. For a given transformation (i) $Q = p,\ p = -q$ and (ii) $Q = p,\ P = q$ where p and q are canonical conjugate variables, which one of the following statement is true?

(*a*) only (i) is canonical (*b*) only (ii) is canonical

(*c*) both (i) and (ii) are canonical (*d*) neither (i) nor (ii) is canonical

6. For what values of a and b the transformation $Q = (a\,p/x)$, $P = b\,x^2$ is canonical

(*a*) $a=1$, $b=2$ (*b*) $a = 2$, $b=1$

(*c*) $a=(1/2)$, $b=-1$ (*d*) $a=-1$, $b=(1/2)$

7. Which transformation is canonical?

(*a*) $Q = p - iaq,\ P = \dfrac{p - iaq}{21a}$ (*b*) $Q = p + iaq,\ P = \dfrac{p - iaq}{21a}$

(*c*) $Q = p - iaq,\ P = \dfrac{p + iaq}{21a}$ (*d*) none of these

8. For what values of a and b do the equation $Q = q^b \cos bp$, $P = q^b \sin ap$ represent a canonical transformation

(*a*) $a = (1/2)$, $b = 2$ (b) $a = 2$, $b = (1/2)$

(*c*) $a = 1$, $b = 1$ (*d*) $a = -1/2$, $b = 2$

9. The generating function for the canonical transformation

$Q = \log\dfrac{\sin p}{q},\ P = q\cot p$ is

(*a*) $\exp(Q)\cos p$ (*b*) $Q \log \sin p$

(*c*) $\exp(-Q)\cos p$ (*d*) $\exp(-Q)\cot p$

10. Which is not correct?

(*a*) The general form of a canonical transformation involves a generating function which controls the transformation

(*b*) The product of two canonical transformation is once more a canonical transformation

(*c*) The canonical transformations are those transformations which leave the Poisson bracket $[f,g]$ invariant no matter how the functions f and g depends on q and p.

(*d*) In the infinitesimal contact transformation $Q_k = q_k + \delta q_k$, $P_k = p_k + \delta p_k$, δq_k and δp_k represent virtual displacements.

11. q_1 and q_2 are generalized coordinates and p_1 and p_2 are the corresponding generalized momenta. The Poisson bracket $[F,G]$ of $F = q_1^2 + q_2^2, G = 2p_1 + p_2$ is

(*a*) $(q_1^2 + q_2^2)p_1$ (*b*) $4q_1 + 2q_2$

(*c*) $3(q_1^2 + q_2^2)$ (*d*) 0

12. A linear transformation of a generalized coordinate q and the corresponding momentum p to Q and P is given as $Q = q + p$. $P = q + \alpha p$ is canonical if the value of constant α is

(*a*) 0 (*b*) –1

(*c*) 1 (*d*) 2

13. The Jacobi identity is

(*a*) $[f, [g,h]]-[h, [g,f]]-[g, [f,h]]=0$ (*b*) $[f, [g,h]]+[h, [g,f]]-[g, [f,h]]=0$

(*c*) $[f, [g,h]]-[h,[g,f]]+[g, [f,h]]=0$ (*d*) $[f, [g,h]]+[h, [g,f]]+[g,[f,h]]=0$

14. Which is not correct?

(*a*) $p_k = \dfrac{\partial F_2}{\partial q_k}, Q_k = \dfrac{\partial F_2}{\partial P_k}$

(*b*) $P_k = -\dfrac{\partial F_3}{\partial Q_k}, q_k = -\dfrac{\partial F_3}{\partial p_k}$

(*c*) $q_k = \dfrac{\partial F_4}{\partial P_k}, Q_k = -\dfrac{\partial F_4}{\partial p_k}$

(*d*) $q_k = \dfrac{\partial F_1}{\partial p_k}, P_k = -\dfrac{\partial F_1}{\partial Q_k}$

PROBLEMS

1. The transformation equations between two sets of coordinates are

   $Q = ln(1+q^{1/2} \cos p), P = 2(q^{1/2} + q\cos p)\sin p$

   Show from these transformation equations that Q and P are canonical variables if q and p are.
   Obtain the generating function.

2. Show that the transformation

   $Q = p + iaq, P = (p - iaq)/2ia$ is canonical.

3. For which constants a and b is the transformation

   $Q = \frac{\alpha p}{x}, P = \beta x^2$ canonical.

4. Show that the transformation $Q = \sqrt{q}\, \cos 2p, P = \sqrt{q}\, \sin 2p$ is canonical.

5. Show that the transformation defined by

   $Q = \sqrt{2q}\, exp(k)\cos p, P = \sqrt{2q}\, exp(-k)\sin p$ is canonical.

6. For what values of α and β do the equation

   $Q = q^{\alpha} \cos \beta\, p, P = q^{\alpha} \sin \beta\, p$ represent a canonical transformation. What is the form of generating function?

7. Show that the transformation

   $Q = q\cos\theta - p\sin\theta; P = q\sin\theta + p\sin\theta$ is canonical.

8. Evaluate $[L_i, A_{jk}]$ and $[A_{jk}, A_{il}]$ where $A_{jk} = x_j x_k + p_j p_k$.

9. Show that the transformation $Q = q \tan p$, $P = \ln \sin p$ is canonical.

10. Show that

    $(\varepsilon_{nmi}\varepsilon_{jln} - \varepsilon_{lki}\varepsilon_{jkm} = \delta_{mj}\delta_{il} - \delta_{ml}\delta_{ij} - \delta_{im}\delta_{lj} + \delta_{ij}\delta_{lm})$

11. Consider a motion of a free particle of mass m. Given its constant of motion $F = x - (pt/m)$.

    Show that $\frac{\partial F}{\partial t} = -[F, H] = -\frac{p}{m}$

12. Given $H = \frac{p^2}{2m} - \frac{1}{2q^2}$ and $F = \frac{pq}{2} - Ht$, show that F is a constant of motion.

❑❑❑

CHAPTER 9

Hamilton Jacobi Equation

9.1 HAMILTON JACOBI EQUATION

The solution of the equation of motion of a canonical system becomes elementary if we succeed in making all coordinates q_k cyclic ones so that all p_k are constants of motion. Let these constants be denoted by α_k. For a conservative system

$$H = H(\alpha_1, ..., \alpha_n)$$

$$\dot{q}_k = \frac{\partial H}{\partial \alpha_k} = \mathrm{w}_k \quad (k = 1, ..., n)$$

where w_k are constant. The above equation on integration gives

$$q_k = \mathrm{w}_k t + \beta_k$$

where β_k are constant of integration.

An alternative technique is to look for canonical transformation which makes q_k and p_k functions of initial values. In this case

$$q_k = q_k(q_0, p_0, t)$$
$$p_k = p_k(q_0, p_0, t)$$

The Hamilton Jacobi theory aims to get a solution in this form.

The equation of motion in terms of the new Hamiltonian $\hat{H}$ and the relation between $\hat{H}$ and H are

$$\dot{Q}_k = \frac{\partial \hat{H}}{\partial P_k} \qquad ...(9.1)$$

$$\dot{P}_k = -\frac{\partial \hat{H}}{\partial Q_k} \qquad ...(9.2)$$

$$\hat{H}(Q,P,t) = H(q,p,t) + \frac{\partial F}{\partial t} \qquad ...(9.3)$$

where F is the generating function of the transformation. If new variables Q_k and P_k are constants then

$$\dot{Q}_k = 0 = \frac{\partial \hat{H}}{\partial P_k} \qquad ...(9.4)$$

$$\dot{P}_k = 0 = -\frac{\partial \hat{H}}{\partial Q_k} \qquad ...(9.5)$$

This implies that $\hat{H}$ depends neither on P nor on Q. $\hat{H}$ is a constant and we can set it equal to zero. A transformation from H to $\hat{H} = 0$ is possible if we use a generating function that depends on time t.

The generating function must satisfy the equation

$$H(q,p,t) + \frac{\partial F}{\partial t} = 0 \qquad ...(9.6)$$

we choose the generating function of the form

$$F = F_2(q,P,t) \qquad ...(9.7)$$

The Eq. (9.6) is therefore

$$H(q,p,t) + \frac{\partial F_2(q,P,t)}{\partial t} = 0 \qquad ...(9.8)$$

In this equation P's are constant as shown by Eq. (9.5). We have

$$p_k = \frac{\partial F_2}{\partial q_k} \qquad ...(9.9)$$

Substituting these values of p_k from Eq. (9.9) in Eq. (9.8)

$$H\left(q_1, q_2, ..., q_n, \frac{\partial F_2}{\partial q_1}, \frac{\partial F_2}{\partial q_2}, ..., \frac{\partial F_2}{\partial q_n}, t\right) + \frac{\partial F_2}{\partial t} = 0 \qquad ...(9.10)$$

where in the Hamiltonian the momenta have been expressed in terms of derivatives of F by using the Eq. (9.9). The Eq. (9.10) is known as the Hamilton-Jacobi partial differential equation. It is an equation of the first order, in $(n+1)$ independent variables q's and t. The solution of the equation is denoted by S and is called Hamilton's principal function. We shall therefore, use S instead of F_2. S and F_2 can differ at most by an irrelevant constant since only the derivative of F_2 appears. Its complete solution must involve $(n+1)$ constant of integration, but S itself does not appear in Eq. (9.10), one of the constants α_k is purely additive because if S is a solution then $S+\alpha$ is also a solution of Eq. (9.10). The other n constants may be taken as a_k $(k = 1,2,..,n)$. The complete solution of Eq. (9.10) is therefore

$$S(q_1,.....,q_n,\alpha_1,........,\alpha_n,t) \qquad ...(9.11)$$

where none of the n constants is additive and there are new constants P_k. For p_k we have

$$p_k = \frac{\partial S(q,\alpha,t)}{\partial q_k} \qquad ...(9.12)$$

at $t=0$ these constitutes n equations relating q_0, p_0 and α_k. These may be solved to yield

$$\alpha_k = \alpha_k(q_0, p_0) \qquad ...(9.13)$$

Consider Eq.(8.18)

$$Q_k = \frac{\partial F_2}{\partial P_k} \qquad ...(9.14)$$

Since Q_k are also constant and let these constants are designated by β_k. In view of $P_k = \alpha_k$, we obtain

$$Q_k = \beta_k = \frac{\partial S(q_k,\alpha_k,t)}{\partial \alpha_k} \qquad ...(9.15)$$

at $t = 0$, these constitute n equation relating q_0, p_0 and β_k. These may be solved to yield

$$\beta_k = \beta_k(q_0, p_0) \qquad ...(9.16)$$

Eq. (9.15) is the implicit solution from which we have

$$q_k = q_k(\alpha_k, \beta_k, t) \qquad ...(9.17)$$

which solves the problem by giving the coordinates as function of time and the initial conditions.

Since $\hat{H} = 0$ and Q_k are constants of the motion, the new Lagrangian is

$$\hat{L} = P_k\dot{Q}_k - \hat{H} \qquad ...(9.18)$$

The $\hat{L}$ is also zero. The total time derivative of $S(q_k, \alpha, t)$

$$\frac{dS}{dt} = \sum_k \frac{\partial S}{\partial q_k}\dot{q}_k + \frac{\partial S}{\partial t} = \sum_k p_k \dot{q}_k - H = L \qquad ...(9.19)$$

On integration

$$S = \int L\,dt + \text{constant} \qquad ...(9.20)$$

The Hamilton's principal function differ from the indefinite time integral of the Lagrangian by a constant.

9.2 HARMONIC OSCILLATOR PROBLEM AS AN EXAMPLE OF HAMILTON-JACOBI METHOD

Consider a simple harmonic oscillator in one dimension. The Hamiltonian of the oscillator is

$$H = \frac{p^2}{2m} + \frac{1}{2}kq^2 = \frac{1}{2m}\left(p^2 + mkq^2\right) = \frac{1}{2m}\left(p^2 + m^2\omega^2 q^2\right) = E \qquad ...(9.21)$$

where k is the spring constant and $\omega = \sqrt{(k/m)}$ is the frequency of the oscillator.

Putting $F_2 = S$ in Hamilton-Jacobi Eq. (9.10) we have

$$H\left(q_1, q_2, \ldots, q_n, \frac{\partial S}{\partial q_1}, \frac{\partial S}{\partial q_2}, \ldots\ldots, \frac{\partial S}{\partial q_n}, t\right) + \frac{\partial S}{\partial t} = 0 \qquad ...(9.22)$$

Now

$$p = \frac{\partial S}{\partial q} \qquad ...(9.23)$$

Eq. (9.22) for harmonic oscillator is

$$\frac{1}{2m}\left[\left(\frac{\partial S}{\partial q}\right)^2 + m^2\omega^2 q^2\right] + \frac{\partial S}{\partial t} = 0 \qquad ...(9.24)$$

The explicit dependence of S on t involved only in $\frac{\delta s}{\partial t}$, thus a solution is of the form

$$S(q, \alpha, t) = W(q, \alpha) - \alpha t \qquad ...(9.25)$$

The Eq. (9.24) is

$$\frac{1}{2m}\left[\left(\frac{\partial W}{\partial q}\right)^2 + m^2\omega^2 q^2\right] = \alpha \qquad ...(9.26)$$

Thus α is identified with total energy E. The Eq. (9.26) is

$$\left(\frac{\partial W}{\partial q}\right)^2 = 2\,m\alpha - m^2\,\omega^2\,q^2 = 2\,m\,\alpha\left(1-\frac{m\,\omega^2\,q^2}{2\alpha}\right) \qquad ...(9.27)$$

$$\frac{\partial W}{\partial q} = \sqrt{2m\alpha}\sqrt{1-\frac{m\omega^2\,q^2}{2\alpha}} \qquad ...(9.28)$$

on integration

$$W = = \sqrt{2m\alpha}\int\sqrt{1-\frac{m\omega^2\,q^2}{2\alpha}}\;dq \qquad ...(9.29)$$

Substituting Eq. (9.29) in Eq. (9.25)

$$S(q,\alpha,t) = \sqrt{2m\alpha}\int\sqrt{1-\frac{m\omega^2\,q^2}{2\alpha}}\;dq - \alpha\,t \qquad ...(9.30)$$

$$S(\,q,\alpha,t\,) = \int\sqrt{\frac{mk\,2\alpha}{k} - \frac{m\mathrm{k}\,2\alpha\,q^2}{2\alpha}}\;dq - \alpha\,t$$

$$S(\,q,\alpha,t\,) = \sqrt{mk}\int\sqrt{\frac{2\alpha}{k} - q^2}\;dq - \alpha\,t \qquad ...(9.31)$$

Differentiating with respect to the arbitrary constant α and equating the derivative to new constant β

$$\frac{\partial S}{\partial \alpha_k} = \beta_k \qquad ...(9.32)$$

These are n algebraic equations. Differentiating Eq. (9.31)

$$\frac{\partial S}{\partial \alpha} = \sqrt{\frac{m}{k}}\int\left(\frac{2\alpha}{k} - q^2\right)^{-\frac{1}{2}} dq - \,t = \beta \qquad ...(9.33)$$

$$\beta + t = \sqrt{\frac{m}{k}}\int\left(\frac{2\alpha}{k} - q^2\right)^{-\frac{1}{2}} dq \; = \sqrt{\frac{m}{k}}\,\sin^{-1} q\sqrt{\frac{k}{2\alpha}} = \frac{1}{\omega}\sin^{-1} q\sqrt{\frac{k}{2\alpha}}$$

$$q = \sqrt{\frac{2\alpha}{k}}\,\sin\omega\,(\mathrm{t}+\beta) = \sqrt{\frac{2\alpha}{m\omega^2}}\,\sin\omega\,(\mathrm{t}+\beta) \qquad ...(9.34)$$

which is a familiar solution for a simple harmonic oscillator.

From Eqs. (9.23) and (9.25)

$$p = \frac{\partial S}{\partial q} = \frac{\partial W}{\partial q} \qquad ...(9.35)$$

From Eqs. (9.28) and (9.34)

$$\frac{\partial W}{\partial q} = p = \sqrt{2m\alpha}\sqrt{1 - \frac{m\omega^2\, 2\alpha}{2\alpha m\omega^2}\sin^2\omega(\mathrm{t}+\beta)} = \sqrt{2m\alpha}\sqrt{1-\sin^2\omega(t+\beta)}$$

$$p = \sqrt{2m\alpha}\,\cos\omega\,(t+\beta) \qquad ...(9.36)$$

9.3 ACTION AND ANGLE VARIABLES

The Hamilton-Jacobi method is useful for dealing with periodic system. Two kinds of periodic system may be distinguished. Consider a trajectory of a system in phase space which is closed curve. The system passes through the same state, that is p and q repeat their values after a certain time interval. Such a motion is designated by the name liberation. The examples of such kind of a motion are simple harmonic oscillator, simple pendulum. In the second type of periodic motion q itself is not periodic, but is such that q is increased by some value, say q_0, the configuration of the system remains essentially unchanged. As an example consider the rotation of a rigid body about a given axis. In this case q can be taken as the angle of rotation and q_0 can be taken equal to 2π. Such a motion is called rotation. The value of q are no longer bounded but can increase indefinitely libration and rotation are not mutually exclusive, for example simple pendulum exhibit both liberation and rotation.

We now define a new set of canonical variables to deal with the periodic systems. The variables are denoted by J and θ, J is the conjugate momentum to θ. The set of defining equation for the generating function is

$$p = \frac{\partial S(q, J)}{\partial q} \qquad ...(9.37)$$

$$\theta = \frac{\partial S(q, J)}{\partial J} \qquad ...(9.38)$$

The Hamilton-Jacobi equation is

$$H\left(q, \frac{\partial S}{\partial q}\right) = \alpha = H(\mathbf{J}) \qquad ...(9.39)$$

Differentiating θ with respect to q, for a trajectory with fixed α

$$\frac{d\theta}{dq} = \frac{\partial}{\partial J}\left(\frac{\partial S}{\partial q}\right) \qquad ...(9.40)$$

If the trajectory is completely traversed then θ should increase by 2π, that is,

$$\oint_c d\theta = 2\pi = \frac{\partial}{\partial J}\oint_c\left(\frac{\partial S}{\partial q}\right)dq = \frac{\partial}{\partial J}\oint_c p\,dq \qquad ...(9.41)$$

The condition is satisfied if

$$J = \frac{1}{2\pi}\oint_c p(q,\alpha)\,dq \qquad ...(9.42)$$

The Eq. (9.42) is the defining relation of the action variable. Eq. (9.42) is independent of the choice of integration path *c*.

The canonical equations of motion are

$$\dot{J} = -\frac{\partial H(J)}{\partial \theta} = 0 \qquad ...(9.43)$$

$$\dot{\theta} = -\frac{\partial H(J)}{\partial J} = \omega(\text{J}) \qquad ...(9.44)$$

On solving Eqs. (9.43) and (9.44)

$$J = \text{constant} \qquad ...(9.45)$$

$$\theta = \omega(J)\text{t} + \delta \qquad ...(9.46)$$

where $\omega(J)$ is the characteristic frequency of the motion and $\delta = \theta(0)$ is determined by the initial condition.

Solved Examples

Example 1. *Find frequency of a linear harmonic oscillator using action angle variables. Write Hamilton's equation of motion.*

Solution: The Hamiltonian for the simple harmonic oscillator is

$$H = \frac{p^2}{2m} + \frac{1}{2}kq^2 = \frac{p^2}{2m} + \frac{1}{2}m\omega^2 q^2$$

The Hamilton-Jacob equation is [Eq. (9.24)]

$$\frac{1}{2m}\left[\left(\frac{\partial S}{\partial q}\right)^2 + m^2\omega^2 q^2\right] + \frac{\partial S}{\partial t} = 0$$

The explicit dependence of *S* on *t* involved only in $\frac{\partial S}{\partial t}$, thus a solution is of the form [Eq. (9.25)]

$$S(q,\alpha,t)=W(q,\alpha)-\alpha t$$

Thus Hamilton-Jacobi equation take the form

$$\frac{1}{2m}\left[\left(\frac{\partial W}{\partial q}\right)^2+m^2\omega^2q^2\right]=\alpha$$

Thus α is identified with total energy E. From Eq. (9.42)

$$J=\frac{1}{2\pi}\oint_c p(q,\alpha)\,dq=\frac{1}{2\pi}\oint_c\frac{\partial W(q,\alpha)}{\partial q}\,dq=\frac{\sqrt{mk}}{2\pi}\oint\sqrt{\frac{2\alpha}{k}-q^2}\,dq$$

Putting $q=\sqrt{\frac{2\alpha}{k}}\,sin\,\theta,\quad dq=\sqrt{\frac{2\alpha}{k}}\,cos\,\theta\,d\theta$

$$J=\frac{\sqrt{mk}}{2\pi}\left(\frac{2\alpha}{k}\right)\int_0^{2\pi}\cos^2\theta\,d\theta=\frac{\alpha}{\pi\omega}\int_0^{2\pi}\left(\frac{1+\cos 2\theta}{2}\right)d\theta=\frac{\alpha}{\pi\omega}\left[\frac{\theta}{2}+\frac{\sin 2\theta}{4}\right]_0^{2\pi}=\frac{\alpha}{\omega}$$

$$\alpha=H=J\,\omega$$

The frequency of oscillation is

$$\frac{\partial H}{\partial J}=\omega$$

OBJECTIVE TYPE QUESTIONS

1. Which is true about Hamilton's principal function *S?*

(*a*) $S=\int L\,dt$ (*b*) $S=L\,dt$

(*c*) $S=\int L\,dt+\text{constant}$ (*d*) none of the above

2. Hamilton -Jacobi equation is

(*a*) $H\left(q_k,\frac{\partial F_2}{\partial q_k},t\right)+\frac{\partial F_2}{\partial t}=0$ (*b*) $H\left(q_k,\frac{\partial F_2}{\partial q_k},t\right)=0$

(*c*) $H=\sum_k q_k p_k-L$ (*d*) none of the above

3. Hamilton-Jacobi equation for simple harmonic oscillator is

(*a*) $\frac{1}{2m}\left[\left(\frac{\partial S}{\partial q}\right)^2 + m^2\omega^2 q^2\right] = 0$

(*b*) $\frac{1}{2m}\left[\left(\frac{\partial S}{\partial q}\right)^2 + m\omega^2 q^2\right] = 0$

(*c*) $\frac{1}{2m}\left[\left(\frac{\partial S}{\partial q}\right)^2 + m^2\omega^2 q^2\right] + \frac{\partial S}{\partial t} = 0$

(*d*) $\frac{1}{2m}\left[\left(\frac{\partial S}{\partial q}\right)^2 + m\omega^2 q^2\right] + \frac{\partial S}{\partial t} = 0$

4. The solution of Hamilton-Jacobi equation of simple harmonic oscillator is

(*a*) $S(q,\alpha,t) = W(q,\alpha) - \alpha$

(*b*) $S(q,\alpha,t) = W(q,\alpha) + \alpha t^2$

(*c*) $S(q,\alpha,t) = W(q,\alpha) - \alpha t^2$

(*d*) $S(q,\alpha,t) = W(q,\alpha) - \alpha t$

5. Simple pendulum exhibits

(*a*) rotation
(*b*) liberation
(*c*) rotation and liberation
(*d*) none of these

6. Which is not true?

(*a*) rigid body exhibits rotation
(*b*) rigid body exhibits liberation
(*c*) rotation and liberation are not mutually exclusive
(*d*) simple pendulum exhibits liberation

7. The Hamilton-Jacobi equation for a single particle moving under the Hamiltonian ($p^2/2$) is

(*a*) $\frac{1}{2}\left[\left(\frac{\partial S}{\partial q}\right)^2 + \omega^2 q^2\right] + \frac{\partial S}{\partial t} = 0$

(*b*) $\frac{1}{2m}\left[\left(\frac{\partial S}{\partial q}\right)^2 + m^2\omega^2 q^2\right] - \frac{\partial S}{\partial t} = 0$

(c) $\frac{1}{2m}\left[\left(\frac{\partial S}{\partial q}\right)^2 + \omega^2 q^2\right] = 0$

(d) $\frac{1}{2}\left[\left(\frac{\partial S}{\partial q}\right)^2\right] + \frac{\partial S}{\partial t} = 0$

8. Action variable is defined as

(a) $\frac{1}{4\pi}\oint p(q,\alpha)\, dq$

(b) $\frac{1}{2\pi}\oint p(q,\alpha)\, dq$

(c) $\frac{1}{2\pi}\oint q(p,\alpha)\, dp$

(d) $\oint q(p,\alpha)\, dp$

9. J has the dimension of

(a) time
(b) energy
(c) energy × time
(d) none of these

10. The canonical equations of motion are

(a) $\dot{J} = -\frac{\partial H}{\partial \theta}, \dot{\theta} = -\frac{\partial H}{\partial J}$

(b) $\dot{J} = -\frac{\partial H}{\partial \theta}, \dot{\theta} = \frac{\partial H}{\partial J}$

(c) $\dot{J} = \frac{\partial H}{\partial \theta}, \dot{\theta} = -\frac{\partial H}{\partial J}$

(d) $\dot{J} = \frac{\partial H}{\partial \theta}, \dot{\theta} = \frac{\partial H}{\partial J}$

PROBLEMS

1. A particle of mass m moves in a force field whose potential in spherical polar coordinates is

$$V = -\frac{k\cos\theta}{r^2}$$

write the Hamilton-Jacobi equation.

2. Solve the Hamilton-Jacobi equation for the system whose Hamiltonian is

$$H = \frac{p^2}{2m} - \frac{k}{q}$$

3. Consider a particle projected in a uniform gravitational field. The field is in the x direction. Obtain Hamilton-Jacobi equation.

4. Obtain Hamilton-Jacobi equation for a three dimensional harmonic oscillator.

5. Obtain Hamilton-Jacobi equation for a particle moving under the potential

$$V = A(r) + \frac{B(\theta)}{r^2} + \frac{C(\varphi)}{r^2 \sin^2\theta}$$

where A,B and C are some functions of their arguments.

❑❑❑

CHAPTER 10

Central Forces

10.1 CENTRAL FORCE

A force which is directed always towards or away from a fixed centre and whose magnitude is a function only of distance from the centre is called a central force. In spherical polar coordinates

$$\mathbf{F} = \mathbf{n}\,F(r) \qquad \text{...(10.1)}$$

where

$$\mathbf{n} = \frac{\mathbf{r}}{r}$$

The force F represents an attraction [if $F(r) < 0$] and repulsion [if $F(r) > 0$] from the fixed point located at $r = 0$. Examples of attractive forces are (i) the gravitational forces acting on a planet due to sun (ii) force on electron due to nucleus of an atom. The example of repulsive forces is the force between proton or alpha particle and the nucleus. In these examples, none of the two interacting particle is fixed to a certain position. However, it is assumed that one of the particle is stationary. This is true if one of the particle is very heavy in comparison to the another one. The magnitude of the force acting on the two particles is same therefore by Newton's third law, the acceleration of heavy particle is much smaller than the lighter particle. The motion of heavy particle is therefore can be neglected. The two body problems can thus be reduced to equivalent one body problem. Thus, we need to consider only one particle moving about a fixed centre of force. We assume that this fixed centre of force is at the origin of the coordinate system. The equation of motion is

$$m\ddot{\mathbf{r}} = \mathbf{n}\,F(r) = F(r)\,\frac{\mathbf{r}}{r} \qquad ...(10.2)$$

consider the angular momentum **L**

$$\mathbf{L} = \mathbf{r} \times \mathbf{p} = \mathbf{r} \times m\dot{\mathbf{r}} \qquad ...(10.3)$$

and

$$\dot{\mathbf{L}} = \dot{\mathbf{r}} \times m\dot{\mathbf{r}} \;+\; \mathbf{r} \times m\ddot{\mathbf{r}} = 0 + \mathbf{r} \times F(r)\,\frac{\mathbf{r}}{r} \;=\; 0 \qquad ...(10.4)$$

$$\mathbf{L} = \text{constant}$$

as **L** is perpendicular to **r** and $\dot{\mathbf{r}}$, the motion takes place in a plane perpendicular to **L**. Since there is no force component normal to this plane, motion once started in it will continue in it.

10.2 REDUCTION TO THE EQUIVALENT ONE BODY PROBLEM

Consider a conservative system consisting of two particles of mass m_1 and m_2. The position of the particle of mass m_1 is specified by the radius r_1 having components (x_1, y_1, z_1) while that of m_2 by r_2 having components (x_2, y_2, z_2). Alternatively, the system has six degrees of freedom. The system can also be described by three components of the centre of mass vector **R** and the three components of the difference vector $\mathbf{r} = \mathbf{r}_1 - \mathbf{r}_2$ as shown in the Fig. (10.1). The Lagrangian for such a system is

$$L = \frac{1}{2}m_1\,\dot{\mathbf{r}}_1^2 + \frac{1}{2}m_2\,\dot{\mathbf{r}}_2^2 - V(\mathbf{r}) \qquad ...(10.5)$$

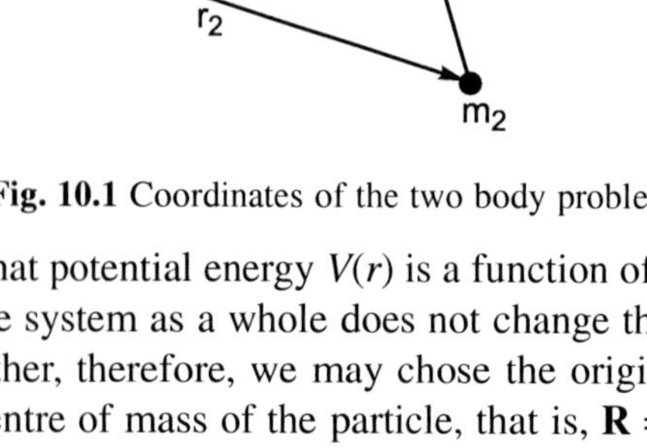

Fig. 10.1 Coordinates of the two body problem

It is assumed that potential energy $V(r)$ is a function of only r. The translational motion of the system as a whole does not change the particle orbit with respect to one another, therefore, we may chose the origin for the coordinate system to be the centre of mass of the particle, that is, $\mathbf{R} = 0$ and we have

$$m_1\mathbf{r}_1 + m_2\,\mathbf{r}_2 = 0 \qquad ...(10.6)$$

and

$$\mathbf{r} = \mathbf{r}_1 - \mathbf{r}_2 \qquad ...(10.7)$$

From relations (10.6) and (10.7)

$$m_1(\mathbf{r}_1 + \mathbf{r}_2) + m_2\,\mathbf{r}_2 = 0$$

$$\mathbf{r}_2 = -\frac{m_1\,\mathbf{r}}{m_1 + m_2} \qquad ...(10.8)$$

From Eqs. (10.7) and (10.8)

$$\mathbf{r}_1 = \frac{m_2\,\mathbf{r}}{m_1 + m_2} \qquad ...(10.9)$$

From Eqs. (10.5), (10.8) and (10.9)

$$L = \frac{1}{2}m_1\left(\frac{m_2}{m_1 + m_2}\right)^2 \dot{\mathbf{r}}^2 + \frac{1}{2}m_2\left(\frac{-m_1}{m_1 + m_2}\right)^2 \dot{\mathbf{r}}^2 - V(\mathbf{r})$$

$$L = \frac{1}{2}\left(\frac{m_1\,m_2}{m_1 + m_2}\right)^2 \dot{\mathbf{r}}^2 + \; - V(\mathbf{r}) = \frac{1}{2}\mu\dot{\mathbf{r}}^2 - V(\mathbf{r}) \qquad ...(10.10)$$

where μ is reduced mass

$$\mu = \frac{m_1\,m_2}{m_1 + m_2} \qquad ...(10.11)$$

Thus, the problem of the motion of two bodies is reduced to equivalent one body problem.

10.3 CONSERVATION THEOREMS-FIRST INTEGRAL OF THE MOTION

The system of two particles of mass m_1 and m_2 can be considered reduced to a particle of mass m which moves in a central force field described by the potential function $V(r)$. As described in Sec.10.1, the motion takes place in a plane perpendicular to angular momentum vector and angular momentum vector is conserved.

Consider that motion is in the xy plane. The kinetic energy is

$$T = \frac{1}{2}\mu(\dot{x}^2 + \dot{y}^2) \qquad ...(10.12)$$

It is convenient to introduce polar coordinates in the xy plane, that is,

$$x = r\cos\theta, \;\; y = r\sin\theta$$

$$\dot{x} = \dot{\mathrm{r}}\cos\theta - \mathrm{r}\sin\theta\,\dot{\theta}\,,\; \dot{y} = \dot{\mathrm{r}}\sin\theta + \mathrm{r}\cos\theta\,\dot{\theta}$$

Kinetic energy is therefore,

$$T = \frac{1}{2}\mu\left[(\dot r\cos\theta - r\sin\theta\,\dot\theta)^2 + (\dot r\sin\theta + r\cos\theta\,\dot\theta)^2\right] = \frac{1}{2}\mu(\dot r^2 + r^2\dot\theta^2) \quad ...(10.13)$$

The Lagrangian L is therefore,

$$L = T - V = \frac{1}{2}\mu(\dot r^2 + r^2\dot\theta^2) - V(r) \quad ...(10.14)$$

The coordinate θ is absent in the Lagrangian, therefore, θ is a cyclic coordinate and the momentum conjugate to θ is constant

$$\dot p_\theta = \frac{\partial L}{\partial\theta} = 0 = \frac{d}{dt}\left(\frac{\partial L}{\partial\dot\theta}\right) \quad ...(10.15)$$

From Eq. (10.14)

$$\frac{\partial L}{\partial\dot\theta} = \mu r^2\dot\theta \quad ...(10.16)$$

Eq. (10.15) is therefore

$$\frac{d}{dt}p_\theta = \frac{d}{dt}(\mu r^2\dot\theta) = 0 \quad ...(10.17)$$

$$p_\theta = \mu r^2\dot\theta = \text{constant} = l \quad ...(10.18)$$

where l is the constant magnitude of the angular momentum.

In describing the path $r(t)$ the radius vector sweeps out an area (Fig. 10.2) in time interval dt is

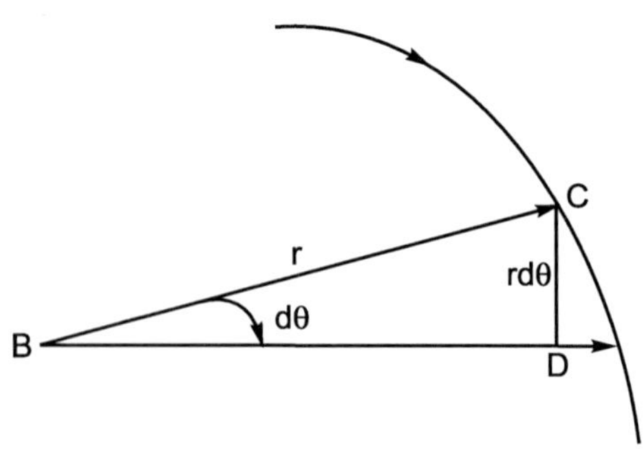

Fig. 10.2 The area sweptout by the radius vector in a time *dt*.

$$dA = \frac{1}{2}BC\times CD = \frac{1}{2}r^2\,d\theta$$

and upon dividing by the time interval dt, the areal velocity is

$$\frac{dA}{dt} = \frac{1}{2} r^2 \frac{d\theta}{dt} = \frac{1}{2} r^2 \dot{\theta} \qquad ...(10.19)$$

From Eqs. (10.18) and (10.19)

$$\frac{dA}{dt} = \frac{l}{2\mu} = \text{constant} \qquad ...(10.20)$$

The areal velocity is thus constant. The conservation of angular momentum is thus equivalent to saying that areal velocity is constant. Conservation of areal velocity is a general property for central force motion.

The total energy of the system is conserved, which means that

$$E = T + V = \frac{1}{2}\mu(\dot{r}^2 + r^2\dot{\theta}^2) + V(r) \qquad ...(10.21)$$

From relations (10.18) and (10.21)

$$E = \frac{1}{2}\mu \dot{r}^2 + \frac{l^2}{2\mu r^2} + V(r) \qquad ...(10.22)$$

10.4 EQUATION OF MOTION

When $V(r)$ is known, the Eq.(10.22) completely describes the system. From Eq. (10.22)

$$\frac{dr}{dt} = \dot{r} = \sqrt{\frac{2}{\mu}\left(E - V - \frac{l^2}{2\mu r^2}\right)} \qquad ...(10.23)$$

$$dt = \frac{dr}{\sqrt{\frac{2}{\mu}\left(E - V - \frac{l^2}{2\mu r^2}\right)}} \qquad ...(10.24)$$

Let $r = r_0$ at $t = 0$, the Eq. (10.24) on integration

$$t = \int_{r_0}^{r} \frac{dr}{\sqrt{\frac{2}{\mu}\left(E - V - \frac{l^2}{2\mu r^2}\right)}} \qquad ...(10.25)$$

The Eq. (10.25) yields the solution t as a function of r. An inversion of this result will then give the equation of motion in the form $r = r(t)$.

Consider the Eq. (10.18) from where

$$\dot{\theta} = \frac{l}{\mu\, r^2}$$

$$d\theta = \frac{l\, dt}{\mu\, r^2} \qquad ...(10.26)$$

On substitution of Eq. (10.24) in Eq. (10.26)

$$d\theta = \frac{(l/r^2 \mu)\, dr}{\sqrt{\frac{2}{\mu}\left(E - V - \frac{l^2}{2\mu r^2}\right)}}$$

On integration

$$\theta = \int_{r_0}^{r} \frac{(l/r^2 \mu)\, dr}{\sqrt{\frac{2}{\mu}\left(E - V - \frac{l^2}{2\mu r^2}\right)}} + \theta_0 \qquad ...(10.27)$$

where $q = q_0$ at $t = 0$.

Since l is constant in time, therefore, $\dot{\theta}$ cannot change sign and hence $q\ (t)$ must increase monotonically with time. The equation of motion for the coordinate r is

$$\frac{d}{dt}\left(\frac{\partial L}{\partial \dot{r}}\right) - \frac{\partial L}{\partial r} = 0 \qquad ...(10.28)$$

From the Lagrangian (10.14)

$$\frac{\partial L}{\partial \dot{r}} = \mu\, \dot{r} \qquad ...(10.29)$$

$$\frac{\partial L}{\partial r} = \mu\, r\, \dot{\theta}^2 - \frac{\partial V}{\partial r} \qquad ...(10.30)$$

On substitution of Eqs. (10.29) and (10.30) into Eq.(10.28)

$$\frac{d}{dt}(\mu \dot{r}) - \mu r \dot{\theta}^2 + \frac{\partial V}{\partial r} = 0$$

$$\mu(\ddot{r} - r\dot{\theta}^2) = -\frac{\partial V}{\partial r} = F(r) \qquad ...(10.31)$$

Let

$$u = \frac{1}{r} \qquad (10.32)$$

$$\dot{r} = \frac{dr}{dt} = -\frac{1}{u^2}\frac{du}{d\theta}\frac{d\theta}{dt} = -\frac{\dot{\theta}}{u^2}\frac{du}{d\theta} \qquad ...(10.33)$$

From Eqs.(10.18) and (10.32)

$$\dot{\theta} = \frac{l}{\mu r^2} = \frac{l}{\mu}u^2 \qquad ...(10.34)$$

On substitution of (10.34) in (10.33)

$$\dot{r} = -\frac{l}{\mu}\frac{du}{d\theta} \qquad ...(10.35)$$

$$\ddot{r} = -\frac{l}{\mu}\frac{d^2u}{d\theta^2}\dot{\theta} = -\frac{l}{\mu}\frac{d^2u}{d\theta^2}\frac{l}{\mu}u^2 = -\frac{l^2}{\mu^2}\frac{d^2u}{d\theta^2}u^2 \qquad ...(10.36)$$

On substitution of Eqs. (10.34) and (10.36) in Eq. (10.31)

$$\mu\left(-\frac{l^2}{\mu^2}\frac{d^2u}{d\theta^2}u^2 - \frac{1}{u}\frac{l^2u^4}{\mu^2}\right) = F\left(\frac{1}{u}\right)$$

$$\frac{d^2u}{d\theta^2} + u = -\frac{\mu}{l^2u^2}F\left(\frac{1}{u}\right) \qquad ...(10.37)$$

This form of the equation of motion is particularly useful, if the orbit is given and one wishes to find the force law.

10.5 THE EQUIVALENT ONE-DIMENSIONAL PROBLEM AND CLASSIFICATION OF ORBITS

The Eqs. (10.23) and (10.27) have the common term

$$\sqrt{\frac{2}{\mu}\left(E - V - \frac{l^2}{2\mu r^2}\right)} \qquad ...(10.38)$$

The term $l^2/2m\ r^2$ has the dimension of the energy and from Eq.(10.18)

$$\frac{l^2}{2\mu r^2} = \frac{1}{2}\mu r^2 \dot{\theta}^2 \qquad ...(10.39)$$

Interpreting this quantity as potential energy

$$V_c = \frac{l^2}{2\mu r^2} \qquad ...(10.40)$$

and the force

$$F_c = -\frac{dV_c}{dr} = \frac{l^2}{\mu r^3} = \mu r \dot{\theta}^2 \qquad ...(10.41)$$

F_c is called centrifugal force. Thus $l^2/2\mu\ r^2$ can be interpreted as the centrifugal potential energy. The effective potential energy is thus

$$V_{eff.}(r) = V(r) + \frac{l^2}{2\mu r^2} \qquad ...(10.42)$$

Since V_{eff} depends on the value of l, there is no unique effective potential but one potential for every value of l.

Let us consider the inverse square form of force, that is,

$$F = -\frac{k}{r^2} \qquad ...(10.43)$$

where k is a constant. The potential energy is

$$V = -\int F\,dr = \int \frac{k}{r^2}\,dr = -\frac{k}{r} \qquad ...(10.44)$$

The effective potential energy is

$$V_{eff.} = -\frac{k}{r} + \frac{l^2}{2\mu r^2} \qquad ...(10.45)$$

A plot of $V_{eff.}$ vs. r is shown in the Fig. 10.3. The value of the potential is arbitrarily taken to be zero at $r = \infty$. In $V_{eff.}$ The term $l^2/2\mu\ r^2$ dominates near $r \to 0$ whereas $-k/r$ term dominates for large values of r. Since term in right hand side of Eq. (10.45) have opposite sign, therefore V_{eff} has a minimum.

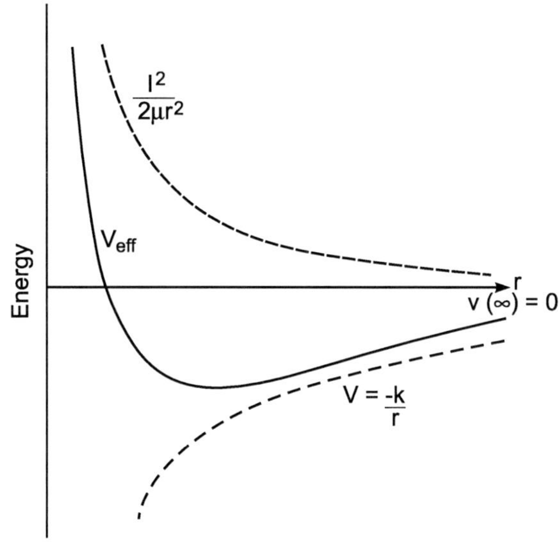

Fig. 10.3

The Eq. (10.22) is

$$E = \frac{1}{2}\mu \dot{r}^2 + V_{eff.}(r) \quad ...(10.46)$$

$$\dot{r} = \sqrt{\frac{2}{\mu}[E - V_{eff.}(r)]} \quad ...(10.47)$$

In Eq.(10.47) there should have been both positive and negative sign in front of the square root. However, the two sign signify motion in opposite direction and the two together complete the orbit of the particle. Therefore, the sign has been dropped. From Eq. (10.47) it is clear that the motion of the particle is possible only if $E > V_{eff.}$. The point at which $\dot{r} = 0$ is the apse of the motion. Let us now consider the various cases (Fig. 10.4)

Case I: $E \geq 0$ ($E = E_1$, 0)

If the total energy is positive or zero the particle moves towards the force centre (located at $r = 0$) from infinitely far away until it strikes the potential barrier at $r = r_1$ and is reflected back towards the infinitely large r. At turning point $r = r_1$, $E_1 = V_{eff.}$ and $\dot{r}$ vanishes. The distance $E - V_{eff}$. On the plot is kinetic energy $(1/2)mv^2$ at the given value of r. The distance between V and $V_{eff.}$ curve is $l^2/2\,\mu\, r^2$.

Case II: $E = E_2$

Let the total energy is negative (negative value of the total energy arises because we have taken $V = 0$ at $r = \infty$) and lies between zero and the minimum value of $V(r)$. In this case, in addition to a lower bound r_2, there is also a maximum value r_4 which cannot be exceeded by r with positive kinetic energy. The motion is then bounded and there are two turning points r_2 and r_4. These points are known as apsidal distances. In this case the motion is bounded contained between two circles of radius r_2 and r_4 (Fig. 10.5). This does not necssairly mean that orbits are closed.

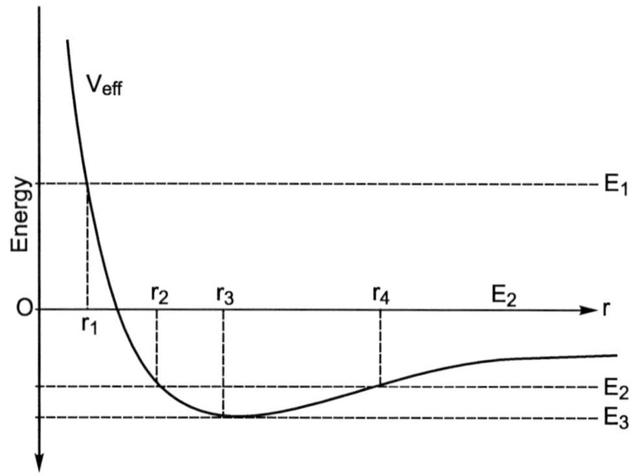

Fig. 10.4

Case III: $E = E_3$

The energy E_3 is just at the minimum of $V_{eff.}$, then the two are bound to coincide. The motion is possible at only one radius and $\dot{r} = 0$. The orbit is circular.

The case $E < E_3$ does not correspond to physically possible motion since for such cases $\dot{r}^2 < 0$, and velocity would be imaginary

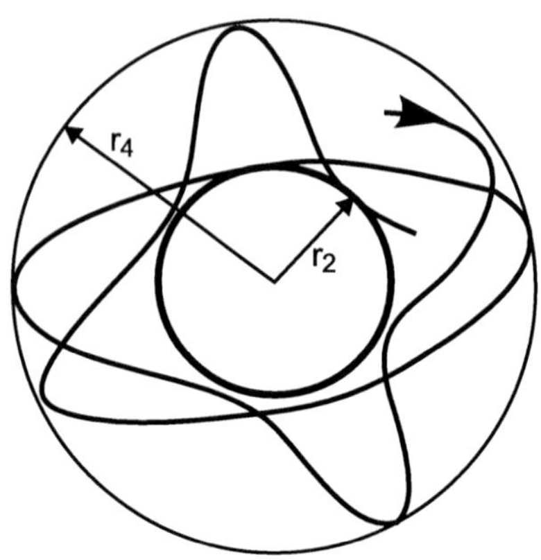

Fig. 10.5 Nature of the orbit for bounded motion

10.6 VIRIAL THEOREM

Consider a system of N particles whose position vectors r_l and whose momentum $\boldsymbol{p}_i$ remains finite for all values of the time, that is, the system is closed. Further, potential forces are not necessarily central forces. Let us define a quantity

$$G = \sum_{i=1}^{N} r_i \cdot p_i \qquad \text{...(10.48)}$$

The function G is called the virial. Defining the time average of the function f

$$\langle f \rangle = lim(t \to \infty)\frac{1}{\tau}\int_0^{\tau} f(t)dt$$

The time derivative of G is

$$\frac{dG}{dt} = \sum_i (\dot{r}_i \cdot p_i + r_i \cdot \dot{p}_i) \qquad \text{...(10.49)}$$

The average value of dG/dt is

$$\left\langle \frac{dG}{dt} \right\rangle = lim(t \to \infty)\frac{1}{\tau}\int_0^{\tau} \frac{dG}{dt}dt$$

$$\left\langle \frac{dG}{dt} \right\rangle = lim(t \to \infty)\ \frac{G(\tau) - G(0)}{\tau} \qquad \text{...(10.50)}$$

In the event that the motion of the system is periodic, and if τ is some integer multiple of the period, then $G(\tau) = G(0)$ and $\langle dG/dt \rangle$ vanishes. If the system does not exhibit periodicity, then such G is a bound function, we can make $\langle dG/dt \rangle$ to become sufficiently long. Therefore, the time average of right hand side of Eq. (10.49) can be made to vanish or at least approaches zero.

Thus

$$\frac{dG}{dt} = \sum_i (m_i \dot{\mathbf{r}}_i \cdot \dot{\mathbf{r}}_i + \mathbf{r}_i \cdot \mathbf{F}_i)$$

$$\frac{dG}{dt} = \sum_i [m_i \dot{\mathbf{r}}_i^2 - \mathbf{r}_i \cdot \nabla_i V(r_1, r_2, \ldots\ldots, r_N)]$$

$$\frac{dG}{dt} = 2\sum_i T_i - \sum_i \mathbf{r}_i \cdot \nabla_i V$$

$$\left\langle \frac{dG}{dt} \right\rangle = \left\langle 2\sum_i T_i \right\rangle - \left\langle \sum_i \mathbf{r}_i \cdot \nabla_i V \right\rangle = 0$$

$$\left\langle 2\sum_i T_i \right\rangle = \left\langle \sum_i \mathbf{r}_i \cdot \nabla_i V \right\rangle \quad ...(10.51)$$

Sum over T_i is total kinetic energy T. The Eq. (10.51) is

$$\langle T \rangle = -\frac{1}{2}\left\langle \sum_i \mathbf{r}_i \cdot \mathbf{F}_i \right\rangle \quad ...(10.52)$$

The right hand side of the Eq. (10.52) is called the virial of the system and the virial theorem thus states that the average kinetic energy of the of the particles is equal to its virial.

The Eq. (10.52) takes a simple form when V is a homogeneous function of degree N in its arguments (r_1, r_2, ..., r_N). For such a case

$$\sum_i \mathbf{r}_i \cdot \nabla_i V = NV \quad ...(10.53)$$

The Eq.(10.51) reduces to

$$2\langle T \rangle - N\langle V \rangle = 0$$

$$\langle T \rangle = \frac{1}{2} N \langle V \rangle$$

If the potential is of the form $V = r^{N+1}$

$$\sum_i \mathbf{r}_i \cdot \nabla_i V = (N+1)V$$

and Virial theorem becomes

$$\langle T \rangle = \frac{1}{2}(N+1)\langle V \rangle \quad ...(10.54)$$

If the particle have a gravitational interaction then $N = -2$ and Eq. (10.54) is

$$\langle T \rangle = -\frac{1}{2}\langle V \rangle \quad ...(10.55)$$

10.7 THE KEPLER PROBLEM

In the early years of the seventeenth century, Kepler formulated three important laws based on the observed data on planetary motion. The laws are

1 The planets move in ellipse with the sun at one focus.

2. Area swept out by the radius vector from the sun to a planet in equal times are equal.

3. The square of the period of revolution is proportional to the cube of the semi major axis.

The force is given by

$$F = -\frac{k}{r^2} = -k\,u^2 \qquad \text{...(10.56)}$$

where u is given by Eq. (10.32).

The potential energy is

$$V = -\int \mathbf{F}\cdot d\mathbf{r} = -\frac{k}{r} = -k\,u \qquad \text{...(10.57)}$$

Substituting Eq. (10.56) in Eq. (10.37)

$$\frac{d^2u}{d\theta^2} + u = \frac{\mu}{l^2 u^2} k\,u^2$$

$$\frac{d^2u}{d\theta^2} + u - \frac{\mu}{l^2} k = 0 \qquad \text{...(10.58)}$$

Let

$$y = u - \frac{\mu k}{l^2} \qquad \text{...(10.59)}$$

$$\frac{d^2y}{d\theta^2} = \frac{d^2u}{d\theta^2}$$

The Eq. (10.58) is therefore

$$\frac{d^2y}{d\theta^2} + y = 0 \qquad \text{...(10.60)}$$

The solution of the above equation is

$$y = D\cos(\theta - \theta') \qquad \text{...(10.61)}$$

where D and θ' are constants of integration. Using Eq. (10.59) in (10.61)

$$u - \frac{\mu k}{l^2} = D\cos(\theta - \theta')$$

$$\frac{1}{r} = \frac{\mu k}{l^2} + D\cos(\theta - \theta')$$

$$\frac{1}{r} = \frac{\mu k}{l^2}\left[1 + \varepsilon\cos(\theta - \theta')\right] \qquad \text{...(10.62)}$$

where

$$\varepsilon = \frac{D l^2}{\mu k} \qquad ...(10.63)$$

Putting

$$r = \frac{1}{u} \text{ and } dr = -\frac{1}{u^2} du$$

in Eq. (10.27)

$$\theta = -\frac{l}{\mu} \int_{u_0}^{u} \frac{du}{\sqrt{\frac{2}{\mu}\left(E - V - \frac{l^2 u^2}{2\mu}\right)}} + \theta'$$

$$\theta = \theta' - \int_{u_0}^{u} \frac{du}{\sqrt{\left(\frac{2\mu}{l^2} E - \frac{2\mu}{l^2} V - u^2\right)}}$$

using Eq. (10.57) the above equation is

$$\theta = \theta' - \int_{u_0}^{u} \frac{du}{\sqrt{\left(\frac{2\mu}{l^2} E + \frac{2\mu k u}{l^2} - u^2\right)}} \qquad ...(10.64)$$

where θ' is determined by the initial condition and will not necessarily be the same as initial angle θ_0 at $t = 0$. Consider the integral

$$\int \frac{dx}{\sqrt{a + bx + cx^2}} = \frac{1}{\sqrt{-c}} \cos^{-1}\left[-\frac{b + 2cx}{\sqrt{b^2 - 4ac}}\right] \qquad ...(10.65)$$

The integral of Eq. (10.64) is of the same form as integral of Eq. (10.65). On comparing the two we have

$$a = \frac{2\mu E}{l^2}, b = \frac{2\mu k}{l^2}, \; c = -1, \; b^2 - 4ac = \frac{4\mu^2 k^2}{l^4} + \frac{8\mu E}{l^2} \qquad ...(10.66)$$

$$b^2 - 4ac = \left(\frac{2\mu k}{l^2}\right)^2 \left(1 + \frac{2El^2}{\mu k^2}\right) \qquad ...(10.67)$$

The Eq. (10.64) with the help of (10.65)-(10.67) is

$$\theta = \theta' - \cos^{-1}\left(\frac{-\frac{2\mu k}{l^2} + 2u}{\frac{2\mu k}{l^2}\sqrt{\left(1 + \frac{2El^2}{\mu k^2}\right)}}\right)$$

$$\theta - \theta' = -\cos^{-1}\left(\frac{-1 + \frac{l^2 u}{\mu k}}{\sqrt{\left(1 + \frac{2El^2}{\mu k^2}\right)}}\right)$$

$$-1 + \frac{ul^2}{\mu k} = \sqrt{\left(1 + \frac{2El^2}{\mu k^2}\right)} \quad \cos(\theta - \theta')$$

$$u = \frac{1}{r} = \left(\frac{\mu k}{l^2}\right)\left[1 + \sqrt{\left(1 + \frac{2El^2}{\mu k^2}\right)} \quad \cos(\theta - \theta')\right] \quad ...(10.68)$$

which is of the same form as Eq. (10.62). Here eccentricity ε is evaluated in terms of E and l. On comparing Eqs. (10.62) and (10.64)

$$\varepsilon = \sqrt{1 + \left(2El^2/\mu k^2\right)} \quad ...(10.69)$$

writing

$$\frac{l^2}{\mu k} = \alpha \quad ...(10.70)$$

The Eq. (10.68) is

$$\frac{\alpha}{r} = 1 + \varepsilon \cos(\theta - \theta') \quad ...(10.71)$$

This is a conic section with one focus at the origin. 2α is termed as latus rectum of the orbit. Various values of eccentricity (and hence energy E) classify the orbit according to different conic section as given in Table 10.1

Table 10.1 Various values of Eccentricity

Eccentricity ε	**Energy *E***	**Orbit**
$\varepsilon > 1$	$E > 0$	hyperbola
$\varepsilon = 1$	$E = 0$	parabola
$0 < \varepsilon < 1$	$V_{min} < E < 0$	ellipse
$\varepsilon = 0$	$E = -(\mu k / l^2) = V_{min}$	circle
$\varepsilon < 0$	$E < V_{min}$	not allowed

This classification agrees with the qualitative discussion of the orbits based on the energy diagram of equivalent one dimensional potential $V_{eff.}$.

Consider the case of elliptic orbits. The semi major axis of the ellipse is one-half the sum of two apsidal distances r_1 and r_2 and from Eq. (10.71)

$$\frac{1}{r_1} = \frac{1}{\alpha}[1 + \varepsilon \cos(\theta - \theta')]$$

$$\frac{1}{r_2} = \frac{1}{\alpha}[1 - \varepsilon \cos(\theta - \theta')]$$

The minimum value of r occur when cos $(q - \theta')$ is maximum, that is, $(\theta - \theta') = 0$ and the maximum value of r occur when $(\theta - \theta') = p$. The position corresponding to r_{min} is called pericentre while r_{max} corresponds to apicentre.

$$r_1 + r_2 = \frac{\alpha}{1 + \varepsilon \cos(\theta - \theta')} + \frac{\alpha}{1 - \varepsilon \cos(\theta - \theta')}$$

$$a = \frac{r_1 + r_2}{2} = \frac{1}{2}\left[\frac{\alpha}{1+\varepsilon} + \frac{\alpha}{1-\varepsilon}\right] = \frac{\alpha}{1-\varepsilon^2}$$

$$a = \frac{\alpha}{1-\varepsilon^2} = \frac{l^2}{\mu k\left[1 - 1 - \frac{2El^2}{\mu k^2}\right]} = -\frac{k}{2E} \qquad ...(10.72)$$

The eccentricity is

$$\varepsilon = \sqrt{1 + \frac{2El^2}{\mu k^2}} = \sqrt{1 - \frac{2kl^2}{2a\mu k^2}} = \sqrt{1 - \frac{l^2}{a\mu k}} \qquad ...(10.73)$$

The minor axis is

$$b = a\sqrt{1-\varepsilon^2} = \frac{k}{2E}\sqrt{1 - 1 + \frac{l^2}{a\mu k}} = \sqrt{\frac{l^2}{2E\mu}} \qquad ...(10.74)$$

The major axis depends only on the energy E of the particle. On the other hand minor axis is a function of both E and l.

To obtain the period of elliptic motion, we rewrite the Eq. (10.19) as

$$\frac{dA}{dt} = \frac{1}{2} r^2 \dot{\theta} = \frac{1}{2} r^2 \frac{l}{\mu r^2} = \frac{l}{2\mu} \qquad \text{...(10.75)}$$

Since the entire area A of the ellipse is swept out in one complete period τ . Area A is found by integrating Eq.(10.75)

$$\int_0^\tau \frac{dA}{dt} dt = A = \int_0^\tau \frac{l}{2\mu} dt = \frac{l\tau}{2\mu} \qquad \text{...(10.76)}$$

$$\tau = \frac{2\mu}{l} A \qquad \text{...(10.77)}$$

The area of the ellipse A is πab.Therefore, Eq. (10.77) is by using Eqs. (10.72) and (10.74)

$$\tau = \frac{2\pi \mu ab}{l} = \frac{2\pi \mu a^2 \sqrt{1-\varepsilon^2}}{l} = \frac{2\pi \mu a^2}{l} \sqrt{\frac{\alpha}{a}}$$

$$\tau = \frac{2\pi \mu a^{\frac{3}{2}}}{l} \sqrt{\frac{l^2}{\mu k}} = 2\pi a^{\frac{3}{2}} \sqrt{\frac{\mu}{k}}$$

$$\tau^2 = 4\pi^2 a^3 \frac{\mu}{k} \qquad \text{...(10.78)}$$

Thus, the square of the periods of the various planets are proportional to the cube of their major axis with the same proportionality constants for all the planets. The statement is only approximately correct since the reduced mass is different for each planet. The gravitational force is given by

$$F = -G\frac{m_1 m_2}{r^2} = -\frac{k}{r^2}$$

and $k = G\, m_1 m_2$. Therefore,

$$\tau^2 = 4\pi^2 a^3 \frac{m_1 m_2}{(m_1 + m_2) G m_1 m_2} = \frac{4\pi^2 a^3}{G(m_1 + m_2)} \approx \frac{4\pi^2 a^3}{G m_2} (\text{if } m_1 << m_2)$$

The Kepler's law is valid only if mass m_1 of a planet can be neglected with respect to the mass m_2 of the sun.

10.8 STABILITY OF THE CIRCULAR ORBITS

Let the force is given by

$$F(r) = -\mu g(r) = -\frac{\partial V}{\partial r}$$

The Lagrangian is

$$L = T - V = \frac{1}{2}\mu(\dot{r}^2 + r^2\dot{\theta}^2) - V(r)$$

The equation of motion for r

$$\frac{d}{dt}\left(\frac{\partial L}{\partial \dot{r}}\right) - \frac{\partial L}{\partial r} = 0$$

gives

$$\frac{d}{dt}(\mu\dot{r}) - \mu r\dot{\theta}^2 + \frac{\partial V}{\partial r} = 0$$

$$\mu\ddot{r} - \mu r\dot{\theta}^2 + \mu g(r) = 0$$

$$\ddot{r} - r\dot{\theta}^2 = -g(r) \qquad ...(10.79)$$

Using Eq.(10.18)

$$\ddot{r} - \frac{l^2}{\mu^2 r^3} = -g(r) \qquad ...(10.80)$$

Suppose the particle is initially in a circular orbit of radius r_0 and on applying a small perturbation to r_0 we have

$$r = r_0 + x \quad (x << r_0)$$

Eq. (10.79) is then

$$\ddot{x} - \frac{l^2}{\mu^2 r_0^3}\left(1 + \frac{x}{r_0}\right)^{-3} = -g(r_0 + x) \qquad ...(10.81)$$

expansion of left hand side of the Eq. (10.81) gives

$$\ddot{x} - \frac{l^2}{\mu^2 r_0^3}\left(1 + \frac{x}{r_0}\right)^{-3} = \ddot{x} - \frac{l^2}{\mu^2 r_0^3}\left(1 - \frac{3x}{r_0} \cdots\cdots\cdots\right) \qquad ...(10.82)$$

Expansion of right hand side of Eq. (10.81) by Taylor expansion gives

$$g(r_0 + x) = g(r_0) + x \left.\frac{\partial g}{\partial r}\right|_{r=r_0} + \ldots\ldots\ldots\ldots\ldots \qquad \ldots(10.83)$$

Ignoring the x^2 and higher order terms and substituting the Eqs. (10.82) and (10.83) in Eq. (10.81)

$$\ddot{x} - \frac{l^2}{\mu^2 r_0^3} + \frac{3l^2 x}{\mu^2 r_0^4} = -g(r_0) - x g'(r_0) \qquad \ldots(10.84)$$

Since the particle initially is in circular orbit of radius $r = r_0$, under such condition

$$\dot{r}\Big|_{r=r_0} = 0, \quad \ddot{r}\Big|_{r=r_0} = 0$$

From Eq. (10.80) we have

$$\frac{l^2}{\mu^2 r_0^3} = g(r_0) \qquad \ldots(10.85)$$

On substitution of Eq. (10.85) in Eq. (10.84)

$$\ddot{x} - \frac{l^2}{\mu^2 r_0^3} + \frac{3l^2 x}{\mu^2 r_0^4} = -\left[\frac{l^2}{\mu^2 r_0^3} + x g'(r_0)\right]$$

Using Eq.(10.79) and putting $\ddot{r} = 0$ we have

$$\ddot{x} + \left[\frac{3g(r_0)}{r_0} + g'(r_0)\right] x \cong 0 \qquad \ldots(10.86)$$

Let

$$\frac{3g(r_0)}{r_0} + g'(r_0) = \omega^2 \qquad \ldots(10.87)$$

Eq. (10.86) is

$$\ddot{x} + \omega^2 x = 0 \qquad \ldots(10.88)$$

The solution of Eq. (10.88) is of the form

$$x(t) = c_1 e^{i\omega t} + c_2 e^{-i\omega t} \qquad \ldots(10.89)$$

If $\omega^2 < 0$, ω is imaginary, then the second term of the Eq.(10.89) is $c_2\, e^{i\omega t}$. This term increases without limit as t increases. The condition for oscillation is that $\omega^2 > 0$ or we have

$$\frac{3\,g(r_0)}{r_0} + g'(r_0) > 0 \qquad \text{...(10.90)}$$

Since

$$\frac{l^2}{\mu^2 r_0^3} = g(r_0) > 0$$

The Eq. (10.90) on dividing by $g(r_0)$ is

$$\frac{3}{r_0} + \frac{g'(r_0)}{g(r_0)} > 0 \qquad \text{...(10.91)}$$

Since $g(r_0)$ and $F(r_0)$ are related by a constant multiplication factor, therefore Eq. (10.91) is

$$\frac{3}{r_0} + \frac{F'(r_0)}{F(r_0)} > 0 \qquad \text{...(10.92)}$$

Suppose that the force law is

$$F(r) = -\frac{k}{r^n}$$

$$F'(r_0) = \frac{nk}{r_0^{n+1}}$$

Eq. (10.92) gives

$$\frac{3}{r_0} - \frac{(nk/r_0^{n+1})}{k/r_0^n} > 0$$

$$(3-n)/r_0 > 0 \qquad \text{...(10.93)}$$

or n < 3.

10.9 KEPLERS' EQUATION

Suppose the motion takes place in the elliptical orbit with the force centre located at the focus O which is also the origin for a rectangular coordinate system (Fig. 10.6). In this system the equation of orbit is

$$\frac{(x+a\varepsilon)^2}{a^2}+\frac{y^2}{b^2}=1 \qquad ...(10.94)$$

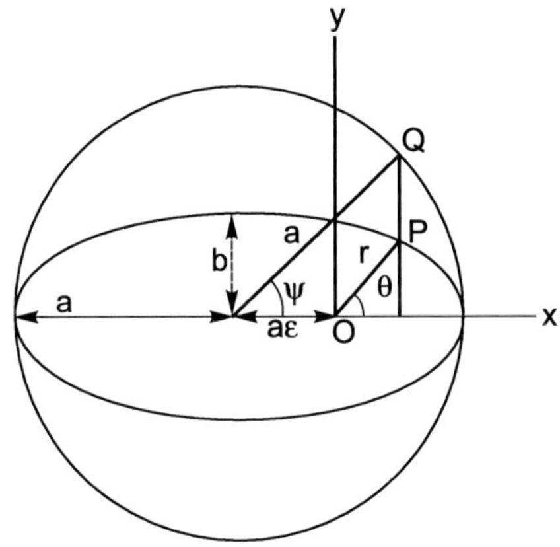

Fig. 10.6

consider a circle of radius a circumscribing the ellipse. The coordinates of point P on the ellipse are r, θ and project of point P on the circle is Q. The angle between the x axis and the line connecting the centre of the circle with the point Q is called eccentricity anomaly ψ and is

$$\cos\psi=\frac{x+a\varepsilon}{a} \qquad ...(10.95)$$

From Eq. (10.94)

$$\frac{y^2}{b^2}=1-\frac{(x+a\varepsilon)^2}{a^2}=1-\cos^2\psi=\sin^2\psi$$

$$\sin\psi=\frac{y}{b} \qquad ...(10.96)$$

From Eqs. (10.95) and (10.96)

$$x=a(\cos\psi-\varepsilon),\qquad y=b\sin\psi=a\sqrt{1-\varepsilon^2}\,\sin\psi$$

and

$$r^2=x^2+y^2=a^2(\cos^2\psi+\varepsilon^2-2\varepsilon\cos\psi)+a^2(1-\varepsilon^2)\sin^2\psi$$

$$r^2=a^2(1-\varepsilon\cos\psi)^2$$

$$r=a(1-\varepsilon\cos\psi) \qquad ...(10.97)$$

From Eqs. (10.71) and (10.72) by putting $\theta'=0$, we have

$$r = \frac{a(1-\varepsilon^2)}{1+\varepsilon\cos\theta} \qquad ...(10.98)$$

Equating Eqs. (10.97) and (10.98)

$$\frac{a(1-\varepsilon^2)}{1+\varepsilon\cos\theta} = a(1-\varepsilon\cos\psi)$$

$$1+\varepsilon\cos\theta = \frac{1-\varepsilon^2}{1-\varepsilon\cos\psi}$$

$$\varepsilon\cos\theta = \frac{1-\varepsilon^2}{1-\varepsilon\cos\psi} - 1 = \frac{\varepsilon(\cos\psi-\varepsilon)}{1-\varepsilon\cos\psi}$$

$$\cos\theta = \frac{\cos\psi-\varepsilon}{1-\varepsilon\cos\psi} \qquad ...(10.99)$$

From Eq. (10.99)

$$2\sin^2\frac{\theta}{2} = 1 - \frac{\cos\psi-\varepsilon}{1-\varepsilon\cos\psi} = \frac{(1+\varepsilon)(1-\cos\psi)}{1-\varepsilon\cos\psi} \qquad ...(10.100)$$

and

$$1-\sin^2\frac{\theta}{2} = \cos^2\frac{\theta}{2} = 1 - \frac{1}{2}\frac{(1+\varepsilon)(1-\cos\psi)}{1-\varepsilon\cos\psi}$$

$$2\cos^2\frac{\theta}{2} = \frac{(1-\varepsilon)(1+\cos\psi)}{1-\varepsilon\cos\psi} \qquad ...(10.101)$$

From Eqs. (10.100) and (10.101)

$$\tan^2\frac{\theta}{2} = \frac{1+\varepsilon}{1-\varepsilon}\frac{1-\cos\psi}{1+\cos\psi} = \frac{1+\varepsilon}{1-\varepsilon}\frac{\sin^2(\psi/2)}{\cos^2(\psi/2)}$$

$$\tan\frac{\theta}{2} = \sqrt{\frac{1+\varepsilon}{1-\varepsilon}}\tan\frac{\psi}{2} \qquad ...(10.102)$$

which gives ψ uniquely in terms of θ.

On differentiating Eq. (10.102)

$$d\theta = \sqrt{\frac{1+\varepsilon}{1-\varepsilon}}\ \frac{cos^2(\theta/2)}{cos^2(\psi/2)}\, d\psi \qquad ...(10.103)$$

adding 1 on both side of the Eq. (10.99) and also multiplying by *r* on both sides using Eq. (10.97)

$$r = a(1-\varepsilon)\frac{cos^2(\psi/2)}{cos^2(\theta/2)} \qquad ...(10.104)$$

Multiplying (10.104) by *r* given by Eq.(10.97) and using Eq. (10.103) we have

$$r^2\, d\theta = [a(1-\varepsilon\cos\psi)]\left[a(1-\varepsilon)\frac{\cos^2(\psi/2)}{\cos^2(\theta/2)}\right]\left[\sqrt{\frac{1+\varepsilon}{1-\varepsilon}}\ \frac{\cos(\theta/2)}{\cos(\psi/2)}\, d\psi\right]$$

$$r^2\, d\theta = a^2\sqrt{1-\varepsilon^2}\ (1-\varepsilon\, cos\psi)\, d\psi \qquad ...(10.105)$$

Let in time τ, the radius vector of the body sweep out the entire area pab. Since the areal velocity is constant therefore the area swept out by the radius vector in time t is

$$\frac{\pi ab}{\tau}t = \int dA$$

If $\theta = 0$ at $t = 0$, we have by using Eq. (10.105)

$$\frac{\pi ab}{\tau}t = \frac{1}{2}\int_0^\theta r^2\, d\theta = \frac{1}{2}\int_0^\psi a^2\sqrt{1-\varepsilon^2}\ (1-\varepsilon\, cos\psi)\, d\psi$$

$$\frac{\pi ab}{\tau}t = \frac{1}{2}\int_0^\theta r^2\, d\theta = \frac{ab}{2}\int_0^\psi (1-\varepsilon\, cos\psi)\, d\psi = \frac{ab}{2}\left[\psi\Big|_0^\psi - \varepsilon\, sin\psi\Big|_0^\psi\right]$$

$$\frac{2\pi t}{\tau} = \ = \psi - \varepsilon\, sin\psi \qquad ...(10.106)$$

$$wt = \psi - \varepsilon\, sin\psi \qquad ...(10.107)$$

where $\omega t = (2\pi t/\tau)$ is called the mean anomaly, since it measures the angular deviation of a body moving in a circular orbit with period τ. The Eq. (10.107) is known as Kepler's equation.

Solved Examples

Example 1. *Prove that speed v of a particle moving in an elliptical path in an inverse square field is given by*

$$v^2 = \frac{k}{\mu}\left(\frac{2}{r} - \frac{1}{a}\right)$$

a is semi-major axis.

Solution: From Eq.(10.72)

$$E = -\frac{k}{2a}$$

kinetic energy T is

$$T = \frac{1}{2}\mu v^2 = E - V = -\frac{k}{2a} + \frac{k}{r}$$

$$v^2 = \frac{k}{\mu}\left(\frac{2}{r} - \frac{1}{a}\right)$$

Example 2. *Show that particle moving in a centre of force travels in a path which is cycloid $r = a(1 - \cos\theta)$, the force varies as r^{-4}.*

Solution: The orbit equation is $r = a(1 - \cos\theta)$, Putting $u = r^{-1}$ we have

$$u = \frac{1}{r} = \frac{1}{a(1-\cos\theta)} = \frac{1}{2a}\operatorname{cosec}^2\frac{\theta}{2}$$

$$\frac{du}{d\theta} = \frac{1}{2a}\left(-2\operatorname{cosec}^2\frac{\theta}{2}\cot\frac{\theta}{2}\frac{1}{2}\right) = -\frac{1}{2a}\operatorname{cosec}^2\frac{\theta}{2}\cot\frac{\theta}{2}$$

$$\frac{d^2u}{d\theta^2} = -\frac{1}{2a}\left[-2\operatorname{cosec}^2\frac{\theta}{2}\cot^2\frac{\theta}{2}\frac{1}{2} - \operatorname{cosec}^4\frac{\theta}{2}\frac{1}{2}\right] =$$

$$\frac{1}{2a}\operatorname{cosec}^2\frac{\theta}{2}\left[\cot^2\frac{\theta}{2} + \frac{1}{2}\operatorname{cosec}^2\frac{\theta}{2}\right]$$

$$\frac{d^2u}{d\theta^2} + u = -\frac{1}{2a}\operatorname{cosec}^2\frac{\theta}{2}\left[\cot^2\frac{\theta}{2} + \frac{1}{2}\operatorname{cosec}^4\frac{\theta}{2} + 1\right] =$$

$$\frac{1}{2a}\operatorname{cosec}^2\frac{\theta}{2}\left[\operatorname{cosec}^2\frac{\theta}{2} + \frac{1}{2}\operatorname{cosec}^2\frac{\theta}{2}\right]$$

$$\frac{d^2u}{d\theta^2} + u = \frac{3}{4a}\operatorname{cosec}^4\frac{\theta}{2}$$

Using Eq. (10.37)

$$\frac{d^2u}{d\theta^2}+u=-\frac{\mu}{l^2u^2}F\left(\frac{1}{u}\right)=\frac{3}{4a}\cos ec^4\frac{\theta}{2}$$

$$F\left(\frac{1}{u}\right)=-\frac{l^2u^2}{\mu}\frac{3}{4a}\cos ec^4\frac{\theta}{2}=-\frac{l^2u^2}{\mu}\frac{3}{4a}(2au)^2=-\frac{3al^2}{\mu}u^4$$

$$F(r)=-\frac{3al^2}{\mu r^4}\propto\frac{1}{r^4}$$

Example 3. *Two particles move about each other in circular orbit under the influence of gravitational force with a period* τ. *Their motion is suddenly stopped at a given time and they are then released and allowed to fall into each other. After what time they collide.*

Solution: The time period is given by Eq. (10.78)

$$\tau^2=4\pi^2a^3\frac{\mu}{k}$$

The particle is suddenly stopped in its orbit, it means that its velocity is reduced to zero. Consequently the particle will start to move towards the centre of force in a straight line under the law of inverse square and equation of motion is, therefore

$$\mu\frac{d^2x}{dt^2}=-\frac{k}{x^2}$$

Multiplying both side by *2dx/dt*

$$2\frac{dx}{dt}\frac{d^2x}{dt^2}=-\frac{k}{\mu}\frac{dx}{dt}\frac{1}{x^2}$$

$$\frac{d}{dt}\left(\frac{dx}{dt}\right)^2=-\frac{k}{\mu}\frac{1}{x^2}\frac{dx}{dt}$$

On integration

$$\left(\frac{dx}{dt}\right)^2=-\frac{2k}{\mu}\frac{x^{-2+1}}{-2+1}+A=\frac{2k}{\mu x}+A$$

Initially when $x = a$, $dx/dt = 0$, hence $A = -(2k/a)$

$$\left(\frac{dx}{dt}\right)^2=\frac{2k}{\mu}\left(\frac{1}{x}-\frac{1}{a}\right)=\frac{2k}{\mu}\left(\frac{a-x}{ax}\right)$$

$$\sqrt{\frac{2k}{\mu}}\,dt = \sqrt{\frac{a\,x}{a-x}}\;d\,x$$

On integration

$$\sqrt{\frac{2k}{\mu}}\,t = \int_0^a \sqrt{\frac{a\,x}{a-x}}\;d\,x$$

Let $x = a\ sin^2\ \theta$, $dx = 2a\ sin\ \theta\ cos\ \theta$

$$\sqrt{\frac{2k}{\mu}}\,t = \int_0^{\pi/2} \frac{\sqrt{a}\ sin\theta}{cos\theta}\,2a\ sin\theta\ cos\theta\ d\,\theta = 2\,a^{3/2}\int_0^{\pi/2} sin^2\,\theta\,d\,\theta$$

$$\sqrt{\frac{2k}{\mu}}\,t = 2\,a^{3/2}\,\frac{\Gamma 3/2\,\Gamma 1/2}{2\,\Gamma 2} = a^{3/2}\,\frac{1}{2}\sqrt{\pi}\sqrt{\pi} = \frac{\pi}{2}\,a^{3/2}$$

$$t = \sqrt{\frac{\mu}{2k}}\,\frac{\pi}{2}\,a^{3/2} = \sqrt{\frac{\mu}{2k}}\,\frac{\pi}{2}\,\frac{\tau}{2\pi}\sqrt{\frac{k}{\mu}} = \frac{\tau}{4\sqrt{2}}$$

The particle collides after time $\dfrac{\tau}{4\sqrt{2}}$.

Example 4. *Investigate stability of circular orbit when*

$$V(\,r\,) = -\frac{k}{r}\,exp(-r\,/\,a\,)$$

Solution. We have

$$F(\,r\,) = -\frac{\partial V}{\partial r} = -k\left[\frac{1}{r^2}+\frac{1}{a\,r}\right]exp(-r\,/\,a\,)$$

$$F'(\,r\,) = k\left[\frac{1}{a^2 r}+\frac{2}{a\,r^2}+\frac{2}{r^2}\right]exp(-r\,/\,a\,)$$

The condition for stability is from Eq. (10.92)

$$\frac{3}{r_0}+\frac{F'(\,r_0\,)}{F(\,r_0\,)} > 0$$

$$\frac{3}{r_0}+\frac{k\left[\dfrac{1}{a^2 r}+\dfrac{2}{a\,r^2}+\dfrac{2}{r^2}\right]exp(-r\,/\,a\,)}{-k\left[\dfrac{1}{r^2}+\dfrac{1}{a\,r}\right]exp(-r\,/\,a\,)} > 0$$

$$\frac{a^2}{r_0^2}+\frac{a}{r_0}-1>0$$

Putting $p = a/r_0$

$$p^2+p-1>0$$

The stability will result or all p which exceeds the values that satisfies

$$p^2+p-1=0$$

The roots are

$$p=\frac{-1\pm\sqrt{1+4}}{2}$$

$$p=\frac{-1-\sqrt{5}}{2},\quad \frac{-1+\sqrt{5}}{2}$$

The only meaningful solution is

$$p=\frac{-1+\sqrt{5}}{2}\approx 0.62$$

Therefore

$$\frac{a}{r_0}>0.62$$

$$r_0\le 1.62\,a$$

Example 5. *For Kepler problem*

$$V=-\frac{k}{r}$$

show that

$$\langle V\rangle = 2E$$

Solution: We have

$$F=-\frac{dV}{dr}=-\frac{k}{r^2}$$

From Virial theorem (10.52)

$$\langle T\rangle = \frac{1}{2}\frac{k}{r}$$

Total energy E is

$$E=T+V=\frac{k}{2r}-\frac{k}{r}=-\frac{k}{2r}=-\langle T\rangle$$

$$\langle V \rangle = -\frac{k}{r} = 2E$$

This is valid for the variable r. The origin where the force becomes infinite should be excluded.

Example 6. *An object of unit mass orbits in a central potential V(r). Its orbit is r = a exp(-α θ), where θ is the azimuthal angle measured in the orbital plane. Find V(r) .*

Solution: Let $u = r^{-1}$

$$u = \frac{1}{r} = \frac{exp(\alpha\,\theta\,)}{a}$$

$$\frac{d\,u}{d\,\theta} = \frac{\alpha}{a}\,exp(\,\alpha\,\theta\,) = \alpha\,u$$

$$\frac{d^2\,u}{d\,\theta^2} = \frac{\alpha^2}{a}\,exp(\,\alpha\,\theta\,) = \alpha^2 u$$

From Eq. (10.37)

$$\frac{d^2 u}{d\theta^2} + u = (1+\alpha^2\,)u = -\frac{1}{l^2\,u^2}\,F\left(\frac{1}{u}\right)$$

$$F\left(\frac{1}{u}\right) = -l^2(1+\alpha^2\,)u^3$$

$$F(r) = -l^2(1+\alpha^2\,)\frac{1}{r^3} = -\frac{dV}{dr}$$

$$V = l^2(1+\alpha^2\,)\int\frac{1}{r^3}\,d\,r = -\frac{l^2(1+\alpha^2\,)}{2r^2}$$

Example 7. *A particle of mass m is bound by a linear potential V = k r. What is the frequency of small oscillations if the particle is slightly disturbed from circular motion.*

Solution: From Eq. (10.42)

$$V_{eff.} = k\,r + \frac{l^2}{2m\,r^2}$$

$$\left.\frac{d\,V_{eff.}}{d\,r}\right|_{r=r_0} = \left(k - \frac{l^2}{m\,r^3}\right)_{r=r_0} = 0$$

$$r_0 = \left(\frac{l^2}{m\,k}\right)^{1/3}$$

$$\left.\frac{d^2 V_{eff.}}{d\,r^2}\right|_{r=r_0} = \left.\left(\frac{3l^2}{m\,r^4}\right)\right|_{r=r_0} = 3\,k\left(\frac{m\,k}{l^2}\right)^{1/3} > 0$$

$$\omega^2 = \frac{1}{m}\left.\frac{d^2 V_{eff.}}{d\,r^2}\right|_{r=r_0} = 3\,k\left(\frac{k}{m^2 l^2}\right)^{1/3}$$

Example 8. *A particle moves in a circular orbit in a central force field given by the potential*

$$V = -\frac{k}{r} \quad (k > 0)$$

suddenly k becomes k/2. Show that the orbit becomes parabolic.

Solution: The kinetic energy is given by

$$T = \frac{1}{2}\mu\,\dot{r}^2 + \frac{1}{2}\mu\,r^2\,\dot{\theta}^2$$

For circular motion $\dot{r} = 0$. The kinetic energy is therefore

$$T = \frac{1}{2}\mu\,r^2\,\dot{\theta}^2$$

Consider Eq. (10.31)

$$\mu\,(\ddot{r} \; - r\dot{\theta}^2\;) = \; -\mu\,r\dot{\theta}^2 = -\frac{\partial V}{\partial\,r} = -\frac{k}{r^2}$$

$$\dot{\theta}^2 = \frac{k}{\mu\,r^3}$$

Using the above relation in the expression for kinetic energy we have

$$T = \frac{1}{2}\mu\,r^2\,\frac{k}{\mu\,r^3} = \frac{k}{2r}$$

when k is changed to $k/2$, the potential energy is

$$V = -\frac{k}{2\,r}$$

Total energy E is

$$E = T + V = \frac{k}{2r} - \frac{k}{2r} = 0$$

Putting $E = 0$ in the expression for eccentricity (10.69) we have

$$\varepsilon = \sqrt{1 + \left(2El^2/\mu k^2\right)} = 1$$

Thus, the orbit becomes parabolic.

OBJECTIVE TYPE QUESTIONS

1. A particle is moving under a central force. Of the kinetic energy T, total energy E, linear momentum p and angular momentum l, the following remain constant through the motion

   (*a*) E, p (*b*) E, l
   (*c*) T, p (*d*) T, l

2. A central force always conserves

   (*a*) energy (*b*) linear momentum
   (*c*) angular momentum (*d*) none of these

3. In motion under a central force we always have a circular motion when

   (*a*) E is least (*b*) Potential energy is least
   (*c*) Effective potential energy is least (*d*) The angular momen tum is least

4. The magnitude of the radial velocity is

   (*a*) $\dot{r}$ (*b*) $\left|\dot{r} - r\dot{\theta}\right|$
   (*c*) $\sqrt{\dot{r}^2 + r^2\dot{\theta}^2}$ (*d*) $\sqrt{\dot{r}^2 + 2r\dot{r}\dot{\theta} + r^2\dot{\theta}^2}$

5. The Lagrangian for planetary motion is

   (*a*) $\frac{1}{2}\mu(\dot{r}^2 + r^2\dot{\theta}^2) + \frac{k}{r}$

   (*b*) $\frac{1}{2}\mu(\dot{r}^2 + r^2\dot{\theta}^2) - \frac{k}{r}$

(c) $\frac{1}{2}\mu(\dot{r}^2 + \dot{r}^2\dot{\theta}^2) + \frac{k}{r}$

(d) $\frac{1}{2}\mu(r^2 + \dot{r}^2\dot{\theta}^2) + \frac{k}{r}$

6. Motion which repeats itself after a definite interval of time is

(a) periodic motion
(b) circular motion
(c) translational motion
(d) oscillation motion

7. If a particle of mass m moving in a circle of radius a under an inverse square attraction $F = -(k/r^2)$, the total energy at any point of the orbit of the particle is

(a) $\frac{k}{a}$
(b) $-\frac{k}{a}$
(c) $-\frac{k}{2a}$
(d) none of these

8. If the r motion is non-oscillatory, the orbit of the particle is

(a) not bounded
(b) ellipse
(c) circle
(d) none of these

9. For orbits under inverse square law of attractive force, the effective potential energy is

(a) $\frac{k}{r^2} + \frac{l^2}{2mr^2}$
(b) $-\frac{k}{r^2} + \frac{l^2}{2mr^2}$
(c) $-\frac{k}{r} - \frac{l^2}{2mr^2}$
(d) $-\frac{k}{r} + \frac{l^2}{2mr^2}$

10. The force which is always directed away or towards a fixed centre and magnitude of which is a function only of the distance from the fixed centre is known as

(a) central force
(b) coriolis force
(c) centrifugal force
(d) centripetal force

11. For repulsive inverse square forces, the shape of the orbit is

(a) hyperbolic
(b) elliptical
(c) circular
(d) all of these

12. Kepler's second law says that

(*a*) areal velocity is zero
(*b*) areal velocity is constant
(*c*) angular momentum is not constant
(*d*) none of these

13. The value of eccentricity ε for an elliptical orbit is

(*a*) $\varepsilon > 0$
(*b*) $\varepsilon = 1$
(*c*) $\varepsilon = 0$
(*d*) $0 < \varepsilon < 1$

14. Which is not conserved in centre force motion?

(*a*) energy
(*b*) linear momentum
(*c*) angular momentum
(*d*) none of the above

15. If a particle of mass m moving in a circle of radius a under an inverse square attraction $F = -(k / r^2)$, the velocity of the particle at any point of the orbit is

(*a*) $\frac{k}{m}$
(*b*) $\sqrt{\frac{k}{m a}}$
(*c*) $\sqrt{\frac{k}{a}}$
(*d*) none of the above

16. If we eliminate r and its derivative from

$$E = \frac{1}{2}\mu \dot{r}^2 + \frac{l^2}{2\mu r^2} + V(r)$$

$$\mu r^2 \dot{\theta} = l$$

the resulting equation is independent of

(*a*) l
(*b*) m
(*c*) e
(*d*) V

17. For Kepler's problem

(*a*) $< V > = E$
(*b*) $V = < E >$
(*c*) $< V > = 2E$
(*d*) $< V > = 0$

18. In the case of elliptical orbit, energy is proportional to

(*a*) a
(*b*) a^{-3}
(*c*) a^{-1}
(*d*) a^3

19. The conservation of angular momentum in the central force field leads us to

(*a*) Kepler's first law (*b*) Kepler's second law
(*c*) Kepler's third law (*d*) None of these

20. The eccentricity of the particle moving under the central force field is

(*a*) $\varepsilon = \sqrt{1+(2E/\mu)}$ (*b*) $\varepsilon = \sqrt{(1+2El^2)/\mu k^2}$

(*c*) $\varepsilon = \sqrt{1+(2El^2/\mu k^2)}$ (*d*) $\varepsilon = \sqrt{1-(2El^2/\mu k^2)}$

21. The areal velocity of the particle in a central force field is

(*a*) zero (*b*) maximum
(*c*) minimum (*d*) constant

22. At an apse, the radial velocity is

(*a*) zero (*b*) maximum
(*c*) minimum (*d*) none of these

23. For the potential $V = kr^2$ $(k>0)$, the closed orbit is

(*a*) circle (*b*) parabola
(*c*) hyperbola (*d*) ellipse

24. A particle describes a circular orbit given by $r = 2a \cos\theta$ under the influence of an attractive central force directed towards a point on the circle. Then the force is

(*a*) $F(r) \propto r^{-4}$ (*b*) $F(r) \propto r^{-5}$

(*c*) $F(r) \propto r^{-2}$ (*d*) $F(r) \propto r^{-3}$

25. A particle moves under a central force with angular momentum l, total energy E, the radial equation of the motion is

$$E = \frac{1}{2}\mu \dot{r}^2 + \frac{l^2}{2\mu r^2} + V(r)$$

For a bound state, we have for all r that

(*a*) $E<V$ (*b*) $E>V$

(*c*) $E < \frac{l^2}{2\mu r^2} + V(r)$ (*d*) $E > \frac{l^2}{2\mu r^2} + V(r)$

26. Which is not true?

(*a*) the effective potential has at least one minimum between the turning points.

(b) for bounded motion isotropic harmonic oscillator potential yields periodic orbits for all values of the force constant and initial conditions.

(c) motion of the particle under the force $-k\ r$ obeys Kepler's third law.

(d) Motion of the particle under the force $-(3k/r^4)$ obeys Kepler's second law.

27. The value of r for which $V_{eff.}$ (for $k<0$) is minimum is

(a) $-\frac{l^2 k}{\mu}$ (b) $\frac{l^2 k}{\mu}$

(c) $-\frac{l^2}{\mu k}$ (d) $\frac{l^2}{\mu k}$

28. The product $r_{min.}(V_{eff.})_{min}$ for $k<0$ is

(a) $\frac{l^2}{k}$ (b) $\frac{k}{2}$

(c) $\frac{2}{k}$ (d) $\frac{k}{l^2}$

29. For $V_{eff.} = \frac{k}{r} + \frac{l^2}{2\mu r^2}$ $(k>0)$, the orbit is

(a) circle (b) hyperbola
(c) ellipse (d) all of them

30. If the orbit is $exp\ (-\theta)$ the force law is proportional to

(a) r^{-3} (b) r^2

(c) r^{-7} (d) r^{-5}

31. An atom is displaced from its mean position in a crystal lattice is under a force which is always directed towards the mean position and is proportional to its distance from it . The force is of the form

(a) $kr\,\hat{r}$ (b) $kr\,\hat{r}$

(c) $-kr\,\hat{r}$ (d) $kr\,\hat{r}$

32. An atom is displaced from its mean position in a crystal lattice is under a force which is always directed toward the mean position and is proportional to its distance from it . The force is obtained from the potential energy (V_0= constant)

(*a*) $V_0 + \frac{1}{2} k r^2$ (*b*) $V_0 + k r^2$

(*c*) $V_0 - \frac{1}{2} k r^2$ (*d*) cannot be derived

33. Which is not true?

(*a*) When the central force is repulsive, the orbit is convex to the origin.
(*b*) If the *r* motion is oscillatory, the orbit is bounded.
(*c*) For attractive inverse square force law, the orbit is circle for $E = 0$.
(*d*) If the value of eccentricity is equal to one, the shape of the orbit is parabola.

34. Consider the motion of a particle of mass m under the influence of force $F = -kr$, where *k* is a positive constant, *r* is the position vector of the particle. The motion of the particle does not obey

(*a*) Kepler's first law (*b*) Kepler's second law
(*c*) Kepler's third law (*d*) Kepler's first and second law

35. Under inverse square law of attractive force, for elliptical orbit

(*a*) $v^2 = \frac{k}{\mu}\left(\frac{2}{r} + \frac{1}{a}\right)$ (*b*) $v^2 = \frac{\mu}{k}\left(\frac{2}{r} - \frac{1}{a}\right)$

(*c*) $v^2 = k \frac{2}{\mu r}$ (*d*) $v^2 = \frac{k}{\mu}\left(\frac{2}{r} - \frac{1}{a}\right)$

PROBLEMS

1. Show that when a particle describes a circle under a central attraction directed to a point in its circumference, the law of force is inverse fifth power of distance.

2. Show that when a particle describes a path *r* = *exp(-q)*, the law of force is proportional to r^{-3}.

3. Show that when a particle describes a path $r^2 = 2a^2 \cos 2q$, the law of force is proportional to r^{-7}.

4. Investigate the stability of circular orbit when

$$f(r) = -\frac{k}{r^2} + \frac{\alpha}{r^3}$$

5. Investigate the stability of circular orbit when

$$f(r) = -\frac{k}{r^2} - \frac{\alpha}{r^4}$$

6. Discuss the qualitative nature of motion of the particle in a central force field given by the harmonic oscillator potential $V = (kr^2/2)$ where $k>0$.

7. Discuss the qualitative nature of motion of the particle in a central force field given by the potential

$$V(r) = -\frac{a}{r^3}$$

where a is a positive constant

8. Discuss the qualitative nature of motion of the particle in a central force field given by the potential

$$V(r) = -\frac{k\,exp(-\alpha r)}{r}$$

where α and k are positive constants.

9. Find the force law for a central force field which allows a particle to move in a spiral orbit given by $r = k\,\theta^2$, where k is a constant.

10. A particle is attracted to a force centre by a force which varies inversely as the cube of the distance from the centre. Obtain the equation of the orbit.

11. The orbit of a particle moving under the influence of a central force is $r\,\theta$ = constant.
Determine the potential energy.

12. Consider a particle of mass m moving in a bound orbit with potential $V = -k/r$ .Using the Virial theorem show that

$$\oint p_r dr + \oint p_\theta d\theta = \pi k \sqrt{\frac{2m}{-E}}$$

❑❑❑

CHAPTER 11

Rutherford Scattering

11.1 CENTRE OF MASS AND LABORATORY COORDINATE SYSTEMS

When two particles interact, the motion of one particle relative to the other is governed by the force law which describes the interaction. For example, an alpha particle may be scattered by the electric, field of an atomic nucleus. In describing physical processes, the coordinate system chosen are centre of mass coordinate system (C system) or laboratory coordinate system (L system). The system in which one particle is moving and other is initially at rest is called L system. On the other hand a coordinate system that is at rest relative to the centre of mass of the system is called C system.

Let m_1 be the mass of the particle 1 and m_2 is the mass of the particle 2. The position of the particle in C system are located by the vectors $\mathbf{r}_1'$ and $\mathbf{r}_2'$ (Fig.11.1) with respect to the centre of mass as origin. We have

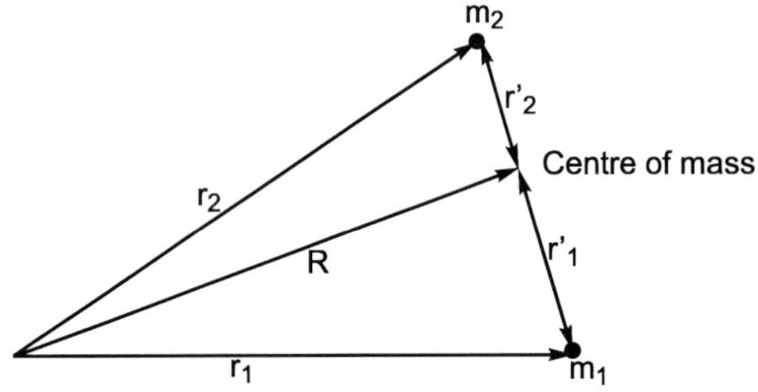

Fig. 11.1

$$\mathbf{r}_1' = \mathbf{r}_1 - \mathbf{R} \qquad ...(11.1)$$

$$\mathbf{r}_2' = \mathbf{r}_2 - \mathbf{R} \qquad ...(11.2)$$

or

$$\mathbf{r}_1 = \mathbf{r}_1' + \mathbf{R} \qquad ...(11.3)$$

$$\mathbf{r}_2 = \mathbf{r}_2' + \mathbf{R} \qquad ...(11.4)$$

where

$$\mathbf{R} = \frac{m_1\mathbf{r}_1 + m_2\mathbf{r}_2}{m_1 + m_2} \qquad ...(11.5)$$

From the Fig. 11.1

$$\mathbf{r} = \mathbf{r}_1 - \mathbf{r}_2 \qquad ...(11.6)$$

From Eqs.(11.3) and (11.6)

$$\mathbf{r}_1' = \frac{m_2\mathbf{r}}{m_1 + m_2} = \frac{\mu}{m_1}\mathbf{r} \qquad ...(11.7)$$

$$\mathbf{r}_2' = -\frac{m_1\mathbf{r}}{m_1 + m_2} = -\frac{\mu}{m_2}\mathbf{r} \qquad ...(11.8)$$

Consider that particle 1 moves while particle 2 is hit by particle 1. Let in the L system velocity of particle 1 is u_1 and v_1 before and after the collision while for particle 2, these are u_2 and v_2. In C system the velocities of particle 1(2) before and after the collision are $u_1'(v_1')$ and $u_2'(v_2')$. V is the velocity of centre of mass in the L system. In the L system the particle 1 is deflected by an angle ψ and particle 2 is deflected by angle η (Fig. 11.2). In C system particles 1 and 2 are deflected by angle θ (Fig. 11.3). In C system, particles 1 and 2 approach each other and after collision they move in exactly opposite direction. Thus, total linear momentum of such a system is zero.

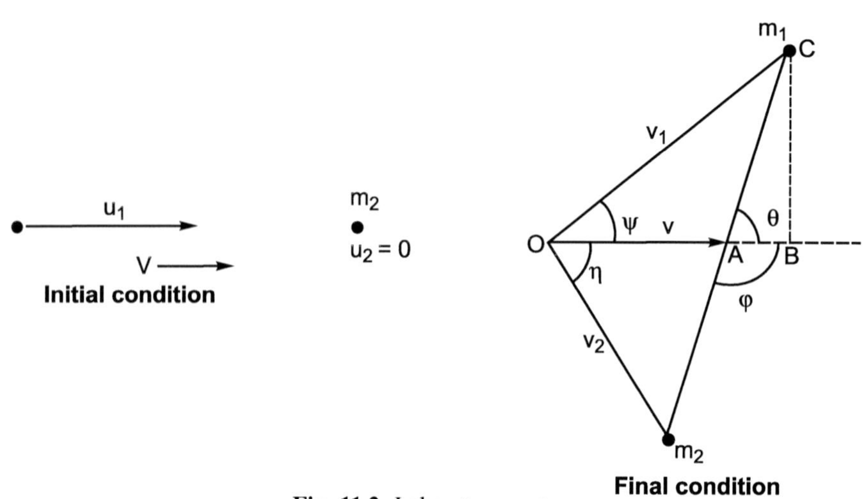

Fig. 11.2 Laboratory system

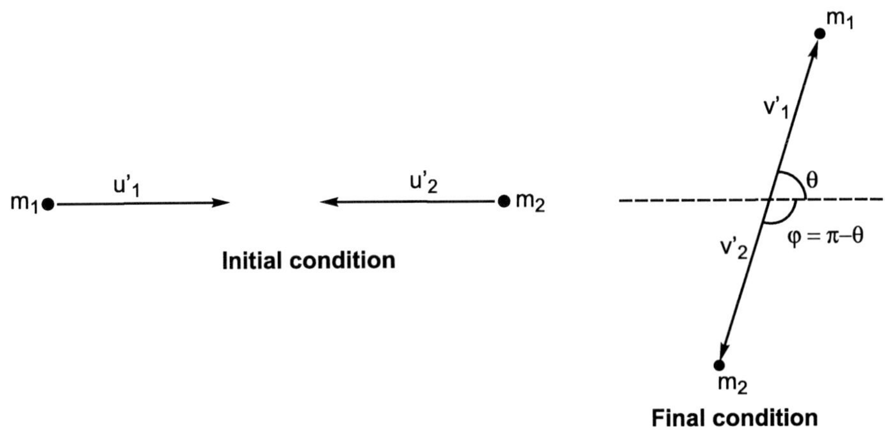

Fig. 11.3 Centre of Mass system

In the L system, the particle 2 is at rest, therefore, $u_2 = 0$. The velocity of centre of mass from Eq. (11.5) is

$$\dot{\mathbf{R}} = \mathbf{V} = \frac{m_1 \dot{\mathbf{r}}_1}{m_1 + m_2} = \frac{m_1 \mathbf{u}_1}{m_1 + m_2} \qquad ...(11.9)$$

Since the particle 2 is initially at rest, therefore, the initial centre of mass velocity of particle 2 must just equal V

$$\mathbf{u}_2' = \mathbf{V} = \frac{m_1 \mathbf{u}_1}{m_1 + m_2} \qquad ...(11.10)$$

however,

$$\mathbf{u}_2' = -\mathbf{V} \qquad ...(11.11)$$

since the motion are in opposite direction. In C system velocities before and after collisions are equal, that is,

$$u_1' = v_1' \qquad ...(11.12)$$

$$u_2' = v_2' \qquad ...(11.13)$$

The relative velocity of two particles in C system before the collision is

$$u_1' + u_2' \qquad ...(11.14)$$

The relative velocity of two particles in L system before the collision is u_1. Therefore,

$$u_1' + u_2' = u_1 \qquad ...(11.15)$$

In C system, the velocities after collision is therefore from Eqs. (11.7),

(11.13) and (11.15)

$$v_2' = u_1 - u_1' = u_1 - \frac{m_1 u}{m_1 + m_2}$$

$$v_2' = \frac{m_1 u_1}{m_1 + m_2} \qquad ...(11.16)$$

$$v_1' = u_1 - u_2' = u_1 - v_2' = \frac{m_2 u_1}{m_1 + m_2} \qquad ...(11.17)$$

From Fig. 11.2

$$BC = AC \sin\theta = OC \sin\psi$$

$$v_1' \sin\theta = v_1 \sin\psi \qquad ...(11.18)$$

and

$$OB = (OA + AB) = (V + AB) = v_1 \cos\psi \qquad ...(11.19)$$

$$AB = v_1' \cos\theta \qquad ...(11.20)$$

From Eqs. (11.19) and (11.20)

$$AB = v_1' \cos\theta = -V + v_1 \cos\psi$$

$$v_1' \cos\theta + V = v_1 \cos\psi \qquad ...(11.21)$$

From Eqs.(11.18) and (11.21)

$$\tan\psi = \frac{v_1' \sin\theta}{v_1' \cos\theta + V} = \frac{\sin\theta}{\cos\theta + (V/v_1')} \qquad ...(11.22)$$

From Eqs. (11.9) and (11.17)

$$\frac{V}{v_1'} = \frac{m_1 u_1 / m_1 + m_2}{m_2 u_1 / m_1 + m_2} = \frac{m_1}{m_2} \qquad ...(11.23)$$

substituting Eq. (11.23) in Eq. (11.22)

$$\tan\psi = \frac{\sin\theta}{\cos\theta + (m_1/m_2)} \qquad ...(11.24)$$

For $m_1 << m_2$

$$\tan\psi \approx \tan\theta \qquad ...(11.25)$$

that is scattering angle in L and C systems are approximately equal.

If $m_1 = m_2$, Eq. (11.24) gives

$$tan\,\psi = \frac{sin\,\theta}{cos\,\theta + 1} = \frac{2\,sin\frac{\theta}{2}\,cos\frac{\theta}{2}}{2\,cos^2\frac{\theta}{2} - 1 + 1} = tan\frac{\theta}{2}$$

$$\psi = \frac{\theta}{2} \qquad \text{...(11.26)}$$

In L system, scattering angle is one half the scattering angle in C system. Since $q_{max.} = 180^o$, therefore for there can be no scattering in L system at angles greater than 90°.

11.2 CROSS SECTION

Consider the scattering of a particle of mass m by a fixed force centre. The particle interact via a specified force. The particle of mass m comes in from infinity with velocity $\mathbf{v}_0$ and momentum $m\mathbf{v}_0$. It approaches the vicinity of force centre. If there were no force acting between them, then m would pass with a distance of closest approach s. The quantity s is called impact parameter. Energy of the particle of mass m is

$$E = \frac{1}{2} m\,\mathbf{v}_0^2 \qquad \text{...(11.27)}$$

and momentum p is

$$\mathbf{p} = m\,\mathbf{v}_0 \qquad \text{...(11.28)}$$

the angular momentum l is

$$l = \mathbf{r} \times \mathbf{p} = \mathbf{s} \times \mathbf{p} = s\,p = m\,\mathbf{v}_0\,s \qquad \text{...(11.29)}$$

From Eqs. (11.27) and (11.29)

$$l = s\,\sqrt{2mE} \qquad \text{...(11.30)}$$

If there is interaction between the particle m and fixed force centre, the particle m on approaching the force centre will be either be attracted or repelled depending on the nature of the interaction. As a result of this the path of the particle m will deviate from the incident line trajectory. After passing the particle force centre the force acting on m decreases and at large distances the orbit of the incident particle approaches a straight line with a well defined angle θ between the initial and final direction of the motion. In general the final direction of motion is not the same as the incident direction and the particle is said to be scattered.

Consider a narrow uniform beam of particles each of which has a mass m and energy E directed towards a centre of force. Let the incident beam has intensity (or flux density) I. It gives the number of particles crossing per unit area normal to the direction of the beam in the unit time. The incident beam is scattered by the centre of force. The cross-section for scattering in a given direction is given by

$$\sigma(\Omega)\,d\Omega = \frac{n}{I} \qquad \text{...(11.31)}$$

where

$d\Omega$ = element of solid angle in the direction of

n = number of particles scattered into solid angle d Ω per unit time

$\sigma(\Omega)$ = differential scattering cross section

Total scattering cross-section σ_T is defined as

$$\sigma_T = \int \sigma(\Omega)\,d\Omega = \frac{N}{I} \qquad \text{...(11.32)}$$

where N is total number of particles scattered per unit time.

Suppose that the scattered particles are in some way detected at a very large distance from the scatterer. Then the whole scatterer can be considered as a point and after scattering the particles move in a straight lines from the centre of force. Consider those particles which occupy the space between two cones that have the same apex and a common axis (Fig. 11.4), the half angle of the inner cone is equal to θ and the external cone is $\theta + d\theta$. The space between the two cones is called solid angle. The solid angle is a measure of the area of a sphere of unit radius drawn about the centre of the cone. Solid angle is that part of the surface of a sphere covered by an element of are $d\theta$ when it is rotated about OC. Since $OC = 1$, the radius of rotation of the element $d\theta$ is equal to sin θ. Therefore, the surface of the sphere which it covers is equal to

$$d\Omega = 2\pi \sin\theta\, d\theta \qquad \text{...(11.33)}$$

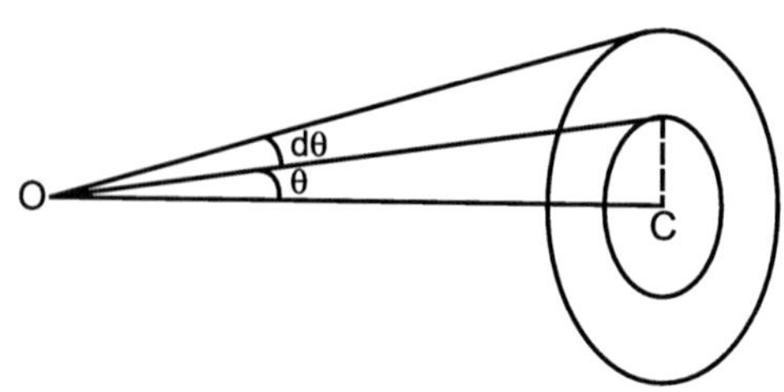

Fig. 11.4

The number of particles with impact parameters within a range ds at a distance s is

$$2\pi I s\,ds \qquad \text{...(11.34)}$$

The number of particles scattered between θ and $\theta + d\theta$ is from Eqs. (11.31) and (11.33) is

$$2\pi I \sigma(\theta) \sin\theta\, d\theta \qquad \text{...(11.35)}$$

The number of particles scattered into a solid angle lying between θ and θ + dθ must be equal to the number of incident particles with impact parameter between the corresponding s and $s + ds$. Equating Eqs. (11.34) and (11.35)

$$2\pi I s\,ds = -2\pi I \sigma(\theta) \sin\theta\, d\theta \qquad \text{...(11.36)}$$

The minus sign is introduced because an increase in s means less force is exerted on the particle resulting in a decrease in the scattering angle q. From Eq. (11.36)

$$\sigma(\theta) = -\frac{s}{\sin\theta}\frac{ds}{d\theta} = \frac{s}{\sin\theta}\left|\frac{ds}{d\theta}\right| \qquad \text{...(11.37)}$$

11.3 RUTHERFORD SCATTERING

Let the scattering force field is produced by the fixed charge Ze acting on the incident particle having a charge $Z'e$, the force is

$$f = \frac{ZZ'e^2}{r^2} \qquad \text{...(11.38)}$$

that is, repulsive inverse square law of force. Let $k = -ZZ'e^2$. The equation of the orbit is given by Eq. (10.68)

$$u = \frac{1}{r} = \left(\frac{mk}{l^2}\right)\left[1 + \sqrt{\left(1 + \frac{2El^2}{mk^2}\right)} \cos(\theta - \theta')\right] \qquad \text{...(11.39)}$$

Now $k = -ZZ'e^2$ and therefore Eq. (11.39) is

$$u = \frac{1}{r} = -\left(\frac{mZZ'e^2}{l^2}\right)\left[1 + \sqrt{\left(1 + \frac{2El^2}{mZ^2Z'^2e^4}\right)} \cos(\theta - \theta')\right]$$

$$\frac{1}{r} = -\left(\frac{mZZ'e^2}{l^2}\right)[1 + \varepsilon \cos\theta] \qquad \text{...(11.40)}$$

where the coordinates have been rotated so that $\theta' = 0$, and

$$\varepsilon = \sqrt{\left(1+\frac{2\,El^2}{mZ^2\,Z'^2\,e^4}\right)} \qquad ...(11.41)$$

From Eqs.(11.30) and (11.41)

$$\varepsilon = \sqrt{\left(1+\frac{4\,E^2\,s^2}{Z^2\,Z'^2\,e^4}\right)} = \sqrt{1+\left(\frac{2\,E\,s}{Z\,Z'e^2}\right)^2} \qquad ...(11.42)$$

Since $\varepsilon > 1$, The Eq. (11.40) represent a conic section which is a hyperbola.

From the Fig. 11.5, 2 α is the angle between the asymptotes for incident and scattered path. Thus α is the value of θ for $r \to \infty$ or $u = 0$. With this limit Eq. (11.40) is

$$\frac{1}{\infty} = -\left(\frac{mZZ'e^2}{l^2}\right)[1+\ \varepsilon\cos\alpha\ ] = 0$$

$$\cos\alpha = -\frac{1}{\varepsilon} \qquad ...(11.43)$$

From the Fig. (11.5)

$$2\alpha + \theta = \pi$$

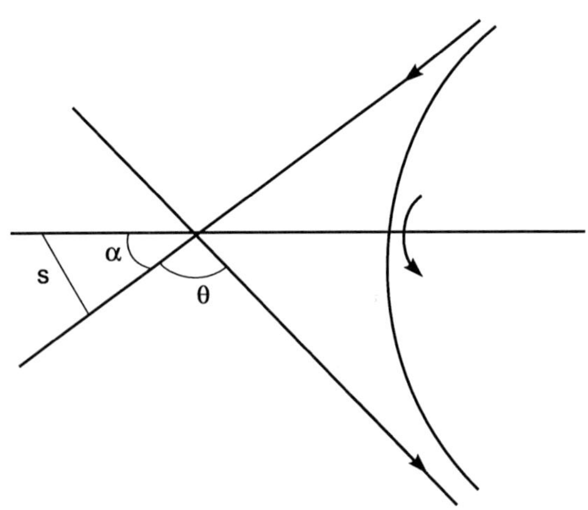

Fig. 11.5 Rutherford scattering

$$\alpha = \frac{\pi}{2} - \frac{\theta}{2} \qquad ...(11.44)$$

The Eq. (11.43) is therefore

$$\cos\alpha = \cos\left(\frac{\pi}{2} - \frac{\theta}{2}\right) = \sin\frac{\theta}{2} = -\frac{1}{\varepsilon} \qquad ...(11.45)$$

$$\cot^2\frac{\theta}{2} = \varepsilon^2 - 1 = 1 + \left(\frac{2Es}{ZZ'e^2}\right)^2 - 1 = \left(\frac{2Es}{ZZ'e^2}\right)^2$$

$$\cot\frac{\theta}{2} = \frac{2Es}{ZZ'e^2} \qquad ...(11.46)$$

$$s = \frac{ZZ'e^2}{2E}\cot\frac{\theta}{2} \qquad ...(11.47)$$

Differentiating Eq.(11.47) with respect to θ

$$\frac{ds}{d\theta} = -\frac{1}{4}\frac{ZZ'e^2}{E\sin^2(\theta/2)} \qquad ...(11.48)$$

Substituting Eqs. (11.47) and (11.48) in Eq. (11.37)

$$\sigma(\theta) = \frac{s}{\sin\theta}\left|\frac{ds}{d\theta}\right| = \frac{ZZ'e^2}{2E}\frac{\cot(\theta/2)}{2\sin(\theta/2)\cos(\theta/2)}\frac{ZZ'e^2}{4E\sin^2(\theta/2)}$$

$$\sigma(\theta) = \frac{1}{4}\left(\frac{ZZ'e^2}{2E}\right)^2\frac{1}{\sin^4(\theta/2)} \qquad ...(11.49)$$

$\sigma(\theta)$ is independent of the sign of k so that the form of the scattering distribution is the same for an attractive force as for a repulsive one.

The total scattering cross section for Rutherford scattering comes out to be infinite. This arise from the fact that the effect of Coulomb field extend to infinity. Therefore, even for indefinitely large impact parameter, a very small deflection occurs. Hence, all particles in an incident beam of infinite cross section will experience some scattering and must be included in the total cross-section resulting the diverging of the integral (11.32). However, the finite result for total scattering cross-section can be obtained if the range of Coulomb force/potential is effectively cut off at large distances. For example, the inclusion of screening term *exp(-r/a)* in the potential yield a finite value of total scattering cross-section.

Solved Examples

Example 1. *Show that the cross section for elastic scattering of point particle from an infinitely massive sphere of radius R is isotropic.*

Solution: For elastic scattering, the incident angle equals the angle of reflection. The angle of scattering is then $\alpha = 2\theta$. as shown in the Fig. 11.2. Let s is the impact parameter, then from the Figure

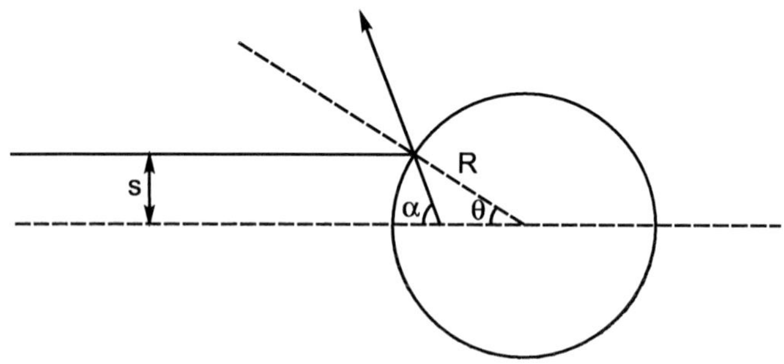

Fig. 11.6

$$s = R \sin\theta$$

$$ds = R\cos\theta\, d\theta = \frac{1}{2} R\cos(\alpha/2)\, d\alpha$$

Differential scattering cross section from Eq. (11.37) is

$$\sigma = \frac{s}{\sin\alpha}\left|\frac{ds}{d\alpha}\right| = \frac{R\sin(\alpha/2)}{\sin\alpha}\frac{R\cos(\alpha/2)}{2} = \frac{R^2 \sin\alpha}{4\sin\alpha} = \frac{R^2}{4}$$

The differential scattering cross section is independent of angle and is therefore isotropic.

Example 2. *Show that (for $m_1 = m_2$) $\sigma(\psi) = 4\sigma(\theta)\cos\psi$ where $\sigma(\psi)$ is the scattering cross section in laboratory system while $\sigma(\psi)$ is the scattering cross section in centre of mass system.*

Solution: The number of particles scattered into a given element of solid angle must be the same in the laboratory system as well as in centre of mass system, that is

$$2\pi I\sigma(\theta)\sin\theta\, d\theta = 2\pi I\sigma(\psi)\sin\psi\, d\psi$$

$$\sigma(\psi) = \sigma(\theta)\frac{\sin\theta\, d\theta}{\sin\psi\, d\psi} = \sigma(\theta)\frac{d(\cos\theta)}{d(\cos\psi)}$$

Substituting the value of θ from Eq. (11.26) in the above expression

$$\sigma(\psi) = \sigma(\theta)\frac{d(\cos 2\psi)}{d(\cos\psi)} = 4\sigma(\theta)\cos\psi$$

OBJECTIVE TYPE QUESTIONS

1. In centre of mass coordinate system, total linear momentum is

(*a*) zero before and after the collision
(*b*) zero before the collision, non zero after the collision
(*c*) non zero before the collision, zero after the collision
(*d*) non zero before and after the collision

2. θ_L is lab scattering angle and θ_C is centre of mass scattering angle .Which of the following is true when the mass of the target particle is equal to the mass of the incident particle.

(*a*) $\theta_L = \theta_C$ (*b*) $\theta_L = 2\,\theta_C$
(*c*) $\theta_L = (\theta_C/2)$ (*d*) none of these

3. θ_L is lab scattering angle and θ_C is centre of mass scattering angle. Which of the following is true when the mass of the target particle is infinitely large in comparison with the mass of the incident particle?

(*a*) $\theta_L = \theta_C$ (*b*) $\theta_L = 2\,\theta_C$
(*c*) $\theta_L = (\theta_C/2)$ (*d*) none of these

4. If θ_L is lab scattering angle then which value of θ_L is not possible when the mass of the target particle is equal to the mass of the incident particle.

(*a*) $\theta_L = 30^\circ$ (*b*) $\theta_L = 60^\circ$
(*c*) $\theta_L = 90^\circ$ (*d*) $\theta_L = 120^\circ$

5. The impact parameter *s* varies with energy of the incident particle as

(*a*) E (*b*) E^{-1}
(*c*) $E^{(-1/2)}$ (*d*) $E^{1/2}$

6. The desired relationship between the impact parameter and the scattering angle is

(*a*) $\frac{ZZ'e^2}{2E}\cot^2\frac{\theta}{2}$ (*b*) $\left(\frac{ZZ'e^2}{2E}\right)^2 \operatorname{cosec}^4\frac{\theta}{2}$

(*c*) $\frac{ZZ'e^2}{2E}\cot\frac{\theta}{2}$ (*d*) $\frac{ZZ'e^2}{2E}\frac{1}{\sin^4(\theta/2)}$

7. In Rutherford scattering, the scattering cross-section for alpha particles is proportional to the energy E as

(*a*) E^2 (*b*) E

(*c*) $1/E$ (*d*) $1/E^2$

8. Rutherford scattering formula fails to agree with the data for

(*a*) small impact parameter (*b*) small scattering angle

(*c*) both (a) and (b) (*d*) none of these

9. Departure from predicted scattering is observed for

(*a*) light nuclei
(*b*) heavy nuclei
(*c*) heavy nuclei, small impact parameter
(*d*) heavy nuclei, large scattering angle.

10. Rutherford scattering cross-section is

(*a*) independent of atomic number (Z) of the target
(*b*) varies as Z
(*c*) varies as Z^2
(*d*) varies as $Z^{-1/2}$

11. Total scattering cross-section for the Rutherford scattering can be deduced if the field of

(*a*) target nuclei is not screened by the electron orbiting it
(*b*) Nuclei are screened by the electron orbiting it
(*c*) both (a) and (b) are true
(*d*) none of these

12. On what type of orbit of alpha particle does Rutherford scattering formula depend?

(*a*) hyperbola (*b*) ellipse
(*c*) parabola (*d*) none of these

13. In the expression for Rutherford scattering cross-section, the differential scattering cross section is proportional to charge e as

(*a*) e (*b*) e^2
(*c*) e^3 (*d*) e^4

PROBLEMS

1. Obtain the cross-section for elastic scattering of small sphere of mass m and radius r from a massive sphere of mass M and radius R $(m<<M)$.

2. Show that Rutherford scattering cross-section in laboratory system for $m_1 = m_2$ is

$$\sigma(\psi) = \left(\frac{ZZ'e^2}{2E}\right)^2 \frac{\cos\psi}{\sin^4\psi}$$

❑❑❑

CHAPTER 12

Dynamics of Rigid Body

12.1 DEFINITION OF RIGID BODY

A rigid body can be defined in two ways:

1. A system of N mass points m_1, m_2, ..., m_N such that the distance between the particles do not vary. Fig 1.4 shows the example for $N = 3$. The total mass M is given by

$$M = \sum_{k=1}^{3} m_k = m_1 + m_2 + m_3$$

2. A body with a given continuous distribution $\rho(r)$ (Fig. 12.1) whose shape does not change. The mass is given by

$$M = \int \rho(r)\, d^3r$$

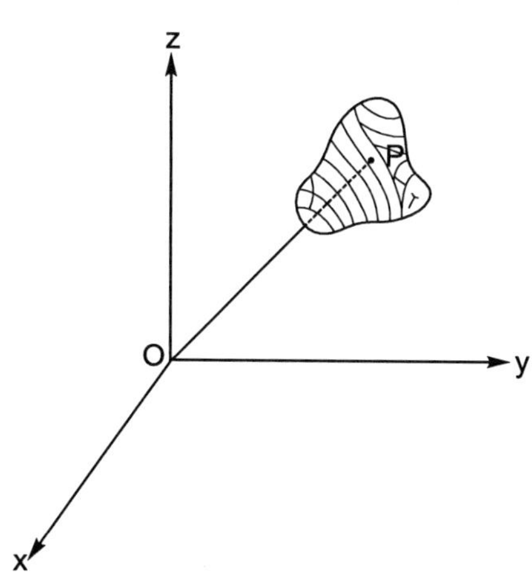

Fig. 12.1 A rigid body consisting of fixed variable mass distribution

For the description of rigid bodies and their motion, two classes of coordinate systems are used. A coordinate system S(Oxyz) that is fixed in space and assume to be inertial. A coordinate system $S'(O'x'y'z')$ which is fixed in the body called body fixed coordinate system and is in general not an inertial system. The origin O' of the body fixed coordinate system may conveniently be taken to coincide with the centre of mass of the body.

Let **R** be the position vector O' of S' system with respect to origin O of S. Another point P of the body has position vector **r** in S coordinate system (Fig. 12.2). As it describes P relative to S, **r′** is independent of time by construction.

The position of rigid body in space is completely determined by **R** of O' in S'. The orientation of axis of S' system relative to S system is given by three independent angles. Therefore, we need six quantities, the three components of vector **R** and three angles. Thus, a rigid body is a system

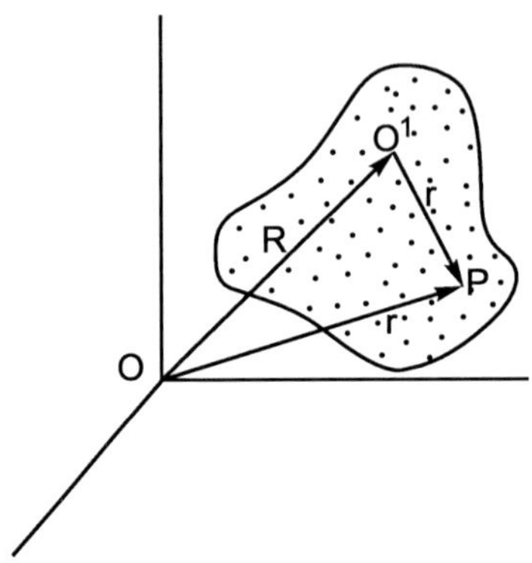

Fig. 12.2 Coordinate system S' fixed in body and S fixed in space

with six degrees of freedom. The number of degrees of freedom may be less when the rigid body is subjected to various conditions. If a point of the rigid body is fixed it has only three degrees of freedom. The rigid body also has three degrees of freedom if it is moving parallel to a plane. On the other hand, if a rigid body is in contact with a fixed plane it has five degrees of freedom. If the rigid body rotates around a single axis, there is only one degree of freedom.

12.2 INERTIA TENSOR

Consider a rigid body which is composed of N particles of masses m_1, m_2, ..., m_N. Let the body rotates with an instaneous angular velocity ω about some point which is fixed relative to S′ coordinate system. Suppose the point moves with a linear velocity **V** relative to S coordinate system, that is, fixed coordinate system. The velocity relative to fixed axes is given by the relation (7.18)

$$\mathbf{v} = \mathbf{V} + \mathbf{v}' + \omega \times \mathbf{r}' \qquad ...(12.1)$$

The velocity of the ith particle is obtained from Eq. (12.1) by putting velocity relative to S′ coordinate equal to zero (v′ =0) as the body is rigid and $\mathbf{r}_i'$ is fixed in S' system. Therefore Eq. (12.1) is

$$\mathbf{v} = \mathbf{V} + \omega \times \mathbf{r}' \qquad ...(12.2)$$

The kinetic energy of the ith particle is

$$T_i = \frac{1}{2} m_i \text{v}_i^2 \qquad ...(12.3)$$

Substituting Eq. (12.2) in Eq.(12.3) and summing over all the particles

$$T = \sum_i T_i = \sum_i m_i \text{v}_i^2 = \frac{1}{2} \sum_i m_i (\mathbf{V} + \omega \times \mathbf{r})^2 \qquad ...(12.4)$$

$$T = \frac{1}{2} \sum m_i \text{V}^2 + \sum m_i \mathbf{V} \cdot (\omega \times \mathbf{r}_i) + \frac{1}{2} \sum m_i (\omega \times \mathbf{r}_i)^2 \qquad ...(12.5)$$

Since V and ω are not characteristic of the ith particle, then we write

$$\sum m_i \mathbf{V} \cdot (\omega \times \mathbf{r}_i) = \mathbf{V} \cdot \left(\omega \times \sum_i m_i \mathbf{r}_i \right) \qquad ...(12.6)$$

Now

$$\left(\sum_i m_i r_i \right) = M\, R \qquad ...(12.7)$$

which vanishes in the S' system since r_i are measured from centre of mass. Eq. (12.5) is therefore

$$T = \frac{1}{2} \sum m_i \text{V}^2 + \frac{1}{2} \sum m_i (\omega \times \mathbf{r}_i)^2$$

$$T = \frac{1}{2} M\, \text{V}^2 + \frac{1}{2} \sum m_i (\omega \times \mathbf{r}_i)^2 = T_t + T_r \qquad ...(12.7)$$

The first term on the right hand side of the Eq. (12.7) is translational energy and second term is rotational kinetic energy.

By using the vector identity

$$(\mathbf{A} \times \mathbf{B})^2 = (\mathbf{A} \times \mathbf{B}) \cdot (\mathbf{A} \times \mathbf{B}) = A^2 B^2 - (\mathbf{A} \cdot \mathbf{B})^2$$

The second term on the right hand side of Eq. (12.7) is

$$T_r = \frac{1}{2} \sum m_i (\omega \times \mathbf{r}_i)^2 = \frac{1}{2} \sum_i m_i \left[\omega^2 r_i^2 - (\omega \cdot \mathbf{r}_i)^2 \right] \qquad ...(12.8)$$

Let ω_1, ω_2 and ω_3 are components of ω along *x,y* and z axes (*or* x_1, x_2, x_3) and is denoted by ω_k and $\mathbf{r}_{ik}$ ($k=1,2,3$) are the components of the $\mathbf{r}_i$ along the x,y,z of rotating system S′ (however now prime symbol over axes are omitted) and written $\mathbf{r}_i$ as (x_{i1}, x_{i2}, x_{i3}). The rotational kinetic energy is

$$T_r = \frac{1}{2}\sum_i m_i \left[\sum (\omega_k^2)(\sum_j x_{ij}^2) - \left(\sum_k \omega_k \cdot x_{ik}\right)\left(\sum_l \omega_l \cdot x_{il}\right)\right]$$

$$\omega_k = \sum_l \omega_l \delta_{kl} \qquad \text{...(12.9)}$$

$$T_r = \frac{1}{2}\sum_{,i,k,l} m_i \left[\omega_k \omega_l \delta_{kl} (\sum_j x_{ij}^2) - \omega_k \omega_l x_{ik} x_{il} \right]$$

$$T_r = \frac{1}{2}\sum_{k,l} \omega_k \omega_l \sum_i m_i \left[\delta_{kl} (\sum_j x_{ij}^2) - x_{ik} x_{il} \right] \qquad \text{...(12.10)}$$

Let

$$I_{kl} = \sum_i m_i \left[\delta_{kl} (\sum_j x_{ij}^2) - x_{ik} x_{il} \right] \qquad \text{...(12.11)}$$

Eq. (12.10) is

$$T_r = \frac{1}{2}\sum_{k,l} I_{kl} \omega_k \omega_l \qquad \text{...(12.12)}$$

$$T_r = \frac{1}{2} I \omega^2 \qquad \text{...(12.13)}$$

where I is scalar and is moment of inertia about the axis of rotation. I_{kl} has nine components and is denoted by I, $\{I\}$ whose components from Eq. (12.10) are

$$I_{11} = \sum_i m_i [x_{i2}^2 + x_{i3}^2] = \sum m_i [y_i^2 + z_i^2]$$

$$I_{22} = \sum_i m_i [x_{i1}^2 + x_{i3}^2] = \sum_i m_i [x_i^2 + z_i^2]$$

$$I_{33} = \sum_i m_i [x_{i1}^2 + x_{i2}^2] = \sum m_i [x_i^2 + y_i^2]$$

$$I_{21} = -\sum_i m_i x_{i2} x_{i1} = -\sum_i m_i x_i y_i = I_{12}$$

$$I_{23} = -\sum_i m_i x_{i2} x_{i3} = -\sum_i m_i y_i z_i = I_{32}$$

$$I_{13} = -\sum_i m_i x_{i1} x_{i3} = -\sum_i m_i x_i z_i = I_{31}$$

TheEq. (10.12) in matrix form is

$$\{\mathrm{I}\} = \begin{pmatrix} \sum_i m_i [x_{i2}^2 + x_{i3}^2] & -\sum_i m_i x_{i2} x_{i1} & -\sum_i m_i x_{i1} x_{i3} \\ -\sum_i m_i x_{i2} x_{i1} & \sum_i m_i [x_{i1}^2 + x_{i3}^2] & -\sum_i m_i x_{i2} x_{i3} \\ -\sum_i m_i x_{i1} x_{i3} & -\sum_i m_i x_{i2} x_{i3} & \sum_i m_i [x_{i1}^2 + x_{i2}^2] \end{pmatrix} \quad \text{...(12.15)}$$

The diagonal elements are called the moment of inertia about x_1, x_2, x_3 (x', y', z) axes respectively and off diagonal elements are product of inertia. Further

$$I_{kl} = I_{lk} \quad \text{...(12.16)}$$

There are therefore only six independent elements of inertia tensor.

12.3 ANGULAR MOMENTUM

Consider a rigid body moves with one point stationary. The fixed point is taken as the origin of the body set of axes. Suppose the body is rotating with an angular velocity ω about an axis through the origin. The total angular momentum of the body about the fixed point is

$$\mathbf{L} = \sum_i \mathbf{r}_i \times \mathbf{p}_i = \sum_i m_i (\mathbf{r}_i \times \mathbf{v}_i) \quad \text{...(12.17)}$$

where r_i and v_i are the radius vector and velocity of the ith particle relative to a given point. r_i is the fixed vector relative to the body, the velocity v_i with respect to the S system arises from the rotational motion of the rigid body about the fixed point. From Eq. (7.16)

$$\frac{d\mathbf{r}_i}{dt} = \frac{d'\mathbf{r}_i}{dt} + \omega \times \mathbf{r}_i$$

Now $\frac{d'\mathbf{r}_i}{dt} = 0$, because $\mathbf{r}_i$ is fixed in S′ system. Hence

$$\mathbf{v}_i = \frac{d\mathbf{r}_i}{dt} = \omega \times \mathbf{r}_i \quad \text{...(12.18)}$$

From Eqs. (12.17) and (12.18)

$$\mathbf{L} = = \sum_i m_i \{\mathbf{r}_i \times (\omega \times \mathbf{r}_i)\}$$

Using the vector identity

$$\mathbf{A} \times (\mathbf{B} \times \mathbf{C}) = \mathbf{B}(\mathbf{A} \cdot \mathbf{C}) - \mathbf{C}(\mathbf{A} \cdot \mathbf{B})$$

we have

$$\mathbf{L} = \sum_i m_i [\omega \, \mathrm{r}_i^2 - \mathbf{r}_i (\mathbf{r}_i \cdot \omega)] \qquad ...(12.19)$$

The component of L along the axes of S' system (omitting the prime symbol on x, y, and z) we have

$$\mathbf{L} = \sum_i m_i [(\omega_x \mathbf{i} + \omega_y \mathbf{j} + \omega_z \mathbf{k}) \mathrm{r}_i^2 - (x_i \mathbf{i} + y_i \mathbf{j} + z_i \mathbf{k})(x_i \omega_x + y_i \omega_y + z_i \omega_z)]$$

x component of L is

$$\mathrm{L_x} = \sum_i m_i [\omega_x \mathrm{r}_i^2 - (x_i^2 \omega_x + x_i y_i \omega_y + x_i z_i \omega_z)]$$

$$\mathrm{L_x} = \sum_i m_i [\omega_x (\mathrm{r}_i^2 - x_i^2) - x_i y_i \omega_y - x_i z_i \omega_z]$$

$$\mathrm{L_x} = \omega_x \sum_i m_i (y_i^2 + z_i^2) - \omega_y \sum_i m_i x_i y_i - \omega_z \sum_i m_i x_i z_i \qquad ...(10.20)$$

Similarly

$$\mathrm{L_y} = -\omega_x \sum_i m_i x_i y_i + \omega_y \sum_i m_i (x_i^2 + z_i^2) - \omega_z \sum_i m_i y_i z_i \qquad ...(10.21)$$

$$\mathrm{L_z} = -\omega_x \sum_i m_i x_i z_i - \omega_y \sum_i m_i y_i z_i + \omega_z \sum_i m_i (x_i^2 + y_i^2) \qquad ...(10.22)$$

Thus each component of angular momentum is a linear function of all the components of angular velocity. Eqs. (12.20)-(12.22) with the help of Eq. (12.14) can be written as (writing 1 for x, 2 for y and 3 for z)

$$L_1 = I\,\omega_1 = I_{11}\omega_1 + I_{12}\omega_2 + I_{13}\omega_3 \qquad ...(12.23)$$

$$L_2 = I\,\omega_2 = I_{21}\omega_1 + I_{22}\omega_2 + I_{23}\omega_3 \qquad ...(12.24)$$

$$L_3 = I\,\omega_3 = I_{31}\omega_1 + I_{32}\omega_2 + I_{33}\omega_3 \qquad ...(12.25)$$

or

$$L_k = \sum_l I_{kl}\omega_l \qquad ...(12.26)$$

$$\mathbf{L} = \mathbf{I}\omega \qquad ...(12.27)$$

Eq. (12.27) represent that I acting upon the vector ω results in the physically new vector. The ω and L are physically different vectors. Multiplying Eq. (12.26) with (1/2) ω_k

$$\frac{1}{2}\sum_k \omega_k L_k = \frac{1}{2}\sum_{k,l} \omega_k I_{kl}\omega_l = T_r \qquad ...(12.28)$$

$$T_r = \frac{1}{2}\omega \cdot \mathbf{L} = \frac{1}{2}\omega \cdot \mathbf{I} \cdot \omega$$

The product of a tensor and two vectors yields a scalar.

Eqs. (12.23)-(12.25) can be rearranged as

$$(I_{11} - \mathrm{I})\ \omega_1 + I_{12}\omega_2 + I_{13}\omega_3 = 0$$

$$I_{21}\omega_1 + (I_{22} - \mathrm{I})\omega_2 + I_{23}\omega_3 = 0$$

$$I_{31}\omega_1 + I_{32}\omega_2 + (I_{33} - \mathrm{I})\omega_3 = 0$$

The condition that they have a non-trivial solution is that the determinant of coefficients vanish

$$\begin{vmatrix} I_{11} - I & I_{12} & I_{13} \\ I_{21} & I_{22} - I & I_{23} \\ I_{31} & I_{32} & I_{33} \end{vmatrix} = 0 \qquad ...(12.29)$$

On expansion of this determinant, equation which is cubic in I is obtained. There are three roots corresponding to the moment of inertia about the principal axes. These are denoted by I_1, I_2 and I_3 and are called principal moment of inertia. The rigid bodies are classified according to the principal moment of inertia

1. If $I_1 \neq I_2 \neq I_3$, the body is termed as asymmetrical top.

2. If $I_1 = I_2 \neq I_3$, the body is termed as symmetric top.

3. If $I_1 = I_2 = I_3$, the body is termed as spherical top.

4. If $I_1 = I_2$. $I_3 = 0$, the body is termed rotor for example diatomic molecule like HCl, rigid rod.

There are two important theorems concerning moment of inertia.

1. Theorem of parallel axis

It states that the moment of inertia of a body about any given axis is the moment of inertia about a parallel axis through the centre of mass plus the moment of inertia about the given axis if all the mass of the body were located at the centre of mass.

2. Theorem of perpendicular axis:

It states that the sum of moment of inertia of a plane lamina about any perpendicular axis in the plane of the lamina is equal to the moment of inertia about an axis through their point of intersection perpendicular to the lamina.

The Moment of Inertia of some common symmetric rigid bodies are tabulated in Table 12.1.

Table 12.1 Moment of inertia of some common symmetric rigid bodies about an axis coincident with the symmetric axis through the centre of mass

Rigid body	Moment of Inertia
Thin cylindrical shell or hoop of radius R and mass M	MR^2
Solid cylinder of radius R and mass M	$MR^2/2$
Thick cylindrical shell or hoop of inner and outer radii R_1 and R_2 and of mass M	$M(R_1^2+R_2^2)/2$
Rectangle plate of sides a and b and of mass M	$M(a^2+b^2)/12$
Long thin rod of mass M and length l	$Ml^2/12$
Sphere of radius R and mass M	$(2/5)MR^2$
Thin spherical shell of mass M and radius R	$(2/3)MR^2$

12.4 THE EULERIAN ANGLES

The transformation from one coordinate system to another can be represented by a matrix equation of the form

$$x' = A\,x$$

where fixed system is identified by x and body system with x' then the rotational matrix A completely describes the relative orientation of the two systems. The matrix A contains three independent angles. In order to describe the rotation of a rigid body we use three angular coordinates called Euler's angle. These coordinates are denoted by θ, φ and ψ. The x,y,z system of coordinates can be rotated into $x'y'z'$ system by successive rotations through the angles φ and then θ and then ψ.

1. Let the initial system of axes xyz is rotated by an angle φ counterclockwise about the z axis and the resultant coordinate system will be labeled by x_1, y_1, z_1 (Fig. 12.3). Since the rotation takes place in the xy plane, the transformation matrix is

$$D = \begin{pmatrix} \cos\varphi & \sin\varphi & 0 \\ -\sin\varphi & \cos\varphi & 0 \\ 0 & 0 & 1 \end{pmatrix} \qquad ...(12.30)$$

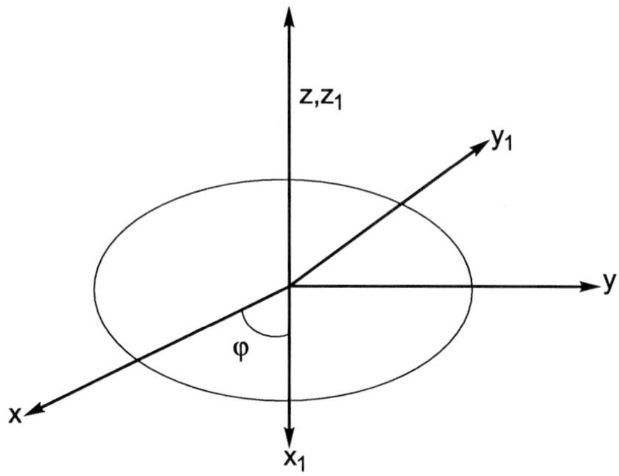

Fig. 12.3 Euler angle φ.

2. The second rotation is counterclockwise through an angle θ about the x_1 axis as shown in the Fig. 12.4. The rotation produces another set of axes x_2, y_2, z_2. The x_2 or x_1 axis is at the intersection of the xy and x_1y_1 planes and is known as the line of nodes. Since the rotation is now in the y_1z_1 plane, the transformation matrix is

$$C = \begin{pmatrix} 1 & 0 & 0 \\ 0 & \cos\theta & \sin\theta \\ 0 & -\sin\theta & \cos\theta \end{pmatrix} \qquad ...(12.31)$$

3. Finally the $x_2y_2z_2$ axes are rotated counterclockwise by an angle ψ about z_2 axis to produce $x'y'z'$ system of axes (Fig. 12.5). The transformation matrix is

$$B = \begin{pmatrix} \cos\psi & \sin\psi & 0 \\ -\sin\psi & \cos\psi & 0 \\ 0 & 0 & 1 \end{pmatrix} \qquad ...(12.32)$$

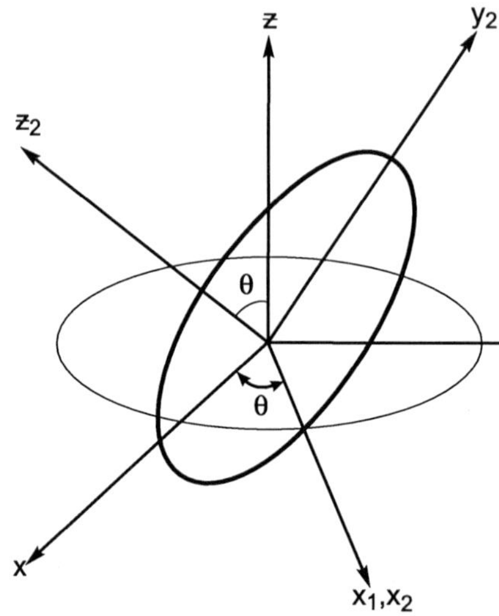

Fig. 12.4 Euler angle θ.

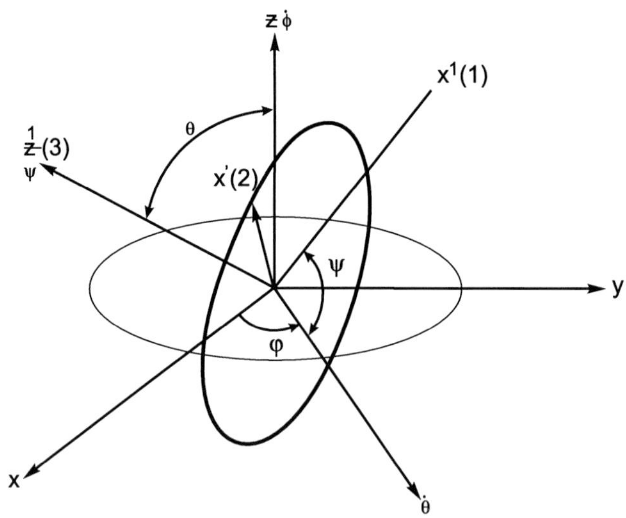

Fig.12.5 Euler angle ψ.

The complete transformation from xyz system to $x'y'z'$ system is given by the rotation matrix

$$A = BCD \qquad ...(12.33)$$

The matrix A with the use of Eqs. (12.30)-(12-33) is

$$A = \begin{pmatrix} \cos\psi & \sin\psi & 0 \\ -\sin\psi & \cos\psi & 0 \\ 0 & 0 & 1 \end{pmatrix} \begin{pmatrix} 1 & 0 & 0 \\ 0 & \cos\theta & \sin\theta \\ 0 & -\sin\theta & \cos\theta \end{pmatrix} \begin{pmatrix} \cos\varphi & \sin\varphi & 0 \\ -\sin\varphi & \cos\varphi & 0 \\ 0 & 0 & 1 \end{pmatrix} \quad ...(12.34)$$

$$A = \begin{pmatrix} \cos\psi & \sin\psi & 0 \\ -\sin\psi & \cos\psi & 0 \\ 0 & 0 & 1 \end{pmatrix} \begin{pmatrix} \cos\varphi & \sin\varphi & 0 \\ -\cos\theta\sin\varphi & \cos\theta\cos\varphi & \sin\theta \\ \sin\theta\sin\varphi & -\sin\theta\cos\varphi & \cos\theta \end{pmatrix}$$

$$A = \begin{pmatrix} \cos\phi\cos\psi - \cos\theta\sin\phi\sin\psi & \cos\psi\sin\phi + \cos\theta\cos\phi\sin\psi & \sin\theta\sin\psi \\ -\sin\psi\cos\phi - \cos\theta\sin\phi\cos\psi & -\sin\psi\sin\phi + \cos\theta\cos\phi\cos\psi & \cos\psi\sin\theta \\ Sin\theta\sin\phi & -\sin\theta\cos\phi & \cos\theta \end{pmatrix}$$

...(12.35)

The inverse transformation from body coordinates to space coordinates is

$$x = A^{-1}x' \quad ...(12.36)$$

where

$$A^{-1} = \begin{pmatrix} \cos\phi\cos\psi - \cos\theta\sin\phi\sin\psi & -\sin\psi\cos\phi - \cos\theta\sin\phi\cos\psi & \sin\theta\sin\phi \\ \cos\psi\sin\phi + \cos\theta\cos\phi\sin\psi & -\sin\psi\sin\phi + \cos\theta\cos\phi\cos\psi & -\sin\theta\sin\phi \\ Sin\theta\sin\psi & \cos\psi\sin\theta & \cos\theta \end{pmatrix}$$

...(12.37)

The matrix is orthogonal. The range of Eulerian angles is

$$0 \le \varphi \le 2\pi, \quad 0 \le \theta \le \pi, \quad 0 \le \psi \le 2\pi$$

Since it is possible to associate a vector with an infinitesimal rotation, therefore the time derivatives of these rotation angles φ, θ and ψ can be associated with the components of the angular velocity ω. Thus

$$\omega_\phi = \dot{\phi}, \quad \omega_\theta = \dot{\theta}, \quad \omega_\psi = \dot{\psi}$$

The quantities $\dot{\varphi}, \dot{\theta}$ and $\dot{\psi}$ are the angular velocity vector along the space z axis, the line of nodes and the body z axis (i.e.z'axis). The angular velocity ω can be expressed in terms of Euler's angles. The angular velocities may be added like vectors. Let **B** be any vector at rest in the starred coordinate system, that is

$$\frac{d^*\mathbf{B}}{dt} = 0 \quad ...(12.38)$$

Let the starred coordinate system is rotating with an angular velocity ω_2 relative to primed coordinate system then by Eq. (7.15)

$$\frac{d'\mathbf{B}}{dt} = \frac{d^*\mathbf{B}}{dt} + \omega_2 \times \mathbf{B} = \omega_2 \times \mathbf{B} \qquad ...(12.39)$$

Suppose primed coordinate system is rotating with an angular velocity w_l relative to unprimed coordinate system, then from Eq. (7.15)

$$\frac{d\mathbf{B}}{dt} = \frac{d'\mathbf{B}}{dt} + \omega_1 \times \mathbf{B} = \omega_2 \times \mathbf{B} + \omega_1 \times \mathbf{B} = (\omega_1 + \omega_2) \times \mathbf{B} \qquad ...(12.40)$$

Thus $(\omega_1 + \omega_2)$ is the angular velocity of the starred system relative to unprimed coordinate system.

Let us consider the components of the angular velocity ω along the body axes $(x', y' z')$

The component of $\dot{\varphi}$ along the z' axis is

$$\dot{\varphi} \cos\theta \qquad ...(12.41)$$

The component of in $x'y'$ plane is

$$\dot{\varphi} \sin\theta \qquad ...(12.42)$$

The component of along x' axis is

The component of $\dot{\varphi} \sin\theta$ along x' axis is

$$\dot{\varphi} \sin\theta \sin\psi \qquad ...(12.43)$$

The component of along y' axis is

$$\dot{\varphi} \sin\theta \cos\psi \qquad ...(12.44)$$

The component of along the x' axis is

$$\dot{\theta} \cos\psi \qquad ...(12.45)$$

The component of along the y' axis is

$$-\dot{\theta} \sin\psi \qquad ...(12.46)$$

The component of along the z' axis is zero. Further, the component of along x' and y' axes is zero while the component of along z' axis is

$$\dot{\psi} \qquad ...(12.47)$$

The components of these angular velocities along the body coordinate axes are

The components of these angular velocities along the body coordinate axes are

$$\dot{\varphi}_{x'} = \dot{\varphi} \sin\theta \sin\psi \qquad ...(12.48)$$

$$\dot{\varphi}_{y'} = \dot{\varphi}\, sin\theta\ cos\psi \quad ...(12.49)$$

$$\dot{\varphi}_{z'} = \dot{\varphi}\, cos\,\theta \quad ...(12.50)$$

$$\dot{\theta}_{x'} = \dot{\theta}\ cos\psi \quad ...(12.51)$$

$$\dot{\theta}_{y'} = -\,\dot{\theta}\ sin\psi \quad ...(12.52)$$

$$\dot{\theta}_{z'} = 0 \quad ...(12.53)$$

$$\dot{\psi}_{x'} = 0 \quad ...(12.54)$$

$$\dot{\psi}_{y'} = 0 \quad ...(12.55)$$

$$\dot{\psi}_{z'} = \dot{\psi} \quad ...(12.56)$$

Collecting the individual components of ω, we have

$$\omega_{x'} = \omega_1 = \dot{\phi}\ \sin\theta \sin\psi + \dot{\theta}\cos\psi \quad ...(12.57)$$

$$\omega_{y'} = \omega_2 = \dot{\phi}\ \sin\theta\cos\psi + \dot{\theta}\ \sin\psi \quad ...(12.58)$$

$$\omega_{z'} = \omega_3 = \dot{\phi}\cos\theta + \dot{\psi} \quad ...(12.59)$$

12.5 EULER'S EQUATION OF MOTION FOR A RIGID BODY

Suppose the motion is subject to torque **N** then

$$\frac{d\mathbf{L}}{dt} = \mathbf{N} \quad ...(12.60)$$

where L is angular momentum. The time derivative here refer to the space axes. From Eq. (7.15)

$$\frac{d\mathbf{L}}{dt} = \frac{d'\mathbf{L}}{dt} + \omega \times \mathbf{L} \quad ...(12.61)$$

If we let $(dt's/dt)$ denote the time derivative with reference to the axes fixed in the body, then by Eq. (12.60)

$$\mathbf{N} = \frac{d'\mathbf{L}}{dt} + \omega \times \mathbf{L} \quad ...(12.62)$$

$$\frac{d\omega}{dt} = \frac{d'\omega}{dt} + \omega \times \omega = \frac{d'\omega}{dt} \quad ...(12.63)$$

Substituting the value of **L** from Eq. (12.27) in Eq. (12.62) and using Eq. (12.63)

$$\mathbf{N} = \mathbf{I}\frac{d\omega}{dt} + \omega \times (\mathbf{I}\omega) \quad ...(12.64)$$

I is constant relative to body axes.

Choosing the body axes as the principal axes, we have from Eq.(12.64)

$$I_1\omega_1 + (I_3 - I_2)\omega_3\omega_2 = N_1 \quad ...(12.65)$$

$$I_2\omega_2 + (I_1 - I_3)\omega_1\omega_3 = N_2 \quad ...(12.66)$$

$$I_3\omega_3 + (I_2 - I_1)\omega_2\omega_1 = N_3 \quad ...(12.67)$$

These are Euler's equations of motion of a rigid body. If one point of the body is held fixed, that point is taken as the origin for the body axes and moment of inertia and torque are relative to the fixed point. In case of unconstraint motion, the origin of the body axes is centre of mass.

12.6 FORCE FREE MOTION OF A SYMMETRICAL TOP

Consider a freely rotating symmetrical body, with no applied torque. Let the symmetry axis of the body is z' axis (or axis 3), so that $I_1 = I_2 \neq I_3$. The Eqs.(12.65)-(12.67) takes the form

$$I_1\omega_1 + (I_3 - I_1)\omega_3\omega_2 = 0 \quad ...(12.68)$$

$$I_2\omega_2 + (I_1 - I_3)\omega_1\omega_3 = 0_2 \quad ...(12.69)$$

$$I_3\omega_3 = 0 \quad ...(12.70)$$

From Eq.(12.70)

$$\omega_3 = \text{constant} \quad ...(12.71)$$

From Eq. (12.68)

$$\omega_1 = -\left[\frac{(I_3 - I_1)}{I_1}\omega_3\right]\omega_2 \quad ...(12.72)$$

From Eq.(12.69)

$$\omega_2 = \left[\frac{(I_3 - I_1)}{I_2}\omega_3\right]\omega_1 \quad ...(12.73)$$

The terms in the square bracket of Eqs. (12.72) and (12.73) are identical and composed of constants. Let

$$\left[\frac{(I_3 - I_1)}{I_2}\omega_3\right] = \beta \quad ...(12.74)$$

The Eqs. (12.72) and (12.73) are

$$\omega_1 = -\beta\,\omega_2 \qquad ...(12.75)$$

$$\omega_2 = \beta\,\omega_1 \qquad ...(12.76)$$

Eqs. (12.75) and (12.76) are coupled equations. Multiplying the Eq. (12.76) by i and adding with Eq. (12.75)

$$\omega_1 + i\omega_2 - i\beta(\omega_1 + i\omega_2) = 0 \qquad ...(12.77)$$

Let

$$\omega_1 + i\omega_2 = \alpha \qquad ...(12.78)$$

$$\omega_1 + i\omega_2 = \dot{\alpha} \qquad ...(12.79)$$

From Eqs.(12.77)-(12.79)

$$\dot{\alpha} - i\beta\alpha = 0 \qquad ...(12.80)$$

The solution of the Eq.(12.80) is of the form (assuming phase equal to zero)

$$\alpha(t) = A\,exp(i\beta t) \qquad ...(12.81)$$

$$\omega_1 + i\omega_2 = A\exp(i\beta t) = A(\cos\beta t + i\sin\beta t) \qquad ...(12.82)$$

$$\omega_1 = A\cos\beta t \qquad ...(12.83)$$

$$\omega_2 = A\sin\beta t \qquad ...(12.84)$$

The magnitude of ω is

$$|\omega| = \sqrt{\omega_1^2 + \omega_2^2 + \omega_3^2} = \sqrt{A^2 + \omega_3^2} = \text{constant} \qquad ...(12.85)$$

as ω_3 is constant.

Eqs.(12.83) and (12.84) show that the component of ω perpendicular to z axis (3 axis) has a constant magnitude and rotates about the 3 axis with constant frequency β. Thus to an observer in the body coordinate system ω traces out a cone around the body symmetry axis, that is, axis 3. Since ω_3 itself is a constant, the vector ω maintains a constant magnitude and trace out a cone in space- the so called body cone around 3-axis. Thus, the symmetric top while rotating about the symmetry axis (3-axis) with frequency ω_3 also wobble about it with frequency β. The latter motion is called the free precession of the top.

In force free motion the torque is zero and therefore the angular momentum vector **L** is stationary in the fixed coordinate system and is constant in time. Further the centre of mass of the body is fixed, therefore, rotational kinetic energy is constant

$$T_{rot.} = \frac{1}{2}\omega \cdot \mathbf{L}$$

Since **L** is constant therefore ω moves in such a manner that its projection on **L** is constant. Thus ω precess around **L** at a constant angle and traces out a cone-the so called space cone- in space. As ω is common to both the cones and **L** has a fixed direction in space, hence one cone rolls on the other cone (Fig. 12.6)

12.7 THE SYMMETRICAL TOP

The symmetrical top shown in Fig. 12.7 is a body for which $I_1 = I_2$. Consider the motion of a symmetrical top in a gravitational field with one point on the symmetry axis is fixed in space (Fig. 12.7). The centre of mass lies on the symmetry axis Oz' and is at a distance h from the fixed point. Let the mass of the top is M. The only external force are the forces of constraint at O and the force of gravity. Let the origin of space set of axes x,y,z and body set of axes x′y′z′ (1,2,3) coincide. Then the translational kinetic energy vanish since

$$\mathbf{V} = \dot{\mathbf{R}} = 0$$

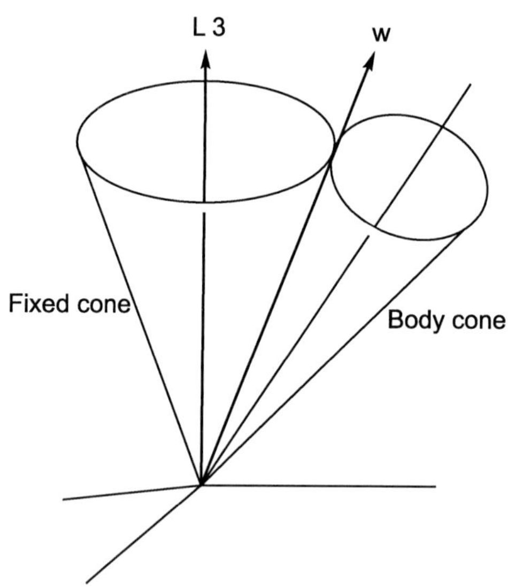

Fig. 12.6

The configuration of the top is completely specified by the Euler′s angles (θ gives the inclination of z axis from the symmetry axis, φ measures the azimuth of top about the vertical)

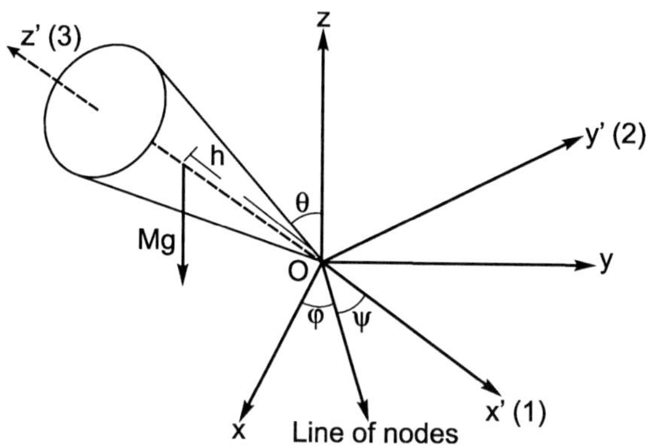

Fig. 12.7

The kinetic energy is given by

$$T = \frac{1}{2} I_1 (\omega_1^2 + \omega_2^2) + \frac{1}{2} I_3 \omega_3^2 \qquad ...(12.86)$$

Substituting the values of ω_1, ω_2 and ω_3 from Eqs.(12.57)-(12.59) in Eq.(12.86)

$$T = \frac{1}{2} I_1 [(\varphi \sin\theta \sin\psi + \dot{\theta} \cos\psi)^2 + (\dot{\varphi} \sin\theta \cos\psi - \dot{\theta} \sin\psi)^2] + \frac{1}{2} I_3 (\dot{\varphi} \cos\theta + \dot{\psi})^2 \qquad ...(12.87)$$

$$T = \frac{1}{2} I_1 [(\dot{\varphi}^2 \sin^2\theta \sin^2\psi + \dot{\theta}^2 \cos^2\psi + 2\dot{\varphi}\dot{\theta} \cos\psi \sin\theta \sin\psi)$$

$$+ (\dot{\varphi} \sin^2\theta \cos^2\psi + \dot{\theta}^2 \sin^2\psi - 2\dot{\varphi}\dot{\theta} \sin\psi \sin\theta \cos\psi] + \frac{1}{2} I^3 (\dot{\varphi} \cos\theta + \dot{\psi})^2$$

$$T = \frac{1}{2} I_1 (\dot{\varphi}^2 \sin^2\theta + \dot{\theta}^2) + \frac{1}{2} I_3 (\dot{\varphi} \cos\theta + \dot{\psi})^2 \qquad ...(12.88)$$

Potential energy is

$$V = Mgh \cos\theta \qquad ...(12.89)$$

The Lagrangian is

$$L = T - V = \frac{1}{2} I_1 (\dot{\varphi}^2 \sin^2\theta + \dot{\theta}^2) + \frac{1}{2} I_3 (\dot{\varphi} \cos\theta + \dot{\psi})^2 - Mgh \cos\theta \qquad ...(12.90)$$

In the Lagrangian φ and ψ do not appear explicitly. They are therefore ignorable coordinates. The moment conjugate to these coordinates are integrals of the motion.

$$\frac{\partial L}{\partial \psi} = \frac{\partial L}{\partial \varphi} = 0 \qquad ...(12.91)$$

From the Lagrange's equations

$$\frac{d}{dt}\left(\frac{\partial L}{\partial \dot{\psi}}\right)-\frac{\partial L}{\partial \psi}=0 \quad ...(12.92)$$

$$\frac{d}{dt}\left(\frac{\partial L}{\partial \dot{\varphi}}\right)-\frac{\partial L}{\partial \varphi}=0 \quad ...(12.93)$$

We have

$$\frac{d}{dt}\left(\frac{\partial L}{\partial \dot{\psi}}\right)=\frac{d}{dt}(p_\psi)=0$$

$$\left(\frac{\partial L}{\partial \dot{\psi}}\right)=p_\psi=I_3(\dot{\phi}\cos\theta+\dot{\psi})=I_3\omega_3=\text{constant} \quad ...(12.94)$$

$$\dot{\psi}=\frac{p_\psi-I_3\dot{\varphi}\cos\theta}{I_3} \quad ...(12.95)$$

From Eqs. (12.91) and (12.93)

$$\frac{d}{dt}\left(\frac{\partial L}{\partial \dot{\varphi}}\right)=\frac{d}{dt}(p_\varphi)=0$$

$$\left(\frac{\partial L}{\partial \dot{\varphi}}\right)=p_\varphi=\text{constant}$$

$$p_\varphi=\left(\frac{\partial L}{\partial \dot{\varphi}}\right)=I_1\,\dot{\varphi}\sin^2\theta+I_3[\,\dot{\varphi}\cos\theta+\dot{\psi}\,]\cos\theta=I_1\,\dot{\varphi}\,\sin^2\theta+p_\psi\,\cos\theta$$

...(12.96)

$$\dot{\varphi}=\frac{p_\varphi-p_\psi\cos\theta}{I_1\sin^2\theta} \quad ...(12.97)$$

The total energy E is

$$E=T+V=\frac{1}{2}I_1(\dot{\varphi}\,\sin^2\theta+\dot{\theta}^2)+\frac{1}{2}I_3(\dot{\varphi}\,\cos\theta+\dot{\psi})^2+Mgh\cos\theta=constant$$

...(12.98)

The energy is conserved as long as frictional forces are neglected.

Eliminating $\dot{\psi}$ and $\dot{\varphi}$ from Eq.(12.98) using Eqs.(12.94) and (12.97)

$$E = \frac{1}{2} I_1 \dot{\theta}^2 + \frac{(p_\varphi - p_\psi \cos\theta)^2}{2I_1 \sin^2\theta} + \frac{p_\psi^2}{2I_3} + Mgh\cos\theta \qquad ...(12.99)$$

Let

$$E' = E - \frac{p_\psi^2}{2I_3} \qquad ...(12.100)$$

$$V_{eff.} = \frac{(p_\varphi - p_\psi \cos\theta)^2}{2I_1 \sin^2\theta} + Mgh\cos\theta = \frac{\eta^2}{2I_1 \sin^2\theta} + Mgh\cos\theta \qquad ...(12.101)$$

where

$$\eta = (p_\varphi - p_\psi \cos\theta)$$

Fig. 12.8 shows the form of $V_{eff.}$ in the physically limited range for θ, that is, between 0 and π. For any value of E', for example E_1' the motion is between θ_1 and θ_2 while for $E' = (V_{eff})_{min}$, θ is limited only to θ_0 and there is steady precession of the top.

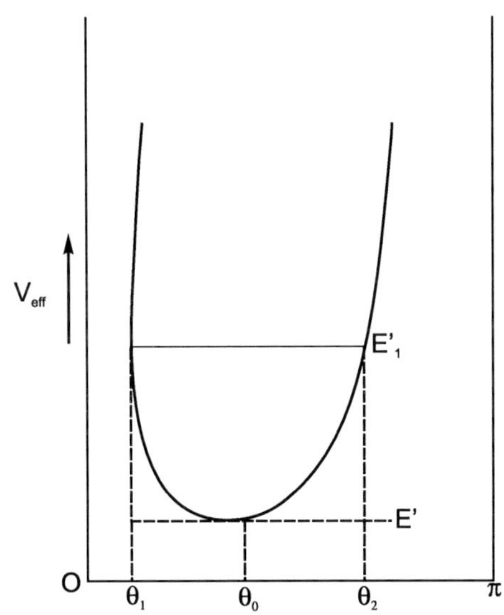

Fig. 12.8

then

$$E' = \frac{1}{2} I_1 \dot{\theta}^2 + \frac{(p_\varphi - p_\psi \cos\theta)^2}{2I_1 \sin^2\theta} + Mgh\cos\theta$$

Multiplying by $\frac{2}{I_1} sin^2 \theta$

$$\frac{2}{I_1} sin^2 \theta E' = \dot{\theta}^2 sin^2 \theta + \frac{(p_\varphi - p_\psi cos\theta)^2}{I_1^2} + \frac{2Mgh}{I_1} cos\theta \, sin^2 \theta \quad ...(12.102)$$

Let

$$\frac{2E'}{I_1} = a, \quad \frac{2Mgh}{I_1} = b \quad ...(12.103)$$

The Eq.(12.102) is then

$$a \, sin^2 \theta = \dot{\theta}^2 sin^2 \theta + \frac{(p_\varphi - p_\psi cos\theta)^2}{I_1^2} + b \, cos\theta \, sin^2 \theta$$

$$\dot{\theta}^2 sin^2 \theta = (a - b \, cos\theta) sin^2 \theta - \frac{(p_\varphi - p_\psi cos\theta)^2}{I_1^2} \quad ...(12.104)$$

Let

$$u(t) = cos\theta(t) \quad ...(12.105)$$

$$\frac{du}{dt} = - sin\theta \, \dot{\theta} \quad ...(12.106)$$

Eq.(12.104) is

$$f(u) = \dot{u}^2 = (1-u^2)(a-bu) - \frac{(p_\varphi - p_\psi u)^2}{I_1^2} \quad ...(12.107)$$

$$\frac{du}{dt} = \sqrt{(1-u^2)(a-bu) - \frac{(p_\varphi - p_\psi u)^2}{I_1^2}}$$

$$t = \int_{u(0)}^{u(t)} \frac{du}{\sqrt{(1-u^2)(a-bu) - \frac{(p_\varphi - p_\psi u)^2}{I_1^2}}} \quad ...(12.108)$$

Only those values of $u(t)$ are physical which lies in the interval [– 1,1] and for which $f(u) \geq 0$. The boundaries $u = 1$ ($\theta = \theta_1$) or $u = -1$ ($\theta = \theta_2$) can only be physical if in the Eq.(12.107), $p_\varphi = p_\psi$ or $p_\varphi = -\theta_\psi$. For $p_\varphi = p_\psi$, the top is standing vertically while for $p_\varphi = -p_\psi$ the top is suspended vertically. In both the cases top is called sleeping. When condition $p_\varphi = \pm p_\psi$ is not satisfied the symmetry axis of the top is at an angle θ with the vertical. The values of θ lies between θ_1 and θ_2. The motion which is wobbling up and down of the axis between the limits θ_1 and θ_2 is called nutation and takes place at the same time as the precessional motion of the axis of the top about the vertical and spinning of the top about its axis.

Putting $u_0 = (p_\varphi / p_y)$ in the Eq.(12.97)

$$\dot{\varphi} = \frac{p_\psi \left[\dfrac{p_\varphi}{p_\psi} - \cos\theta \right]}{I_1 (1 - \cos^2\theta)} = \frac{p_\psi (u_0 - u)}{I_1 (1 - u^2)} \tag{12.109}$$

where the values of q lies between θ_1 and θ_2. The derivative of φ changes sign if and only if the numerator of Eq.(12.110) changes sign in the range of θ. In case when there is no change in the sign of the numerator, the axis of the top precess monotonically about the vertical at the same time oscillating up and down. When $\cos\theta_1 \neq \cos\theta_2$ $(u_1 \neq u_2)$, the extremity of the symmetry axis moves on the unit sphere between the parallel of latitude. It is customary to represent the motion of the locus of the figure axis on a sphere of unit radius whose centre is at the fixed point of the top. The Euler angles θ and φ are identical with the angular coordinates of a point on the surface of a sphere. Whenever $u_1 \neq u_2$ figure axis moves between the limiting circles defined by

$$\theta_i = \cos^{-1} u_i \quad (i = 1,2)$$

Depending on the position of u_0 relative to u_1 and u_2, we have three cases

1. $u_0 > u_2$ (or $u_0 < u_1$)

From Eq. (12.110), $\dot{\varphi}$ will always have the same sign (positive or negative) for the allowed inclination angle between θ_1 and θ_2. The locus of the figure axis must be tangent to the boundary circles in such a manner that $\dot{\varphi}$ is in the same direction at θ_1 and θ_2 as shown in Fig. (12.9). Thus top precesses monotonically around z axis while the symmetry axis oscillates between θ_1 and θ_2.

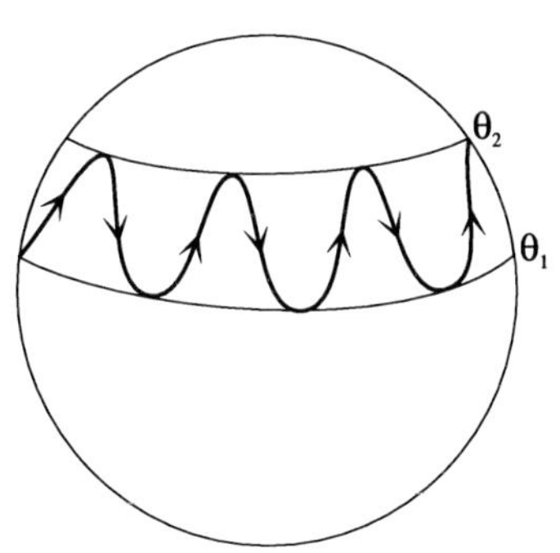

Fig. 12.9

2. $u_1 < u_0 < u_2$

In this case has different signs at q_1 and q_2 and the motion of the symmetry axis looks as shown in Fig. (12.10)

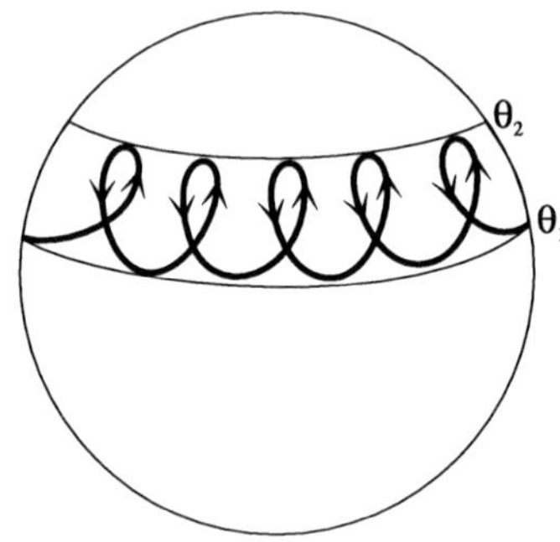

Fig. 12.10

In this case the direction of precession is opposite on the two limiting circles and so the symmetry axis of the top describes loops as it moves round the vertical

3. $u_0 = u_1$ or $u_0 = u_2$

For this case vanishes at the lower and upper circles, respectively and the locus of the symmetry axis is as shown in the Fig. 12.11

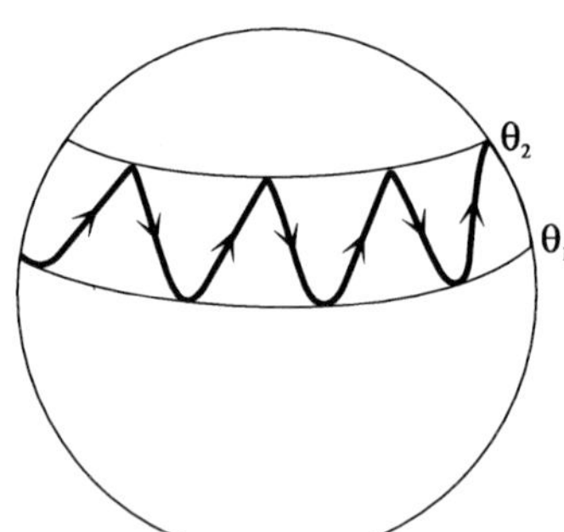

Fig. 12.11

Solved Examples

Example 1. *Find Moment of Inertia, product of inertia of a uniform square plate of length a about the xyz axes chosen as shown in the Fig. 12.12*

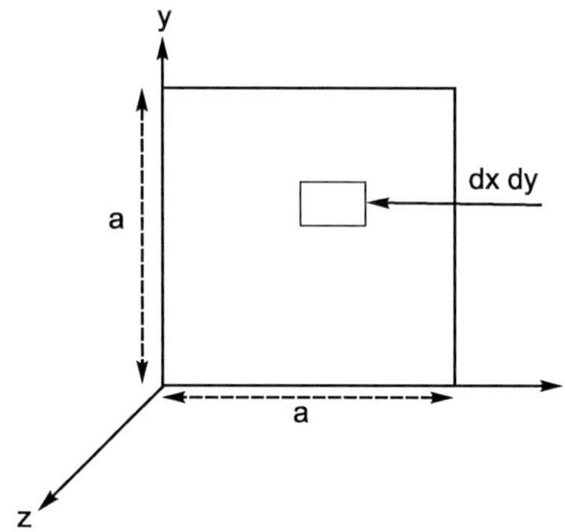

Fig. 12.12

Solution: The moment of inertia of an element *dxdy* of the plate about the *x* axis is $\rho y^2\, dxdy$ where $\rho = (M/a^2)$ is the mass density. The moment of inertia of the entire plate about the *x* axis is

$$I_{xx} = \int_{x=0}^{a}\int_{y=0}^{a} \rho(y^2+z^2)\,dx\,dy = \frac{1}{3}\rho a^4 = \frac{1}{3}Ma^2$$

$$I_{yy} = \int_{x=0}^{a}\int_{y=0}^{a} \rho(x^2+z^2)\,dx\,dy = \frac{1}{3}\rho a^4 = \frac{1}{3}Ma^2$$

$$I_{xx} = \int_{x=0}^{a}\int_{y=0}^{a} \rho(x^2+y^2)\,dx\,dy = \frac{1}{3}\rho a^4 + \frac{1}{3}\rho a^4 = \frac{2}{3}Ma^2$$

Product of inertia

$$I_{xy} = I_{yx} = -\int_{x=0}^{a}\int_{y=0}^{a} \rho\, x\, y\, dx\, dy = -\frac{1}{4}\rho a^4 = -\frac{1}{4}Ma^2$$

The product of inertia of the element *dx dy* of the plate about *x* and *z* axes is the product of ρ *dx dy* by the distance *yz* and *xy* planes which are *x* and zero, respectively. Thus, we have

$$I_{xz} = I_{zx} = 0; \quad I_{yz} = I_{zy} = 0$$

From Eq. (12.29)

$$\begin{vmatrix} \frac{1}{3}Ma^2 - I & -\frac{1}{4}Ma^2 & 0 \\ -\frac{1}{4}Ma^2 & \frac{1}{3}Ma^2 - I & 0 \\ 0 & 0 & \frac{2}{3}Ma^2 - I \end{vmatrix} = 0$$

On solving the above determinant

$$\left(\frac{1}{3}Ma^2 - I\right)\left[\left(\frac{1}{3}Ma^2 - I\right)\left(\frac{2}{3}Ma^2 - I\right)\right] + \frac{1}{4}Ma^2\left[-\frac{1}{4}Ma^2\left(\frac{2}{3}Ma^2 - I\right)\right] = 0$$

$$\left(\frac{2}{3}Ma^2 - I\right)\left[\left(\frac{1}{3}Ma^2 - I\right)^2 - \frac{1}{16}M^2a^4\right] = 0$$

$$\left(\frac{2}{3}Ma^2 - I\right)\left[\left(I - \frac{7}{12}Ma^2\right)\left(I - \frac{1}{12}Ma^2\right)\right] = 0$$

$$I_1 = \frac{1}{12}Ma^2, \quad I_2 = \frac{7}{12}Ma^2, \quad I_3 = \frac{2}{3}Ma^2$$

For $I_1 = \frac{1}{12}Ma^2$, Eqs.(12.23)-(12.25) becomes

$$\frac{1}{4}Ma^2\,\omega_x - \frac{1}{4}Ma^2\,\omega_y = 0$$

$$-\frac{1}{4}Ma^2\,\omega_x + \frac{1}{4}Ma^2\,\omega_y = 0$$

$$\left(\frac{2}{3}Ma^2 - \frac{1}{12}Ma^2\right)\omega_z = 0$$

From the above equations

$$\omega_x = \omega_y, \omega_z = 0$$

thus

$$\omega_x(\mathbf{i} + \mathbf{j}) + \omega_z\mathbf{k} = \omega_x(\mathbf{i} + \mathbf{j})$$

Then the principal axis corresponding to I is $(\mathbf{i} + \mathbf{j})$

Similarly for $I_1 = \frac{7}{12} Ma^2$ we have

$$\omega_x = -\omega_y, \omega_z = 0$$

$$\omega_x (\mathbf{i} - \mathbf{j}) + \omega_z \mathbf{k} = \omega_x (\mathbf{i} - \mathbf{j})$$

Then the principal axis corresponding to I is $(i - j)$

If we let $I = I_3 = \frac{2}{3} Ma^2$, we find $\omega_x = \omega_y = 0$ while ω_z is arbitrary. This gives $\omega_z = \omega_z$ **k** which shows that these principal axis is along **k**.

Example 2. *The inertia tensor of a rigid body is of the form*

$$I = \begin{pmatrix} I_{11} & I_{12} & 0 \\ I_{21} & I_{22} & 0 \\ 0 & 0 & I_{33} \end{pmatrix}$$

with $I_{21}=I_{12}$. *Determine the three moment of inertia. Assuming* $I_{11} = \alpha, I_{22} = 4\alpha, I_{12} = \beta$ *., Find* I_{33}.

Solution: From Eq. (12.29)

$$\begin{vmatrix} I_{11} - I & I_{12} & 0 \\ I_{21} & I_{22} - I & 0 \\ 0 & 0 & I_{33} - I \end{vmatrix} = 0$$

On solving the above

$$(I_{11} - I)(I_{22} - I)(I_{33} - I) - I_{12} I_{21}(I_{33} - I) = 0$$

$$(I_{33} - I)[(I_{11} - I)(I_{22} - I) - I_{12}^2] = 0$$

$$(I_{33} - I)[I^2 - (I_{11} + I_{22})I + (I_{11} I_{22} - I_{12}^2)] = 0$$

The roots are

$$I_{1,2} = \frac{(I_{11} + I_{22}) \pm \sqrt{(I_{11} + I_{22})^2 - 4(I_{11} I_{22} - I_{12}^2)}}{2}, I_3 = I_{33}$$

$$I_{1,2} = \frac{(I_{11} + I_{22}) \pm \sqrt{(I_{11} - I_{22})^2 - 4 I_{12}^2}}{2}, I_3 = I_{33}$$

Putting $I_{11} = \alpha, I_{22} = 4\alpha, I_{12} = \beta$ we have

$$I_{1,2} = \frac{(\alpha + 4\alpha) \pm \sqrt{9\alpha^2 + 16\alpha^2}}{2} = \frac{5\alpha \pm 5\alpha}{2} = 5\alpha, 0$$

From $I_1 + I_2 \geq I_3$ and $I_2 + I_3 \geq I_1$ follows $I_3 = 5\alpha$. The body is axially symmetric with respect to 2-axis.

Example 3. *Show that for a given w_3 there are two possible values of the precessional velocity for a given value of θ_0 ($\theta_0 < \theta/2$)*

Solution: We have from Eq.(12.101)

$$V_{eff.} = \frac{(p_\varphi - p_\psi \cos\theta)^2}{2I_1 \sin^2\theta} - Mgh(1-\cos\theta)$$

From the Figs. 12.9-12.11 it is seen that inclination of the top is confined to the region $\theta_1 \le q \le \theta_2$. For the case $E' = E'_2 = V_{min.}$, $\theta = \theta_0$ and the motion is steady precession at a fixed angle of inclination θ_0. Therefore, at $\theta = \theta_0$, $\frac{dV_{eff.}}{d\theta}$ equal to zero. Thus

$$\left.\frac{dV_{eff.}}{d\theta}\right|_{\theta_0} = \frac{2(p_\phi - p_\psi \cos\theta)p_\psi \sin\theta}{2I_1 \sin^2\theta} - \frac{2(p_\phi - p_\psi \cos\theta)^2 \cos\theta}{2I_1 \sin^3\theta} - Mgh \sin\theta\Bigg|_{\theta_0} = 0$$

$$\left.\frac{dVe_{ff}}{d\theta}\right|_{\theta 0} = \frac{(p_\varphi - p_\psi \cos\theta)p_\psi \sin^2\theta_0 - (p_\varphi - p_\psi \cos\theta_0}{I_1 \sin^3\theta_0} - Mgh \sin\theta_0 = 0$$

Let $\eta = (p_\varphi - p_\psi \cos\theta_0)$, The above equation becomes

$$\cos\theta_0 \eta^2 - p_\psi \sin^2\theta_0 \eta + Mgh I_1 \sin^4\theta_0 = 0$$

This is a quadratic equation in h^2. Its roots are

$$\eta = \frac{1}{2\cos\theta_0}\left[p_\psi \sin^2\theta_0 \pm \sqrt{(p_\psi \sin^2\theta_0)^2 - 4MghI_1 \sin^4\theta_0 \cos\theta_0}\right]$$

$$\eta = \frac{p_\psi \sin^2\theta_0}{2\cos\theta_0}\left[1 \pm \sqrt{1 - \frac{4MghI_1 \cos\theta_0}{p_\psi^2}}\right] \quad ...(12.110)$$

Since η must be real quantity, therefore the radical must be positive, or

$$p_\psi^2 \ge 4MghI_1 \cos\theta_0$$

From Eq.(12.94)

$$p_\psi = I_3\omega_3$$

or

$$\omega_3 \ge \frac{2}{I_3}\sqrt{MghI_1 \cos\theta_0}$$

There can be a steady precession at the fixed angle of inclination, only if the angular velocity of spin is larger than the limiting value given by the above relation. For $\theta = \theta_0$, the Eq. (12.97) is

$$\dot{\varphi}_0 = \frac{\eta}{I_1 \sin^2 \theta_0}$$

Since η has two values, therefore, there are two possible values of $\dot{\varphi}_0$. If ω_3 is large, then the second term in the radical of Eq.(12.110) is small. Expanding the radical

$$\left(1 - \frac{4MghI_1 \cos\theta_0}{p_\psi^2}\right)^{1/2} = \left(1 - \frac{2MghI_1 \cos\theta_0}{p_\psi^2} + ...\right)$$

Retaining only the first non vanishing term , the Eq. (12.110) is

$$\eta = \frac{p_\psi \sin^2 \theta_0}{2\cos\theta_0}\left[1 \pm 1 - \frac{2MghI_1 \cos\theta_0}{p_\psi^2}\right]$$

$$\eta_+ = \frac{p_\psi \sin^2 \theta_0}{2\cos\theta_0}\left[2 - \frac{2MghI_1 \cos\theta_0}{p_\psi^2}\right] \cong \frac{p_\psi \sin^2 \theta_0}{\cos\theta_0}$$

and

$$\eta_- = \frac{p_\psi \sin^2 \theta_0}{2\cos\theta_0}\left[1 - 1 + \frac{2MghI_1 \cos\theta_0}{p_\psi^2}\right] \cong \frac{MghI_1}{p_\psi} \sin^2 \theta_0$$

we have

$$(\dot{\varphi}_0)_+ = \frac{\eta_+}{I_1 \sin^2 \theta_0} \cong \frac{p_\psi}{I_1} \cos\theta_0 \cong \frac{I_3 w_3}{I_1} \cos\theta_0$$

$$(\dot{\varphi}_0)_- = \frac{\eta_-}{I_1 \sin^2 \theta_0} \cong \frac{MghI_1 \sin^2 \theta_0}{p_\psi I_1 \sin^2 \theta_0} \cong \frac{Mgh}{I_3 w_3}$$

Thus, there are two possible precessional angular velocities for $\theta_0 < \pi/2$. For $\theta_0 > \pi/2$ the radical in Eq. (12.110) is always positive and there is no limiting condition on ω_3.

Example 4. *Discuss Standing Top.*

Solution: For standing top $\theta = 0$, we have from Eq.(12.94) and (12.96)

$$p_\varphi = p_\psi$$

From Eq.(12.99)

$$E = \frac{1}{2} I_1 \dot{\theta}^2 + \frac{(p_\varphi - p_\psi \cos\theta)^2}{2I_1 \sin^2\theta} + \frac{p_\psi^2}{2I_3} + Mgh\cos\theta$$

Writing

$$V_{eff.}(\theta) = \frac{(p_\varphi - p_\psi \cos\theta)^2}{2I_1 \sin^2\theta} Mgh\cos\theta$$

and

$$E' = E - \frac{p_\psi^2}{2I_3} - Mgh$$

$$E' = \frac{1}{2} I_1 \dot{\theta}^2 + V_{eff.}(\theta)$$

For $\theta = 0$, $V_{eff.} = 0$, and therefore $E' = 0$ or

$$E = \frac{p_\psi^2}{2I_3} - Mgh$$

The rotation is stable only if $V_{eff.}$ has a minimum at $\theta = 0$. In the neighbourhood of θ

$$V_{eff.}(\theta) = \frac{p_\psi^2 \left(1 - \left(1 - \frac{\theta^2}{2} + ...\right)^2\right.}{2I_1 \theta^2} + Mgh\left(1 - \frac{\theta^2}{2} + ...\right)$$

$$V_{eff.}(\theta) = \frac{p_\psi^2 \frac{\theta^4}{4}}{2I_1\theta^2} - Mgh\frac{\theta^2}{2} + Mgh = \left[\frac{p_\psi^2}{8I_1} - \frac{Mgh}{2}\right]\theta^2 + Mgh$$

$$\frac{dV_{eff.}}{d\theta} = 2\left[\frac{p_\psi^2}{8I_1} - \frac{Mgh}{2}\right]\theta$$

$$\frac{d^2V_{eff.}}{d\theta^2} = \left[\frac{p_\psi^2}{4I_1} - Mgh\right] > 0$$

$$p_\psi^2 > 4I_1 Mgh$$

$$(I_3\omega_3)^2 > 4I_1 Mgh$$

$$\omega_3^2 > \frac{4I_1 Mgh}{I_3^2}$$

Exmaple 5. *Describe Fast Top.*

Solution: Consider the case when the top spinning about its axis with angular velocity ω_3 is held with its axis initially at rest at an angle θ_l and then release. At this position the top is neither precessing nor nutating that is $\dot{\varphi} = 0, \dot{\theta} = 0$. So θ = θ_1 is a root of $f(u)$ = 0[Eq.(12.107)] as soon; as the top is let go, $\dot{\varphi}$ and $\dot{\theta}$ must become non-zero and Mgh cos must decrease, or θ must increase. The top therefore starts to fall, it continues to do so till θ become equal to θ_2. At that point the falling motion of the top is reversed. The top precesses about the vertical and nutates between θ_l and θ_2.

Initially, we have

$$\theta = \theta_1, \quad \dot{\theta} = 0, \dot{\phi} = 0, \dot{\psi} = \omega_3$$

The Eq.(12.94) is then

$$p_\psi = I_3 \omega_3$$

From Eq.(12.96)

$$p_\phi = I_3 \omega_3 \cos\theta$$

Eq.(12.101) is then

$$V_{eff.} = \frac{I_3^2 \omega_3^2 (\cos\theta_1 - \cos\theta)^2}{2I_1 \sin^2\theta} + Mgh\cos\theta$$

$$V_{eff.} = \frac{I_3^2 \omega_3^2}{2I_1}\left[\frac{(\cos\theta_1 - \cos\theta)^2}{\sin^2\theta} + \alpha\cos\theta)\right]$$

where

$$\alpha = \frac{2I_1 Mgh}{I_3^2 \omega_3^2}$$

Under the given conditions we have for $\theta = \theta_{l,}$ from Eqs.(12.99)-(12.101)

$$E' = \frac{1}{2} I_1 \dot{\theta}^2 + V_{eff.}(\theta) = Mgh\cos\theta_1$$

From the above equation

$$Mgh\cos\theta_1 = \frac{I_3^2 \omega_3^2}{2I_1}\left[\frac{(\cos\theta_1 - \cos\theta)^2}{\sin^2\theta} + \alpha\cos\theta\right]$$

Multiplying by $\sin^2\theta$ and rearranging the terms

$$(cos\theta - cos\theta_1)[\alpha\, cos^2\theta - cos\theta - (\alpha - cos\theta_1)] = 0$$

The roots of the equation are

$$\cos\theta = \cos\theta_1$$

and

$$\cos\theta = \frac{1}{2\alpha}[1 \pm \sqrt{1+4\alpha^2 - 4\alpha\cos\theta_1}\,]$$

Using the negative sign in the root the angle θ_2 is given by

$$\cos\theta_2 = \frac{1}{2\alpha}[1 - \sqrt{1+4\alpha^2 - 4\alpha\cos\theta_1}\,]$$

The plus sign gives a root for $\cos\theta > 1$. For rapidly spinning top, that is, for very large value of ω_3

$$\frac{2I_1 Mgh}{I_3^2\omega_3^2} >> 1$$

Under this condition the second term in the radical is very small. We may expand the radical and ignoring terms higher than α^2, we have

$$\cos\theta_2 \cong \cos\theta_1 - \alpha\sin^2\theta_1$$

$$u_1 - u_2 = \alpha\sin^2\theta_1 = \frac{2I_1 Mgh\sin^2\theta_1}{I_3^2\omega_3^2}$$

The angle θ_2 is slightly greater than θ_1 and the amplitude of nutation is proportional to α. Thus, larger the ω_3 smaller the magnitude of nutation. A fast top therefore appears to precess without nutation.

Example 6. *Verify that the angle of rotation F is given in terms of the Euler angles by the expression*

$$\cos\frac{\Phi}{2} = \cos\frac{\phi+\psi}{2}\cos\frac{\theta}{2}$$

Solution: A rotation about z axis through the angle Φ is represented by the transformation whose matrix has the form

$$\begin{pmatrix} \cos\Phi & \sin\Phi & 0 \\ -\sin\Phi & \cos\Phi & 0 \\ 0 & 0 & 1 \end{pmatrix}$$

Trace of the matrix is = $1 + 2\cos\Phi$

Trace of the rotational matrix in terms of the Eularian angles from the matrix (12.35) is

$$\cos\phi\cos\psi - \cos\theta\sin\phi\sin\psi - \sin\psi\sin\phi + \cos\theta\cos\phi\cos\psi + \cos\theta$$

Equating the two traces

$$1 + 2\cos\Phi = \cos\phi\cos\psi - \cos\theta\sin\phi\sin\psi - \sin\psi\sin\phi + \cos\theta\cos\phi\cos\psi + \cos\theta$$

$$1 + 2\cos\Phi = \cos(\psi + \phi) + \cos\theta\cos(\psi + \phi) + \cos\theta = \cos(\psi + \phi)(1 + \cos\theta) + \cos\theta$$

$$4\cos^2\frac{\Phi}{2} - 1 = \left[2\cos^2\frac{(\psi + \phi)}{2} - 1\right]2\cos^2\frac{\theta}{2} + 2\cos^2\frac{\theta}{2} - 1$$

$$= 4\cos^2\frac{(\psi + \phi)}{2}\cos^2\frac{\theta}{2} - 1$$

$$\cos\frac{\Phi}{2} = \cos\frac{(\psi + \phi)}{2}\cos\frac{\theta}{2}$$

OBJECTIVE TYPE QUESTIONS

1. The number of degrees of freedom for a rigid body with one point fix is

(*a*) three (*b*) five
(*c*) six (*d*) one

2. A body is called asymmetric if the moment of inertia have the relation

(*a*) $I_1 = I_2 = I_3$ (*b*) $I_1 = I_2$, $I_3 = 0$
(*c*) $I_1 = I_2 \neq I_3$ (*d*) $I_1 \neq I_2 \neq I_3$

3. A body is called rotor if the moment of inertia have the relation

(*a*) $I_1 = I_2 = I_3$ (*b*) $I_1 = I_2$, $I_3 = 0$
(*c*) $I_1 = I_2 \neq I_3$ (*d*) $I_1 \neq I_2 \neq I_3$

4. A body is called symmetric top if the moment of inertia have the relation

(*a*) $I_1 = I_2 = I_3$ (*b*) $I_1 = I_2$, $I_3 = 0$
(*c*) $I_1 = I_2 \neq I_3$ (*d*) $I_1 \neq I_2 \neq I_3$

5. Which is not correct?

(*a*) **L** and ω are physically different vectors
(*b*) Product of a tensor and a vector yields a vector
(*c*) Product of a tensor and two vectors yields a scalar
(*d*) In a force free motion of the rigid bodies, the kinetic energy of the rotational motion is not conserved

6. Rigid rod is an example of

(*a*) rotor (*b*) spherical top
(*c*) symmetric top (*d*) asymmetric top

7. The range of Eulerian angle y is

(*a*) $0 \leq \psi \leq 2\pi$ (*b*) $0 \leq \psi \leq \pi$
(*c*) $-\pi \leq \psi \leq \pi$ (*d*) $\pi \leq \psi \leq 2\pi$

8. Moment of Inertia of the solid sphere of mass M and radius R about a tangent is

(*a*) $(1/2)MR^2$ (*b*) $(2/5)MR^2$
(*c*) $(7/5)MR^2$ (*d*) $(2/3)MR^2$

9. Minimum spin angular velocity $\omega_{\min}$. below which the top cannot precess uniformly at angle θ_0 less than $\pi/2$ is

(*a*) $\left(\frac{I_3^2 \cos\theta_0}{4MghI_1}\right)^{\frac{1}{2}}$ (*b*) $\left(\frac{I_1^2 \cos\theta_0}{4MghI_3}\right)^{\frac{1}{2}}$

(*c*) $\left(\frac{4MghI_1 \cos\theta_0}{I_3^2}\right)^{\frac{1}{2}}$ (*d*) $\left(\frac{4MghI_3 \cos\theta_0}{I_1^2}\right)^{\frac{1}{2}}$

10. For spin angular velocity greater than minimum spin angular velocity, the symmetrical top can precess at two values of $\dot{\varphi}_0$, the slow precession and fast precession. The angular velocity of slow precession is

(*a*) $\frac{Mgh}{I_3\omega_3}$ (*b*) $\frac{I_3}{I_1\omega_3 \cos\theta_0}$

(*c*) $\frac{I_1 \cos\theta_0}{I_3\omega_3}$ (*d*) $\frac{I_3 \sin\theta_0}{I_1\omega_3}$

11. Which is not true?

(*a*) The larger the ω_3, the smaller is the magnitude of nutation
(*b*) If the shape and mass distribution of a rigid body is symmetric with respect to reflection in a plane, its centre of mass and two of its principal axes lie in that plane.
(*c*) The inertia tensor is a static property of the body
(*d*) In general angular velocity and the angular momentum of a rigid body point in the same direction.

12. A sphere, a cylinder, a thin walled cylindrical pipe and a thin spherical shell have the same mass and radius and are spinning at the same angular speed about a symmetry axis through their respective centre of mass. Which has the greatest rotational kinitic energy?

(*a*) sphere (*b*) cylinder
(*c*) thin walled cylindrical pipe (*d*) thin spherical shell

PROBLEMS

1. Find the moment of inertia of a thin ring of radius R and mass M about a tangent perpendicular to the plane of the ring.

2. Find the moment of inertia of a disc of mass M and radius R about a tangent in the plane of the disc.

3. Consider a thin rectangular sheet of mass M. Find the moment of inertia about an axis through the centre perpendicular to the plane.

4. Find the moment of inertia of a sphere of mass M and radius R about a tangent.

5. The inertia tensor of a rigid body is of the form

$$\{\mathbf{I}\} = \begin{pmatrix} 2\alpha/3 & -\alpha/4 & -\alpha/4 \\ -\alpha/4 & 2\alpha/3 & -\alpha/4 \\ -\alpha/4 & -\alpha/4 & 2\alpha/3 \end{pmatrix}$$

where $\alpha = Ma^2$. Determine the principal moment of inertia.

6. The inertia tensor of a rigid body is of the form

$$\{\mathbf{I}\} = \begin{pmatrix} 15\alpha & 0 & 0 \\ 0 & 11\alpha & -3\sqrt{2}\,\alpha \\ 0 & -3\sqrt{2}\,\alpha & 8\alpha \end{pmatrix}$$

where $\alpha = Ma^2/40$. Determine the principal moment of inertia

7. A rigid body consists of three particles of masses 2,1,4 located at $(1,-1,1)$; $(2,0,-2)$ and $(-1,1,0)$ respectively. Determine (a) moment of inertia, (b) product of inertia, (c) angular momentum of body if it is rotated about the origin with angular velocity $\boldsymbol{\omega} = 3\,\mathbf{i} - 2\,\mathbf{j} + 4\,\mathbf{k}$, and (d) kinetic energy

8. Obtain the relation (12.37)

9. Obtain the components of the angular velocity along the space set of axes in terms of the Euler angles.

10. Consider a rigid body with $I_1 > I_2 > I_3$. If the body in free space is set to spin around one of the principal axes, it will continue spinning about that axis. Discuss the stability of the motion.

❑❑❑

Answers to Objective Questions

Chapter 1

1. (b) 2. (c) 3. (a) 4. (d) 5. (c) 6. (a) 7. (a)
8. (b) 9.(a) 10.(d) 11. (a) 12. (a) 13. (a) 14. (d)
15.(c) 16.(d) 17. (b)

Chapter 2

1.(a) 2. (a) 3. (a) 4. (a) 5. (a) 6. (d) 7.(b)
8. (c) 9. (a) 10. (a) 11. (b) 12. (b)

Chapter 3

1. (a) 2. (d) 3. (a) 4. (c) 5. (a) 6. (a) 7. (c)
8. (d) 9. (c)

Chapter 4

1. (c) 2. (d) 3. (a) 4. (c) 5. (b) 6. (a) 7. (c)
8. (c) 9. (b) 10. (a) 11. (d)

Chapter 5

1. (a) 2. (b) 3. (a) 4. (b) 5. (d) 6. (d) 7. (c)
8. (c) 9. (c) 10. (b) 11. (c) 12. (c) 13. (a) 14. (d)

Chapter 6

1. (a) 2. (b) 3. (b) 4. (d) 5. (a) 6. (c) 7. (b)
8. (a) 9. (b) 10. (d)

Chapter 7

1. (a) 2. (b) 3. (c) 4. (a) 5. (c) 6. (a) 7. (c)
8. (b) 9. (b) 10. (d) 11. (a) 12. (c)

Chapter 8

1. (b) 2. (c) 3. (d) 4. (d) 5. (a) 6. (c) 7. (a)
8. (b) 9. (b) 10. (d)

Chapter 9

1. (c)	2. (a)	3. (c)	4. (d)	5. (c)	6. (b)	7. (d)
8. (b)	9. (c)	10. (b)				

Chapter 10

1. (b)	2. (c)	3. (a)	4. (c)	5. (a)	6. (a)	7. (c)
8. (a)	9. (d)	10. (a)	11. (a)	12. (b)	13. (d)	14. (b)
15. (b)	16. (b)	17. (c)	18. (c)	19. (b)	20. (b)	21.(d)
22. (a)	23. (d)	24. (b)	25. (d)	26. (c)	27. (c)	28. (c)
29. (c)	30. (a)	31. (b)	32. (a)	33. (c)	34. (c)	35. (d)

Chapter 11

1. (a)	2. (c)	3.(a)	4. (d)	5. (b)	6. (c)	7. (d)
8. (b)	9. (a)	10.(c)	11. (b)	12. (d)	13. (d)	

Chapter 12

1. (a)	2. (d)	3. (b)	4. (c)	5. (d)	6. (a)	7. (a)
8. (c)	9. (c)	10. (a)	11. (d)	12. (c)		

❑❑❑

Selected Bibliography

Bhatia, V.B. *Classical Mechanics*, Narosa Publishing House, New Delhi 1997

Corben, H.C. and Stehle, P. *Classical Mechanics*, 2nd Ed. Dover Publications Inc. New York, 1977

Goldstein, H. *Classical Mechanics*, Addison-Wesley, Reading 1980

Gregory, R.D., *Classical Mechanics*, Cambridge University Press, 2006

Greenwood, D.T., *Advanced Dynamics*, Cambridge University Press 2003

Greenwood, D.T., *Classical Dynamics*, Prentice Hall Inc. 1977

Griffiths, J.B., *The Theory of Classical Dynamics*, Cambridge University Press, Cambridge 1985

Landu, L.D and Lifshitz, E.M. Mecahanics, Pergamon Oxford and Addison Wesley Reading 1971

Marion, J.B., *Classical Dynamics of Particles and Systems*, 2nd Ed. Academic Press, New York 1970

Mc Cauley, J.L. *Classical Mechanics Transformations, flow, integrable and Chaotic Dynamics,* Cambridge University Press, 1977

Panant, P.V. *Classical Mechanics,* Narosa Publishing House, New Delhi 2005

Rana, N.C. and Joag, P.S. *Classical Mechanics*, Tata McGraw-Hill

Scheck, F. *Mechanics from Newton's Laws to Deterministic Chaos*, Springer-Verlag, Berlin 1999.

Slater, J.C. and Frank, N.H. *Mechanics*, McGraw-Hill, New York 1961

Spiegel, M.R. *Theory and Problems of Theoretical Mechanics*, McGraw Hill Book Company 1982

Sudarshan, E.C.G. and Mukunda, N. *Classical Mechanics: A Modern Perspective*, John Wiley & Sons New York 1974

Symon, K.R., *Mechanics* 2nd Ed. Addison-Wesley, Reading, Massachusetts 1960.

Wells, D.A., *Schaum's Outline of Theory and Problems of Lagrangian Dynamics,* Tata McGraw Hill Publication Company Ltd. New Delhi 2005.

Woodhouse, N.M.J. *Introduction to Analytical Dynamics*, Clarendon Press, Oxford 1987

Whittaker, E.T., *A Treatise on the Analytical Dynamics of Particles and Rigid Bodies,* Cambridge University Press, Cambridge 1988.

Index

N

P

R

S

T

V